# BORDERING RUSSIA

# Bordering Russia

Theory and Prospects for Europe's Baltic Rim

*Edited by*
HANS MOURITZEN

## Ashgate

Aldershot • Brookfield USA • Singapore • Sydney

Published by
Ashgate Publishing Ltd
Gower House
Croft Road
Aldershot
Hants GU11 3HR
England

Ashgate Publishing Company
Old Post Road
Brookfield
Vermont 05036
USA

**British Library Cataloguing in Publication Data**
Bordering Russia : theory and prospects for Europe's Baltic
    rim
    1. Russia (Federation) - Foreign relations - Baltic States
    2. Baltic States - Foreign relations - Russia (Federation)
    3. Russia (Federation) - Foreign relations - Finland
    4. Finland - Foreign relations - Russia (Federation)
    5. Russia (Federation) - Foreign relations - Poland  6. Poland
    - Foreign relations - Russia (Federation)
    I. Mouritzen, Hans, 1952-
    327.4'7'0479

**Library of Congress Cataloging-in-Publication Data**
Bordering Russia : theory and prospects for Europe's Baltic Rim /
    edited by Hans Mouritzen.
        p.    cm.
    Includes bibliographical references.
    ISBN 1-85521-959-X (hardbound)
    1. Russia (Federation)--Foreign relations--Baltic States.
2. Baltic States--Foreign relations--Russia (Federation) 3. Russia
(Federation)--Foreign relations--Finland. 4. Finland--Foreign
relations--Russia (Federation) 5. Russia (Federation)--Foreign
relations--Poland. 6. Poland--Foreign relations--Russia
(Federation) 7. European Union. 8. World politics--1989-
I. North Atlantic Treaty Organization. II. Mouritzen. Hans.
DK502.715.B67    1998
327.479047--dc21                                                97-39119
                                                                        CIP

ISBN 1 85521 959 X

Printed in Great Britain by The Ipswich Book Company, Suffolk.

# Contents

List of Figures                                                        vi
List of Abbreviations                                                 vii
List of Contributors                                                   ix
Preface                                                                xi

1    Focus and Axioms
     *Hans Mouritzen*                                                    1

2    The Russia Dimension
     *Alexander Sergounin*                                              15

3    The West Dimension
     *Hans Mouritzen*                                                   73

4    Finland
     *Hans Mouritzen*                                                   91

5    Estonia
     *Mare Haab*                                                       109

6    Latvia
     *Zaneta Ozolina*                                                  131

7    Lithuania
     *Grazina Miniotaite*                                              165

8    Poland
     *Wojciech Kostecki*                                               195

9    Foreign Military Assistance
     *Michael Clemmesen*                                               227

10   Prospects for Europe's Baltic Rim
     *Clive Archer*                                                    259

11   Lessons for Alliance Theory
     *Hans Mouritzen*                                                  283

*Bibliography*                                                        295
*Index*                                                               315

# List of Figures

Fig. 1.1: *Europe's Baltic Rim and Adjacent Areas*     3

Fig. 3.1: *Core-Periphery Europe and Beyond*     81

Fig. 4.1: *The Relevant Environment Scenarios for Finland*     103

Fig. 7.1: *Lithuania: Historically Disputed Territories*     184

Fig. 7.2: *The Relevant Environment Scenarios for Estonia, Latvia, and Lithuania*     188

Fig. 8.1: *The Relevant Environment Scenarios for Poland*     222

Fig. 11.1: *Degrees of Bandwagoning 1988-1998*     289

# List of Abbreviations

| | |
|---|---|
| BALTBAT | Baltic Peacekeeping Battallion |
| BALTDEFCOL | Baltic Staff College |
| BALTNET | Baltic Air Surveillance Network |
| BALTRON | Baltic Naval Squadron |
| BE | Baltic Entente |
| CAP | Common Agricultural Policy |
| CBM | Confidence Building Measures |
| CBSS | Council of Baltic Sea States |
| CEFTA | Central European Free Trade Agreement |
| CFE | Conventional Forces in Europe |
| CFSP | Common Foreign and Security Policy |
| CIS | Commonwealth of Independent States |
| CJTF | Combined Joint Task Force |
| CMEA | Council of Mutual Economic Assistance |
| CPRF | Communist Party of the Russian Federation |
| CSCE | Conference on Security and Cooperation in Europe |
| EAPC | Euro-Atlantic Partnership Council |
| EC | European Community |
| EEA | European Economic Area |
| EFTA | European Free Trade Agreement |
| EMU | Economic and Monetary Union |
| ESC | European Security Council |
| EU | European Union |
| FCMA | Treaty of Friendship, Cooperation and Mutual Assistance |
| FEZ | Free Economic Zone |
| FSU | Former Soviet Union |
| G-7 | Group of Seven |
| GATT | General Agreement on Trade and Tariffs |
| GDP | Gross Domestic Product |
| GNP | Gross National Product |
| IGC | Inter Governmental Conference |
| IM | Internal Market |

| | |
|---|---|
| IMF | International Monetary Fund |
| IR | International Relations Theory |
| KOR | Kaliningrad Special Defence District |
| LDPR | Liberal Democratic Party of Russia |
| LPF | Latvian Popular Front |
| MD | Military District |
| MFN | Most Favoured Nation |
| MP | Member of Parliament |
| NACC | North Atlantic Cooperation Council |
| NATO | North Atlantic Treaty Organization |
| NCO | Non-Commissioned Officer |
| NGO | Non-Governmental Organization |
| OMRI | Open Media Research Institute |
| OSCE | Organization for Security and Cooperation in Europe |
| PfP | Partnership for Peace |
| RSFSR | Russian Soviet Federative Socialist Republic |
| SEZ | Special Economic Zone |
| SKAT | Volunteer National Defence Organization of Lithuania |
| SOP | Standard Operating Procedure |
| START | Strategic Arms Limitations Talks |
| UN | United Nations |
| WEU | Western European Union |
| WTO | World Trade Organization |

# List of Contributors

**Clive Archer,** b. 1947, PhD, research professor at Manchester Metropolitan University, UK, Department of Politics and Philosophy.

**Michael Clemmesen,** b. 1944, colonel, historian, Danish defence attaché to the Baltic states during the writing of his contribution.

**Mare Haab,** b. 1957, research fellow at the Institute of International and Social Studies, Estonian Academy of Sciences, during the writing of her contribution.

**Wojciech Kostecki,** b. 1956, PhD, senior research fellow at the Institute for Political Studies, Polish Academy of Sciences.

**Grazina Miniotaite,** b. 1948, PhD, senior research fellow at the Lithuanian Institute of Philosophy and Sociology.

**Hans Mouritzen,** b. 1952, Dr.scient.pol., senior research fellow at DUPI, the Danish Institute of International Affairs.

**Zaneta Ozolina,** b. 1957, PhD, research fellow at the Latvian Institute of International Affairs.

**Alexander Sergounin,** b. 1960, PhD, professor at the University of Nizhny Novgorod, Russia.

# Preface

A key dilemma in Western policy towards Russia these years is whether to admit all those countries into NATO and the EU that wish to join, or to respect Russian sensitivities and be more selective. The dilemma is put on its peak for the countries bordering Russia; they are the ones who fear Russia the most, but they are also the ones whose integration into the West provokes Russia the most, and is likely to strengthen Russian non-democratic forces. This is the dilemma that the present volume evolves around; the discussion is focused on five countries bordering Russia: Finland, Estonia, Latvia, Lithuania, and Poland.

A core axiom is that nation-state behaviour should be understood primarily on the basis of the power polarity in their geographical environments, rather than attributes of any overarching international system. Whereas such "salient environments" differ from state to state, they are remarkably stable for each state. This makes the soil fertile for inertia and states' learning of lessons from their historical experiences. The book is also future-oriented, however: systematic scenarios for the countries in focus are formulated and eventually synthesized for Europe's Baltic rim as a whole.

One major audience of this book should be those interested in Russian foreign policy, EU and NATO enlargement and, of course, the five countries in Europe's Baltic rim. Another audience should be those interested in the book's contributions to theory of regional integration or alliance theory and the underlying assumptions of these theories.

We have aimed towards the coherence of a monograph for this book, while still benefiting from the expertise of a range of individual authors. Whether we have succeeded in fulfilling this dual ambition is up to the reader to judge, of course.

The book is the result of co-operation between COPRI, the Copenhagen Peace Research Institute and DUPI, the Danish Institute of International Affairs. Almost all contributors are part of the COPRI international "family", having for shorter or longer periods stayed at COPRI and benefited from its grants. Several contributors are grateful to Pertti Joenniemi for practical and intellectual support. COPRI arranged an authors' conference in January 1997 in Copenhagen that greatly helped put the book on track. In spite of the contributors' different national backgrounds, we have been able to treat the issues in a detached academic

xi

way, in no way self-evident at scholarly conferences or in publications on the sensitive issues at stake.

While initiating this work as a project director at COPRI, I have edited the volume and written my contributions to it being employed by DUPI. Whereas COPRI has carried out the technical preparation of the manuscript in a highly satisfactory way, DUPI has been helpful in various stages of the process, for instance in preparing the figures and the index. Steven Rubin of DUPI has offered linguistic assistance to most of the chapters. The book project was supported by a NATO Science Fellowship.

Hans Mouritzen,
Editor.
Copenhagen,
February 1998.

# 1 Focus and Axioms

HANS MOURITZEN

The potential power of Russia militarily and politically combined with the instability of its situation confer an element of unpredictability to the whole of Central and Eastern Europe. Therefore, developments in Russian foreign policy and its domestic determinants (chapter 2) constitute the big "X" in any scenario construction for these areas. The countries in the Baltic Sea rim space from Finland through Estonia, Latvia, and Lithuania to Poland all border mainland Russia or the Kaliningrad enclave (cf. fig. 1.1). The interaction of Russian developments with Western EU or NATO enlargements (chapter 3) and the inputs from the rim space countries themselves are vital determinants for the eventual outcome of the process. These countries may become "outposts of the West" with an iron curtain to their East, they may come to constitute an extensive grey zone, or they may become Western bridge-builders eastwards, just to mention the most clear-cut outcomes. Moreover, it is in no way certain that the same outcome will apply to all of them.

What the countries selected for study (chapters 4-8) have in common are their borders with Russia and their serious candidacy in relation to Western alliance arrangements. Apart from this common basis, their preconditions and aspirations are more or less different. Finland is an established Nordic/Western state and since 1995 has belonged to the EU, currently staying put in relation to NATO. Poland as a former Warsaw Pact member has been invited into NATO and realistically stretches out also for EU membership. The Baltic countries, as former Soviet republics, likewise aspire for these two types of Western co-operation and commitment. Firstly, this book accounts for the alliance policies of these five countries since the end of the Cold War; apart from the geopolitical fundamentals we stress the countries' different legacies and perceptions: Finland's Paasikivi-Kekkonen heritage and Finland's negative lessons from being an anti-Soviet outpost before and during World War II, the Polish inter-war legacy and anti-Soviet heritage from the postwar period, and the Baltic countries finding much of their identities in their inter-war independencies and from their fate during Soviet occupation. Military assistance to the Baltic countries with a UN and, more important, a NATO/PfP connection is analysed; the obstacles to its implementation are reported in-depth (chapter 9). Secondly, we consider for each country its likely posture in various 10-year scenarios, presupposing alternative developments in Russian foreign policy (a status quo vs. a revisionist orientation) and in Western integration (various patterns of EU and NATO enlargement). Subsequently, the individual country scenarios are synthesized for Europe's Baltic rim as a whole (chapter 10), whereas the final chapter considers the lessons for alliance theory from the five rim state cases.

## ALLIANCE POLICY

Our focus on alliance policy encompasses not only a state's basic choice of military/political alliance, but also the preparatory stages that may lead up to alliance membership, proper, and the alliance profile *within* the framework of membership, once attained (e.g. Kupchan 1988). Even though we have selected states being as yet non-members, a certain future alliance profile is often discussed or hinted already at the pre-alliance stage as part of the entrance game. Regarding the basic choice, preferring a non-aligned or neutral status, for instance, are also seen as "alliance choices" and thereby as alliance policy. We cover both military alliances, proper, as NATO and the WEU, and such a non-military membership as that of the EU, being of significant importance for belongingness in the overall power structure. In this way, we deal with European/Western integration in its broadest sense.

The main purpose of a state's alliance policy is to safeguard external state security/autonomy, here understood as ability to avoid other actors' influence on the state's behaviour. This is done by borrowing military or political deterrence from a perceived friendly actor, thereby hopefully adding to its own capability vis à vis a perceived threat (e.g. Rothstein 1968: 49). "Security policy" is broader than "alliance policy," covering also the establishment of the state's own defence forces and, in some of its modern uses, policies aiming towards ecological or societal security or other good purposes. Conversely, alliance policy may be instrumental beyond external security, in that it may affect domestic military/societal structures in a desired (democratic) direction (chapter 9); this was one of the arguments for Spanish NATO membership, for instance. In sum, hence,

**Fig. 1.1: Europe's Baltic Rim and Adjacent Areas**

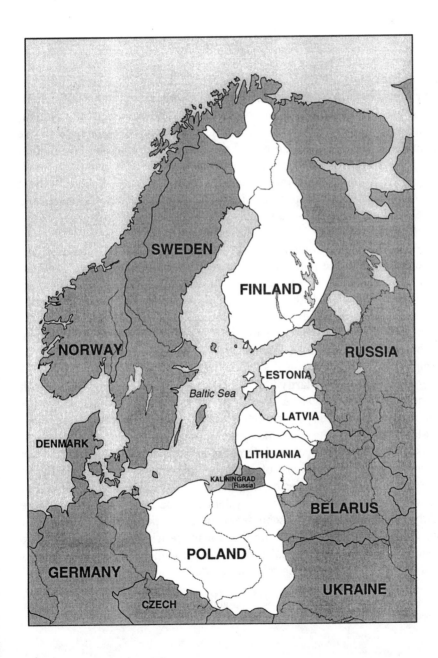

whereas there is a significant overlap between alliance policy and security policy, the two have each their own domains in addition.[1]

## POLARITY AND STATES' SALIENT ENVIRONMENT

Nation-state actors are mutually non-mobile as distinct from molecules in a gas or consumers in a market, for instance (Mouritzen 1980, 1998: ch.2). After some drifting around in various segments and corners of the system, the "average" environment of all mobile units can be equated with the system, they form part of: the gas or the market. By contrast, non-mobile units face a specific and relatively stable geographical neighbourhood, differing from unit to unit, rather than any overall system. Such a "salient environment" is likely to possess significant explanatory power regarding their behaviour, since *power and incentives wane with distance from states' home base* (cf. Boulding 1962: ch. 12 regarding the power aspect).

In particular the *combination* of anarchy and units' non-mobility characterizing the international system reinforces the importance of units' salient environments at the expense of the overall systemic structure (Mouritzen 1980: 172, 180; 1998 ch. 2). By contrast, a global police-actor with sufficient capabilities and recognition, like some visions of the UN, would to some extent overrule the importance of units' specific salient environments, as universal norms would be enforced everywhere, in principle.

By "environment polarity" is understood the number of poles with paramount positive/negative sanctions that can be projected in the neighbourhood of the environed nation-state. It may be labelled "unipolar," "bipolar," "tripolar," etc., just like systemic polarity (Waltz 1979). Even if this is a frog perspective on international politics, it is different from decision-makers' *perceptions* of polarity; as with systemic polarity, it requires the counting of poles by the analyst, as objectively as possible. For instance, whereas the international system may be unipolar, because there is only one superpower as seen from an eagle perspective, the salient environment of state "X" may simultaneously be tripolar, as in addition to the superpower two local great powers have roughly the same incentives and ability to project power in relation to "X."

---

1. Even though our focus in this book is on alliance policy as here delimited, the term "security policy" may be used occasionally.

IR (international relations) theory has typically overlooked the implications of non-mobility; it has often borrowed its models from systems of mobile units (e.g. mobile consumers and firms in micro economic theory, Waltz 1979). This has entailed an over-confidence in the explanatory capability of one overarching "international system," allegedly facing all actors. By contrast, the implications of non-mobility have always been (tacitly) recognized by journalists, historians, inter-disciplinary conflict research with its roots in geopolitics (e.g. Spykman 1944) or, for that matter, political scientists in their empirical analyses. The difference between an environment polarity and the familiar notion of systemic polarity could be illustrated from World War II: already from December of 1941 (the US entering the war, and the Germans being stopped in front of Moscow) and even more with war events during 1942 (Stalingrad notably), it was apparent that the Allied powers would eventually win the war. Still, Germany continued to possess military hegemony on the European Continent until mid-1944. In other words, there was a tangible discrepancy for two and a half years, at least, between the systemic polarity (bipolar with an increasing bias to the Allied powers) and the polarity facing European actors (unipolar German). These actors–satellites, neutrals, or resistance movements alike–had to take primary account of the prevailing unipolar structure, because Germany possessed marked physical preponderance here and now–i.e. forceful negative sanctions. The systemic balance of power was of psychological importance, primarily, and increasingly also for planning purposes. But neglect of the prevailing power structure might entail that there would be no long run to bother about whatsoever for the actor in question, due to its physical destruction in the meantime.

Let me add one further illustration of polarity difference. The Gulf conflict 1990-91 was a US/UN "police action" against an aggressor, in this case the Iraqi regime. As seen from a systemic perspective, this marked US/UN unipolarity ("the new world order") to those, who had not yet understood its implications. However, the polarity in Jordan's salient environment was bipolar during the whole Gulf crisis; the US/UN and Iraq could both project significant power and influence to bear on Jordan. An implication of this was that Jordan could not participate in UN sanctions against Iraq. *Even* in moments of "new world order" triumph–as, for instance, the initial decision in 1935 in the League of Nations on sanctions against Italy after her attack on Abyssinia–geopolitics prevailed at the local level. Italy's immediate neighbours voted "no"to sanctions or abstained–

although they could have more reason than others to hope for the curbing of the aggressor.[2]

Even if one recognizes the environment concept of polarity, it does not entail that one should completely disregard the systemic–or even less the regional–meanings of it.[3] They can be useful for the initial mapping and, thus, as an antecedent to proper explanation of nation-state behaviour. Under special circumstances the salient environment of a unit may equal the system (apart from itself). This can be so for pole actors, notably (in particular the two poles in bipolarity): being themselves essential elements in the systemic polarity, their behaviour is both significantly conditioned by it (as well as by domestic factors, presumably), and they are also delivering important feedbacks to it.[4] If we wish, however, to explain the behaviour of non-pole actors like those in the Baltic Sea rim space–our purpose in this book–it should be obvious that the environment meaning of polarity is indispensable. Although the systemic polarity currently seems to be some modified form of US unipolarity (an issue of controversy, though), the environment polarities in Talinn, Riga, and Vilnius are still Moscow unipolar. Even though the Russian armed forces are currently in bad shape, the actor possessing the most credible (negative) sanctions that can be applied to the Baltic countries remains Russia.

Small powers being subject to bullying from a neighbouring great power (their environment unipole) cannot "escape" to a more benign environment. Bordering Russia, for instance, is a parameter for a range of states in this book; they cannot sail out into the Atlantic Ocean, should they wish to. Of course, exile governments may exist during extreme conditions, but their

---

2. Only Austria, Hungary, and Albania (apart from Italy herself) voted against sanctions.

3. For some minor modifications to the above argument, cf. Mouritzen 1998: 14-17. The neglect of the salient environment and its polarity in IR theory has also been documented here (ch. 3).

4. The United States being one of the power poles, the distinction between systemic polarity and environment polarity was of no practical relevance for the explanation of US behaviour. If the system as a whole was bipolar, then it surely was so also from a Washington perspective. It may be a point in the sociology of science that many trend setting American IR scholars, being understandably preoccupied with analysing the challenges facing their own country, do not perceive the distinction between the two meanings of polarity, because they do not need it for most of their own empirical purposes. What is regrettable, then, is that their allegedly general theories tend to neglect it. This is exacerbated by the fact that the US is, by far, the largest producer of IR theories in the world.

raison d'être is the hope that they will once be able to return to their geographical home-base.

Respecting the parameter of non-mobility, however, alliance policy as studied in this book can modify its significance *somewhat,* if it leads to membership. In the terms used here, the primary purpose of joining an alliance is to modify an unfavourable environment polarity. Typically, the incentives and power projection ability of a threatening unipole is sought reduced through the offering of incentives to a conflicting pole, so that it may improve its power projection ability in the area. In this way, the alliance candidate hopes to replace an unpleasant environment unipolarity by bipolarity or perhaps even by a pleasant unipolarity under the wings of the protective pole. However, an alliance option does not always exist, or it may be unfavourable (too high a price for protection!) or lack the necessary credibility. This latter alternative, or even rumours about it, may actually be dangerous. For instance, if the power projection ability of the future ally is militarily dubious at the time in question, the threatening unipole may be tempted to a pre-emptive military attack before the alliance has become effective. In any case, even if an alliance should appear to be successful, membership does not offer the newcomer a new salient environment. Also in the future it will be costly not to relate to its geographical neighbours, both in the security field and in other spheres of acticity that are spatially conditioned, such as trade or ecological degradation. At most, therefore, the implications of non-mobility and distance have been *modified.*

In the rhetoric of most states, however, distance and power assymmetries (sometimes even power as such) are described as "old-fashioned" and unimporant in the world of today (e.g. Hunter 1996: 19-20, as cited on p.88). The slogan that "security is indivisible"–entailing that there can only be "real" security if there is security everywhere–is empirically more inaccurate in the regionalized world of today than during the bipolar period; for instance, local wars like the one in ex-Yugoslavia has actually been contained (e.g. Heurlin 1995: 63-4). Even though spheres of interest may be tacitly implied by what many Western statesmen are saying and doing, their aim seems to be to eradicate or weaken such spheres by denying their existence–in particular a Russian sphere of interest. Rhetoric probably expresses wishes for the future rather than descriptions of traditional or existing states of affairs. From a normative point of view, one might wish to replace power politics with the rule of international organizations and their universal norms. For the purely analytical purpose of understanding *actual* state behaviour, however, it is seen as essential here that the phenomena of distance and power assymetries are respected, irrespective of one's normative assumptions.

## INERTIA AND LEARNING

Heterogeneity rather than homogeneity is likely to prevail, as we compare the situations of various state-units in international politics. Exposing identical units to identical stimuli will often lead to different reactions, given the different characteristics of units' salient environments. By contrast, the picture is one of homogeneity and stability, if we follow one and the same unit over time. Of course, salient environments are transformed in the wake of major wars or state dissolutions–as when states fell apart in Central and Eastern Europe post-1989. This created new neighbours for others, evidently. Still, the *general* picture is that salient environments–and thereby foreign policy orientations–keep relatively constant for whole "eras" like 1949-89 in Europe. They are stable–but mutually different. Stability over time for the units means that the soil is fertile for inertia and units' learning of historical lessons.

Stable salient environments invite inertia in the form of custom and habit at all levels; one gets used to a certain external constellation and the challenges that it poses. Certain SOPs (standard operating procedures) are developed, not only in bureaucracies but also among top decision-makers. Essentially the same parliamentary or other foreign policy debates are repeated over and over again, decade after decade. The same goes for a gradually more specific bureaucratic code language.[5] Stable environments also entail that national stereotypes may be applied to units in the neighbourhood: "big brother complexes" (at the popular level, notably) or the "hereditary enemy." By being unable to circle freely around, nations are forced to remain in conflictual symmetric dyads with a "hereditary enemy" or in conflictual asymmetric dyads, in which at least the weaker party would probably prefer to drift away, if possible. Top decision-makers as well as bureaucracy learn "lessons" from the past (how to deal with the "hereditary enemy," for instance). They repeat behaviour defined as "successes" or shun behaviour defined as "failures" (e.g. Steinbruner 1974; Jervis 1976; Stenelo 1981; Levy 1994). Present behaviour depends not only

---

5.  On foreign policy inertia in general, cf. Goldmann 1982 or Mouritzen 1988, part IV.

on present conditions, but also on the way incoming information is interpreted in terms of theories inherited from the past. Decision-makers may overlook that evidence supporting their theory may also be consistent with other theories or express sheer coincidence (Jervis, ibid.)

Applying a theory requires historical analogy (Stenelo 1981; Steinbruner 1974: 115-16): a current situation is said to be somehow "similar" to a historical situation. A particular risk facing successful states is that "nothing fails like success" (Jervis 1976: 278-9); one is tempted to use an old, successful remedy the next time one faces a seemingly "corresponding" situation. Its peculiarities are overlooked. As formulated by Jervis (1976: 234):

> When the aspects of a situation that make it distinctive are not detected, policies that failed previously will be shunned, and policies that succeeded will be applied again even under conditions that are so different that the earlier outcomes tell little about what the results will be if the policies are repeated.

As should be apparent, "learning a lesson" as here understood does not necessarily "improve" future foreign policy; we just neutrally observe that decision-makers have been affected in one or the other direction by their country's past experiences.

As we remember, the stressing of perception so vital in this *historical* salient environment perspective was absent in the "pure" salient environment focus introduced above. Evidently, any salient environment has to be perceived and interpreted by nation-state decision-makers in order to affect foreign policy. As expressed by Brecher, "decisions are made by men, not by environments" (1972: 556). However, this descriptive truism diverts attention from the relative explanatory potency of the environment level as argued above; perception or decision-making factors have only explanatory potency, if there is something *peculiar* about them–as in the historical analogy explanation. Of course, if the logic of a current salient environment competes with a historical lesson, we have to add the two perspectives in specific foreign policy explanations. Under such circumstances we have to stress also how the current salient environment is perceived, in order to make such an addition logically meaningful.

## PRE-THEORY AND ALLIANCE THEORY

The stressing of states' salient environment, including the past salient environment, as crucial for their behaviour does not in itself add up to a theory. Given the axioms of states' mutual anarchy (or non-hierarchy, at any rate) and their mutual non-mobility, the searchlight should be directed towards their geographical neighbourhood when looking for an explanation of their behaviour, as argued above. However, nothing has been said about *how* this behaviour should be affected, let alone why, as a theory should do (the historical analogy mechanism referred to above is an exception). We are dealing with a *pre-theory*, giving explanatory priority to a set of factors by saying "look in this direction." This priority will be followed, by and large, throughout the five "rim state chapters." In the chapter "Lessons for Alliance Theory", however, it will be discussed which conclusions can be drawn from our empirical evidence regarding the viability of *specific* alliance theories. Which theoretical expectations are confirmed and which are disconfirmed, and what does this teach us about the theories' underlying assumptions?

## ENVIRONMENT SCENARIOS

We shall construct mid-term scenarios for the rim states, looking a decade or so into the future. There is no divine justification for this time perspective, of course. Roughly speaking, however, in the long run anything is possible (almost!), and the short run is normally too similar to the present to bear interesting implications. So by exclusion, a mid-term perspective has been chosen.

"Environment scenarios" are at stake. In contrast to global or regional scenarios, this type of scenarios predict the situation and behaviour of *one* specific nation-state on the basis of assumptions pertaining to selected characteristics of its salient environment. These assumptions, in turn, may be based on assumptions concerning the broader regional or perhaps even global context. As in the 1990-97 "historical" analysis, the dimensions are Russia's foreign policy orientation and patterns in West enlargement. Depending on not least internal developments in Russia (cf. chapter 2), its basic foreign policy orientation will be either revisionist or status quo oriented (Wolfers 1962: 18-9) in the region at stake here. A revisionist orientation means that the re-establishment of an old order is being sought. In this case, Russia perhaps expanding to the old Soviet borders (or even old Tsarist borders). An assertive foreign policy supported by regained military strength will be necessary to attain this long-term objective. By contrast, a status quo orientation is basically conservative in being satisfied with the existing order in the region. Regarding the West dimension, it is argued in chapter 3 that future integration "depth" is not likely to deviate more than marginally from the current one; the EU will hardly integrate much further, nor will it fall apart. So the interesting question will be the pattern of EU geographic widening–not least of course for those subject to the process. Combined with the equally crucial question of NATO widening, we get a comprehensive West enlargement dimension. Its detailed construction varies between countries, depending on whether they already are members of the EU (Finland) and depending on the likely sequence between memberships. For Poland we know that NATO membership is under way prior to EU membership, whereas the sequence will probably be the reverse for the Baltic countries (if NATO membership will ever be attained). With this way of structuring the future, we get 4 scenarios for Finland and Poland (2 Russia orientations x 2 membership patterns) and 6 for each of the Baltic countries (2 Russia orientations x 3 membership patterns). There *may* be a certain interaction among the two dimensions, for instance in the sense that Russian revisionism in the wake of a Moscow coup leads to quicker NATO enlargement, or that the latter phenomenon strengthens revanchist forces in Moscow, and thereby leads to foreign policy revisionism. However, this is in no way so by necessity; one could as well imagine, for instance, that Finnish alliance cautiousness would increase in the face of Russian revisionism. In any case, interaction between the dimensions is so hypothetical that none of the "boxes" (scenarios) are apriori ruled out. Some are more likely than others, but all are worth considering.

As should appear we have limited ourselves to a few clearcut, but not too far-fetched assumptions in the environment scenarios. These pertain both to the selection of dimensions and "values" on these dimensions; they have been consciously selected in the light of arguments in chapters 2 and 3. This selection means, evidently, that developments *not* covered by the two dimensions are seen as being of minor importance and/or as scenario-dependent. For instance, Sweden's importance to Finland, Nordic-Baltic co-operation, inter-Baltic co-operation, or domestic politics in each country are phenomena that are highly scenario-dependent: their importance varies strongly according to which specific scenario that we are considering. Such phenomena are precisely what makes scenario analysis worthwhile: that it makes a *difference* to other important features/developments, whether we are considering one or the other scenario.

Our parsimony and priority to a few environment features make us vulnerable to accusations of over-simplification, "box thinking," etc. However, according to the philosophy of science followed here, simplification (complexity reduction) is not only a necessary instrument to make analysis manageable; the very purpose of inquiry is actually to simplify reality rather than the opposite (e.g. Mouritzen 1997a). This applies both to explanation/theory-building and to prediction/scenario construction.

Adding, for instance, one "value" to each dimension would entail proliferation from six Baltic scenarios to twelve, and from four Finnish/Polish scenarios to nine. As should be apparent, following such a temptation would quickly make the whole exercise unmanageable. We could then as well revert to a purely verbal discussion as in most books, in which distinctions and disagreements can be easily swept under the carpet. Even though this would feel more comfortable, we would lose the explicitness and disciplining of thought that a few scenarios force upon us.

In chapter 10 a synthesis of the country-by-country scenarios will be made, in order to discuss the likelihood of alternative futures for Europe's Baltic rim.


FIVE SIMILAR SALIENT ENVIRONMENTS?

We focus in this book on a range of countries with apparently similar salient environments. Finland, Estonia, Latvia, Lithuania, and Poland have two essential traits in common pertaining to their salient environments: (1) they border Russia, be it mainland Russia or the Kaliningrad enclave, and (2) they are seriously considered in relation to Western alliance options–NATO and the European Union/WEU. For instance, Georgia also borders Russia, but is not seriously considered in Western alliance discussions. Norway likewise borders Russia, but is an established NATO member. The two requirements being fulfilled, the countries in question are exposed to an autonomy threat (the nature of which is subject to controversy, of course) and they are, more or less, within the range of alliance protection vis à vis that threat. That opens the field for several alliance options: seeking "full" alliance, low profile alliance, neutral status, "good relations" with the perceived threat, or theoretically even alliance with it.

Moreover, the countries in question also happen to share a third common characteristic: their Baltic beaches. This means in practice possibilities for co-operation with other countries around the Baltic Sea such as Sweden and Denmark (and Finland for the four other cases), or for being coupled to various forms of institutionalized Nordic co-operation.[6] This hardly opens the possibility for credible alliance arrangements, but it is obviously relevant both for low politics concerns and for catalyst activities in relation to Western alliance arrangements. For instance, Denmark can serve as an insider advocate for the Baltic countries' NATO and EU memberships, and Sweden and Finland can function likewise within the EU.

With salient environments being roughly similar, major differences in alliance policy, if any, should probably be accounted for by the countries' respective historical lessons, as described above: repeat this or that alleged "success" or avoid this or that alleged "failure" in the past. This is a major thesis of this book. It is not the whole story, however. Similarity is, of course, a concept that is relative to one's level of abstraction. Closer inspection in the rim state chapters will reveal differences between the five salient environments at stake, differences that in themselves can explain significant variances in alliance behaviour.[7]

First of all, however, we shall turn to analyses of the two major factors in the countries' salient environments: the Russia factor and the West factor. One chapter will be devoted to each. Since Russia is, after all, a bigger "X" than Western integration and enlargements, the Russia chapter will be the largest and most detailed of the two. We shall not only analyse developments regarding the Russia and the West factors from the end of the Cold War; supported by theory and extrapolation, we shall also evaluate the prospects for the coming decade or so. This is done in order to provide the necessary raw materials for the scenario construction in the rim state chapters.

---

6. One might add Germany and even Russia as possibilities here, as formalized in the Council of Baltic Sea States.
7. This tendency is even more marked, of course, as past salient environments are considered in connection with the respective historical heritages.

# 2   The Russia Dimension

ALEXANDER SERGOUNIN

With the break-up of the Soviet Union and the re-emergence of the Russian Federation as an independent state Russia has had to redefine both its national interests and role in the post-Cold War international relations system. Trying to do this, in an environment where effective regional and global security structures do not exist, the Russian leadership faces almost insurmountable difficulties. The leaders have often been compelled to make decisions before a clear consensus on national priorities has been reached. These decisions, in turn, have affected the political elites in neighbouring states, who also have been taking only the first tentative steps on the international arena. Russia's search for a new security identity is far from reaching a constructive phase both in theoretical and practical senses. Combined with internal socio-economic and political instability this spreads anxiety and misunderstanding among the neighbours, including the Baltic Sea area.

What is the Russian foreign policy in the Baltic Sea rim space about? What are the major forces shaping Moscow's strategy in the area? What is the future of Russian security policies in the rim space? What type of alliance policy is preferable for Moscow? Is there any possibility to create a co-operative security system in the area or should we be prepared for the worse-case scenario? These and related questions confronting policymakers and analysts are addressed in this paper.

RUSSIAN NATIONAL INTERESTS IN THE BALTIC SEA RIM SPACE

*The historical background*

The Baltic lands have always been a zone of interaction (or "contact zone")—in peaceful or confrontational form—between Russia and the external world. For a number of historical and geopolitical reasons Russia's perceptions of the Baltic Sea area have always been influenced by security considerations. Since the times of Kievan Rus (9th century), when Lord

15

Novgorod the Great gained a limited outlet to the Baltic Sea around today's St. Petersburg, to the present Russia has been concerned with strengthening its positions in the area and preventing the rise of hostile powers (Baranovsky 1996: 167-168).

It was Peter the Great who conquered some Baltic provinces from the Swedes and opened the "window on Europe." The Russian expansion continued under Empress Elisabeth (when the south-eastern part of Finland and East Prussia were put under Moscow's sovereignty) and Catherine the Great (who incorporated the remainder of modern Latvia and today's Lithuania after the partition of Poland). It culminated in the beginning of the 19th century when Finland was annexed from Sweden.

In the 20th century, Russia (and the Soviet Union) retained its perception of the Baltic Sea rim space as a front-line against Western expansion either in the form of German *Drang nach Osten* or NATO's "aggressive plans." Moscow's diplomacy, military doctrines and armed forces posture in the area were subordinated to the objectives of the global confrontation with the West.

*The doctrinal background*

With the collapse of the USSR and the disappearance of most dangerous threats from the West, the Russian policy makers suddenly found themselves in a new strategic and geopolitical situation. According to a majority of Russian theorists, main external threats to Russian security will originate–in the foreseeable future–from the South or East rather than the West (Vladislavlev and Karaganov 1992: 35; Zhirinovskiy 1993; Arbatov 1994: 71; Lukin 1994: 110). Russia is neither geopolitically nor militarily able to dominate in the Baltic Sea area any longer.

Under these circumstances, quite animated discussions on Russia's national interests have been started by the Russian political, military and intellectual elites. Do any constant Russian interests exist? Or should they be completely re-defined? What place in the set of the Russian foreign policy priorities should the area take? Some suggest that the Baltic Sea region is no longer as important for Moscow as it was during Soviet times (Fadeev and Razuvayev 1994: 114; Baranovsky 1996: 167). Others argue that the area will retain its traditional meaning as a border zone or bridge between the East and the West (Uspensky and Komissarov 1993: 83; Institute of Europe 1995: 21-23; Sergounin 1996: 112-115). Some believe that the rim space is becoming strategically important again as NATO and the EU are moving to the Baltic States. To their minds, north-west Russia is vulnerable for potential Western encroachments again as in the times of German crusaders or Hitler's *Blitzkrieg* (Gromov 1995: 9-13; Trynkov 1995: 65-68; *Komsomolskaya Pravda* 29 September 1995; *Nezavisimaya Gazeta* 11 April 1996).

As for Russia's official threat perceptions it should be noted that there is no official published document–either presidential or Foreign Ministry's– that specially defines Russian interests and strategy in the Baltic Sea area. It is possible only to reconstruct Moscow's official concept basing on numerous documents, declarations and interviews with high-ranking Russian officials.

It seems Russia's official foreign policy "doctrine" shares the experts' ambiguity as regards the significance of the Baltic Sea rim space. On the one hand, as it put by the Foreign Ministry's document (1993), the three Baltic States and Nordic Europe are ranked fifth (as a part of Europe) on a list of fifteen priorities. Europe follows the CIS, arms control and international security, economic reform, and the United States; at the same time it precedes the Asia-Pacific region, the Near East, Latin America and so on (Ministry of Foreign Affairs of the Russian Federation 1993: 3-23). That means that the area is not a very important priority for Moscow. On the other hand, the new Russian Foreign Minister Yevgeni Primakov put Eastern Europe (including Poland and the Baltic States) on the second position in the list of four Russian priorities (the CIS, Eastern Europe, Asia-Pacific, Europe and the United States) (*Izvestiya* 6 March 1996; Stupavsky 1996: 10).[1]

It is, however, unclear whether these priorities are *real* priorities for the Russian foreign policy and military machinery or rather, they should serve as signals to certain domestic and foreign audiences. It is obvious, for instance, that Asia-Pacific was put forward by Primakov to send a message to NATO that Russia is able to find new allies in the East (China, South Korea, India, etc.) to cope with a shifting balance in Europe. But it does not mean, of course, that Asia-Pacific is really more important and preferable for Russia than Europe and the United States. The CIS is also declared as a priority No. 1, but half of the 800 accords signed by leaders of the member-

---

1. By the way, Primakov preferred to use the term "post-Soviet space" rather then "CIS" *(Nezavisimaya Gazeta,* 9 February 1996). It remains unclear whether he implied the Baltic States as well or not.

states remain only on paper. For the same reasons, it is safe to assume that the above official priorities can be misleading as regards the Baltic Sea rim space.

## The set of priorities

There are at least four dimensions which make the area important for Russia regardless the above-mentioned geostrategic shifts in the world's post-Cold War landscape:

1. In *geopolitical and strategic* terms there have been major changes. With the collapse of the USSR Russia's access to the Baltic Sea was significantly reduced to the small areas around Kaliningrad and St. Petersburg. Russia lost approximately two-thirds of the former Soviet Baltic coastline. The total length of the outer boundary of the country's territorial waters is now only just over 200 km. Also important, Moscow has lost its strategic allies from the adjacent regions. As Baranovsky notes, the new geopolitical situation is psychologically traumatic for Russians: indeed, what Russia possesses now in the Baltic Sea area is only slightly more than it did in the time of Ivan the Terrible (Baranovsky 1996: 168). In fact, Russia feels itself pushed back several centuries.

This feeling of increasing isolation from Europe was added by expanding the "buffer zone" between Russia and Central and Western Europe in the result of secession by Belarus, Moldova and Ukraine in 1991. Russia's access to the industrially developed European countries thus became more difficult than in the recent past. In fact, Russia now has a land frontier only with two North European countries–Finland and Norway– which are seen by the Russian political and business elites as "lucrative pieces" to develop economic ties with the "core" of Europe.

Paradoxically, the same geopolitical catastrophe which reduced Russia's influence in the Baltic Sea rim space made the latter rather attractive for Moscow in terms of economic co-operation with Europe. Due to numerous barriers (socio-economic and political instability, tariffs, the lack of co-ordination between custom services and border guards of different countries, organised crime, underdeveloped infrastructure, isolation from the European markets and others) Russia's CIS partners (Belarus, Moldova and Ukraine) are less preferable than other countries. The Visegrad countries and even the Baltic States look more promising because they are ahead of other post-socialist countries in conducting reforms; they are economically viable and potentially welcome to the European "club." For these reasons, the Baltic Sea countries might again assume the role of a Russian "window on Europe" which they have had since the time of Peter the Great.[2]

The region is also an important transport junction by sea, land and air. As a result of Russia's loss of its main ports on the Black Sea (Odessa, Nikolayev, Sevastopol, Kerch, Sukhumi and Batumi) and on the Baltic (Klaipeda, Riga, Tallinn and Ventspils) which formerly connected Russia with the West, the role of the Kaliningrad and St. Petersburg harbours has become crucial.

On the Baltic Sea, as much as 56 per cent of the former Soviet harbour capacity reverted to the possession of the new independent states. Russia's shortage of harbour capacity in the Baltic will be an acute problem for many years to come. Commercial harbour statistics for the 1980s indicate that some 30 per cent of all visits by Soviet ships were made to the harbour of Leningrad and the rest, just under 70 per cent, to harbours of the former Baltic socialist republics and the Kaliningrad Region. This means that the numbers of vessels using the harbours of St. Petersburg and its nearby areas will now have to be increased substantially in order to ensure that all transport takes place via the country's own harbours. It is well-known, however, that these harbours are already overcrowded. The number of commercial visits to the Baltic ports of the former USSR amounted to some 12,000 per year in the mid-1980s, of which 4,000 were to Leningrad. On the other hand, the quantity of goods passing through the latter port decreased in the early 1990s, so that having been 11 million tonnes in 1990 it was only some 5 million tonnes in 1992 (Viitasalo and Österlund 1996: 12, 23). Due to overall decline of Russian foreign trade and Lithuanian high transit tariffs, only 63 per cent of the Kaliningrad ports' capacity was used in 1995 (Trynkov 1996: 8).

Russian foreign trade still relies to a great extent on the ports of the Baltic States. Russia can continue to make use of the harbours in the Baltic States, but this will mean transit payments and will have to be based on the existence of good political relations. Use of the railways and harbours of these countries for military transportation would be much more problematic, as it would require negotiations and agreements between individual countries. Presently, Russia has an agreement on military transit

---

2.  The 'Visegrad countries' refer to Poland, the Czech Republic, Slovakia and Hungary.

only with Lithuania. Both countries are not happy with the conditions and the ways for practical implementation.

The new geopolitical situation influences greatly the development of Russian land and sea transport infrastructure. Moscow is planning to develop the above-mentioned ports and land transport communications in North-west Russia. Russia announced in the early 1990s that it planned to construct new large-scale harbours close to St. Petersburg on the bays of Ust-Luga, Primorsk and Batareinaya by the year 2000 (Viitasalo and Österlund 1996: 23-24). There are also some plans to develop a direct transport line between St. Petersburg-Baltiysk to supply raw materials and consumer goods to the Kaliningrad exclave. As for land transport communications, Russia is going to develop, for example, a high-speed railway between Moscow, St. Petersburg and Murmansk (Nordic Council 1992: 23-24). Moscow has repeatedly offered the Balts and Poles the extension of the proposed *Via Baltica* (high-speed motorway) to St. Petersburg and Kaliningrad. The Russian proposals, however, were rejected for various reasons (financial, environmental, political, etc.).

As mentioned, the new geopolitical situation has posed not only economic but also political, military and even psychological challenges to Russia. The Kaliningrad problem exemplifies such a combination of different factors. The Kaliningrad Region (Oblast) has, since 1991, become an exclave separated from Russia by Belorussian, Latvian and Lithuanian territories. The Region is fully dependent on external sources of raw materials, energy, fuel, foodstuff, etc. It can meet only 5-6 per cent of local industry's needs with its own resources. The Region lost 300 billion roubles in 1994 and 440 billion roubles in the first half of 1995 because of the Lithuanian transit fees (Trynkov 1996: 8). There is also a difference of opinion among Russian politicians and experts with regard to the future status and role of Kaliningrad. Some suggest its transformation into the Baltic "Hong Kong," others propose to retain its status as Russia's main military outpost on the Baltic Sea (Szajkowski 1993: 164; *The Baltic Independent* 4 – 10 November 1994; Trynkov 1996: 1-4, 14-16). Regardless, there is no simple solution for this geopolitical puzzle.

The Russian political and military leadership emphasises the need to protect the most important industrial and administrative centres of North-west Russia, which have become more vulnerable since the emergence of independent states–the separation of Kaliningrad from Russia and the shift of the border close to St. Petersburg, Pskov and Novgorod. In his speech to the sailors of the Russian navy at Baltiysk in March 1993, the Russian

Foreign Minister Andrei Kozyrev pointed out that Russia must hold on to its powerful position in the Baltic Sea area to be able to protect Kaliningrad from any territorial claims that might be advanced by the Germans or other "right-wing" powers. He also announced that he was in favour of a continuous, effective Russian army presence in the Baltic Sea area.

North-west Russia is a region which has accommodated some troops who have been withdrawn from former Warsaw Pact countries and Soviet republics. The same is true for the Russian Navy. The Baltic Sea Fleet faced the problem of redeployment of vessels and facilities from the Baltic States to the Kaliningrad ports and Kronshtadt (near St. Petersburg).

The role of the Baltiysk base (near Kaliningrad), which was estimated in 1993 to be used by 75 per cent of the surface interception vessels, 60 per cent of the anti-submarine vessels, 20 per cent of the minesweepers and all the landing craft, seems likely to increase still further (Viitasalo and Österlund 1996: 33). The area also has a vital shipbuilding and repairs industry, and the Jantar shipyard in Kaliningrad, which builds the *Udaloi* and *Neustrashimyi*-class vessels, is of vital importance to the Baltic Fleet and to the Russian navy in general. In addition, the Kaliningrad area is located at the ice-free zone of the Baltic Sea while St. Petersburg area can be surrounded by ice for as long as six months of the year.

At the same time, St. Petersburg retains its leadership in military shipbuilding on the Baltic Sea. Its shipyards build battle cruisers, anti-submarine destroyers, submarines of all classes (from strategic to tactical), etc. The vessels are produced not only for the Baltic Sea Fleet but for the Northern Fleet and export purposes as well (*Jane's International Defense Review* September 1996; *Pointer* October 1996; *The Economist* 30 November 1996).

The Baltic Sea is still a field of NATO-Russian military confrontation. Comparing to the Cold War era, both sides have reduced their activities in the area though they are still fairly intensive. "Submarine incidents" occur from time to time. Naval intelligence operations are sometimes even more active: NATO and Russia are still interested in each other's intentions. According to data, the naval activities in the Baltic Sea have significantly increased in accordance with the PfP programme. A number of NATO military aircraft revealed in the air defence zone of the Kaliningrad Special Defence District (KOR) has increased by 250 per cent during 1995 (Trynkov 1996: 5). In turn, Russia pushed forward an idea of a CIS unified air defence system. An agreement "On creation of a unified air defence system of CIS member states" was signed by Commonwealth leaders on

February 10, 1995 in Almaty (*Rossiyskaya Gazeta* 25 February 1995; *FBIS-SOV-95-040* 1 March 1995). It first became effective on the CIS western air border; on 1 April 1996, Russia and Belarus started joint patrolling on that border.

KOR's strategic-military importance may even grow in view of NATO enlargement. According to many experts, since Poland has been invited to join NATO the further demilitarisation of Kaliningrad will inevitably be stopped regardless of Warsaw's promises not to deploy foreign troops and nuclear weapons on its territory. If the Baltic States join NATO, the re-militarisation of the KOR, Leningrad Military District (MD) and Belarus is predicted (*Komsomolskaya Pravda* 29 September 1995; *Nezavisimaya Gazeta* 11 April 1996; Trynkov 1996: 5).

Moreover, some provisions of the Russian military doctrine adopted by President Yeltsin in November 1993 (*Jane's Intelligence Review Special Report* January 1994) (for example, the assumption of use of military force for the protection of Russian citizens abroad and repeal of the principle of no first use of nuclear weapons) should be taken into account.

The Baltic Sea countries paid attention to two exceptions from Russia's promise not to use nuclear weapons against any state party to the Nuclear Non-Proliferation Treaty. Russia will never use it against them, unless: "a) such a state, which is connected by an alliance agreement with a nuclear state, attacks the Russian Federation, its territory, Armed Forces and other services or its allies; b) such a state collaborates with a nuclear power in carrying out, or supporting, an invasion or an armed aggression against the Russian Federation, its territory, Armed Forces and other services or its allies" (*Jane's Intelligence Review Special Report* January 1994: 6).

Somehow, all the Baltic Sea and Nordic countries (especially NATO members such as Germany, Denmark, Iceland and Norway) fall under these provisions. For that reason, their reaction was contradictory. On the one hand, they considered this change to a Western style concept of deterrence as Russia's inclination to openness and frankness in military matters (few people in the West took seriously the old Soviet "no first use" doctrine). In addition, they understood that Russia's new nuclear doctrine reflected Moscow's intention to rely mainly upon nuclear deterrence to compensate for its conventional weakness in an effort to maintain great power status. On the other hand, they perceived this change as a clear message to them (especially to the three Baltic States and Poland): they will fall into the said categories if they will join NATO or the WEU or "support" any Western intervention in Russia or the "near abroad," for example, by giving rights of passage or bases (*Jane's Intelligence Review Special Report* January 1994; SIPRI 1994: 648).

In turn, these concerns have stimulated discussions on different variants of a common defence (Nordic, Baltic or Nordic/Baltic) and on joining NATO.

2. *Politically,* the Baltic Sea area is significant for Russia as well. Moscow has different approaches to the three ex-Soviet Baltic republics and the rest of the Baltic Sea countries. The former are important if Moscow is to keep its influence in the region and protect the Russian-speaking minorities. In addition, Russia wants to demonstrate that it is still a major player in this part of Europe; the player which is able, for instance, to veto the Balts' joining NATO or to regulate the pace and scope of their entering other European institutions.

As regards Denmark, Finland and Sweden, Moscow hopes to use them: (a) as a vehicle for Russia's participation in the European economic, political and military institutions; (b) in the diplomatic game against any potential rival in Europe (e.g., Germany, France or the UK); and (c) to avoid Russia's isolation on the continent (Uspensky and Komissarov 1993: 83; Sergounin,1993: 20; Institute of Europe 1995: 21-23). In general, Russia may be expecting these states to be more tolerant of and responsive to its intentions than other European countries; at the same time it has to keep in mind their sensitivity to Russian pressure on the Baltic States. Furthermore, they may be more intransigent with respect to violations of human rights and democratic principles by Russia.

3. In *economic* terms, Moscow looks to some Baltic Sea countries as a possible source of investment, advanced technology and training assistance and as a promising trading partner. Geographically this area is closer to Russia than other Western countries. Moscow hopes to attract the Baltic Sea countries' attention to the development of regions adjacent to them–the Kola Peninsula, St. Petersburg, Kaliningrad, the Northern Sea Route, the autonomous districts on the Arctic coast and so on. With regard to the three Baltic States, Moscow hopes that they will retain their interest in Russian natural resources and will be a promising market for Russian industrial goods.

According to some estimates, Russian trade through the Baltic ports will increase to 55.5 million tonnes by the year 2000 and to as much as 98.0 million tonnes in 2005 (it was only 39 million tonnes in 1992 and 46 million tonnes in 1993) (Viitasalo and Österlund 1996: 23). Some experts suggest that the routes which could most conveniently be used to meet the increasing flow of goods may be divided into three categories: (a) direct deliveries to Russian harbours, including those under construction; (b) deliveries to harbours in the Baltic States and transport to Russia from there; and (c) deliveries via Finnish harbours, primarily Hamina, Kotka and Kokkola. According to the Finnish Ministry of Transport, as much as 10 million tonnes of Russian exports and imports could be transported via Finland in addition to the current 5 million tonnes. It is also stated in the ministry's report that competition between the harbours of Russia, the Baltic States and Finland will become more fierce (Viitasalo and Österlund 1996: 24). In addition, there is overt competition between St. Petersburg and Kaliningrad for becoming the leader of Russian merchant shipping on the Baltic Sea (Wellman 1996: 176).

On the other hand, if Moscow's political relations with the Balts improve, the focus of Russia's goods traffic will be via the Baltic States. To meet this possibility, improvements in infrastructure are being already designed in the Baltic States, including the harbour of Muuga east of Tallinn in Estonia. If the costs of transporting goods via the Baltic States remain low, the pressures upon Russia to build new ports around St. Petersburg will be alleviated.

4. There are two important *humanitarian* issues in Russian relations with the Baltic Sea rim space. The first and most acute is the rights of the Russian-speaking minorities in the three Baltic States. This is very important from the points of view both of foreign policy (Russia's international authority) and of domestic policy (the confrontation between the government and opposition, the issue of refugees and displaced persons and so on).

The second issue is cultural co-operation between the related (Finno-Ugrian) nations of the north. The Russian leadership understands the need for this co-operation and favours the establishment of cultural ties between, for instance, Finns and Karelians, Mordva, Saami, Komi, Mansi and others (Osherenko and Young 1989: 84-86; *Nordic Council of Ministers Newsletter* January 1993).

For those four sets of reasons the Baltic issues were relatively important in Russian national debates on foreign policy in the 1990s. Obviously, they will retain their significance for Moscow in the foreseeable future.

However, the Russian leadership, being preoccupied with other problems, has sometimes underestimated the importance of the region. For example, the Nordic countries were not identified as a priority in the early drafts of the Russian foreign policy doctrine (Ministry of Foreign Affairs of the Russian Federation 1992). The three Baltic States are perceived predominantly through the prism of military and human rights issues while political, economic, environmental and cultural aspects are often ignored. Russian leaders prefer strong language regarding the Baltic States instead of quiet diplomacy. This incomplete view arises from failure to define the basic concepts of Russian diplomacy towards the Baltic/Nordic countries. The doctrinal principles of Russian strategy must be defined before a proper intellectual framework for shaping Moscow's policy in the region can be set up.

## *Wanted: a new Russian Baltic/Nordic security doctrine*

First of all, the Baltic States and the Nordic countries should be perceived as a united, indivisible region with its own historical traditions and basic characteristics rather than as two separate regions. Current Russian strategic thinking, in fact, ignores the existence of such a region (Rogov 1993: 76).

Second, there is a strong case for Russia identifying itself as part of this region-in-the-making and not as an external or intrusive power. For Russia to view its Baltic/Nordic policy solely as a policy *towards* the region is not adequate. It is conducted *within* the region as well.

Third, Russia's emotional attitudes to the Baltic problems sometimes have led to exaggeration of the significance of the Baltic issues and to a vision of the Baltic States as "a source of threat to Russia" (*Statement of the Russian Foreign Minister Kozyrev* 19 January 1994). The Baltic States, incidentally, are very skilful in using Russia's blunders to present Moscow as being in the wrong in the conflict.

Fourth, in dealing with its Baltic/Nordic problems, Russia acts from a unique place in the world security order. Russia's role will be crucial in the maintenance of order and stability within the Eurasian strategic space as well in establishing a link between the European and Eurasian security systems. Russia is in the process of changing its security role and image from being a force threatening European countries to being a mediator and guarantor. Russia's politico-military potential and great-power status can be instruments for the consolidation of the security order on the continent, not for winning unilateral advantages. The Baltic Sea and Nordic countries in fact constitute a border region between the European and Eurasian security regimes. This means a special responsibility for Moscow and a need for balance and restraint.

In fact, a new Baltic/Nordic security sub-system is emerging now in the region as a part of the European security order. This is natural as the countries of the region draw increasingly close for economic and political reasons. There is much discussion of its status, identity, orientation, role and concrete form in a contemporary scholarship (Kukk, Jervell, and Joenniemi 1992: 211–38; Øberg 1992: 20–26; Joenniemi and Vares 1993: 1–31, 39–65) but the existence of the sub-system is a matter of fact, which every regional actor should take into account.

It appears that Russia wishes to contribute to the development of this security sub-system and become a recognised member of it. To be realistic, it will not be simple for the Baltic and Nordic countries to accept the participation of Moscow. It will only be acceptable if Russia abandons its imperial traditions and interprets its membership in the security community as a duty rather than a natural privilege. Clearly, this cannot be realised immediately. Moscow should change the foundations of its foreign policy in order to put right former misperceptions among the countries of the region and to provide its diplomatic and military undertakings with a solid economic basis.

To summarise, a special and clearly pronounced Russian security doctrine for the Baltic/Nordic region is needed. Since Yeltsin's decree on relations with the Nordic countries (April 1992) and Kozyrev's speech at the Kirkenes meeting to establish the Barents Sea Council (January 1993) (*Statement of the Russian Foreign Minister Kozyrev* 19 January 1994), Moscow has not updated or clarified its security strategy toward the Baltic/Nordic region. The diplomatic initiative proposed by the Russian Prime Minister Victor Chernomyrdin at the Visby summit (May 1996) is targeted at economic and transregional rather than security co-operation in the area (Chernomyrdin 1996: 9–12). A coherent regional strategy is at present lacking.

## RUSSO-BALTIC SECURITY RELATIONS SINCE 1991

Russia's relations with the Baltic States came through several stages in the post-Communist epoch. In 1990-91, when both Russia and the Baltic republics struggled with the Soviet centre for independence, these relations were based on a co-operative basis. In 1992-94, two issues–withdrawal of Russian residual troops and Russian-speaking minorities rights–dominated in Moscow's security policies towards the Baltic Sea rim space. Since 1995 NATO and the EU's eastward expansion pre-occupied the area's security agenda.

*From friendship to a troubled neighbourliness?*

In 1990, all of the Baltic countries declared their intent to restore independence. In the spring of the same year, the Balts initiated negotiations with Moscow on the withdrawal of the Baltic republics from the USSR. The RSFSR, which presented itself as a sovereign state, supported the Balts in their striving for independence. In July 1990, at the Jurmala meeting of the Russian President Boris Yeltsin with the heads of the Baltic republics, horizontal relations between the four republics were established. The Russian leader signalled to his Baltic colleagues that Gorbachev's federative policy was less than constructive (Zhuryari 1994: 77).

In opposition to the Soviet centre, the RSFSR started negotiations with the Baltic republics on principles of inter-state relations. Talks with Estonia and Latvia were concluded in January 1991 (after the tragic events in Lithuania) and in July with Vilnius itself. Russia accepted that troops stationed in the Baltic republics had to be withdrawn, and that a solution to the Baltic problem had to be found at an international level.

Russian-Baltic friendly relations culminated on 20 August 1991, when amidst the power struggle in Moscow Yeltsin announced recognition of the independence of the Baltic republics and appealed to the world community to join him. Again, as in 1920, Russia paved the way for the Baltic republics' independence.

Nonetheless, the re-birth of the national statehood has brought to an end the former alliance between Russia and the Balts. A number of factors have aggravated Russo-Baltic security relations:

Despite the friendly rhetoric Moscow did not give up a geopolitical leadership in the area. Instead, Moscow proclaimed itself a guarantor and protector of security in the entire post-Soviet space. A concept of "enlightened post-imperialism" was adopted as guideline for the Russia's policy in the post-Soviet space (Vladislavlev and Karaganov 1992: 35).

In turn, the Balts made it clear that they would not follow Russia in their foreign policy orientations. Contrary to Moscow's expectations, they seemed not very obliged to Russia for liberation from the Soviet domination and subsequently did not hurry to express their gratitude.

Part of the Baltic political elites and broad public transformed their negative attitudes toward the Soviet centre into anti-Russian sentiment. For them, Russia will be a source of eternal threat posed by Moscow's historical inclination to expansion and imperialism. In turn, Moscow can not understand why the Balts do not trust it and why "democratic" Russia must be responsible for what the totalitarian regime did. In fact, a new enemy image was created by both sides.

A number of bilateral problems such as troop withdrawal, national minorities rights, territorial disputes, etc., has also contributed to the worsening of Russo-Baltic relations. All parties wanted their demands satisfied as soon as possible, regardless of real capabilities of a partner. This added kerosene to conflicts between Moscow and the Balts.

*Military issues*

There were four main problems in Russian-Baltic military relations: (a) the withdrawal of Russian troops from the Baltic States and related issues; (b) Russian military transit; (c) Russian military activities in the area; and (d) NATO enlargement.

*Withdrawal of Russian residual forces.* There were three main problems concerning withdrawal: (a) political–the linkage with human rights; (b) financial–costs of redeployment of forces and dismantling of military installations; and (c) technical–a future of Russian military property in the Baltic States and the accommodation of the withdrawn troops in Russia. Unfortunately, financial and technical issues were often hostages of grand policy. Quiet and pragmatic diplomacy gave way to political contingency and nerves.

Initially, Russia and the three Baltic States (except Lithuania) had completely different views of the problem. Russia had three main conditions: a) the Baltic States must guarantee the civil rights of the Russian minorities; b) the final date for withdrawal should be determined by the ability of the Russian Defence Ministry to accommodate the withdrawn forces; and c) the Baltic States should provide the Russian military with access to the bases and with transit rights. The Baltic States, however, insisted that the withdrawal should be a precondition for negotiations on other problems.

To the extent that Lithuania adopted citizenship legislation which has satisfied Russia, Moscow and Vilnius reached an agreement on withdrawal of residual forces relatively quickly. Russia completed withdrawal of its troops from Lithuania by 1 September 1993.

It was more difficult for Moscow to conclude agreements on troop withdrawal with Estonia and Latvia. Both sides, under pressure from domestic public opinion and hoping to gain more advantages, used tough tactics instead of a pragmatic search for a compromise.

For some time Russian Foreign Minister Andrei Kozyrev pursued a tactic of "linkage" between the issue of minorities and that of troop withdrawals which was a main instrument of Russian policy toward Estonia and Latvia. In 1993-94 Moscow postponed troop withdrawal several times, linking its decision with Russian-speaking minorities and financial issues (*Krasnaya Zvezda* 25 December 1993). However, its pressure on Estonia and Latvia had contradictory consequences. On the one hand, both conceded some liberalisation of their citizenship and language legislation and resolved the problem of retired Russian servicemen. On the other hand, it became apparent that Moscow's power to affect the Baltic countries' policy towards Russian minorities is limited, and Russian pressure evoked irritation and countermeasures. This cast doubt on the effectiveness of the tactic. The linkage tactic also proved to be very harmful for future Russian-Baltic relations. The Baltic States perceive Moscow's current policy as a continuation of Russian (or Soviet) imperial policy. They do not believe that the new Russian foreign policy has a truly democratic character.

Along with the ineffectiveness of the linkage tactics, two other factors have changed the Russian position: first, Western pressure on Moscow, and, second, Western promises to cover some of the expenses connected with force withdrawal. In July 1994, for example, when President Yeltsin declared a postponement of Russian withdrawal from Estonia, the US Senate amended a bill which would have provided $839 million in aid to Russia by making the departure of all Russian troops from Estonia and Latvia by 31 August a condition of the aid being disbursed (*The Baltic Independent* 22-28 July 1994). On the other hand, President Clinton at the Vancouver G-7 summit meeting in April 1993 promised Yeltsin $160 million to pay for housing Russian troops leaving the Baltics (*The Baltic Independent* 23 February 1995). At the same time, the USA, the UK, Germany and the Nordic countries exerted pressure (visibly and behind the scenes) upon the Baltic States to make them more flexible in negotiating with Moscow (*The Baltic Independent* 6-12 May 1994).

Finally, after lengthy and difficult negotiations, Russia concluded agreements with Latvia (30 April 1994) and Estonia (26 July 1994) and had withdrawn its troops from both countries by 31 August 1994. Small Russian contingents remained to maintain Skrunda radar station in Latvia for another five years and to dismantle nuclear reactors at the submarine training base in the Estonian port of Paldiski (*The Baltic Independent* 29 July – 4 August 1994, and 6–12 May 1994, and 5–11 August 1994).

The Baltic States are still concerned about the future of Russian military property left behind after force withdrawal, about the environmental consequences of the former Russian military presence in the region, and about the several thousands Russian servicemen still residing in Estonia and Latvia and waiting for housing to be built for them in Russia (*The Baltic Independent* 23 February 1995).

To summarise, compromise was finally reached on the basis of mutual concessions. Russia had failed to force Estonia and Latvia to grant citizenship automatically to all Russian-speaking inhabitants, to prolong troop withdrawal for years, to get compensation for its military property and to keep strategically important naval bases in the region. Estonia and Latvia had had to agree to guarantee the social rights of Russian military pensioners and to provide them with residence permits, to give Moscow some limited access to base facilities (Skrunda radar station), and to abandon their claims to financial compensation for ecological damage caused by the Russian military.

*Russian military transit.* This problem first emerged in relation to the Russian troop withdrawal from Germany in 1991. In 1993, Russia and Lithuania signed an agreement regulating the use of Lithuania's railway system and other transportation facilities, especially the ferry line from Mukran (Rügen) to Klaipeda for the withdrawal of the Russian troops from Germany up to 1995. According to the agreement, Russia had to ask permission for every transport, submit to inspection and pay fees. The troops must not to leave the wagons or carry weapons and the trains could only make authorised stops (Joenniemi 1996b: 13-14).

The above agreement was never ratified by the Lithuanian Parliament. There was a powerful opposition both to the 1993 agreement and a concluding new one in the legislature. Some factions were generally opposed to Russia's military transit through Lithuania. They argued that Russia may provoke incidents and then use them against Lithuania. They also believed that Russia does not perceive Lithuania as a sovereign state because its military aircraft repeatedly violated the country's airspace.

Other politicians insisted the agreement should not be prolonged upon withdrawal of troops from Germany. They pointed out that since 1995, Moscow would be able to use the ferry line from St. Petersburg to Kaliningrad built specially for this purpose. Costs of shipment of military personnel and materials via St. Petersburg would be much lower than by rail through Lithuania. Some were not against military transit in principle but opposed to concluding a formal agreement with Moscow. Instead, they proposed to establish unilateral general rules for military and other dangerous transit (Nekrasas 1996: 72).

The latter point of view was close to the Cabinet's position. On 3 October 1994, Lithuania's Labour government–under strong pressure from the conservatives led by ex-President Landsbergis–adopted the resolution No. 938 that made military transit virtually impracticable. Under new rules, the Russian military needed special permission from Lithuanian authorities for each border crossing (Nekrasas 1996: 72; Wellman 1996: 175-176). However, yielding to Russia's pressure, the government has also agreed to prepare a bilateral document specifying some financial and other details of Russia's military transit.

Moscow, however, wanted both a new accord on military transit and a comprehensive political agreement. Trying to compel Lithuania to sign new documents Russia doubled import duties on Lithuanian goods in 1994 and postponed putting into force the 1993 trade agreement containing most favoured nation status. Moscow asked the EU countries to put pressure on Vilnius to resolve the problem.

Finally, a compromise was reached. In January 1995 Moscow and Vilnius exchanged the diplomatic notes by which Lithuania agreed to extend the current rules for Russian military transit to Kaliningrad Region until the end of 1995, and Russia stated that the agreement giving Lithuania MFN status, signed in November 1993, had come into force (*The Baltic Independent* 3–9 February 1995). The agreement on military transit has since been later extended on a yearly basis. Russia, however, was not satisfied with a partial solution. It is still looking for a comprehensive agreement to settle along with the transit issue a number of other disputable questions.

*Russian military activities.* The Russian military has considerably reduced its activities in the region, motivated both by political and economic considerations.

The Baltic Military District (MD) has been abolished. The Leningrad (Northern) MD has been provided with a more defensive configuration. In

1990-96 the number of motor rifle divisions in the MD fell from 11 to 5, the number of tanks was reduced from 1,200 to 870, and the numbers of artillery, multiple rocket launchers and mortars fell from 2,140 to 1,000. Over the same period the KOR reduced its number of tank divisions from 2 to 1, the artillery division was transformed into three brigades, the airborne brigade was dismissed, the number of surface-to-surface missile brigades fell from 3 to 1, the number of artillery pieces was reduced from 677 to 426, and the number of combat aircraft fell from 155 to 28. Over the same period the Baltic Fleet reduced its number of submarines from 42 (2 strategic and 40 tactical) to 6 (all tactical) and the number of surface ships from 450 (39 principal combatants, 150 patrol and coastal combatants, 120 mine warfare, 21 amphibious and 120 support vessels) to 259 (31 principal combatants, 42 patrol and coastal combatants, 60 mine warfare, 8 amphibious and 118 support ships) (International Institute for Strategic Studies 1990: 39-40; 1996: 114-115, 118).

Most of Russia's submarines and major surface vessels are no longer on the alert and are stationed in their bases. They often have no fuel to stay out at sea. At the same time the Russian Navy's operational capacity has been reduced. According to some reports, only 30 per cent of the Navy's needs for repairs and ship maintenance can be met (Dellenbrant and Olsson 1994: 168). Military shipbuilding has been reduced or in some cases stopped.

This has reduced Baltic concerns regarding a Russian military threat. However, the Russian military presence and activities in the region are still fairly intensive.

Russia is to expand its naval facilities at Baltiysk in a plan linked to the withdrawal of warships from the Baltic States, according to Admiral Vladimir G. Yegorov. The naval presence at Baltiysk will be expanded to include more conventional submarines and new barracks to house a 1,100-strong maritime border guard unit (*Jane's Defence Weekly* 13 March 1993). In addition to a motor rifle division stationed in the KOR, one more was redeployed from ex-Czechoslovakia. In 1990-95 the number of tanks increased from 802 to 893 (850–in 1996), the number of armoured combat vehicles increased from 1081 to 1156 (925–in 1996), and the number of attack helicopters increased from 48 to 52 (International Institute for Strategic Studies 1995: 105; 1996: 114).

Some Scandinavian military experts believe that the lack of cohesion and precisely defined military purposes makes Russia's considerable forces in the region useless in a military sense (Clemmesen 1993). However, most of the Baltic leaders consider this potential as sufficient to create a significant threat to their countries' security in the event of possible tension.

*NATO extension.* Russia varies its policies towards the Baltic Sea countries as regards the question of NATO enlargement.

Russia is content with Finland and Sweden's positions in this regard. Despite occasional discussions of the pro-NATO perspective in some political quarters, Finland's official position is that Helsinki is neither seeking NATO membership nor actively promoting NATO enlargement in Eastern Europe. In Helsinki's view, changes in Europe's military configuration could create new security problems or inequalities, particularly in the relationship between itself, Russia and the Baltic States. Finland acknowledges that Russia is opposed to hasty enlargement of NATO, fearing that expansion towards its borders will, among other things, encourage extreme anti-democracy and nationalist forces inside the country. Finland is keen not to alienate Russia over NATO, preferring to wait and see what future strategic partnership between the two might bring (*Jane's Defence Weekly* 19 August 1995). As the Finnish delegation noted in its statement resulted from the meeting at the NATO secretariat (May 1996), "It is essential to European security that NATO and Russia are able to co-operate in accordance with the principles adopted by the OSCE. Creation of new spheres of influence in Europe must be avoided. Every country has the right to choose or change its security arrangements. Security interests are not to be pursued at the expense of others." (Finnish Ministry of Foreign Affairs 1996: 2).

The Swedish approach to the security problem has much in common with the Finnish one. In its report, the Swedish parliamentary defence committee said: "Swedish membership in NATO and/or the WEU would not benefit Swedish security interests, or stability in our part of the world." (*Jane's Defence Weekly* 19 August 1995).

Helsinki and Stockholm have praised the 1997 Paris Russia-NATO charter (cf. below) as an act of good will oriented to the creation of a co-operative security system in Europe.

Since Finland and Sweden joined the PfP programme and obtained observer status in the WEU, the two countries are no longer neutral states. However, Russia is interested in securing the non-alignment status of Finland and Sweden and strongly opposes the very idea of their possible joining NATO in the foreseeable future.

Poland's eagerness to join NATO has led to worsening of the overall Russo-Polish relations (in particular, in security issues). However, the

Russian leadership realised from the very beginning that it would be unable to prevent Warsaw from going into the alliance. Long before the Paris accords and Madrid summit, Moscow has decided that Russia's tacit consent with Poland's adhesion to NATO would be exchanged for NATO's promises not to accept the Baltic States and the CIS countries.

As for the Baltic States, their desire to join NATO has evoked Moscow's painful reaction. There is consensus in Russia regarding NATO extension as a serious threat to national security. Russian arguments against NATO enlargement could be summarised as follows:

NATO enlargement would destroy the existing "security buffer" between Russia and NATO and shift strategic balance in favour of the West; it could bring NATO military presence to the Russian borders, potentially including foreign military bases and nuclear weaponry; NATO extension could evoke a Russian military build-up on the western and north-western borders to protect Kaliningrad, Novgorod, St. Petersburg and other vulnerable areas; it would strengthen a "war party" inside Russia which could demand a stoppage of military reforms and re-militarise the country; NATO enlargement could accelerate a creation of the military alliance within the CIS and resume confrontation in Europe on the military block basis; it would challenge Ukraine and Moldova's status of neutral states; The alliance's extension could generate a new crisis and even potential collapse of the CFE Treaty; it would undermine the OSCE's role as a main backbone of the European security system, etc. (*International Affairs* [Moscow] 41 (11-12): 3-23; Arbatov 1995: 146).

The Russian leadership believes the East and Central European countries' NATO membership would not enhance their security. On the contrary, it could compel Moscow to perceive them as a potential threat to Russia's security. Presently, Moscow's concerns are mostly related to the soft security issues (minorities rights, territorial disputes, smuggling, etc.) in the case of the Baltic States. Russia's relations with the Visegrad countries are not burdened with any serious security problems at all. Their membership, however, would shift Russian threat perceptions to the hard security issues.

Some experts suggest that Russia mainly poses challenges to neighbours' security by its internal instability rather than by aggressive external policy. To cope with such threats Russia's neighbouring countries do not need to respond by military means. The best way to prevent confrontation is to develop bilateral relations and multilateral co-operation targeted at the creation of an inter-dependence mechanism. The latter could be the best safeguard against any mutual mistrust or fluctuations in the political conjuncture (Sergounin 1996: 115).

At the institutional level, options other than NATO are available. Moscow does not oppose EU (and WEU) enlargement. Some Western and Nordic politicians and experts think that the Baltic States (at least Estonia) could be brought into the EU quite soon and without posing an enormous economic burden on EU members (Asmus and Nurick 1996: 134). Along with economic benefits the Baltic States could enjoy enhanced security because even a hypothetical authoritarian regime in Russia would not dare to attack a EU member-state. In addition, the Nordic countries could enhance their military co-operation with the Baltic States. This is also more acceptable for Moscow than NATO extension.

Some Russian experts proposed to change the entire European security architecture to prevent a new clash between East and West. The OSCE should become a main collective security organisation on the continent. The OSCE has to create a European Security Council (ESC) with permanent members possessing veto power and a number of rotating non-permanent members, representing smaller European and CIS states. NATO and the WEU should be subordinated to the ESC and serve as its military arms in maintaining regional security (especially in peace-keeping operations) (Arbatov 1996: 248-249).

Since those proposals proved to be unrealistic, most of the Russian experts have focused on the search for a compromise with the West. They proposed to delay NATO enlargement for some years and limit it to the Visegrad countries but not extend its membership to the Baltic States. They also proposed a special Russia-NATO charter to ensure Moscow's security (no further expansion to the CIS countries, no military bases and nuclear weapons on the territory of new members, continuation of arms control dialogue, etc.) (Arbatov 1994: 70-71; Arbatov 1995: 146; Rogov 1995: 10-11; Trenin 1995: 20-26).

The Paris charter[3] and the decisions adopted by the Madrid summit (*International Herald Tribune* 9 July 1997) have generally satisfied the Russian foreign policy elite. Moscow was content with NATO's decision to limit the first round of extension to the three Visegrad countries only, as well as with the guarantees of Russia's security and prospects for a revised

---

3. For the text of the NATO-Russia Founding Act see *Rossiyskaya Gazeta*, 28 May 1997: 3; and for the brief summary of the document see *International Herald Tribune*, 28 May 1997: 1, 16.

CFE Treaty. Moscow was particularly delighted with delaying the Baltic States admission to NATO for an indefinite future.

In July 1997 the NATO leaders declared at the Madrid summit that "the door is open" to new candidates. During her July 1997 visit to Vilnius, US State Secretary Madeleine Albright assured the Baltic States that they were not permanently excluded from membership in the alliance, even though the summit meeting in Madrid neither invited them to join nor identified them as candidates for the next round of enlargement. "We have said all along that NATO is open to all democratic market systems in Europe," Mrs. Albright replied when asked in a Russian TV interview whether the three former Soviet republics could become members of the alliance. "All those kind of countries are eligible," she said. "It doesn't matter where a country is on the map, they are eligible for membership in NATO." (*International Herald Tribune* 14 July 1997: 7)

For this reason, Russia's security concerns over the future developments remain. Commenting on the Madrid meeting, Primakov asserted that "NATO enlargement is a big mistake, possibly the biggest mistake since the end of the Second World War" (*International Herald Tribune* 9 July 1997: 10)

Moscow continues to insist that there is no need for the Baltic States to come to NATO because many other security options are available. A number of influential Western experts are tending to such a point of view as well. As Asmus and Nurick of RAND put it, the outline of a compromise and an interim step could be: (a) Estonia's early full membership in the EU, partial membership in the WEU and expanded co-operation with NATO under PfP; (b) burdens sharing between NATO and the Nordic states; and (c) acknowledgement of Russian sensitivities (Asmus and Nurick 1996: 139-140). The Balts themselves, however, do not accept such a solution and vigorously protest against such proposals (*International Herald Tribune* 6 December 1996 & 30 May 1997).

With regard to the Baltic States' security concerns, a partial solution could probably be found if all interested sides–NATO, the Nordic Council, the Baltic Sea Council and Russia, not just one country or alliance–were to make joint efforts to strengthen the security of the Baltic States. On Russia's side, a valuable next step in the formation of a more stable security system in the region would be an effort diplomatically and psychologically to calm the fears of at least those Baltic States which worry about a Russian military doctrine which foresees the use of military force to protect ethnic Russians in the "near abroad".

In September 1994, Russia offered the Baltic States bilateral security agreements like those signed that month with Norway, Finland and Denmark. According to Russian Defence Minister Pavel Grachev, another possibility was one multilateral security agreement signed by the three Baltic States and Russia (*The Baltic Independent* 22 September 1994). However, the prime ministers of the Baltic States, meeting in Riga on 13 September, had earlier said such a Russian proposal should be rejected because it was premature and old problems should be resolved first (*The Baltic Independent* 29 September 1994).

The above-mentioned measures could be complemented by intensification of the arms control process if governments combined to push the arms control issues through the OSCE negotiation agenda and through the meetings of Nordic foreign ministers, the Baltic Sea Council and the Barents Sea Council.

The first problem, naval arms, are mostly excluded from the negotiation process. Unilateral measures were taken for the reduction of naval armaments and naval activities, especially under the Gorbachev Administration, but they related mainly to obsolete weapons (Heininen and Käkönen 1991: 7-8; Norwegian Ministry of Foreign Affairs 1992: 16). Regional initiatives so far have ranged from the numbers and location of troops in the Baltic Sea area, to the deployment of forces withdrawn from Eastern Europe and the former Soviet republics, to submarine activities on the Baltic Sea (this is especially important for Sweden) and the prevention of military incidents.

Negotiations on confidence-building measures (CBMs) at sea could be a useful addition to the said initiatives. Co-ordination of naval exercises schedules, any increase in naval power or essential naval activities by NATO, Russia and non-NATO Baltic Sea countries, inspections and study missions, exchanges and visits between the fleets and military academies or discussions of the naval doctrine and force posture of all sea powers of the region could contribute to mutual understanding. Russia could amend these initiatives by analogous steps regarding land forces, in the way, for instance, it has already given the forces of the Leningrad MD a more defensive configuration. An important point for the future negotiating agenda is the issue of accident assistance. At a minimum, assurances ought to be exchanged that help will be provided and accepted when needed. It might prevent or reduce the risks of accidents like *Komsomolets* submarine disaster.

The first signs of Russia's co-operation with the Baltic Sea countries in the military field have appeared already. In June 1994, the US led a flotilla of 42 warships from 15 countries in multinational joint exercise manoeuvres on the Baltic (*Military and Arms Transfers News* 17 June 1994). Three months later Lithuania, Poland, Russia and Sweden and the naval forces of NATO countries all joined for Co-operation Venture '94, a naval exercise in the North Sea and Norwegian Sea (*The Baltic Independent* 23 – 29 September 1994). Danish Defence Minister Hans Haekkerup visited his Russian counterpart Pavel Grachev (for the first time in the history of Danish-Russian relations) in March 1993 and concluded an agreement for exchange visits involving naval fleets and military cadets (*DanNews* 16–23 March 1993). On 11 September 1994, Defence Minister Grachev signed agreements on military co-operation with Denmark, Finland and Norway during a visit to Copenhagen (*The Baltic Independent* 16 – 22 September 1994).

However, a number of factors make negotiations and the implementation of arms control and CBMs initiatives nearly impossible. First, the three Baltic States do not trust Russian promises and guarantees and prefer to rely upon the protection of NATO and the Nordic countries. Second, because Russia has no consistent foreign and military policy towards the region, threats follow goodwill initiatives and vice versa. Third, in the last five years Moscow's attention has turned from arms control issues to national conflicts on the southern and south-western boards of the former Soviet Union at a time when the West has been preoccupied by peacekeeping in the former Yugoslavia and other problems.

## National minorities

Russian-speaking minorities are a serious problem for most of the Baltic States. The same countries which have accused the Soviet Union of violating the rights of national minorities have now themselves established numerous restrictions regarding non-citizens. There are several arguments in support of those restrictions that are common to all the Baltic States.

First, according to Baltic constitutional and legal thinking, all Soviet legislation on citizenship and human rights since 1940, i.e., from the beginning of "Soviet occupation," is illegal. The restoration of Baltic citizenship legislation, therefore, meant a choice between the "1940 option" (citizenship would be granted automatically to those who were Baltic citizens before the occupation and their descendants) and the "zero option" (citizenship would be granted automatically to all inhabitants of the three former Soviet republics). Estonia and Latvia have decided in favour of the 1940 option; Lithuania has chosen the zero option. Second, the Baltic States refer to the Russia's imperial legacy and authoritarian nationalism. Baltic politicians point out that there are many chauvinistic leaders even in democratic Russia. If they came to power the Russian communities in the Baltic States could become both a pretext for intervention and a "fifth column". Third, the Baltic States worry about the Baltic national cultures and identities which were very much under attack during the Soviet era. According to Baltic perceptions, the Russians have very limited knowledge of Baltic languages, history and culture and are seen as a threat to the national cultures (Joenniemi and Vares 1993: 140-142). In turn, this serves as an excuse for discrimination on the basis of language. The nature of the restrictions varies from country to country.

In accordance with Estonian legislation, persons who took up residence after the country was incorporated into the Soviet Union in 1940 and their descendants (474,000 or 30 per cent of the population) (*Vestnik Moskovskogo Universiteta* [5] 1992: 67) were not permitted to participate in the constitutional referendum or the elections and do not have the right to an Estonian passport because they are not citizens. A law of February 1992 which has covered naturalisation requirements provided for a two-year residency requirement to be followed by a one-year waiting period and knowledge of the Estonian language (US Department of State 1993: 765). According to the Estonian Department for Citizenship and Migration, by the beginning of 1995 nearly 50,000 people had been naturalised. According to the Russian embassy in Tallinn, approximately 60,000 people have taken Russian citizenship in Estonia by that moment (*The Baltic Independent* 27 January–2 February 1995).

On 19 January 1995 Estonia passed a second, stricter citizenship law which stipulates five years' residence plus a one-year waiting period to process applications and a test on the basics of the Estonian constitution and the citizenship law, in addition to the Estonian-language test. According to Estonian experts, the law, which took effect on 1 April 1995, has no retroactive force. This means the changes would not affect the country's current non-citizen population (*The Baltic Independent* 27 January–2 February 1995). The authorities established a deadline of 12 July 1995 for application for work and residence permits. About 80 per cent of non-citizens have applied for permits.

Although discrimination on the basis of race, sex, or other grounds is prohibited by the Estonian Constitution, relationships between Estonians and the large ethnic Russian population remain tense. Non-Estonians, especially Russians, have continued to allege discrimination in jobs, salaries and housing based on language requirements.

On 21 February 1995 Estonia adopted a new language law. It left unchanged the system of language testing and categorisation by which non-Estonians qualify for citizenship and work permits and added a declaration that Estonian is the only official language. It provided for the regulation of public signs and announcements, specifying fines for the use of foreign or irregular (ungrammatical) language and prohibits the use of foreign languages without an Estonian translation on television and radio broadcasts unless a programme is clearly targeted at a foreign-speaking audience (as the Russian-language news programmes are) (*The Baltic Independent* 3 – 9 March 1995). The new legislation met with an angry reaction from non-citizens and from Moscow.

In Latvia ethnic Latvians now make up only 52 per cent of the population, and none of the country's seven largest cities boasts an ethnic Latvian majority (*Mirovaya Ekonomika i Mezhdunarodnye Otnosheniya* (12) 1993; *The Baltic States: A Reference Book* 1991: 92). The possibility that non-Latvians who entered the country during the Soviet period could control the balance of political power made citizenship and naturalisation issues particularly contentious here as well. Under the citizenship act passed by parliament in October 1991, only those who were citizens prior to 17 June 1940 and their direct descendants could to claim citizenship. The citizenship status of other residents of Latvia, including those who arrived or were born there during the Soviet period, was unresolved.

In 1994 a revision of this citizenship act became a hostage of the political debate regarding the withdrawal of Russian troops: the parliament passed a law that Latvia would not naturalise new citizens until the Russian Army had left. On 21 June 1994 the parliament passed a tough citizenship law including the controversial quota system,[4] which gave rise to concerns both in Moscow and at the Council of Europe and was amended after the Council of Europe gave some hints that it could prevent Latvia's joining the latter. Most applicants will thus now be naturalised by 2003 (*The Baltic*

---

4. Non-citizens born in Latvia could gain naturalisation from 1 January 1995 until the year 2000. This figure was estimated at 230,000. After the turn of the century there would be 500,000 remaining non-citizens who under the quotas were estimated to gain naturalization at a rate of 2,000 per year (*The Baltic Independent*, 24-30 June 1994: 1).

*Independent* 29 July – 4 August 1994). Latvia became a member of the Council of Europe in February 1995, and, finally, on 12 April 1995, the parliament passed a long-awaited law applying to citizens of the former USSR who were permanent residents of Latvia prior to 1 July 1992. It outlined non-citizens' freedom to choose their place of residence, their right to leave and re-enter Latvia, their preservation of language and culture in Latvia and established that non-citizens cannot be expelled except under special circumstances and safeguarded their personal security. Non-citizens of Latvia over the age of 16 will now be eligible for a non-citizen's passport which allows them to travel to and from the country (*The Baltic Independent* 21-27 April 1995).

The implementation of the law has led to new controversies. Human rights organisations and some members of the Latvian Parliament have criticised the Citizenship and Immigration Department for repeated abuses of power, including the unlawful confiscation of passports, the issuing of subsequent deportation orders, and demands for documents not actually required by law from persons applying for citizenship (*The Baltic Independent* 28 April – 4 May 1995).

Even some Baltic observers admit that Estonian and Latvian legislation on citizenship, official languages and civil rights based on the majority rule principle is not fully in conformity with democratic standards. They make at least three reservations about these laws: (a) there is a considerable difference between formal law and justice; (b) majority rule is not the one and only principle of democratic legislation; and (c) the citizenship laws are, in a sense, retroactive legislation (Joenniemi and Vares 1993: 134).

Unlike the other Baltic States, Lithuania passed a citizenship law (US Department of State 1993: 835) that is fully in line with European standards except for a residence requirement of 10 years. As a result over 90 per cent of the ethnic Poles, Russians, Belarussians, Ukrainians and Jews who make up 20 per cent of the Lithuanian population were granted citizenship. The reason for this tolerance is fairly simple: non-Lithuanians do not threaten control over power in the country where native inhabitants essentially outnumber others.

The Yeltsin Government has been heavily criticised by Russians in the Baltic States and by nationalists in Russia itself for neglecting the human rights situation in the Baltic States in 1991-92. As a result, Yeltsin has changed his policy on this problem. On 1 October 1991 the Russian State Council declared that the Russian leadership was responsible for all Russians living in the former Soviet republics. In February 1992 Foreign

Minister Kozyrev made it clear in his speech at a UN conference on human rights that Russia regarded this issue as a very high priority in its foreign policy (Kukk, Jervel and Joenniemi 1992: 99-100). In 1992-94 Russian officials, contrary to declared government policy, referred several times to the issue of national minorities as a reason to delay withdrawal of the remaining forces. Following the demands of Russia and international human rights organisations, the Council of Baltic Sea States in its meeting in Helsinki in March 1993 decided to appoint a High Commissioner for Human Rights and Minorities who would monitor the situation not only in Estonia and Latvia but in all 10 member countries (*The Baltic Independent* 25 March 1993).

The problem of national minorities has damaged Russian-Baltic relations, delayed Russian troop withdrawal and destabilised the whole regional system of international relations.

What steps could be undertaken by Russia to improve the human rights situation in the Baltic States when it has limited resources to influence the Baltic States in this regard? The use of force is ruled out. Russia has only diplomatic and economic instruments at its disposal as a last resort to prevent discrimination against Russians there.

The resolution (or non-resolution) of this complex problem depends mainly on the Baltic States themselves, their wisdom, soberness and goodwill. However, Russia can assist to some extent in solving the problem, by continuing its efforts together with the Nordic and other European countries, on a bilateral basis and through the international institutions, to stimulate Latvia and Estonia to complete the process of naturalisation of non-citizens, to soften authorities' attitude to a dual citizenship, to guarantee the right of national minorities to cultural autonomy and to observe human rights standards. That could create favourable conditions for the achievement of social consensus and the integration of national minorities into society.

## Territorial disputes

There are various causes of territorial conflicts in the region–historical, economic, ethnic, political and technical. Some are old, others relatively new.

*Karelia.* The Karelia issue is quite old. It has both a historical and an ethnic background. The Karelians are a nation related to the Finns and constitute only 10 per cent of the population in their eponymous republic. Karelia developed as a part of Finland from the 14th century, Finland itself being first a part of Sweden and then of Russia. Shortly after it achieved independence, in 1918–20 Finland occupied a part of Karelia belonging to Soviet Russia, was defeated and was forced to sign the Tartu Peace Treaty (of 14 October 1920) which legitimised the division of Karelia (Sukianen 1948). The repressive national and agricultural policy of the Soviet authorities in Soviet Karelia led to a rebellion in 1921–22, supported by Finland and cruelly suppressed by the Red Army, as result of which many Karelians migrated to Finland. Under the Moscow Peace Treaty of 12 March 1940 which followed the Soviet–Finnish war of 1939–40, the rest of Karelia (including Vyborg) and the western and northern coasts of Lake Ladoga were transferred to the Soviet Union. The subsequent Soviet–Finnish agreements (the 1944 Moscow armistice and the 1947 Paris peace treaty) confirmed the status of Karelia as an autonomous republic of the RSFSR (Szajkowski 1993: 41; Joenniemi 1996a: 2-4).

There has been much discussion on the Karelia question in Finland during the past few years. The collapse of the Soviet Union, the restoration of the independence of the Baltic countries and the negotiations between Japan and Russia concerning the return of the Kurile Islands to Japan served as an additional spur to the discussion (Joenniemi 1996a: 5-11). Finland has taken a rather negative attitude towards the idea of initiating official negotiations on the return of Karelia. In December 1991, the Finnish Government officially renounced all claims to Karelia (Szajkowski 1993: 170) although some groups in Finland and the Karelian Association in the Karelian Autonomous Republic have continued to press both Helsinki and Moscow for Karelia to be returned to Finland.

It should be emphasised that it is impossible for Russia even to recognise officially the existence of the question. Any negotiations on territorial problems with other countries could undermine Yeltsin's domestic political position; and the Russian leadership is cautious about generating a "chain reaction" in the region. If Moscow recognises the Karelia issue it could seem to lend legitimacy to other claims. During his official visit to Finland in July 1992 President Yeltsin made it clear that there was no such issue. Finland stated that, at that point, the question would not be raised, but at the same time reminded President Yeltsin that the principles of the OSCE made it possible to change borders by peaceful means.

More recently the Russian leadership signalled that it is ready to make at least symbolic concessions on the Karelian issue even though any talks on border shifts have been avoided. In May 1994 Yeltsin for the first time acknowledged that the annexation of Finnish Karelia was an aggressive act of Stalin's policy (Joenniemi 1996a: 11-12). The Russian Ambassador to Helsinki, Yuriy Deryabin, stated that in reality the future position of Karelia called for discussion, but instead of changes to the border the aim should be to lower the level of border controls (Finnish Institute of International Affairs 1992: 30-31). Russia prefers to develop direct ties between Finland and Karelia rather than to recognise the problem officially (Nordic Council 1992: 43). It hopes that intensive trans-border co-operation will ease tensions and prevent any official claims in the future.

*Kaliningrad.* The origins of the Kaliningrad issue lie in decisions taken after World War II. By decision of the Potsdam Peace Conference (1945) a part of former East Prussia, including its capital, Königsberg, was given to Russia. In 1946 the Kaliningrad Region was formed as a part of the RSFSR. Ethnic Germans were moved away from this territory (most of them left the city before the arrival of the Red Army) and the region was populated mainly by Russians, who today make up 80 per cent of the inhabitants (Joenniemi 1996b: 6-7). The overall population of the region is now 900,000 civilians plus an unspecified number of military personnel and demobilised soldiers (estimates range from 60,000 to 400,000) (Szajkowski 1993: 163; SIPRI 1994: 177; *Jane's Intelligence Review* December 1994). Ten per cent of the population are Belarussians. According to some accounts, in 1994 approximately 17,000–18,000 Germans were resident in the region, although their passports often state that they are Russian or Ukrainian (the official figure was 6,000) (*Jane's Intelligence Review* December 1994).

A completely new situation has arisen following the collapse of the Soviet Union and the Baltic States' achievement of independence, which separated the Kaliningrad Region from Russian territory. Some German politicians (and even some Russian leaders before German reunification) have considered the exclave as a possible place for the creation of a German autonomous area in Russia in order to prevent further German emigration from Russia (Blanc-Noël 1992: 62–63; Szajkowski 1993: 165). This is resisted by the present inhabitants of the region, although they favour German assistance to the region and the development of a free economic zone. Some extremist groups in Germany claim the return of Königsberg to the "Vaterland" (Calabuig 1991). Although officially Bonn does not support these proposals they make Moscow nervous because the issue is very sensitive for Russians. A number of German organisations in Russia have proposed solutions to the Kaliningrad issue. Freiheit (Freedom), an association which emerged in the spring of 1993 as a radical voice for the interests of Russian Germans, decided to press for the formation (between 1995 and 1997) of a sovereign Baltic German republic under Russian jurisdiction in the Kaliningrad Region. At the same time the association stated that "it should not be ruled out that this territory will eventually again be incorporated into Germany" (Szajkowski 1993: 118). The Society of Old Prussia, set up in 1990 and comprising activists of several nationalities including ethnic Germans, aims to restore the pre-Soviet traditions and in the long run achieve independence for the region (Szajkowski 1993: 393).

Interestingly, in contrast with Moscow, the Kaliningrad authorities are not afraid of a possible influx of Russian Germans from the territory of the former Soviet Union. According to some experts, there is sufficient room for 100,000 Germans in the Kaliningrad Region (*Jane's Intelligence Review* December 1994). However, Germany has refrained from highlighting Kaliningrad in its official assistance to ethnic Germans in Russia. This programme is restricted to selected regions, and Kaliningrad is not one of them.

Russia's policy is to stimulate economic and cultural contacts and tourism between Kaliningrad and Germany as well as with other countries of the Baltic Sea area and at the same time to prevent a mass migration of Germans to the strategically important region. In November 1991, President Yeltsin issued a decree granting the city of Kaliningrad the status of a free economic zone. Under the Russian scenario, the area could become an West–East trade bridge, Russia's Hong Kong.[5] Several hundred joint ventures have been registered (45 per cent of them with German companies), mostly small service operations (Szajkowski 1993: 164; Matochkin 1995: 11).

However, there was a difference of opinion between Moscow and the Kaliningrad local authorities about the status of the region and the prospects for its economic co-operation with foreign countries. The

---

5. According to Yuri Matochkin, Head of Administration of the Kaliningrad Region, the FEZ was established to speed the socio-economic growth of the region and raise the standard of living by expanding trade, economic, scientific and technological co-operation with foreign countries, attracting foreign investments and technologies, etc. (Matochkin, 1995: 9).

regional government has proposed to transform the FEZ into a Special Economic Zone (SEZ) provided with even more autonomy and privileges. Russian Deputy Prime Minister Sergey Shakhrai has complained that foreign investors there get significant tax and other concessions while investing insignificant amounts of money. As of 1 September 1994, a total of 885 enterprises with foreign investments were registered in the Kaliningrad Region, 239 of them fully foreign-owned. Foreign investors accounted for less than $2 million (*The Baltic Independent* 4–10 November 1994). According to Shakhrai, the region is already being turned into a channel for the export of raw materials, including strategic resources, and for the creeping expansion of foreign influence in the economic and ethnic spheres, with the prospect of the creation of a "fourth independent Baltic state" (*The Baltic Independent* 10 November 1994). As a compromise Shakhrai proposed, instead of making the whole of the region a free economic zone, the creation of limited zones of free trade activity near ports and main roads in the region, stressing that "we have again to declare clearly the priority of Russia's military–strategic interests in the Kaliningrad *oblast*" (*The Baltic Independent* 10 November 1994).

Under the pressure of the "centralists," the federal authorities tried to tighten their control over the Kaliningrad Region. In May 1995 Yeltsin suddenly abolished the customs exemptions and this led to annulment of a large number of contracts. Moscow disavowed a trade agreement signed between Kaliningrad and Lithuania and control was retained over border and visa questions (Joenniemi 1996b: 19).

The regional leadership was able, however, to persuade the President to continue with the FEZ. On 18 May 1995, Yeltsin issued a decree on social and economic development of the Kaliningrad Region which provided the FEZ with broad powers in foreign economic policy, tax privileges and state support in protection of region's producers, creating ferry line between Kaliningrad and Vyborg and establishing a unified maritime administration of the Port of Kaliningrad (Shumeiko 1995: 7).

In 1996, however, the power struggle between the centre and the region continued. By the presidential decree the FEZ was transformed into SEZ. On the one hand, the latter got back some customs privileges; on the other hand, the regional authorities lost part of their foreign policy powers. The centre took control over the defence industry, mineral resources, energy production, transport and mass media. Foreigners are not allowed to purchase land, but it can be leased for periods yet to be settled (Joenniemi 1996b: 19). The outcome of this "tug-of-war" remains unclear.

The concentration of the Russian military in Kaliningrad (although substantially reduced in recent years) is another matter of concern for neighbouring Poland and Lithuania. According to *The Military Balance,* in 1996 Kaliningrad hosted 24,000 ground forces equipped with 850 tanks, 925 armoured combat vehicles, 426 artillery pieces, 12 *Scud* missiles, and 52 attack helicopters. Air defence had 28 Su-27s and 50 surface-to-air missiles (International Institute for Strategic Studies 1996: 114). Baltiysk (50 km from Kaliningrad) is the main naval base for the Baltic Sea. Admiral Yegorov told the *Jane's Intelligence Review* correspondent that, despite the speculation of foreign specialists, there were only about 60,000 military men stationed in the Kaliningrad Region (*Jane's Intelligence Review* December 1994).

Lithuania, which is especially concerned with the Russian military potential in Kaliningrad, has demonstrated its understanding of the strategic importance of the exclave for Russia. It was thus possible for military transit agreements to be agreed between the two countries in 1993 and 1995. At the same time the Baltic States and Poland have repeatedly proposed the demilitarisation of the region. For example, in November 1994 the Baltic Assembly, the parliamentary body of the three Baltic countries, adopted a resolution calling for an international round table conference on the demilitarisation of Kaliningrad (*The Baltic Independent* 18 – 24 November 1994). Moscow interprets such appeals as open interference in its internal affairs. According to ex-Foreign Minister Kozyrev, "the Russian side will never and with no one discuss in this context the 'future' of the Kaliningrad Region and its status" (ibid.). As mentioned, Moscow does not even rule out the possibility for re-militarisation of the KOR should NATO be enlarged in this area.

To summarise, the Russian leadership still considers Kaliningrad as an important military–strategic outpost of Russia in the Baltic region and will keep the Russian military presence at a significant level.

*The Baltic States.* Other disputes have been generated or reactivated by the Baltic States' achieving independence. Some of the Baltic States consider their existing borders unjust and have claims on neighbouring territories.

Some of these claims are political in nature and are being used as bargaining-counters. For example, Estonia pointed out that under the Tartu peace treaty of 2 February 1920 approximately 2000 sq km east of the Narva River and the Pechory (Petseri) district, part of the Pskov Region, should belong to Estonia. Estonia included reference to the Tartu Treaty in its 1992 constitution.

The Estonian authorities issued thousands of passports for the ethnic Estonians resident in the Pechory district. Russia suspected it of intending to create a "critical mass" of Estonians in the district to lay the legal foundations for calling a referendum and subsequently annexing the territory. The Estonian border regulations are considered in Moscow to be unjust to Russians; maps have been issued which indicate some Russian territories as being under Estonian jurisdiction and Moscow has threatened Tallinn with retaliation. Russia has refused to discuss territorial issues with Estonia, officially declaring the principle of the *status quo*.

In summer 1994, following a presidential decree, Russia began unilateral demarcation of the border in the Pechory district. "This border was, is and will be Russian, and not a single inch of the land will be given to anyone," President Yeltsin declared at the newly constructed border checkpoint on 23 November 1994. He said the border had to be made a "reliable shield" against "smugglers from the Baltic's and foreign intelligence services" (*The Baltic Independent* 25 November–1 December 1994).

Estonia tried to raise the issue in the OSCE but failed to attract any serious attention to the problem (*The Baltic Independent* 19 – 25 August 1994). As a result of Russia's unilateral measures and lack of international support, the majority of the Estonian political parties have begun to become inclined to compromise with Russia over the border issue. At the end of 1994, Prime Minister Andres Tarand said Estonia was prepared to make concessions on the border if Russia at least agreed to recognise the Tartu Treaty as the basis for relations between the two countries (*The Baltic Independent* 9 – 15 December 1995, and 10 – 16 February 1995). According to Alexander Udaltsov, head of the Baltic desk at the Russian Foreign Ministry, Russia is prepared to recognise the historical importance of the treaty, but so are all countries (*The Baltic Independent* 10 – 16 February 1995).

Insofar as the EU and NATO require potential candidates for membership to resolve all their border and national minority problems, Estonia was eager to settle its territorial disputes with Moscow. By November 1996 Russia and Estonia almost reached a compromise on border issues except for some technical details. According to the draft of an Estonian-Russian border agreement, Estonia renounced its territorial claims to Russia. Russian and Estonian experts then began to draw a map of the border with an aim to finish their work by 1997 (*Diplomaticheskiy Vestnik* 1996: 53, 68-69).

Latvia also has some territorial disputes with Russia. In January 1992 the Latvian Supreme Council adopted a resolution on the Non-Recognition of the Annexation of the Town of Abrene (Pytalovo) and Six Districts of Abrene (Pskov Region) by Russia in 1944 and confirmed its adherence to the borders established under the 1920 treaty with Russia (*Boundary Bulletin* 1992: 43). However, initially Riga has not made the claim officially and has not insisted on putting the issue on the Russian–Latvian negotiation agenda. Instead, in December 1994, Latvia and Russia signed four agreements to simplify border regulations (Birzulis 1994/1995: 4).

On 22 August 1996 the Latvian Parliament adopted a Declaration on Occupation of Latvia which officially claimed the above territories. It has evoked Russia's fierce reaction. During his visit to Pskov Region in September 1996, the Russian Prime Minister Viktor Chernomyrdin told Latvia "will get nothing" and ordered the border guards to tighten control over the Russian-Latvian frontier. He also said that Russia would ask the Council of Europe to make a legal assessment of the Latvian declaration. Meantime, the Latvian President Guntis Ulmanis disavowed territorial claims and stressed that the parliamentary declaration should be reconsidered. The Russian-Latvian negotiations on the border issues, however, were stopped (*Moskovskie Novosti* 29 September – 6 October 1996).

Although the territorial disputes are not so important as other problems (military or humanitarian), they are a potential source of dangerous tensions. There is no doubt that they undermine the security order in the region and it would be better to settle them alongside other regional problems.

Approaches to the resolution of these problems depend on the nature of the conflicts themselves.

As Russian-Estonian relations demonstrate, Russo-Baltic territorial disputes can be successfully resolved through bilateral dialogue if the two parties have good will and flexibility. Subregional institutions' mediation can be helpful as well.

Where the Karelia and Kaliningrad issues are concerned, official recognition of the problems and their inclusion on the negotiating agenda could destabilise the situation. For that reason, the principle of the *status quo* is probably the best option for the time being and in the near future. It is clear that the benefits of self-restraint would be considerably greater than those to be gained by simply appeasing nationalistic feelings. Fortunately, all interested parties (Finland, Germany, Lithuania, Poland and Russia) are refraining from any actions which could have a destabilising effect.

The promotion of direct economic and humanitarian contacts between Karelia and Finland, and between Kaliningrad and Germany would probably ease tensions. Free (or special) economic zones, the liberalisation of the visa regime (which has partly happened already), and intensive trans-border co-operation could be appropriate instruments of such a policy.

## DOMESTIC SOURCES OF RUSSIAN POLICY TOWARDS THE BALTIC SEA AREA

There are several determinants of Russian security policy in the area: interest groups, political parties, executive-legislative relationship and security discourse conducted by various schools of thought. It is important to examine these factors to understand better the past, present and future of Russian security policy in the area.

### Interest groups

Compared to other foreign policy priorities, Russia's policy in the Baltic Sea rim space is not subject to particularly strong competition between the different lobbies. To put it more precisely, with rare exception, different pressure groups usually have parallel, not conflicting interests in the area. This gives the Russian foreign policy machinery a relatively free hand in shaping and conducting policy in the Baltic Sea area. A number of informal political actors, however, could be identified.

*The business community.* There are two main business groups which are interested in the maintenance of good relations with the Baltic Sea countries: gas-oil lobby and merchants specialising in export-import operations. The former is a key supplier of energy to the Baltic States and Kaliningrad. It is opposed to economic sanctions against the Baltic States and has pressed the Russian government to normalise its political and economic relations with these countries. Under the gas-oil lobby's pressure, Moscow, for example, insisted on including a special provision on purchases of energy in a larger package into a proposed Russian-Lithuanian agreement (Joenniemi 1996b: 14). The gas-oil lobby has a powerful agent in the Russian government: the Prime Minister Chernomyrdin was the Russian Minister on Gas and Oil Industry; in addition, he was a founding father of Gazprom, a leader of the gas industry (Temirkhanov 1994: 40-44).

Export-import firms vary in nature and by the profile of their businesses. It can be Karelian firms exporting timber to Finland and, in return, importing paper and consumer goods (*Neva News* November 1996; *Moscow News* 28 March – 3 April 1996). It can be small trade firms importing from the Baltic Sea countries, foodstuff, beverages, liquors and other consumer goods for further re-sale on the Russian domestic market. This interest group met with enthusiasm a Russian-Lithuanian trade agreement containing the MFN provision. At the same time, this group was much less effective in exerting pressure on the federal government than the gas-oil lobby due to a lack of finance, organisation and political representation in the governmental bodies.

*Church and human rights organisations.* Formally, the Russian Orthodox Church refrained from active intervention into foreign policy debate. At the same time, on a number of occasions its leaders expressed their concerns over the human rights situation in the "near abroad" including the Baltic States. Referring to Russia's 1993 foreign policy doctrine Archpriest Victor Petlyuchenko, Deputy Chairman, Department of External Church Relations, Moscow Patriarchate, noted: "The concept calls for the protection of minorities, including Russian-speaking people in the ex-Soviet republics. It states explicitly that human rights have priority in our country's foreign policy. We welcome this from the bottom of our hearts" (*International Affairs* [Moscow] 39 (2) 1993: 10).

The Church's concern with minorities rights may be explained not only by its religious doctrine or historical traditions but the Patriarch's personal background as well. Aleksii II (Ridiger), the son of a Russified Baltic German father and Russian mother, had been born in Estonia in 1929. After ordination to the priesthood, he spent eight and a half years serving in the Russian city of Kokhtla-Jarve in north-eastern Estonia, a hotbed of anti-secessionist sentiment in 1989-91. In 1961-64 before acquiring the key position of chancellor of the Moscow Patriarchate, he was Bishop of Tallinn and Estonia. From 1988 through 1990, he served as Metropolitan of Leningrad and Novgorod before being elected Patriarch on 7 June 1990 (Dunlop 1993: 158-159). Therefore, the Patriarch knows from personal experience how complex the problem of inter-ethnic and inter-religious relations in the ex-Soviet republic is and how closely it is connected to the country's security.

The Church ruled out the use of force to protect Russians living in the "near abroad". It proposed that the Russian government must conclude the bilateral agreements on national minorities status with the ex-Soviet republics. The government should also use law-enforcement mechanisms of the UN, OSCE and other international organisations dealing with human rights issues. The Church itself tried to influence the governments involved in human rights violations through its numerous international contacts, especially by participating in the work of the World Council of Churches, the Conference of European Churches and other ecumenical structures (Petlyuchenko 1993: 65).

Right after the break-up of the Soviet Union, the nationalist elites in the ex-Soviet republics pushed the local Orthodox leaders to claim independence from the Moscow Patriarchate. The latter was forced to grant Orthodox Churches in Belarus, Estonia, Latvia, Moldova, and Ukraine autonomy in administrative, economic, educational and civilian affairs. Early in 1996 the Estonian authorities encouraged some parishes to go out of the jurisdiction of the Moscow Patriarchate. This generated a clash among parishes for control over the property (mainly for churches themselves). Despite the mediation of the Finnish Archbishop the conflict was not settled and tensions are still there. As Petlyuchenko stressed, "Actions of this nature are carried out under the banner of the national idea and result in drawing the religious factor into inter-ethnic contradictions. Our Church has never approved of such behaviour and never will, deploring as she does the destructive impact of political processes on church life." (Petlyuchenko 1993: 69). Numerous human rights organisations joined the Church in the campaign to protect ethnic Russians in the Baltic States.

*The environmentalists.* The environmental movement has become rather influential in Russia's domestic politics and security debate in the post-Communist period. It was the environmentalists who first started to re-define the concept of security. Under their pressure nearly all leading schools of foreign policy thought included ecological dimension in their concepts of security. A special section on ecological security was put into the draft of the Russian Law on National Security in 1995 (State Duma 1995).

Apart from monitoring the environment in St. Petersburg, on Kola Peninsula and in the Baltic Sea, the environmentalists initiated some international projects to highlight the most compelling ecological issues in the area. An example of a citizen-based effort to bring people of diverse backgrounds together–including industry representatives, governmental officials and local farmers–is a project called the "Regulation of Boundary Environmental Problems between Estonia and Russia in the Peipsi-Pihkva Lakes Watershed." The project involved 15 to 20 institutions from Estonia, Russia and the United States, with limited funding provided by the IREX in the United States and Central European University (sponsored mainly by the Soros Foundation) in Hungary (Van Buren 1995: 133).

The environmentalists also tried to attract public attention through attempts to take private companies or governmental officials to court on the basis of Russian environmental protection laws. There were two lawsuits being argued against local officials by a NGO organisation in St. Petersburg (the Russian International Centre for Environmental Law); the cases involved alleged violations of the Helsinki Convention on the Protection of the Baltic Sea and illegal dumping of raw sludge (Van Buren 1995: 134).

*The regional elites.* The normal and healthy process of delegating authority to local governments leads to a strengthened influence of regional political elites on the national level. This process, however, was not simple in Russia. Moscow could not prevent the local elites from developing autonomous foreign policy and trade with neighbouring countries. At the same time, the centre tried to influence the local governments through customs and tax regulations as well as by keeping its control over border guard, military and natural resources. The case of Kaliningrad exemplifies such a contradictory relationship between central and local political elites. Relations between Moscow and St. Petersburg were even more complicated given the historical rivalry between the "two capitals".

Up until 1996 three of five Russian regions adjacent to the Baltic Sea area–Kaliningrad, Karelia and St. Petersburg–were controlled by reform-oriented and pro-Western elites. They were interested in opening up the regions to economic, political and humanitarian co-operation with the countries of the Baltic Sea rim space (Vozgrin 1992: 107-119; Matochkin 1995: 8-14). They pushed Moscow to grant them special privileges, including creating FEZs. Some of them succeeded in cultivating contacts with top federal officials who defended regional interests in the centre. For example, Vladimir Shumeiko, ex-Chairman of the Federation Council, Federal Assembly of Russia, was a deputy from the Kaliningrad Region. He assisted the local government in promoting the FEZ idea and obtaining other privileges.

At the same time, the common views did not prevent the regional elites (especially Kaliningrad and St. Petersburg) from competition for influence in the area, access to transport communications, development of infrastructure and even federal subsidies. They were united, however, in their desire to develop direct contacts with the regional players and to join the area's institutions. The Council of the Baltic Sea States was the regions' main vehicle to bring them on to the international arena.

The reformists, however, failed to turn the results of co-operation with the foreign partners into benefits for the common people. They could not prevent further economic decline, the rise of social instability, corruption and organised crime. For that reason, the reformists in Kaliningrad and St. Petersburg were defeated by traditional, more centre-looking politicians during the local elections in spring-summer 1996. The traditionalists were already in power in the Novgorod and Pskov regions. The new political leaders were more concentrated on domestic projects rather than on co-operation with the foreign partners. They have been quite assertive as regards territorial disputes with the neighbouring countries. They have also been trying to build a strategy that takes into account the balance of national and local interests (especially in the case of Kaliningrad).

## Political parties

The Russian political organisations which were able to influence Moscow's security policies in the Baltic Sea rim space can be roughly divided into three main categories: the Democrats, the neo-Communists, and the right radicals.

Despite some tactical differences the Democrats represented by such political organisations as "Yabloko" ("Apple"), led by Grigory Yavlinski, Russia's Choice, headed by Yegor Gaidar, the Party of Russian Unity and Accord, led by Sergei Shakhrai, "Forward, Russia!," headed by Boris Fedorov, etc., initially were sympathetic with the Baltic States. They contributed to achieving independence by the Balts and, for that reason, hoped to develop good-neighbourly relations with them. They believed that after the collapse of the USSR, Russia's relations with the Baltic States would be free of conflict; they did not think that any grave contradictions could arise in Moscow's relations with the new states (Razuvayev 1993: 9, 16-24).

The Democrats were prepared to reckon with the interests of the Baltic States, having agreed, for instance, to an accelerated pullout of the Russian troops from Estonia, Latvia and Lithuania. However, with the rise of tensions over troop withdrawal and human rights, the Democrats began to reconsider their attitude toward the Baltic States. In their view, the realities of the post-Soviet period made it necessary to give up attempts to build Russia's relations with the nationalistic elites of the post-Soviet republics based on models typical of Western liberal democracies (Fadeev and Razuvayev 1994: 115). As a result, they joined other Russian political parties in criticism of the Balts regarding national minorities rights and pro-NATO orientation of their security policies. At the same time, the Democrats hoped that with time, the nationalistic elites in the Baltic States will be replaced by more open-minded and balanced politicians.

The neo-Communists represent the main political and ideological alternative to the Democrats. There are several pro-Communist groups in contemporary Russia. They vary from neo-Stalinist to Socialist-like organisations. The Communist Party of the Russian Federation (CPRF) led by Gennady Zyuganov is the strongest among them. Despite its influential role in the domestic politics CPRF, however, lacks a well-articulated and positive foreign policy platform. It prefers to criticise the former Soviet and current Russian leaders rather than to produce a new concept of its own.

The Communists believe Gorbachev and Yeltsin led the USSR to defeat in the Cold War and to its eventual collapse. For some years they refused to recognise the independence of the former Soviet republics and favoured instead the restoration of the Soviet Union. Finally, they have tacitly submitted to reality. They feel the breakdown of the Warsaw Pact, the Russian troop withdrawal from East Europe and from the Baltic States, and the loss of Moscow's control over East Europe pose new threats to Russia's security.

Insofar as they believe the Soviet Union had been dissolved illegally, the Communists tried to foster the reunification of the former Soviet republics. The Communists, however, ruled out the use of force to restore the USSR. According to Zyuganov, it should be done on the "voluntary basis" (Zyuganov 1995: 67; *Moscow News* 6 – 12 June 1996). The main tools of the reunification are development of economic, political, military, and cultural co-operation between the CIS member-states, creation of the proper institutional framework as well as a gradual transformation of the Commonwealth into a confederation with the final aim to restore a united federative state.

Along with some liberals and nationalists, the Communists put pressure on the Yeltsin government to protect the Russian minorities abroad. In the event of a victory in parliamentary (1995) and presidential (1996) elections, they had planned to sign relevant treaties with Russia's neighbours, "to be closely monitored by the Russian authorities, and demand unflinching compliance with them from our partners." (*International Affairs* [Moscow] 41 (11-12) 1995: 8)

The Communists criticised Yeltsin for his concessions to the Balts in the case of troop withdrawal as well as for his inability to prevent NATO extension (ibid.). To put pressure on the "pro-Western" Yeltsin government, as well as on the Balts and NATO itself, the Communists undertook some measures through their faction in the parliament. The latter proposed to revise the CFE Treaty in accordance with "new realities'. The CPRF faction voiced its negative attitude to the ratification of the START II Treaty until the US and NATO changed their position on the alliance's extension. According to experts close to the CPRF, the Treaty is detrimental to Russia's security because it is grounded on Moscow's unilateral concessions and undermines the country's deterrent potential (Podberezkin 1996: 95-97). The Communists threatened to return again to the discussion of Russia's participation in the *Partnership for Peace* programme. Finally, the CPRF faction, together with the Liberal Democrats, urged the government to oppose "the NATO countries' drive in the Balkans" through bilateral channels and multilateral institutions (*International Affairs* [Moscow] 41 (11-12) 1995: 9).

There is a number of rightist organisations in Russia. The right radicals are united primarily by their rejection of Yeltsin domestic reforms and criticism of his pro-Western foreign policy. At the same time they have major disagreements concerning both the meaning of Russian history, and the appropriate model for the future. Therefore, it is difficult for them to go beyond negativism to develop a coherent, forward looking agenda.

The Liberal Democratic Party of Russia (LDPR), led by Vladimir Zhirinovskiy, is the most important among the right-wing radical organisations. It is difficult to reconstruct Zhirinovskiy's foreign policy concept due to the lack of elementary logic and the extravagant form of expression of his ideas. One should take into account his numerous statements which often contradict each other.

He does not conceal his intents to restore the Russian empire as of 1913 status. The Baltic States, according to Zhirinovskiy, would be part of Russia, except for Tallinn, which would be a separate city republic, and three cities in Lithuania which would form a small Lithuanian state. Königsberg might be returned to Germany some day. Zhirinovskiy said "no problem" with respect to Finland, but if Finland wanted Karelia back, then all of Finland would have to go to Russia (Morrison 1994: 109).

In Zhirinovskiy's vision, Russians living outside Russia would be given dual citizenship and Russia would defend them, primarily with economic instruments of power (*The Washington Post* 15 December 1993; Morrison 1994: 108-109; *International Affairs* [Moscow] 41 (11-12) 1995: 12).

In Eastern Europe, according to Zhirinovskiy's vision, three cities in north-western Poland would become part of Germany, and Lvov in Ukraine might be given to Poland as compensation. He did not oppose Poland's joining NATO. He told Polish reporters: "...if Poland wants to join NATO, that is an internal matter for Poland and NATO.... Until recently, the Russian forces guaranteed the Polish border. Today, in this matter, one should turn to NATO and Germany, which play the greatest part in this section of the continent" (Morrison 1994: 117-118). On the other hand, he warned that Eastern European countries could become Western servants and advised them to remain neutral. He also insisted on dissolving NATO because the Warsaw Pact has been dissolved (Morrison 1994: 122).

Despite the LDPR success on the 1993 parliamentary elections, the trend in 1994-95 was one of declining popularity. In 1993, many Russian citizens in the Baltic States who felt disappointed with Yeltsin's policy, voted in favour of Zhirinovskiy. However, on the 1995 parliamentary elections, only 7 per cent of Russians in Estonia backed the LDPR (*International Affairs* [Moscow] 42 (1) 1996: 54).

### The executive-legislative relationship

According to the Russian Constitution, the President is a key figure in foreign policy making. The State Duma has quite limited powers in this field. It is able, however, to influence the executive power in certain ways. The President needs the legislature's approval of his appointees for diplomatic and military posts. The Duma ratifies international treaties. It has some voice in the budgeting process and may cut or increase appropriations for particular foreign policy agencies. The legislature may undertake investigations. Finally, it can appeal to the public opinion's support to block some executive's initiatives.

Parliament's influence on Russian security policy towards the Baltic Sea area was multi-dimensional.

*National minorities rights.* It was Parliament which along with some political parties and interest groups forced the President to pay more attention to the Russian minorities in the Baltic States.

*Russian troop withdrawal.* The legislature opposed the unconditional pullout unless the Baltic States guaranteed the civil rights of the military pensioners and ethnic Russians in these countries. The Parliament fully supported Kozyrev's "linkage tactics".

*NATO eastward expansion.* Most parliamentary factions were united in the strong opposition to NATO enlargement (especially in case of the Baltic States). As mentioned, under the Communist pressure, the State Duma has undertaken certain steps to make Russian diplomacy more assertive with regard to NATO enlargement (Rybkin 1995: 30-31).

*Tightening control over the Kaliningrad Region.* Along with some centralists in the executive branch the State Duma was reluctant to grant the region extended powers. In 1994, the President proposed the law "On the special status of the Kaliningrad region". However, instead of approving the law, the State Duma renamed it to read "On safeguarding the Russian Federation's sovereignty on the territory of the Kaliningrad region" and placed it on a waiting list (Wellman 1996: 176).

*Promoting integration of the post-Soviet space.* In March 1996 the State Duma passed a Communist-drafted resolution that annulled the 1991 Belovezhskaya Pusha agreements on the dissolution of the USSR and creation of the CIS. Despite its political rather than legal significance (it was not mandatory for the President) this Duma's move accelerated the timetable for the signing of the quadripartite agreement between Russia, Belarus, Kazakhstan and Kyrgyzstan, and the union treaty between Russia and Belarus. At the same time, this action increased the Balts' concerns over the ability of the Russian leadership to counter the neo-imperialist forces in the country.

Assessing the Parliament's role in shaping Moscow's foreign policy, Malcolm and Pravda noted, that the parliamentary actions have usually affected the timing of policy moves and the overall climate of policy rather than determining its strategic direction (Malcolm and Pravda 1996: 544).

## The Russian debate on Baltic security policies

There are several schools of foreign policy thought in Russia differing both by their conceptual foundations and approaches to concrete international issues. It goes without saying that these political and academic groups are still fluid coalitions. Therefore, to bring a complex debate down to several categories may risk oversimplification. They do, however, provide a helpful framework for analysing Russia's domestic discourse on foreign policy.

*Atlanticists (Westernisers).* It was a relatively small group of high-established governmental officials and academics close to the Ministry of Foreign Affairs. Their recognised leader was Russian Foreign Minister Andrei Kozyrev. They considered the West (West Europe and the United States) to be the main orientation for the Russian foreign policy. They insisted that Russia historically belongs to the Western (Christian) civilisation. The main task for the Russian international strategy should be building partnership with the West and country's joining Western economic, political and military institutions–the EU, NATO, IMF, GATT, G-7, etc. Mr. Kozyrev stressed in his article published by the *NATO Review* (February 1993) that Moscow's main guideline is to "join the club of recognised democratic states with market economies, on a basis of equality." He regarded such partnership as a principal source of international support for Russian reforms.

The Atlanticists occupied key positions in the Yeltsin's encirclement (in addition to Kozyrev there were Prime Minister Yegor Gaidar, State Secretary Gennady Burbulis, Minister of Communications Mikhail Poltoranin, deputies of Foreign Minister Vitaly Churkin, Georgy Kunadze and Fedor Shelov-Kovedyaev, etc.) (Arbatov 1993: 9-10; Crow 1993: 22-23). For that reason, from the very beginning of his career as Russian leader, his policy towards the Baltic Sea area differed from Gorbachev strategy. While still Chairman of the Supreme Soviet of the RSFSR before the collapse of the USSR, Yeltsin supported the Baltic republics' aspirations for independence and promised gradual withdrawal of Russian troops. His support for Baltic freedom was increased as the conflict between the RSFSR and the central Soviet authorities intensified. Yeltsin attempted to establish direct contact with the Nordic governments and the Nordic Council as early as the beginning of 1991 in order to further co-operation and exchange (Jonson 1992: 90-91).

In 1991-92 Mr. Yeltsin played down the importance of military force in guaranteeing the security of Russia in Northern and Eastern Europe. He and his Foreign Minister argued that international co-operation and non-military instruments of power were important elements in guaranteeing security for the country and its international status. Moscow's new co-operative strategy in the Baltic Sea area increased co-operation with the countries of the region, as indicated by Russia becoming a member of the Council of Baltic Sea States when it was founded in March 1992.

However, a new geopolitical situation after the breakdown of the USSR and a number of international and domestic developments caused a crisis in the Atlanticist school of thought, as well as its shift to traditional strategic concepts.

It has appeared that the West was not really responsive to Russia's demands of large-scale economic assistance and participation in European economic and politico-military institutions. Moreover, the West often ignored Moscow's position with regard to important security questions (the pace and conditions of Russian troop pull-out from the Baltic States, national minorities rights, NATO extension, Yugoslavian conflict, etc.). Thus, the West did not accept Russia as a part of Europe or Western civilisation in general, i.e the main thesis of the Atlanticists. On a number of occasions Yeltsin and Kozyrev complained of the "non-constructive" policy of the West.

In addition, national conflicts throughout the southern borders of Russia have changed Moscow's security philosophy. It was in relation to the "near abroad" that the Russian leadership started to define its "strategic interests," to speak of "spheres of influence" and to express concern about a possible "power vacuum" to be filled by hostile powers. In fact, Moscow elaborated a sort of a Russian Monroe doctrine when Yeltsin in February 1993 laid claim to responsibility for maintaining peace and stability in the whole post-Soviet space and Kozyrev applied to the international community (the UN and the OSCE) to grant Russia an international mandate of peacekeeping efforts in the former Soviet Union (*Litera* 1994/95: 45-52).

The three Baltic States, however, were treated in a different way from other former Soviet republics. On April 4, 1994 President Yeltsin issued a decree which stressed the need to maintain Russian military bases in the CIS and Latvia. However, following protests from the Baltic States and the West, Foreign Minister Kozyrev and Defence Minister Grachev disassociated themselves from this decree, and later apologised for the technical "error" of including Latvia in this specific document (Van Ham 1995: 76). In general, the Russian Government tried to refrain from coercive diplomacy or use of military power with regard to the Baltic States.

Finally, Russian-speaking minorities in the Baltic States as well as anti-Yeltsin political opposition put a pressure upon the Russian Government to make the latter more assertive regarding the human rights situation in Estonia and Latvia.

These developments resulted in a decrease in Atlanticists' influence on Russian foreign policy and evolution of their leaders (including Kozyrev) closer to traditional security concepts.

Moreover, the Atlanticists split into two groups. While Kozyrev's followers became more assertive as to the West and neo-imperialist as to the "near abroad," a number of liberal politicians, academics and journalists were in favour of "civilised dialogue" both with the West and FSU countries. Liberals opposed to Kozyrev's "linkage tactics" regarding troop withdrawal and Russian national minorities in the Baltic States. They were against maintenance of Russian military bases and the considerable military presence in the region as well (Arbatov 1992; *Izvestia* 25 February 1992).

In 1994-95 the Atlanticists were unable to act as a united political force. At the political level, they sold few ideas to certain liberal and reformist organisations and election coalitions (Chernomyrdin's "Our Home–Russia," "Yabloko," Russia's Choice, the Party of Russian Unity and Accord, etc.).

*Eurasianism.* Eurasianist conception ("evraziistvo" in Russian) was very popular among Russian intellectuals in the 1990s. A conception borrowed from a philosophical school of Russian émigrés from the 1920s who tried to find a compromise with the Stalinist version of Socialism, it stresses the uniqueness of Russia. One of its key postulates is that civilisationally Russia has never been part of Europe (Fedotov 1991; Solonevich 1991). Therefore, it should choose the "third way" between the West and the East. Globally, Russia should become a bridge between these civilisations.

The contemporary proponents of this theory were split into two groups which politically opposed each other: One belonged to the reformist (so-called "democratic") camp, another belonged to the Slavophiles.

The starting point of the Eurasianist philosophy was the thesis on special Russia's mission in history. According to Stankevich, "Russia's role in the world is, in my view, to initiate and maintain a multilateral dialogue between cultures, civilizations and states. It is Russia which reconciles, unites, and coordinates. It is the Good Great Power that is patient and open within borders, which have been settled by right and good intentions, but which is threatening beyond these borders. This land, in which East and West, North and South are united, is unique and perhaps the only one capable of harmoniously uniting many different voices in a historical symphony" (Jonson 1994; Stankevich 1992: 47-51).

Konstantin Pleshakov of the Institute for USA & Canada Studies put it in more pragmatic terms: "...the primary object of Russia's mission today is to be basic to Eurasian continental stability... Another aspect of Russia's mission is to guarantee at least minimum respect for human rights in post-Soviet space" (Pleshakov 1993: 22-23).

The Eurasianists have believed that the government paid too much attention to the western direction of its foreign policy while Russia's most compelling needs were in the south and the east. The Eurasianists argued that, first of all, Moscow should deal with "the arc of crisis" developing on Russia's southern borders and with the problems which had arisen in relations with its own sizeable Muslim population.

The Eurasianist approach gave priority to consolidating the economic, political and security ties between the countries of the FSU, preferably within the context of the CIS (Travkin 1994: 34-35). It was the Eurasianists who persuaded the Yeltsin government to make the CIS priority for Moscow's international policy and to initiate the process of the Commonwealth's integration.

Alongside the nationalists the Eurasianists were the first who vigorously pushed the Yeltsin team to protect the Russian-speaking minorities in the "near abroad". Placing the minorities' issue on the top of the Russian foreign priority list, Stankevich stressed that it involved the fate of 25 million people and stability in the entire post-Soviet space. He denied charges of Russian "imperialism" by pointing out that each great power normally defends its citizens residing abroad. At the same time, he ruled out the use of military force or other imperialist methods to protect the Russian minorities. He suggested that Russia should follow the historical experience of a number of post-imperial countries such as Turkey (under Kemal Atatürk) or contemporary Germany which were able to take care of compatriots in the non-imperialist manner (Stankevich 1994: 26).

Defining the Eurasianist security concept regarding the "near abroad" Vladimir Lukin, the then Russian Ambassador to the United States, called it a Russian variation of the "good neighbour" policy. According to Lukin, democratic Russia was not afraid of the sovereignty and independence of its new neighbours; in fact, Russia helped them become independent. Moscow was not going to force them to adopt its own form of government, nor would it interfere in their internal affairs. At the same time, Russia was entitled to expect them to respect and uphold the human and civil rights of the Russian-speaking residents of their territory. Russia was also justified in expecting its neighbours to prevent threats to Russia from arising on their territory as a result of the activities of third countries. Russia was prepared to provide them with any co-operation necessary to establish their own security, through both bilateral and multilateral arrangements (Lukin 1994: 109).

At the same time, this faction of Eurasianists has not denied the importance of keeping good relations with the West. They admitted Russia's entering into the international economy and "defense structure of the advanced part of the world community" (Bogaturov, Kozhokin, and Pleshakov 1992: 31). To their mind, in Europe, Russia's most important interest was improving relations with the European Union and gradual integration into the European economic and political system. Russia should oppose the transformation of Europe into a closed economic system and military-political union, just as it should oppose the appearance of a dominant regional power (Germany). For Eurasianists, it is best to preserve both the multipolar nature of European politics and the role of the United States in the region. The functions and role of NATO should be reconsidered (Lukin 1994: 115). Instead, they proposed the establishment of a new European community with participation of democratically-transformed Russia and other post-socialist countries.

Initially, the Eurasianists were much less influential than the Atlanticists inside the Yeltsin government and the Russian political elites. Along with Stankevich and Lukin, leaders most closely associated with this view have been Nikolai Travkin, the leader of Democratic Party of Russia, Anatoliy Sobchak, the former St. Petersburg mayor, Yevgeniy Ambartsumov, the head of Committee on International Affairs, Supreme Soviet of the Russian Federation, etc. (Dawisha and Parrott 1994: 200-201)

Starting to coalesce in 1992 the Eurasianist Democrats were able by the year 1993 to influence Russian security debates. The theoretical framework of Russia's foreign policy doctrine of 1993 (especially the setting of regional priorities) was obviously affected by the Eurasianist ideas (Ministry of Foreign Affairs of the Russian Federation 1993: 3-23). Alongside nationalists, Eurasianists were successful in forcing Kozyrev to link Russian military politics and troop withdrawal with national minorities rights in the Baltic States. Echoing Eurasianist themes during his 1992 visit to India, President Yeltsin emphasised Russia's Eurasian identity by pointing out that most of Russia's territory–10 million out of 17 million square kilometres–lay in Asia, and that most Russian citizens lived in the Asian part of Russia (Singh 1995: 71).

In contrast with the "democratic" version of Eurasianism, the

Slavophiles stressed Russia's distinction from both the West and the East rather than country's unique geopolitical position. Elgiz Pozdnyakov, a Russian authority in international relations theory noted: "The geopolitical location of Russia is not just unique (so is that of any state), it is truly fateful for both herself and the world. An important aspect of this situation was that Russia, being situated between two civilizations, was a natural keeper of both a civilised equilibrium and a world balance of power" (Pozdnyakov 1993a: 6).

To the Slavophiles' minds, this predetermined in no small measure the evolution of the statehood of Russia as a great power and the build-up of a strong central authority. Unlike the Democrats, the Slavophiles were not ashamed to name Russia the empire and to support its revival. Pozdnyakov pointed out: "Russia has always been held together by a strong system of state power. I have no doubt that guaranteeing Russia's existence is a top priority today. This can only be done by a strong authority equal to saving the people from arbitrary practices, anarchy, hunger and civil war. It must extend to the whole nation" (Pozdnyakov 1993b: 30).

Contrary to the Democrats, the Slavophiles were opposed to a Western assistance which they considered irrelevant and burdensome, and thus proposed to rely upon Russia's own resources. They opposed Russia's joining the Western economic, political and military institutions which could restrict the country's sovereignty.

They also favoured protection of the Russian minorities in the former Soviet republics as the top foreign policy priority. Contrary to the Democrats, however, the Slavophiles did not rule out the use of force to defend minorities.

Finally, they proposed to change current geopolitical priorities in a way that would pay more attention to the southern and eastern neighbours of Russia and to keep a relatively low profile in the West.

Representatives of this faction were scattered among different political parties and groups. The Slavophiles were grouping around certain newspapers and journals–"Den" ("Day"), "Nash Sovremennik" ("Our Contemporary"), "Molodaya Gvardiya" ("Young Guard"), etc. Politically, they were organised in such associations and election coalitions as the Russian National Assembly (Sobor), the Congress of Russian Communities and so on.

By the end of 1993, both–democratic and Slavophile–variants of Eurasianism found themselves in a critical situation similar to that of Atlanticism.

*The rise of the "derzhavniki."* In June 1992, an important political development occurred on the Russian political arena. A powerful centrist alliance, the Civic Union, was formed. This coalition of centrists finalised a process of consolidation of three major political forces–industrial lobby, federal military and civilian bureaucracy, and moderate Democrats. The three leading figures of the new alliance were Arkadii Volskii, co-leader of the Russian Union of Industrialists and Entrepreneurs; Vice President Aleksandr Rutskoi, the de facto head of the 100,000-member People's Party of Free Russia; and Nikolai Travkin, chairman of the 50,000-member Democratic Party of Russia (Rutskoi 1992: 2). The former Secretary of the Security Council Yuri Skokov and Vice Premiers Oleg Lobov and Mikhail Malei supported the group as well. In the intellectual community its positions have been elaborated by Sergei Karaganov, Andrei Zubov, and Andranik Migranian (Arbatov 1993: 12).

This group was quickly labelled as "derzhavniki" or "gosudarstvenniki" (proponents of state power). The term of "derzhavnik" denotes advocates of a strong and powerful state which can maintain order and serve as a guarantee against anarchy and instability, a rather traditional Russian view of the state's role.

Their domestic political aim was to slow down the pace of market reform and force the government into making major concessions to the powerful interest groups they represented (state-owned enterprises, workers in the defence sector, some leaders of organised labour). They proposed paternalism as a main ideology for the new Russian statehood (Vladislavlev and Karaganov 1992: 31).

As for Russia's foreign policy, the "derzhavniki" proposed that it should be guided by the principle of self-limitation and self-sufficiency. First of all, they pointed out that "the disintegration of the Soviet Union has turned Russia into a medium-sized power. Of course, we still have an immense territory and nuclear potential. Nevertheless, the size of our population and especially the dimensions of our GNP place our country in a different category of nations" (Russia's National Interests 1992: 135). For these reasons, Russia should not compete for influence as a global power. It could not in the foreseeable future pose a meaningful military threat to the West (Blackwill and Karaganov 1994: 20-21).

Along with the Democratic Eurasianists they consider the CIS and the "near abroad" as the top priority for Moscow's security policy. "Russia must bear its cross and fulfil its duty by playing an enlightened post-imperial role throughout the ex-Soviet Union," observed Vladislavlev and

Karaganov, "A decisive component of Russia's new mission in the world is to ensure with help from the world community that the ex-Soviet area does not become a geostrategic hole radiating instability and war and ultimately endangering the very existence of humanity" (Vladislavlev and Karaganov 1992: 35). The need for gradual economic and military integration of the CIS is acknowledged as well.

The "derzhavniki" described Kozyrev's policy of ignoring violations of minority rights in the Baltic republics as "amoral" and "short-sighted". To their mind, it is Russia's duty and mission to defend the rights of all ex-compatriots. This is dictated not only by a sense of moral duty but by practical considerations. They emphasise that to suppress the rights of some is to trigger an inevitable chain reaction.

At the same time, Russia's assertive policy in the "near abroad" should not mean imperialist policy. The "derzhavniki" assume that any attempt forcibly to re-establish the Soviet Union or the Russian Empire is fraught with overstraining Moscow itself and may lead to tough international isolation (Blackwill and Karaganov 1994: 19).

This group regards the West as an important priority of Moscow's foreign policy and favours better relations with the West, but not at the cost of diminishing Russia's role as an independent great power with its own "spheres of influence". They are quite sceptical as regards the West's willingness and capability to help Russia in its realisation of reforms. They argue against excessive reliance on Western economic assistance and political guidance as well (Rutskoi 1992: 2; *Nezavisimaya Gazeta* 19 August 1992).

The "derzhavniki" were the leading critics of Western policies of NATO extension among the Russian elites. They warned that enlargement could lead to the resumption of West-East confrontation although in a milder form than before. They recommended the West should delay its decision on extension for some years. Both Russia and the West should propose a positive programme for Central and Eastern European countries to reduce their security concerns. There could be bilateral or unilateral Western guarantees for their security, and an early enlargement of the EU and WEU. Russia should develop its relations with the EU and WEU to counterbalance NATO's offensive (Karaganov 1995: 63-64).

The "derzhavniki" were influential not only in the theoretical debate; they were able to exert a political pressure upon the Yeltsin government.

Throughout 1992, Yeltsin and Gaidar found themselves forced to make political concessions to the powerful "statist" lobby. In May, three representatives of the industrial lobby (including the future Russian Prime Minister Viktor Chernomyrdin) were brought into the government in an effort to appease the centrists. Under the "statists" pressure Yeltsin had to remove a number of leading Western-oriented Democrats and his loyalists: Gennadi Burbulis, Galina Starovoitova, Mikhail Poltoranin, Yegor Yakovlev, and Fedor Shelov-Kovedyaev. Finally, the author of the Russian economic reform, Yegor Gaidar, was forced to resign in December 1992. He was replaced by the leading representative of the gas lobby, Viktor Chernomyrdin. Karaganov was appointed to the President's Advisory Board.

As a result of the 12 December 1993 elections, which demonstrated the success of Vladimir Zhirinovskiy, the domestic basis for a pro-Western policy shrunk. For many Democrats the "statist" ideology became the only way to save the remnants of Democratic principles and confront extremists, nationalists, and Communists. The conservative faction of the Atlanticists (including Kozyrev) and the Democratic "wing" of the Eurasianists joined the "derzhavniki".

The so-called Kozyrev Doctrine proclaimed by the former Russian Foreign Minister in a speech to Russian diplomatic representatives in the CIS and Baltic States in January 1994 became a symbol of the "derzhavniki" foreign policy concept. He declared that the vital strategic issue for Russian diplomacy was the defence of Russian minority rights in the "near abroad". He affirmed the need for a Russian military presence in this area and advocated the idea of dual nationality (*Nezavisimaya Gazeta* 19 January 1994; *Litera* 1994/95: 45-52).

Russian policy towards the West became more assertive as well. At the same time, as Hannes Adomeit put it, "The neo-imperialist bark has been worse than its bite; aggressiveness has been more a matter of words than deeds. This discrepancy is in all likelihood due to the fact that several of the derzhavniki, Kozyrev among them, are essentially sheep in wolves' clothing. They retain a fundamentally Western outlook but feel obliged to make verbal concessions and tactical adjustments to changes in popular mood and pressures exerted from within the political establishment" (Adomeit 1995: 59).

The year of 1996 started from appointment of the new Russian Foreign Minister. Andrei Kozyrev was replaced by Evgeniy Primakov, the former Director of the Foreign Intelligence Service. Primakov was a less controversial figure than Kozyrev: both the Democrats and the opposition to the government acknowledged his professionalism and eagerness to protect Russia's national interests. He followed the "derzhavniki" course as well. Primakov proposed a slightly different set of Russian geographic priorities–the CIS, East Europe, Asia-Pacific, Europe and the USA–to demonstrate to the West Russia's capability to counterweight NATO and EU enlargement (Stupavský 1996: 10).

## THE FUTURE OF RUSSIA'S SECURITY POLICY IN THE AREA

There is a difference of opinion among experts as regards the possible scenarios for the future development of Russia. The simplest one foresees two options: authoritarian and democratic Russia. Such a scenario is quite popular in various studies, (Fadeyev and Razuvayev 1994: 118) but it hardly reflects the real trends in Russia's domestic and foreign policies. Many Russian scholars distinguish several possibilities fluctuating between the above two extremes.

According to Medvedev, there are five possible scenarios: (1) continuation of present trends including slow economic reforms, strong presidential power, and a more or less aggressive foreign policy; (2) an authoritarian or oligarchic regime resulting in an imperialist foreign policy which, however, might not take the form of aggression outside the CIS; (3) the "red and brown" alternative and/or military coup; (4) economic collapse, social chaos and the complete disintegration of Russia; and (5) the break-up of Russia into separate regions (Medvedev 1994: 80-85). The first scenario, he maintains, is the most believable one.

Based on the political developments of 1995-97, it is possible to single out some other scenarios of Russia's internal policy and their implications for the Baltic Sea security system:

*(a) Democratic Russia.* Under this scenario, Russia and the West will, for the most part, manage to preserve the co-operative tone of their relations. In Russian-Baltic relations, both sides will proceed in their actions from a rational interpretation of their mutual interests, rather than from ideological or nationalist considerations. It could mean a further demilitarisation of the area, building a more stable security regime based on arms control agreements. *The Paris charter* on ensuring Russia's security will be thoroughly implemented. Poland's NATO membership will not result in a new military build-up in the region. A new, revised version of the CFE Treaty will be adopted. A compromise on NATO extension to the Baltic States could be reached: enlargement will be delayed for a number of

years (or avoided at all). The Baltic States choose a clear political course on integration of the Russian-speaking minorities into the local societies, resolution of the territorial disputes on the status-quo basis, enhanced economic and humanitarian co-operation (including transborder co-operation). The area assumes a role of a "bridge" between Russia and Europe.

This scenario, however, is not very realistic given the current weakness of the Democratic camp in Russia. The Democrats are not sure any longer that the Western model of democracy could be implemented according to Russian conditions. They are disappointed both with the lack of Western assistance to Russian democratic reforms and with the anti-Russian positions of significant part of the Baltic political elites.

*(b) An authoritarian regime* (nationalistic radicals or extremists in power). Under this scenario, new politico-military tensions will arise between Russia and the West. This will result in the establishment of a strategic *cordon sanitaire* around Russia, with the Baltic States as active participants. NATO will soon be extended to meet the security concerns of the Baltic States. In turn, it will provoke a fast political and military integration within the CIS framework as well as a military build-up on the western and north-western borders of the Commonwealth. Re-militarization of the Kaliningrad Region is almost inevitable. Deployment of Russian tactical nuclear weapon along the Russian western borders and on the Baltic Sea is possible. Moscow will use the Russian-speaking minorities as the "fifth column" in the Baltic States. In turn, it could create a pretext for Russian military intervention in the area. A sharpening of the territorial disputes is possible as well. Moscow will insist on returning Finland and Sweden to neutral status. The Baltic Sea rim space will become a zone of the renewed confrontation between the East and West.

Although extremely unlikely in the short or medium term, this prospect, according to some experts, should not be excluded altogether (Fadeyev and Razuvayev 1994: 118).

*(c) The Communists in power.* As 1995 parliamentary and 1996 presidential elections showed, the Communists and their allies have a rather serious chance to take over the current regime. Domestically, it could result in re-nationalisation of a significant part of the economy and slowing down market-oriented reforms. In the "near abroad," the Communists will focus on acceleration of the CIS integration including reunification with some post-Soviet republics, as well as its military dimensions. It is easy to predict a confrontation with the West on further NATO enlargement. The

Communist regime, however, will be unable to stop NATO extension. Probably, they will influence the pace and scale of enlargement being able to exclude the Balts from the next stage of enlargement. A modest military build-up on the western borders–taking into consideration the country's limited resources–will most likely take place. The Kaliningrad exclave will retain its military importance; its opening up for co-operation with the West and the Baltic countries will be delayed. An effective arms control and security regime will hardly be created. The Communists will probably implement the Soviet tactics of peace offensives directed to conquering world public opinion but lacking real results. "Divide and rule" tactics will be used in Moscow's bilateral relations with the Baltic and Nordic countries to prevent Russia's isolation in the area. Pressure will be placed on the Balts on human rights issues and territorial disputes. Economic co-operation with the countries of the region will be partially frozen. The Baltic Sea rim space will become a "grey security zone" doomed to strategic competition between the West and East.

(d) *Mixture of democracy and authoritarianism* (continuation of the present regime). Internally, a regime will be based on strong presidential power and a weak parliament. Domestic reforms will be targeted primarily at satisfaction of needs of the new elites comprising the "noveaux riches" and "bureaucratic capital" rather than a majority of population. Apart from Yeltsin, a number of his potential successors such as Chernomyrdin, Luzhkov, and Lebed can continue this type of regime.

As for international affairs, such a regime will be unable to produce a coherent Baltic-Nordic foreign policy doctrine. Degradation of the military infrastructure in Kaliningrad and in the Leningrad MD will continue. Moscow will not present a clear vision of Kaliningrad's future role in the Baltic international relations' system. Russia will keep its aggressive rhetoric on further NATO enlargement, but, as the Paris Russia-NATO deal has demonstrated, will be ready to seek new compromises (for example, late NATO membership and early EU membership for the Baltic States, and additional security guarantees for Russia). A military build-up on the western borders and in the Baltic Sea (including nuclear weapons deployment) is hardly possible. At the same time, Moscow will not attempt to revise existing spheres of influence and alliances (except for the creation of a confederation with Belarus) because of its concentration on domestic problems and a shortage of resources. The occasional playing national minorities "card" combined with a lack of real interest in the resolution of the problem will continue. Moscow will want the territorial disputes in the region to keep a low profile and will try to settle them through bilateral channels. The policy in the region will increasingly become a hostage of the domestic political conjuncture. A "muddling through" model will be the most likely policy concept for the future.

The last scenario is the most likely, given the current trends in Russian politics. If, however, the current regime would fail with economic reforms and stabilising society, (b) and especially (c) are possible.

Among the four scenarios, (a) and (d) are tending to a *status quo* and (b) and (c) entail a *revisionist* orientation (cf. chapter 1 for definitions of these concepts). Since the (c) and (d) scenarios are the most probable ones, they should be taken into account first and foremost. The former would have a destabilising rather than stabilising effect on the regional security system and Russia's bilateral relations with the Balts. Despite some shortcomings the latter provides more opportunities for maintaining the status quo in the area and avoiding a "worst case scenario."

To sum up, none of the realistic scenarios for Russian security policy provides either purely optimistic or pessimistic prospects for the area. Obviously, it will be difficult, or probably impossible, to create at least a stable and predictable security system in the Baltic Sea rim space in the foreseeable future. At the same time, some grounds for cautious optimism remain. As Russia progresses with its reforms, the need for a more constructive and coherent policy in the area could emerge. It should be noted, however, that not only domestic determinants should be taken into account: Russia's foreign policy course depends greatly on the international environment as well. Hence, it is very important to provide Russia with positive external inputs, such as even-handed and balanced policies of the neighbouring countries.[6]

---

6. This research was also supported by grants from the Research Support Scheme, Prague (No. 10/1996).

# 3   The West Dimension

HANS MOURITZEN

From the early 1990s the five states bordering Russia considered the EU, NATO, the WEU and the major states behind these entities as potential suppliers of security. This was markedly so for the Baltic countries and for Poland. Finland was a somewhat special case, since EU membership was actually attained from 1995, whereas NATO membership was not officially desired, even if it figured at times in public debate. Let us first briefly survey EC and NATO developments and their underlying preconditions from about 1990.

THE EUROPEAN REGIONAL POLARITY FROM 1990

From the late 1980s the EC was surrounded by high expectations in its completion of the single market, heading towards its magic "1992." Plans were being worked out for an Economic and Monetary Union (EMU). Japan and the US took "Europe" most seriously as a global competitor. The 1989 revolutions in the East appeared in the name of Europe, too–"coming back to Europe" according to the slogan. As German unification was becoming a fact, it was feared that Germany would search out an independent role at the centre of the continent. However, Germany reacted to unification by reaffirming a strong commitment to the EC. This can be explained, inter alia, as compensation to France and proof of her will to tie herself to the West (Wæver 1990; 1996). German unification triggered a Franco-German initiative for supplementing the already planned EMU with a parallel project for Political Union. According to this EU project, the Commission should be entitled to make proposals just like the member-countries regarding common foreign and security policy (CFSP), but not acquire the exclusive right of initiative that it enjoys in other areas. Decision by consensus would still be the order of the day. The basic influence pattern of the pre-EU period–with much more influence to Brussels in low politics areas such as the common agricultural policy or the internal market process than in common foreign and security policy–was

73

still the one prevailing after the EU Treaty had been ratified in November 1993 (e.g. Mouritzen 1996). The Amsterdam Treaty of 1997 left this basic pattern unchanged.

The EU has few purely negative sanctions and no military means of its own. Already through the gradual downfall of the Eastern power pole from 1988, definitely completed with the disintegration of the Soviet Union in 1991, this absence of military means was no longer an impediment to EC status as the one and only European power pole (= European unipolarity). Its most crucial sanctions are its trade barriers to the world around or, in positive terms, varying degrees of access to its market–the world's largest "internal market." Its pole position is also based on political prestige–being the "good company." This, in turn, is based on two things: being rich, at least relatively speaking, and being "Europe." The EU has managed to acquire almost monopoly on this positively value-loaded term.

Except for foreign and security policy the EU is a supranational power pole with nation-states as voluntary members–a hitherto unseen entity that one could label a "membership pole." Moreover, it wishes further members, and nation-states outside the pole do actually wish to become such. Hence, the pole is gradually expanding. This seems, so far, to be a self-reinforcing process: the bigger the pole, the larger its market, and the more "necessary" it becomes to get inside for those still outside; moreover, growth implies that the "Europe" label becomes increasingly justified.

Still, a newly arrived would-be insider with an open and accommodating mind towards the EU–and there are many–may legitimately ask itself and others: where is the power pole "really"? Whom shall we accommodate? The Commission with its exclusive right of initiative in "the capital of Europe" (Brussels), for instance? Hardly in questions pertaining to high politics, at any rate. In both formal and real terms, the pole is the Council of Ministers, with its voting rules of unanimity or qualified majority depending on issues, and represented by its rotating Presidency. But this implies a somewhat ephemeral pole identity, as accommodating actors must adapt to different nation-states at different times and in different issues. For instance, a would-be insider who fears that its entrance will be vetoed by a specific member may have to appease the latter continuously. Another would-be insider may have to appease yet another member out of the same fear. In other words, the real locus of power is difficult to identify–not only because it is dispersed, and sometimes dispersed differently to different accommodators, but also because the Presidency is rotating. This means that the EU pole has low self-control; it is easy for outsiders to penetrate and play off various sub-units (nation-states, primarily) against each other. Also, the pole's decision procedure (unanimity) in foreign and security policy issues favours, evidently, lowest common denominator decisions and entails sometimes paralysis.

This does not really detract from the EU pole character, as its positive sanctions and prestige seem to remain largely unaffected to the outside world. The number of accommodators, would-be members not least, seems to be increasing rather than decreasing–as does their willingness to accommodate. Europe since the great turbulence 1989-91 can be likened to a *school class*. The membership pole has made (most of) the criteria for membership explicit; the students being the would-be members are more than willing to learn from their teachers–the EU Commission and existing EU member-countries–how to interpret and fulfill these criteria. It is far from new that an organization like the UN or a regional organization develops a set of explicit norms; the special feature in the case of the current European norm system is that it has paramount pole power behind it–that of European unipolarity.

The *US-Europe relationship* has been put to its severest challenge since the beginning of the Cold War: the disappearance of the common potential enemy in the form of the Soviet Union. Neo-realist thinking (Waltz 1979) and much common sense would expect an alliance to break up in such a situation: it would triumph to death. However, it more than survived. There were frictions, as always, in the trans-atlantic relationship: the GATT Uruguay Round negotiations were conflictual, and there were open and strong disagreements over the Bosnia policy during 1994-95. There were the usual waverings in US domestic politics. On the one hand, there was the wish to relieve the US of some of its European military burden by letting the Europeans pay more for their own security. On the other hand, there was the wish to assert US global status–now as the only remaining superpower. The policy that was actually pursued by both the Bush and Clinton administrations gave priority not only to keeping NATO alive, but also healthy, innovative, and expanding. Most of the initiatives to that effect–including the NACC, PfP and EAPC, cf. below–were pushed by the US. The NATO enlargement process with Poland, the Czech Republic, and Hungary in the first round was to a large extent a US initiative. But why is the well-being of NATO so vital to the US, in the absence of its original purpose? For one thing, it provides a vehicle by which the US can maintain influence on European affairs, not least economically (Sweedler 1996: 256-

57). Secondly, it is prudent to keep a military foothold in Europe, should US-Russian relations deteriorate–just to be on the safe side. In a broader formulation, for a globally paramount power like the US the enemy is not a single country, but chaos and risks (Heurlin 1996: 124). Thirdly, Europe can be a staging ground for military operations in the Middle East, North Africa and the Balkans (Sweedler ibid.)

Paradoxically, whereas the Clinton administration took a more relaxed attitude than the previous administration to independent European security assertion as in the WEU, the actual logic of events unfolding–not least the Bosnian experience–was that an independent WEU was militarily and politically unrealistic. WEU that had been planned as the EU defence arm in the EU Maastricht Treaty and a potential competitor to NATO seemed to end up as the European pillar of NATO, instead. An indication of this was that France, the major proponent of an independent WEU, decided for re-entry into NATO military structures and the deployment of troops under NATO command in Bosnia. Also, it seemed that WEU as a kind of "backdoor" to NATO[1] –from EU membership to full WEU membership according to the Maastricht Treaty, and from there to de facto NATO membership, given the military-operational implications of the strong WEU commitment–was locked: any candidate for WEU membership would have to get de facto US approval as a *NATO* member before being let into the WEU. As expressed by Hunter, the US ambassador to NATO, "...before a country is admitted to full membership in the WEU, we would like to be consulted about whether we would also want that country to join NATO at that time" (1996: 105-6). This procedure is another sign of de facto NATO annexation of WEU.

## THE FUTURE: POTENTIAL ALLIES FOR THE RIM STATES

Which "West" actor or actors can the five rim states hope for as ally in a 10-year perspective? What will be the "balance of relevance" between NATO, the EU, the WEU and major nation-states pulling the strings behind the facade? One's answer to this question depends on which basic theory that one supports, of course. Without going too thoroughly into the

---

1. On this "backdoor" cf. Asmus, Kugler & Larrabee 1995: 9; or Asmus & Nurick 1996: 134.

theoretical debates, I shall make a forecast arguing initially which courses of development are *unlikely* to occur:

1) An EU calculated amalgamation, in which EU member-states decide to pool their ressources in foreign and defence policy, so as to become one actor also in high politics.[2] The WEU is incorporated into the EU in this scenario. NATO has become rather redundant for European defence purposes here, but may still exist as a court of last resort to involve the US on the European stage in an emergency situation.

2) Virtually the same scenario, but as a result of an incremental spill-over process from low politics integration to high politics, rather than springing from nation-states' foreign policy calculation. According to neo-functionalists, "nations forgo the desire and ability to conduct foreign and key domestic policies independently of each other" (Lindberg, 1971: 6).

3) A European fragmentation into traditional great power spheres of interest.[3] There would be no EU, NATO, or WEU worthy of their names. The rim states, possibly with the exception of Poland, would obviously be part of a Russian sphere of interest. No alliance option would be available.

I have argued extensively elsewhere (Mouritzen 1996: 290-94), why none of these lines of development are likely. The EU, and thereby Europe, is actually in a quite stable situation *now* as regards the nature of its very core. Its nation-states are simply too cautious to yield significantly more high politics autonomy to the EU, but also too cautious to abandon the whole EU project in favour of some rather unpredictable national gains (fragmentation), given all the prestige that has been invested in the project (the EU "being" Europe, or its "good company" at any rate). This cautiousness is derived both from IR realists' stressing of the role of uncertainty in international politics (Waltz 1979: 126; Grieco 1988: 499), but also the concept of "uncertainty avoidance" in organization theory (e.g. Cyert and March 1963; Thompson 1967; Allison 1971 ch.3; Posen 1984: 44-7): organizations, including governments, strive to avoid uncertainty, often by the sacrifice of considerable benefits. Uncertainty avoidance

---

2. This is the so-called "integration scenario" in security complex theory, cf. Buzan *et al.* 1990: ch. 10.
3. A scenario in security complex theory, cf. Buzan et al. 1990: ch. 11.

develops with a unit's identity. The more identity it carries with it—culturally, linguistically, historically, and in terms of an established state bureaucracy with its own organizational interests–the more it has to lose by amalgamation, so the more cautious it will be (i.e. avoiding uncertainty).[4] The historic unification of American states could take place, exactly because the young and relatively homogeneous states had not developed significant identities and vested interests. The European nation-states at stake here, however, have simply had more than enough time to cultivate their apriori identities/vested interests and consequently develop their governments' uncertainty avoidance. There is reason, therefore, to believe in the persistence of the present EU member-states as high politics actors.[5] Should collective benefits be available in a given situation, these–or some of them–will be reaped through inter-governmental co-operation like in NATO or in something being only marginally different from the present EU "common foreign and security policy." This conclusion is reinforced, evidently, by the fact that questions of integration deepening are determined by "the slowest boat in the convoy"–i.e. the *most* cautious one. Also, it would suit American interests perfectly, since the US would remain a European power as much as ever. The US would be reluctant towards EU high politics integration because it would rival the US position in Europe. Conversely, the US would resist European fragmentation to the best of its abilities due to the risks and instabilities it would entail.

Presupposing the forecast made above, the relevant actors from the viewpoint of rim state alliance will be the same as today, roughly speaking. On the one hand, we shall see a NATO with its US based military deterrence ("hard security"). WEU will be a NATO annex, at best. On the other hand, there will be the EU with its high politics limitations providing what has been labeled "soft security," i.e. all non-military aspects of security (e.g. Helveg Petersen 1996). Apart from the avoidance of renewed rivalry among its own member-states, it can provide security externally through the CFSP and by disciplining those states seeking membership in the Union ("nice behaviour" in the class-room).[6] Whether CFSP will be

---

4. Popular nationalism is, of course, a reinforcing factor in this regard. The same goes for inertia.
5. This is not to deny that ambitous *plans* for hard core integration will continue to pop up, of course. Cautiousness and inertia will seldom prevail in official rhetoric.
6. Such "nice behaviour" is also encouraged by NATO that has developed a set of membership criteria that significantly overlap the EU criteria, cf. below. As examples of nice behaviour could be mentioned the Hungarian-Slovakian and the Hungarian-

adequate vis à vis a country not planning for future membership such as Russia is an issue of contention, of course. It is beyond doubt, however, that the reputation and identity of belonging to the "good company" will heighten the threshold of external aggression significantly (cf. further chs. 4-8).

A further attractive element about both NATO and the EU for the states at stake here is the fact they constitute multilateral diplomacy. The fact that *several* great powers are members means that dependency spreading is a realistic strategy for the less resourceful states (cf. Rothstein 1968: 124-7, 177). Regarding the EU in particular should be added its uniquely low self-control as described above.

Behind NATO and the EU there will be the nation-states pulling the strings. As enlargement decisions in both NATO and the EU must be made by consensus, it means that also minor member-states may play crucial roles in the enlargement process. For instance, they may require considerable compensations for not blocking this or that enlargement.

Apart from the actors emphasized here, it is beyond doubt that also the UN, the OSCE, and other international organizations will be of supplementary significance for the rim states' search for security; they will even be vital in the norm building and norm verification processes. The argument here is, however, that NATO, the EU and their member-states will be the essential actors. Any attempt at scenario construction should take *their* interests and developments as parameters.

## EU ENLARGEMENT

*EU core vs. non-core*

The reasoning so far not only excludes the extremes of EU core amalgamation and fragmentation, it also positively points to the persistence of the core status quo with only marginal adjustments. But what about the relation between EU core and non-core?

There are divergent views in the EU core regarding EU enlargement/widening: France, Belgium and the South fearing that widening might endanger deepening and therefore being against, at heart,

---

Romanian treaties (1996) on the treatment of national minorities, e.g. Such treaties were unthinkable until the countries became candidates for EU and NATO memberships.

and Germany, Britain, the Nordics and the Netherlands with their free-trade traditions being in favour (the Netherlands, though, belonging to both camps; cf. Michalski and Wallace 1992: 53-59). For Germany and the Nordics, neighbouring most of the applicants is an additional widening argument; the salient environment incentive pertains both to trade and soft security. The traditional compromise between "deepeners" and "wideners" has been to accommodate both by introducing major deepening reforms prior to each enlargement and safeguarding that existing depths in various fields have been retained. It is dubious, however, if this kind of compromise will work in connection with the East enlargement. Various means of safeguarding EU "efficiency" (=deepening) in the face of the sheer *number*/heterogeneity of would-be members have been suggested (Maclay 1992: 14, 44-45): the fact that the lowest common denominator is being lowered by the many new members could be compensated for by giving additional voting weights to the large member-countries in the Council of Ministers, and the abolishment of the right of each member to recruit a Commissioner in Brussels or to manage the EU Presidency could be options. The main losers from such proposals would be the present-day "non-large" members. According to the principle of uncertainty avoidance, they should use their formal powers to block such an efficiency reform, due to the significant loss of control that it entails for them compared to the status quo.[7] It is difficult to imagine, how they should be adequately compensated. A second danger to established EU accomplishments springs from the *poverty* of the (potential) applicants in comparison to existing members. For instance, there is resistance among the latter to offer the huge financial transfers to East European agriculture or regions that would follow logically from the current CAP or regional policies of the Community (Michalski and Wallace 1992: 19). Also, the difficulties of current members to qualify for the EMU third phase are negligible compared to the problems encountered by the newcomers in this regard.

The multi-depth solution comes in as a new kind of compromise between the "deepeners" and the "wideners." The fear nurtured by most deepeners that widening would endanger existing EU integration depth can

---

7. These and other theoretical considerations regarding the future of EU deepening (including the CFSP) have been made prior to the EU Intergovernmental Conference and the Amsterdam Summit of June 1997. However, the marginal (if any) deepening achieved here and the postponement of institutional reform fit well with the theoretically based expectations.

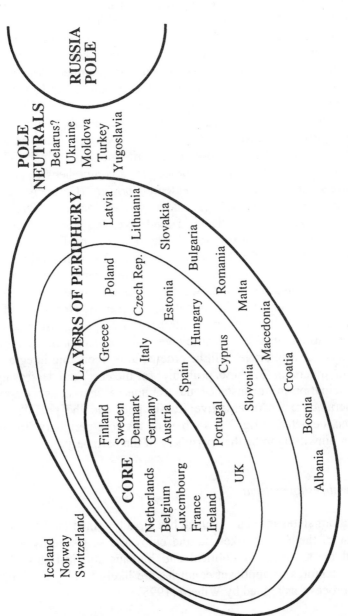

**POLE NEUTRALS**
Belarus?
Ukraine
Moldova
Turkey
Yugoslavia

**RUSSIA POLE**

**LAYERS OF PERIPHERY**

Latvia
Lithuania
Slovakia
Bulgaria
Romania
Malta
Macedonia
Croatia
Bosnia
Albania

Poland
Czech Rep.
Estonia
Hungary
Cyprus
Slovenia

Greece
Italy
Spain
Portugal
UK
Ireland

**CORE**
Finland
Sweden
Denmark
Germany
Austria
Netherlands
Belgium
Luxembourg
France

Iceland
Norway
Switzerland

**Fig. 3.1: Core-Periphery Europe and Beyond**

be accommodated by simply exempting the newcomers–and perhaps even some of the established members–from dimensions of integration which they are not able or willing to engage in ("affiliated members," cf. ibid.: 30, 64; Pedersen 1993: 38, 43). There are, for instance, East and Central European states that go for the political symbols of Europe "belongingness" and thereby soft security–but realize that they lack in economic performance criteria to qualify as conventional members (Maclay 1992: 12-13; Wise and Gibb 1993: 300). But through multi-depth, the process of enlargement will not be allowed to lower the integration achievements that the core members have agreed upon and established for themselves.

As argued by Wæver (1993: 36, 38), however, a "Europe à la carte" where each can pick and choose its favourite menu is unlikely. There has to be a centre, a core that runs the process as a comprehensive package deal, encompassing at least the two essential powers (Germany and France); otherwise "Europe" would lose its most basic actor properties (cf. also Maclay 1992: 4, 26; Michalski and Wallace 1992). Core/periphery encompasses *several* integration depths both among formal members and formal outsiders (cf. fig. 3.1). Even though the EU will surely retain a legal distinction between "members" and "non-members," the *actual* state-of-affairs will be that the boundary between legal members and non-members is less clear-cut and less important than presently. Not much of Southern Europe and even less the new Central/East European "affiliated members" will be willing or able to participate fully in economic integration. The various concentric circles will be ordered after economic integration depth: EMU membership (3. phase, probably) for the core, and decreasing degrees of participation in, for instance, the EU internal market as we approach the peripheral circles. An assertive Russia pole and the pole "neutrals" in-between, depicted in fig. 3.1, are beyond the core-periphery structure, since they are unwilling to be the "periphery of the periphery."

*EU membership criteria*

Among our states in focus, Finland has already joined the EU. The odds for the rest of them to do likewise and enjoy EU soft security will naturally depend on a welter of political and bureaucratic in-fighting. However, various features of applicant countries are likely to play an important part in the process, as argued by Wiberg (1996):

*politico-religious culture;*
*geographical contiguity to the current EU;*
*democracy;*
*conflict potential;*
*capitalism; and*
*budgetary burden.*

Poland scores high on its catholic political culture, it is geographically contiguous to Germany, its new democracy seems relatively well-established, it has no internal ethnonational conflicts or potential neighbour problems, and it is capitalist. The only serious problem seems to be the budgetary burden it presents to the EU (regarding the CAP policy and the structural funds, notably). The ideal EU applicant from this point of view is a small country with a relatively high income per capita; Poland, however, is a big and relatively poor country (ibid.: 51-52 for a quantitative index). The EU multi-depth solution described above should alleviate this problem by having "affiliated members" with modest participation in EU economic integration, at least in a transitory period. Poland could be one such member.

As distinct from Poland, the Baltic countries constitute less of a potential budgetary burden in virtue of their smallness. On the other hand, they have significant Achilles' heels, at least according to some: their geopolitical position and their demographic compositions. In particular Estonia and Latvia have an internal conflict potential with their sizeable Russophone minorities. Lithuania has a more homogeneous population, but it has the special sensitive problem of Russian military transit to the Kaliningrad enclave. Estonia with the most rapid economic reforms and development and with its geographical contiguity to Finland–in turn making the Estonian economy almost a part of the Finnish one–is no.1 in line for membership among the Baltic countries.

There is no Russian opposition to Baltic EU memberships, quite to the contrary (cf. ch.2; Christiansen 1996: 292; Karaganov 1996). Expected economic progress in these countries is seen as an advantage to North-West Russia as well. However, this attitude is surely contingent on the "backdoor" from EU membership to WEU membership and from there to de facto NATO membership being kept locked (Asmus and Nurick 1996: 134). German, French and UK hesitation in the face of Baltic EU memberships seems to be mainly derived from their uncertain security implications.

## NATO ENLARGEMENT

Although there has been significant NATO soulsearching and subsequent reform after the virtual disappearance of its traditional enemy, the inter-governmental status of the organization has not been on the agenda. Unlike the EU enlargement process, in which applicants do not know for sure which kind of entity they will eventually be joining (a "moving target"?), NATO is in this respect a much more static and stable community.[8] Therefore, we can limit our discussion here to the very enlargement question. Which are the pre-dominant views on enlargement among current members, and which are the criteria that applicants are facing? As to various forms of affiliation with NATO, which are the purposes of the NACC/EAPC and PfP arrangements and which role do they play in the NATO enlargement game?

### Enlargement views among current members: multi-depth as compromise?

It was agreed at the NATO summit of July 1997 to invite Poland, the Czech Republic and Hungary to join the alliance. There has been a lot of pulling and hauling among current member countries, however, on the who, how, and when questions of enlargement ever since NATO agreed to the very idea of enlargement (January 1994). Generally speaking France and the UK have been foot-dragging, whereas the US and Germany have taken the lead, although in a somewhat oscillating manner (and depending on applicant). Denmark and Iceland have shown whole-hearted support for the idea all the time.

These disagreements, however, have been postponed through a kind of multi-depth solution. Even if there is no such thing as NATO associated membership, there is actually a NATO analogy to the EU multi-depth development that we expect. This is provided by the NACC/EAPC and PfP arrangements. As formulated by the US ambassador to NATO (Hunter 1996: 22),

> In fact, our ambition with those countries that take this [PfP] very seriously is to make the difference between being a fully engaged partner and being an ally as small as possible.

---

8. Of course, if one accepts the above EU argument the target is not moving that much after all.

Or by the Danish defence minister (Hækkerup 1997):

> Because in the new Europe the clear distinction between countries with a security guarantee according to article 5 of the Washington Treaty and those without is increasingly being blurred.

The "North Atlantic Cooperation Council" (NACC) was a forum of co-operation between NATO and other European states, encompassing the 16 NATO members, the Central and Eastern European states and the Central Asian Republics emerging from the former USSR (Heise 1996). NACC created a certain enthusiasm at its very inauguration in December 1991. It was soon realized, however, that NACC was more of a forum for exchange of views and information, rather than an organization that should solve actual security problems. When the "Partnership for Peace" programme (PfP) was launched in January 1994, it was met with a good deal of disappointment among those who had expected that NATO enlargement was imminent; it was regarded as a consolation prize or a substitute for not being invited to join NATO. However, PfP being open to all NACC members and other OSCE countries, turned out to carry much more substance with it than NACC. It opens up a framework for practical military co-operation, particularly in the planning, training and exercising for peace-keeping missions. For obvious reasons, peace-keeping is always a multinational task, requiring military co-operation of different nations. Forces of some NATO countries co-operate with some non-NATO countries, raising the salient issue of inter-operability due to different equipment, doctrines, and procedures. It is obvious that PfP offers a military and political training ground (e.g. civilian control of the military) for prospective NATO members and transmits a feeling to partner countries of not being left alone in terms of their security. However, it is also an exercise in "common security" vis à vis those countries that do not envision membership, just like the NATO/Russian 16+1 co-operation that was initiated in 1997 (ch. chapter 10). From 1997, the "Euro-Atlantic Partnership Council" (EAPC) has replaced NACC. Apart from strengthening political and security co-operation between NATO and its partners, it encompasses an enhanced PfP as a distinct element within it.

It seems that PfP and now the EAPC have been used by current NATO members to postpone some delicate decisions and disagreements in the enlargement process. As the framework seems to function well both in relation to prospective members and partners, the initial disappointment of Central and East European states has been overcome.

*NATO membership criteria*

Just like in the EU class, the (same) students also get various grades in the NATO class. Strictly speaking, the stressing and weighting of various membership criteria should depend on which specific path to NATO expansion that one has in mind (Asmus, Kugler, and Larrabee 1995): evolutionary expansion along with or after EU expansion, expansion as stability promotion (filling out a security vacuum), and expansion as a strategic response to Russian threats (should such appear). However, as current NATO members prefer various paths (if they prefer any expansion in the first place) and as these paths are to some extent overlapping in practice, it is necessary for would-be members to adapt to a kind of "compromise list" of criteria to make everyone reasonably happy. So whereas the distinction between various paths and their criteria is analytically useful, one combined set of criteria is probably enough as seen from applicants' point of view. Apart from the basic requirements for NATO membership–democracy, market economy, civilian control of the military, and the country's willingness to burden-sharing²–the main factors relevant for an applicant's membership odds (not always stated openly) seem to be the following, adapted from Asmus and Nurick (1996: 124-25):

*Western strategic self-interest.* Whereas Poland is vital to the security of Europe as a whole and Germany in particular (as a former front-line state), Finland and the Baltic states are not seen in the West as forming an area of vital Western strategic interest.[10]

*Russian strategic/political sensitivities.* The Western/NATO rhetoric is that "no country outside the Alliance should be given a veto or droit de regard over the [enlargement] process and decisions"(e.g. NATO 1995: 4; Hækkerup 1997); such would be tantamount to accepting spheres of influence in the contemporary Europe (NATO 1995: 6). However, Russia seems to be ascribed a certain de-facto veto-power, even though this term

---

9. To put it inversely, NATO wants to avoid "freeriders" on the effort of the Alliance, as was implied by the "denmarkization" slogan of the early 1980s. As formulated by Hunter (1996: 19), it is "important that countries be producers and not only consumers of military security". The PfP "waiting room" should ensure that this condition be fulfilled.

10. These countries, and in particular Finland, would probably argue here that they are as much "West" as anybody else, but that argument would hardly count in the kind of cynical considerations at stake here.

would never be used in public.[11] Whereas former Warsaw pact members are being allowed in, in spite of Russian objections (but with no NATO force deployments or stationing of nuclear weapons), it seems that Russian sensitivities will be respected regarding former parts of the USSR, such as the Baltic countries and the Ukraine. NATO enlargement to the Baltic countries in the wake of Polish membership would actually encircle a piece of Russian territory, the heavily armed Kaliningrad enclave. Finland having been once a part of Tsarist Russia Finnish membership is also a sensitive issue, although hardly of Baltic dimensions. Western views have not been put to a test in this question, as the issue has not been on the official agenda.

A related point is that a certain enlargement may have unintended consequences for *other* countries. For instance, it has been assumed in accordance with traditional sphere of interest logic that Russia would compensate for a limited expansion of NATO by an attempt to include the Baltic countries and perhaps Finland in a Russian sphere. This has even been declared by Baltic ministers (e.g. Estonia's foreign minister Hendrik-Ilves, Swedish TV 16 March 1997). Some would argue from such an assumption that a limited expansion should be left undone.

*Minority issues and border disputes.* Analogously to the EU, NATO does not want to import trouble. As formulated by a NATO study,

> States which have ethnic disputes or external territorial disputes, including irredentist claims, or internal jurisdictional disputes must settle those disputes by peaceful means in accordance with OSCE principles. Resolution of such disputes would be a factor in determining whether to invite a state to join the Alliance. (NATO 1995: 4)

Whereas Poland and Finland are unproblematic, the Baltic countries have border issues in relation to Russia as well as minority issues (Estonia and Latvia, notably). Since Russia's security doctrine makes the protection of Russians outside its borders a top priority (cf.ch.2), large Russian populations in Estonia and Latvia tend to nourish Western reluctance to admitting these countries to NATO.

*Defensibility.* The proximity of a future recovered Russian military power to the Baltic countries puts a question-mark behind immediate defensibility, of course. On the other hand, NATO has in the past

---

11. On this duality in Western state rhetoric and security/military bureaucracies, cf. Clemmesen 1996: 9

successfully guaranteed West Berlin, for instance, or admitted countries with correspondingly low immediate defensibility (Carlsen 1996: 98; Clemmesen 1996). Nevertheless, the argument seems to play a role in Western military considerations.

Whereas Poland has actually been welcomed into NATO and whereas attitudes to Finland have not come to any serious test, it is obvious that the Baltic countries do not by far have sufficient support for their candidacies (requiring unanimity). Countries like Germany, France, and the UK, who are hesitant even to Baltic EU memberships, are even more sceptical towards NATO memberships. Only Iceland and Denmark (cf. ch.9) and, hesitantly, the United States have supported Baltic NATO-memberships.[12] As to the US, the Baltic-American communities constitute effective political forces in American domestic politics (Asmus and Nurick 1996: 128); in spite of a certain "Russia first" policy supporting president Yeltsin, as formalized in the 16+1 NATO-Russia Council, no US president would risk being accused of having sold out the Balts through a "new Yalta": a limited NATO expansion, leaving the Baltic countries to a Russian sphere of influence. Therefore, the US has had to compensate the Balts for the limited 1997 expansion (that has actually been anticipated for a couple of years). Embryos of this were frequent presidential statements like "the first NATO enlargement will not be the last" or rhetoric saying that NATO enlargement has not "just...one moment of accession; it is a continuing process and it is open-ended" (Hunter 1996: 19-20). A related attempt at reassurance, expressed by virtually all member-countries, has been to state that:

> we reject the concepts of "grey zone," of "buffer state," or of the old balance of power or spheres of influence. (ibid.)

In the final communiqué of the 1997 summit in Madrid the Baltic countries were *hinted* as possible future member-countries, a few footsteps after Rumania and Slovenia; tellingly, the interpretation of the compromise text is subject to controversy among member-countries.

A type of reassurance that has been suggested, more in line with spheres of influence thinking, are socalled "conditional memberships" (Kamp 1996: 49-50): membership is put into force, *if and only if* the only power with

---

12. For a geopolitical model explaining the five Nordic countries' different Baltic engagement, cf. Mouritzen 1998: 64-79.

adequate power projection capability in the area, Russia, behaves militarily or politically intimidating vis à vis the Baltic, or other relevant, countries. Whereas such conditional memberships might be hoped to encourage Russia to "nice behaviour," their credibility would be subject to speculation, given a rational reluctance to pour oil upon the fire during a crisis escalation.[13] This type of reassurance will hardly find political support. A related but more realistic idea is inherent in the US-Baltic Partnership Charter of January 1998. This will open up for US-Baltic consultations, should one or more of the Baltic countries feel threatened.

Let us now turn to the five rim state cases; one chapter will be devoted to each.

---

13. Cf. also the path of "NATO expansion as strategic response" as formulated by Asmus, Kugler, and Larrabee 1995.

# 4 Finland

HANS MOURITZEN

## A WATERSHED

Apart from "year zero," 1944, when the armistice with the Soviet Union was concluded, the most important watershed in the history of the Finnish Republic may very well have been early September 1991. As it became evident in the aftermath of the failed communist coup in Moscow (August 19-21) that the Soviet Union would disintegrate, the power structure in Finland's salient environment had changed rapidly and dramatically. The Soviet Union with a virtual monopoly on negative sanctions that could potentially be directed against Finland was about to disappear and be replaced by a more fluid structure. Finnish autonomy seemed to benefit greatly from the inward-orientation of the new Russia that was emerging; the end of Soviet infiltration (not least by the Communist party) in Finnish political life marked an important improvement.

Even under the old structure, however, it had increasingly been possible for Finland to be considerably integrated westwards in *low politics*. In 1987 it was declared that the Finnish version of neutrality should no longer be a straitjacket for Finnish EC integration policy. Ties to the West should no longer be balanced off by commitments to the East (Väyrynen 1993). This somewhat revised attitude was probably caused on the one hand by the relaxed posture of the new Soviet leadership, and on the other hand by the danger to Finnish exports of being excluded from the planned EC internal market (IM), included in the Single European Act of 1986. Still, EC membership was not an issue, at all. Instead, the Finnish strategy from the emergence of the IM challenge until September 1991 became to strengthen EFTA as much as possible, so that the organization could function as an asset vis à vis the EC in the expected EEA negotiations[1] (Porevuo 1989;

---

1. The European Economic Area (EEA) implied the extending of the EC internal market also to EFTA countries. As the EC-EFTA negotiations turned out, the EFTAns got no influence on the standards prevailing in the market.

Antola 1991). It was, of course, a hard blow to the EFTA front, as Sweden declared that she intended to apply for full membership (October 1990)– like Austria had done previously. But even as late as August 1991, the Finnish alternative to EEA (that had reached a deadlock at the time) was not EC membership, but instead the further evolution of bilateral relations between Finland and the EC (Antola 1991: 21). One should note here the *relative* unimportance of the German unification 1990 to Finnish strategy[2]

With the disintegration of the Soviet Union that could be discerned from late August 1991, the first Finnish official statements came forward, in which relations eastward were not given special priority compared to, e.g., the EC, Norden, and the CSCE. Not only was "traditional" EC membership seen as being compatible with neutrality, but possibly also membership in a future political Union with a common security policy (3,4 September). In March 1992, the Finnish Parliament decided that Finland should apply for membership. As the EC had agreed to the EU Maastricht Treaty since the Finnish conversion in early September 1991, it was now actually EU membership that Finland applied for–presupposing, of course, that the EU would be ratified by EC member-countries.

The 1948 FCMA-Treaty with the Soviet Union lasted formally until the final dissolution of the Soviet Union, but the Finnish government laid a distance to it on 4 September (*Hbl.* 5 September 1991).[3] Pushed by public opinion referring to the other Nordic countries, Finland came to recognize the re-emerged Baltic republics almost as quickly as these countries in late August 1991, although this had so far been described as a matter between the republics and the central Soviet authorities. Finland was induced also by Yeltsin's recognition, at a moment when the Soviet view was difficult to identify. Influence to public opinion in an important foreign policy issue like the one at stake here was nothing less than a revolution, given the elitist nature of Finnish foreign policy in the post-war era. It also

---

2.  Speeches by Koivisto in the wake of the fall of the Berlin Wall were almost demonstratively downplaying the significance of the transformations taking place (e.g. 27 November 1989, 1 January 1990, in Koivisto 1992: 107, 122). As expressed in the former speech, "When something very unexpected happens, the view is easily formed that further unexpected events are going to occur. I believe...that the general stabilization during the recent decades in Europe does not change so quickly. There are vital interests that impede very drastic transformations from happening..." (ibid.: 110-11).

3.  Also prior to that, certain official Finnish formulations had watered it down (so that it implied, solely, that Finland would never be a bridgehead for an attack on the Soviet Union). However, all claims that the Treaty should be revised or abandoned were rejected.

constituted a revolution through its unprecedented interference in Soviet/Russian "internal affairs." This was seen again, for instance, in connection with Russian President Yeltsin's strife with parliamentary Chairman Chasbulatov of the "old guard" during the spring of 1993. The Finnish government expressed its solidarity with Yeltsin (in a statement resembling the one issued by the EC shortly before).

Summing up developments so far, there were three phases in Finland's *environment polarity*. The post–World War II systemic and European bipolarity had been tantamount to unipolarity as seen from Helsinki, in the sense that the Soviet Union with its overwhelming negative sanctions was the paramount power in Finland's salient environment. This power position was comprehensive in that it could, in principle, be "translated" into pressure on Finland in one or the other sphere. Well before the melting down of this power pole in September 1991, however, the EC had come to constitute a low politics pole; there was, in other words, a phase of simultaneous unipolarity in two different directions (not bipolarity, as they were relatively unrelated!). From September 1991, the EC pole took over the scene as a comprehensive pole, encompassing both high and low politics.[4]

THE EU AND SOFT SECURITY

The "no" in the Danish EU referendum of 2 June, 1992, and the ensuing Edinburgh agreement of 12 December concerning, inter alia, the terms of Danish EU membership led to some clarifications regarding the Finnish membership application. Unlike the reaction of Finnish voters, the *official* Finnish (and Swedish) reactions were ones of stoic calm. As expressed by foreign minister Paavo Väyrynen,

> It is often asked, if we Finns should also seek the Danish solution. Here it must be emphasized that each country tries to find the solutions that best serve its interests. Our objective is the best possible Finnish solution.[5]

---

4. For a more thorough defence of the thesis of September 1991 as an historical watershed in Finnish foreign policy, cf Mouritzen (1994). The Finnish re-orientation is interpreted as bandwagoning behaviour in Chapter 11 below.
5. Speech in Copenhagen, 25 January 1993.

The "Finnish solution" aimed at was, indeed, quite different from the Danish one. Regarding defence, for instance, the foreign minister's formulations were quite "un-Danish" (and "un-Swedish" also):

> We are ready to participate constructively in this development [regarding the defence dimension from Maastricht]...We do not exclude the possibility, either, that we once in the future will participate in the would-be common defence forces of the European Union in the framework of WEU or that we shall become members of NATO. In other words, we join the new Europe with an open mind...[6]

This openness might seem a bit inconsistent with the continued stressing of "neutrality" that one finds in the very same speech. The persistent use of the neutrality label–that had been abandoned in the Swedish case–could lead one to expect that the Danish reservations regarding defence and defence co-operation would be explicitly and energetically exploited by Finland. But the "constructive" attitude cited above pointed in the opposite direction, obviously.

What were, then, the Finnish incentives behind this willingness to concede autonomy to the EU in the first place and, secondly, to sacrifice much more autonomy than Denmark and somewhat more than Sweden (in security and defence matters)? One often heard incentive points to the deficiencies of the EEA agreement for the EFTA-countries: as the latter had been offered no influence in return for the significant infringements on their autonomies, "real" membership became the only possibility for obtaining influence on the many directives, e.g., that pertain to their societies (Törnudd 1993: 32). As expressed by the Finnish prime minister Esko Aho, "by joining...we can best influence our own destinies."[7] This influence, in turn, should help to ward off the deep economic crisis that had been exacerbated by the decline of the economically advantageous trade eastwards. Inherent in this reasoning is also the socalled "Swedish imperative": Sweden having decided to apply for EC/EU membership in October 1990, Finland should follow the Swedish path as soon as her general autonomy allowed it (Törnudd 1993: 31, 85-6). In this way,

---

6. Ibid. Equivalent statements were made by president Koivisto (28 October 1992), minister of foreign trade Salolainen (1 February 1993), and under-secretary of state Blomberg (11 February 1993). As expressed by the latter: "An economic and political union without a military factor would be a strange structure vis à vis the basic philosophy of integration." Swedish officials or politicians were much more cautious and ambiguous on this point.

7. Speech in Helsinki, 16 September 1993.

Swedish industry would not gain advantages that its Finnish competitors were excluded from.

Another concern may have been to emphasize Finland's European identity and status (Wiberg 1994). As expressed by Törnudd (1993: 32),

> The impression of Finland as a distant rim state could be exacerbated, if the Eastern border of the EU followed the Finnish Western border. This could, in turn, have repercussions on economic co-operation, trade, and investments. Such psychological factors have probably played a role...

There does not seem, though, to exist quite the same "core group" ambitions in the Finnish case that characterize Swedish rhetoric. Note that Aho said "influence our own destiny," not "influence the overall European development," for instance.[8]

One Finnish EU incentive that increasingly came in focus pertained to the potential future *security* challenges from the East. From the summer of 1993 onwards, "security" was mentioned as a motive for EU membership in official rhetoric (cf. Salovaara 1993). Not least the success of the Russian ultra-nationalist Zhirinovsky in the Russian parliamentary elections of December 1993 contributed to this. Most of the Russian political spectrum was pushed in a nationalist direction (cf. chapter 2) and Russia became more self-assertive externally. It should be remembered also that the military situation in Northern Europe had not been characterized by the disarmament and disengagement in the first place that had been seen in Central Europe (e.g. Sivonen 1996). Even though Finnish official reactions to the Zhirinovsky success were demonstrably calm[9] compared to other international reactions (the "Zhirinovsky effect"), it is likely that it played a role behind the facade and in the Finnish EU electorate.[10] It would be desirable to face potential future security challenges from Russia on a multilateral basis, i.e. as part of a European Union with its alleged "soft security." Even though there were no prospects for EU defence forces for the foreseeable future, it was believed that the very membership would

---

8. A prescriptive contribution by Joenniemi (1993) is highly critical of the persistence of Finnish low profile behaviour vis à vis the new Europe: "Much of our...heritage, a low profile and a shy and loyal existence in the periphery will fail and lead to self-marginalisation. It is not enough to whisper; in the European debate one must speak loudly and sometimes even shout in order to be heard" (p.5; my translation).

9. Cf. the observations by Yrsa Stenius, "Fascismen kan inte hota Europa", *Aftonbladet*, 21 December 1993.

10. Cf. *Debatt i Finland*, 27 December 1994, Ministry of Foreign Affairs.

heighten the threshold of attack in the calculus of a potential aggressor. Still, the EU deterrence value was not trusted with any real conviction. US military credibility is higher than, e.g., French or British credibility in the high North. As expressed by Törnudd (1993: 30),

> Perhaps, it is rather NATO [than EU] that is able to offer credible guarantees, but is there any willingness in that direction within NATO? It is also conceivable that a future Union, with more members than the present 12 EC member-states, will be looser than what many imagine at this point in time and, in any case, less prepared to function as a real military alliance or an instrument of collective security in Europe.

Therefore, Finland did not exclude NATO membership as a second option.[11] Thirdly, the possibility of Finland standing on her own feet, as in the past, was held open. It is in this light that the persistent use of the neutrality label should be seen. Even if this label sounded a bit outdated outside a bipolar framework, it was difficult to discard and then later reintroduce with credibility intact. So it was retained for the time being, to be on the safe side. Fourthly, Nordic defence co-operation with Sweden and Norway has been somewhat more supported by Finland than the two other countries. This is not because Finland trusts Nordic military assistance in case of an attack, but it refers to co-operation of a lower level nature. This "Nordic" option has developed towards becoming specifically Swedish-Finnish parallel action in security policy, as regarding the EU (the "Swedish imperative" in Finnish politics mentioned above).[12] By being EU members, WEU observers and non-Nato members, but active UN peacekeepers and PfP partners, the two countries obviously have considerable common interests in several areas (but also mutual jealousies accompanying parallel action, cf. Mouritzen 1997b). In relation to the Baltic countries, the common view is that they should be supported in all conceivable ways, but not be given any security guarantees. Sweden and Finland have agreed *not* to take on the kind of security responsibilities in the area that the US, not least, would surely like them to shoulder. As a further example, Finland has recently replaced "neutral" with "military

---

11. It may be more than a coincidence that there was a debate on Finnish NATO membership in Finnish media at the time of Zhirinovsky's visit to Finland in April 1994. No major Finnish politicians wished to meet with Zhirinovsky.
12. A co-authored article by the countries' foreign ministers in daily newspapers (*Helsingin Sanomat* and *Dagens Nyheter* 21 April 1996) is an indicator of the current degree of common foreign policy.

non-alignment" about her line, just as Sweden did some years ago.[13] Semi-jokingly, a personal union under the future Swedish Queen Victoria has been suggested by three former Finnish top-diplomats to give credibility to far-reaching Fenno-Swedish foreign policy co-operation (*Hbl.* 27 August 1996).

Still, there are nuances between the two countries that can be traced ultimately to Finland's bordering Russia with its unpredictable development. Finland is at one and the same time more open towards EU defence/WEU and NATO than Sweden (where these are slightly taboo), but must also be ready to go back to old-fashioned neutrality (cf. the scenarios below).[14] Finland must have more options for would-be future use than Sweden.


## NATO AS A SERIOUS ISSUE

With the referendum "yes" of October 1994, Finland became an EU member from 1 January 1995. However, the preference for "hard security" over "soft," at least in certain circles, together with NATO's decision to enlarge, in principle, kept the issue of NATO membership alive. Finland became an active participant in NATO's PfP programme, also in co-operation programmes involving the Baltic countries.

The debate about proper membership was fuelled by an article in Helsingin Sanomat (6 may 1996) predicting Finnish membership by the highly respected senior diplomat Max Jakobson (*Halsingin Sanomat* 6 May 1996). It was stressed that the EU "backdoor" to NATO through WEU was locked; it had become apparent in connection with Finnish EU membership negotiations that the present WEU members would not have given Finland security guarantees in the absence of a US guarantee through NATO. In other words, full Finnish WEU membership was not possible without Finland wishing and being accepted as NATO member simultaneously. Even if there is no threat to Finland, Finland's special geopolitical

---

13. Only the Centre Party, presently outside government, has retained the neutrality label.
14. Formulations of the form that we "keep all options open," "we do not exclude any security arrangements for the future" occuring in Finnish post-1991 rhetoric are never found in Swedish statements. Cf., for instance, Foreign Affairs Committee of the Finnish Parliament 1995: 12. Also the more positive Finnish attitude towards the EMU (the European Monetary Union) than that of Sweden [1997] may have security reasons.

situation, being the only EU member-country bordering Russia, cannot be compared to that of other EU neutrals like Ireland, Austria, or even Sweden. With actual NATO enlargement beginning in 1997 and the establishment of a NATO-Russian 16+1 security Council, Finland and other "alliance free" countries would be in a grey zone outside the crucial security dialogue affecting this zone. Finland would be absent from crucial decisions affecting her own security. Jakobson predicted, therefore, that Finland together with Sweden and Austria will follow in the footsteps of Poland, Czechia, and Hungary into NATO. This will happen on classic "Danish-Norwegian conditions," i.e. with no stationing of foreign troops or nuclear weapons in the new member-countries.

The official Finnish doctrine, however, continued to be that NATO membership is absent from the Finnish agenda, but that it is not excluded as an option for the future. As part of the Jakobson initiated debate, Centre Party leader Aho suggested a parliamentary commission to evaluate the pros and cons of membership. That idea was rejected by prime minister Lipponen, at least for the time being, referring to the comprehensive party consensus on the present policy.[15] He issued a sharp warning against "loose talk" about NATO (*Hänt i veckan* 20/1996). Also the foreign minister and the President have tried to close the debate by repetitions of the Finnish doctrine, but apparently not with enough credibility. The theme has continued to pop up.[16]

According to opinion polls mid-1996, 21 % of the Finns want membership, whereas 70 % do not (corresponding figures mid-1995 were 25 % vs. 63 %). Two main press explanations have been offered for this opinion: firstly that the Finns have been used to trust their leaders in foreign and security policy questions, and secondly that the Cold War heritage still prevails (*Hänt i veckan* 25/1996).

---

15. As a matter of fact, only a few Conservative MPs support NATO membership. The chairman of the Swedish Liberal Party Ole Norback, however, has predicted that Finland at some time will end up in NATO.

16. During a visit to the US during July 1996, prime minister Lipponen used some new formulations: NATO "will be expanded in any case. Finland should carefully follow events and then draw its own conclusions, as something new happens." Moreover, "Finland cannot stay put in relation to future arrangements that may be made between NATO and Russia..." (Hänt i veckan 1 August 1996). This sounded almost in line with Jakobson's argument; Lipponen's vagueness only tended to fuel debate again ("loose talk"!) At about the same time, president Ahtisaari repeated in a newspaper interview that "Finnish NATO membership would not further Finnish security interests or European security, but would create obstacles to cooperation with our neighbours" (ibid.).

In accordance with the theoretical assumptions (chapter 1) I shall now turn to describe the two basic Finnish foreign policy heritages. Can they account for Finland's reluctant attitude to NATO membership today?

TWO FOREIGN POLICY HERITAGES, BUT ONE LESSON

*1917-44: Ally at any price*

After independence and "White" victory at the expense of the "Reds" in 1918, the military threat to the new Finnish Republic came from the bolshevik state to the east and its ambitions towards world revolution. Under these circumstances, cautiousness would be seen as weakness; with its image of the Soviet Union, Finland had nothing to win from a line of non-provocation. In addition to the safeguarding of Finland's own military capability, Finland attempted to borrow military assistance and deterrence from outside, almost at any price (Kalela 1971; Turtola 1987). Finland adhered to a French conception of the League of Nations, giving priority to the strengthening of collective security and military sanctions against an aggressor–in contrast to the softer British-Scandinavian conception.[17] A logical extension of this strategy was the ambition to get a proper alliance with the Western powers (Kalela 1971: 269)–to become an "outpost of the West." With the British-German naval agreement of 1935, however, Germany was expected to become the major power in the Baltic Sea area. As Finland did not want to become Germany's outpost, Finland approached Nordic foreign policy co-operation.[18] Circles in Finland actually had quite wide-ranging expectations regarding Swedish military assistance during the late 1930s (Turtola 1987). Having stood alone during the Winter War 1939-40, with mainly Swedish non-official military and humanitarian assistance, Nazi-Germany became a co-belligerent and, from June 1944, an ally during the Continuation War 1941-44. This was the only alliance project that actually materialized.

---

17. The Scandinavians assumed that their security was only threatened in case of a *general* European war, so overall European détente was priority no.1. The League should not become a "club of World War I winners."
18. Finland started using the term "neutrality" 1935, thus lining up with the Scandinavian countries. Finnish neutrality 1935-39 did not win credibility, however, neither in Moscow nor in Berlin. The shadows from the outpost role proved too long.

## 1944-91: Trust only yourself

In the summer of 1944, Finland managed to prevent the Soviet army from occupying Helsinki and to convince Moscow to settle for an armistice in September. However, the borders of the peace Treaty of March 1940 were basically re-established, and with the outcome of World War II as a whole the power structure had changed dramatically in Soviet favour in Finland's salient environment. The essence of Finnish post-war policy became to respect this power structure by accepting, to a degree that could only be settled ad hoc, the implications of Finland's political and military dependence upon the Soviet Union. There could be no question of borrowing external counterweight in order to revise this power structure. Finland accepted occasional Soviet infringements on her values, but only with the purpose of safeguarding more basic Finnish values–notably Finland's Western type of society. An essential assumption behind this policy was that the Soviet Union was a status quo power, at least vis à vis Finland. In other words, the image of the Soviet Union from the former period had to be profoundly revised. There was some justification for this "remodeling" in actual reality but, needless to say, it was a difficult and long-lasting process, both at the elite level and the popular level.

Through continuous reassurances of the Soviet leadership, it gradually became possible to make this new Finnish policy credible. The Soviet Union actually at times expressed its support for the Finnish version of neutrality. It was essential that Moscow trusted that Finland would never be a military bridgehead against the Soviet Union or a political "outpost of the West" like previously. Finland had to fight hard for memberships of "Western" organizations (the Nordic Council, EFTA, etc.) that might give rise to Soviet suspicions.

## One and the same lesson

Which were the lessons that Finland learnt from these widely different periods? From the first period was learnt, roughly speaking, that credible allies are difficult or impossible to get, and the ally that one actually gets may lead Finland into war and perhaps even partly spoil her image (as the alliance with Nazi-Germany). Moreover, too much speculation ("loose talk") about alliances may be dangerous, since it will create enemy images about Finland in the Soviet Union and also nourish expectations in Finland that will not be met at a "moment of truth." By contrast, Finland's own military effort in the Winter War and later had impressed the world and, more important, had saved Finland from occupation (the expulsion of the German troops in 1944 was also instrumental in this regard). So the lesson was that for the future, Finland should manage on her own both politically and, if need be, militarily. In Snyder's (1984) theoretical terms (cf. further chapter 11), *abandonment* should be preferred to *entrapment*. It is better to play it "safe" and reassure the eastern neighbour than to invite a Western security alliance that could entrap Finland by provoking a tense situation in the area. It is actually an *advantage* to be abandoned.[19]

Whereas the lesson drawn from the first period was both negative and positive (search for alliance leads to bad outcomes, but Finland's own military capability is significant), the lesson drawn from the second period was altogether positive: with the policy that Finland actually followed 1944-91, Finnish independence and democracy had been preserved under difficult conditions. By being abandoned (or almost so) Finland had managed on its own politically, and the outcome was a de facto success. Even though president Kekkonen has been criticized for *bonapartist* methods, the very orientation of Finnish policy during the circumstances was both necessary and skillfully implemented. So even if 1991 was a behavioural breakpoint, it did not lead to any substantial "rewriting of history" that one has seen elsewhere.

The lessons drawn from both heritages described here amount to one and the same, in Snyder's (1984) terms: for Finland, there is no abandonment/entrapment dilemma. Being entrapped is a risk, whereas abandonment is actually a good thing. Finland should manage her security on her own.[20] As a serious and relevant alliance option seems to present itself, it is likely that this forceful historical lesson can account both for the popular and the elite reluctance reported above (the two, in turn, reinforcing each other mutually).[21] There were several "carriers" that could transmit the lesson of self-reliance across the 1991 watershed: personal continuity in the top leadership —president Koivisto, prime minister Aho and foreign

---

19. Of course, more subtle forms of Western support were appreciated. For instance, Swedish non-membership of NATO and Danish/Norwegian low profile memberships were vital to Soviet restraint vis à vis Finland (the socalled "Nordic balance," a concept that was never used in official Finnish rhetoric).

20. Not surprisingly, the negative lesson from the first period was used by statesmen in their official rhetoric during the second period, justifying their policy reorientation.

21. Historical lessons, vague as they are, do not operate with *types* of alliances.

minister Väyrynen[22] inter alia–is one such factor. Väyrynen actually owes his political upbringing to president Kekkonen, one of the architects of the post-war policy. In addition, apart from the very youngest ones, the diplomats in the Foreign Ministry have been socialized during the previous era. The higher their rank and influence, the longer their time of socialization has been, ceteris paribus. With the Ministry retaining its almost hegemonial position in Finnish foreign policy, the importance of this factor is exacerbated. As to the popular level in particular, there is reason to emphasize Jervis' insight that "the only thing as important for a nation as its revolution is its last major war" (Jervis 1976: 266). Also, why should not the strategy that worked in relation to a totalitarian Soviet Union during the post-war semi-century be good enough vis à vis a democratic Russia? In other words: "don't fix it, if it ain't broke," as the saying goes. Why should roughly 50 years of investment in "good neighbourly relations" eastwards be thrown overboard?

Will the "do it yourself" lesson prevail for a longer time-span, then? Below, I shall touch upon its persistence in various 10-year scenarios. One thing should be stressed already now, however. The fact that there is currently party consensus in the NATO issue is in itself no guarantee against rapid change. As we witnessed regarding EU membership, national "questions of fate" are not solved through much democratic debate among political parties (Mouritzen 1997c, chs. 4, 5); should reorientation become "necessary," all major parties and the President will change their minds at one and the same time, roughly speaking, and virtually over night.[23] In view of the historical lesson that has been internalized, however, it will require a forceful stimulus to happen.

## SCENARIOS FOR THE UPCOMING DECADE

The scenario analysis will follow the general principles, assumptions and definitions that were made for this purpose in chapter 1. The analysis is relatively simple in this chapter, since Finland is already a member of the EU and since withdrawal from the EU is hardly on the agenda. Accor-

---

22. Even though Väyrynen resigned during 1993 "to concentrate on the Presidential campaign," he still seems to have high level ambitions in Finnish political life.
23. The national credibility concern that is one of the reasons for this kind of behaviour, is even more operative in security matters than in connection with the EU.

dingly, it is relevant to discuss Finland's situation and options during the environment scenarios depicted in fig. 4.1:

**Fig 4.1: The Relevant Environment Scenarios for Finland**

| West / Enlargement | Russia Status Quo Orientation | Revisionist Orientation |
|---|---|---|
| Finnish EU Membership | Soft security | Soft insecurity |
| Finnish EU+NATO Memberships | Hard security | Hard insecurity |

*Finland enjoying soft security*

This is in essence an extrapolation of the prevailing situation: a Russian status quo orientation in the region giving top priority to domestic problems combined with Finnish EU membership. Russian state challenges to Finnish autonomy will be rare or absent. In any case, the EU membership will provide "soft security" vis à vis such hypothetical challenges: through its symbolic and prestige value, as member of the European "Champions' League", the threshold vis à vis autonomy challenges, let alone military pressure, will be considerable. Russia will be dependent, not least economically, on EU goodwill. Moreover, it is likely that Finland's current "synchronized swimming" with Sweden will continue. In the absence of any forceful stimulus, the Finnish foreign policy lesson described above will have to be respected. Parallel action with Sweden will not provide the kind of "hard security" wanted by some circles, but it will not violate the historical lesson, either–quite to the contrary.

Finland will continue to be the "outpost of the rich". For the foreseeable future, the Finnish-Russian border will be a border between rich and poor with all its characteristic problems: immigration pressure (not only Russians, but different nationalities), organized crime from the St. Petersburg region, and environmental problems emanating from, e.g., nuclear power plants in Russia. In the face of these challenges, the Finnish role will be not only that of a kind of EU border guard, but also a Russia advocate within the EU in order to mobilize EU ressources for the alleviation of poverty problems in North-West Russia. In other words, specific low politics issues will fill the agenda during this scenario.

In a *longer* time perspective, should the Russian economy develop in a favourable direction, the Finnish-Russian border will no longer be a poverty border. Optimistic prospects will open up for Finnish exports and thereby the Finnish economy as a whole. The psychological expectations in the West will change from Russia being a recipient of assistance to an area of opportunity; the Finnish role as active bridge-builder between the EU core and Russia will be a relatively prestigeous one. In this cooperative atmosphere of mutual advantage, the risks of autonomy challenges from the East will be even more modest.

## Finland enjoying hard security

In this scenario Finland has joined NATO, while still neighbouring a status quo oriented Russia giving top priority to domestic problems (probably, but not necessarily, with democratic rule). Arguments for Finnish NATO membership already under such conditions have been several. For one thing, it is better to join under relaxed conditions than during a tense situation, in which case further escalation will easily be the result. Another argument says that even a status quo oriented Russia will seek to restore such a status quo, if NATO has displaced it by enlarging with Poland, Czechia, Hungary, or others; Finland and the Baltic countries will then be exposed to Russian pressure in compensation.[24] Also, the Finnish image may suffer with the membership of Poland or other ex-Warsaw pact members. The reason for this is that Finland has defined itself during the Cold War as belonging to a different category than that of the Soviet allies and, therefore, as being much more "West" than for instance Poland. This ranking would be turned on its head with Polish NATO and EU memberships.

The view advocated here, however, is that a more tangible stimulus is necessary to surpass the Finnish lesson from history. Presupposing status quo to the East as we do, the most obvious candidate for such a stimulus occurs in Finland's western salient environment: Sweden deciding to join

---

24. This argument could be carried further, but in the opposite direction: Finland should *not* join, as this would put so much extra pressure on the Balts. This altruisitc argument would correspond to the Swedish argument for not joining NATO during the Cold War: then Finland would be "lost" and an iron curtain would be established all the way up through the Gulf of Bottnia.

NATO. Then Finland will rush in as well. Jakobson's argument described above fits in here. Precisely *Swedish* membership would be the triggering event, probably the *sine qua non* for Finnish membership. Firstly, the synchronized Swedish-Finnish behaviour these years would be an argument in itself. Secondly, Sweden's geopolitical location would make compensatory Russian pressure on Finland more likely upon Swedish membership than with other countries. Such a scenario has actually been the Finnish nightmare ever since the creation of NATO; unlike previously, however, Finland can now decide to follow in the Swedish footsteps. Thirdly, Finland relates its prestige/identity in general much more to Sweden than to Poland, as in the above argument. Finland can live with Polish membership, as long as Sweden also stands outside.

There is an entirely different situation that might also eliminate the importance of the historical lesson: that Russia abandons its resistance to NATO enlargement in the area. The reason may be that NATO is developing into a collective security organization, with Russia as a likely future member (as envisioned by current Danish official rhetoric). In this not very likely scenario, Finland gets the best of both worlds: no autonomy challenge from the East and NATO protection from the West. This means that Finland's foreign policy will expand its geographical radius: there will be no pressing "neighbour concerns" in the sphere of high politics, and NATO will provide Finland with an influence on geographically broader security issues (on top of that provided by EU membership).

As with soft security, the low politics issues as described above will probably dominate the agenda; in the short run at least, Finland will take on the twin roles of EU-border guard and Russia-advocate. The latter role will be expanded here, however, so that Russia's interests are advocated *both* within the EU and NATO contexts. As to the latter, Finland is likely to work not only for Russian membership, but also expansion of PfP co-operation with Russia as a preparation for membership.

In a longer time-perspective, there is the same optimistic sub-scenario as dealt with in the preceding section, presupposing a favourable economic development in Russia and giving Finland the prestigeous role as bridge-builder between the EU core and Russia.

*Finland under soft insecurity*

We presuppose here that a revisionist orientation has come to prevail in

Moscow, either as a result of a military coup or through a gradual development. A revision to the old Soviet borders does not directly involve Finland, but obviously a more assertive Russian foreign policy is felt also in Helsinki. NATO membership has not been offered by NATO or accepted by Finland. There is no proper iron curtain to the east of Finland; as in the current situation, EU expansion is not seen as provocative by Russia as NATO expansion would be, given NATO's anti-Soviet legacy. Still, the situation is basically insecure, since Finland is sometimes mentioned as part of the Russian "near abroad," reflecting not only Finland's past as a Russian Grand Duchy pre-1917 but also her political dependency on the Soviet Union in the post-war period. On the positive side, however, there are no border disputes or minority problems in relation to Russia. The major difference to the 1944-91 period is that the symbolic value of EU membership mentioned above significantly heightens the threshold of any Russian autonomy or military challenge; also the Soviet infiltration in Finnish political life will hardly have been re-established. Finland may try to obtain a proper foreign and security policy Union with Sweden, but will hardly succeed, however. Sweden will be too cautious for such an undertaking, just like in 1940 (uncertainty avoidance!)[25] Also, it is doubtful if Swedish-Finnish synchrony can persist in this scenario, given the different challenges they are exposed to. Finland will have to reassure Russia more than Sweden does.

The specific low politics problems filling much of the agenda in the two previos scenarios (environment, immigration, etc.) have probably been swept under the carpet rather than solved. With the Russian orientation presupposed here high politics has taken over, and foreign policy is given top priority.

### Finland under hard insecurity

High politics also prevails in this scenario. Facing a revisionist neighbour to the East (albeit hardly in relation to Finnish territory) and simultaneously being a member of NATO, Finland has become the true "outpost of the

---

25. As investigated by Carlgren (1981), there were specific plans for a Swedish-Finnish state Union with common foreign and security policy during summer and fall of 1940. This was a wideranging plan in an extreme situation, with Hitler in Denmark and Norway and Stalin to the east in an apparent alliance. However, the plan came to nothing and Finland was absorbed into the German orbit from early 1941.

West" that was dreamt of in Finland's alliance policy after World War I. The historical lesson has been overwon, the stimulus being probably a dramatic military take-over in Moscow creating fear of Russian intentions in the region.[26] There will be a mini-bipolarity around Finland's eastern border, being the only border where the two poles confront each other directly (depending on Baltic countries' status, of course). However, there will be no iron curtain, proper. In view of Finland's historical lessons vis à vis her eastern neighbour, the Finnish alliance posture will be one of non-provocation like that of Denmark and Norway during the Cold War: no nuclear weapons and no foreign troops on Finnish territory. Given the sigificant size, for a small power, of the Finnish armed forces together with the nature of the Finnish terrain, foreign forces will hardly be vital for the purpose of deterrence, either. The defensive posture of Finnish troops will also contribute to as relaxed a situation that one can have during the prevailing mini-bipolarity.

---

26. One could also imagine the opposite sequence: Finland joining in the wake of Sweden, this in turn giving revanchist forces in Moscow the necessary momentum.

# 5 Estonia

MARE HAAB

The European states all face the questions, "How much security is enough?" and "How to provide for security in Europe?" The answers, however, greatly depend on whether one is located at the core or on the fringes of the continent. The ultimate outcome rests upon the decisions made within each of the individual states to match the European context and to a certain extent are also conditioned by non-continental actors (the United States being the most significant one). Estonia, one among the new voices eager to have her word on matters of the Old World in the New Time, sees herself culturally, economically and politically as part of Europe and has made this identification the primary political line ever since regaining independence in 1991. Still, in order to determine Estonia's real possibilities in becoming a credible and fully acknowledged partner in the not-too-strictly defined European security space (as well as the more precisely determined Baltic Sea area), one has to consider both the peculiarities of Estonia as a beginner in international relations as well as the basic arguments prevailing in the West and in Russia concerning present and future security and defence issues.

In this chapter an attempt will be made to discuss the security policy and prospects of Estonia with emphasis being put on the political and military aspects of security. While the primary concern lies with the contemporary trends and perspectives, relevant historical experiences are also discussed. Environment scenarios for Estonia covering the upcoming decade are included in the last section of chapter 7.

ESTONIA'S SECURITY ENVIRONMENT

The groundwork for the official security and defence policies of the restored independent Republic of Estonia is much affected by the prevailing threat-perception. This stresses the sensitive geopolitical position of the small country and sees Russia as a source of insecurity. The argument is strongly bound to historical prejudices and inspired by present-day tendencies disclosing themselves in Russia.

Firstly, the relationship between Estonia and Russia has a complex and tense history. Soviet occupation, repression and Sovietization are the influencing factors to provide for mistrust, suspicion and fear in the small neighbouring Estonia. The expansionist ideology, advocated time and again through political rhetoric as well as in numerous official and semi-official documents, which lay out the essence of the foreign and defence policies of the Russian Federation, match the policy used by the Soviet Union and makes it difficult for Estonia to admit any new identity of the Russia which emerged from the collapsed Soviet Union. Russia's refusal to accept the 1920 Tartu Peace Treaty, references made on the Russian side to the Baltic area as "[...] the most explosive region when considering the possibility of the development of new hotbeds of conflict with the participation of the armed forces of the Russian Federation" and describing the Estonian Government as "[...] the ethnocratic regime in Tallinn [...]" (Dementjev and Surikov 1996) are interpreted by Estonia as indicating that Russia has not completely accepted either Estonia's independence or sovereignty and actually aims to restore Great Russia through direct (military) "protection" of the Russian-speaking minorities in the near-abroad countries who "...culturally and ethnically identify themselves with the Russian Federation."[1]

Secondly, Russia having not given up the ideas of superpower policy, insists on viewing the international community through the prism of spheres of influence. Expansionist Russia would definitely be a concern to, say, Great Britain or Denmark, but for Estonia it is estimated to embody a real military threat since Estonia is still included among those areas considered to be Russia's legitimate sphere of interest. The basic argument used to justify this policy is the comparatively large proportion of Russian-speaking minority residing in Estonia. The ethnic composition of the Estonian population as of January 1, 1996 was as follows: 28.5 per cent

---

1. These principles have been formulated most explicitly in the 1993 report On the Security Concept of Russian Federation, compiled by the Russian Institute of Strategic Studies. An even more direct military threat towards the Baltic States is advocated in the document entitled The Conceptual Bases of Countermeasures to the External Threats Directed Against the National Security of the Russian Federation compiled by the Moscow based institute of Strategic Studies in October 1995. According to this document "Russia is having both moral and legal basis for locating troops on the territory of the Baltics."

Russians, 2.6 per cent Ukrainians and 1.5 per cent Belorussians, 0.9 per cent Finns and 1.9 per cent representatives of other nationalities among the 1,476,301 inhabitants (Estonian Statistical Office 1996). Russia's way of thinking in terms of spheres of influence is most clearly demonstrated in its rigid opposition to the dimensional development of NATO which it partly binds to the minority issue in Estonia. As a countermeasure to NATO enlargement in the direction of the Baltic States, Russia has considered nuclear deployment in Belarus, Kaliningrad and on the Norwegian-Russian border. Estonia's aspirations to integrate with the NATO block are defined as "provocative plans" which justify "[...] the preemptive use of force by the armed forces of the Russian Federation against *the nationalistic armed formations* [of Estonia] with the aim of decisively putting down possible practical steps about the[...] plans." The leader of the Russian Communist Party Gennadii Zyuganov has declared that "If the Eastern European States, including the Baltic countries, would join NATO, 80 per cent of the people in North-east Estonia, all Russians, would vote for joining Russia. This would mean the division of Estonia" (*Baltic News Service* 19 December 1995).

Thirdly, the Russian Army is facing extreme economic difficulties and experiencing a deep moral crisis. The Russian military has a mixed picture of their tasks, which makes them vulnerable to political manipulations and hostile intentions. The borders of Russia are seemingly dependent on the context of national, political and economic interests of Russia rather than on the state. Chechnya is the most vivid example of this. The military-political area around Estonia is heavily militarised. The main concrete military threat to Estonia is seen as arising from the Russian 76th Guards Airborne Division located in Pskov. This division of 8,000 has the experiences of both Afghanistan and Chechnya. Similarly, the 450-men Russian peace-keeping Battalion, sent to Bosnia, was compiled on the basis of this division.[2] Several of the officers of the division are known to have formerly served in Estonia and are well aware of the local Estonian conditions. In addition, the allowance within the Treaty on Conventional Forces in Europe (CFE) to increase Russian force levels in the Pskov region from 180 armoured combat vehicles to 600, counts for the Balts as

---

2. This data has been discussed in Estonian daily papers. For more details see i.e. *Postimees,* 2 April, 1996.

an indication of growing aggressiveness on the part of Russia against Estonia.[3]

Furthermore, associated with the general threat-perception there exist in Estonia certain fears which are indirectly associated with Russia and directly with the Russian minority in Estonia. The population structure of Estonia, with a comparatively large proportion of Russian-speaking non-Estonians living permanently or temporarily in Estonia and forming approximately 33 per cent of the total population as of January 1996 (*Estonia Today* 16 Oct. 1996) account for these anxieties. Although these people do not constitute a homogeneous community, their uneven distribution on the territory of Estonia and high concentration together with foreigners primarily in the North-eastern part of the state can be perceived as an indicator of potential inter-state risks. First and foremost, the majority of the Russian community in Estonia is socially isolated from the Estonians and generally speaks modest Estonian (if at all). Living in the Russian-language dominated environment the Estonian-language requirements and the laws on citizenship and language are perceived as illogical demands by authorities exercising political pressure. Consequently, the trend among the non-Estonians is to acquire a Russian citizenship which poses no additional requirements. If in 1994 approximately 35,000 citizens of the Russian Federation were living in Estonia, then according to data from the Russian Embassy in Tallinn there were 89,174 Russian citizens living in Estonia by April 1996 (*Postimees* 28 Apr. 1996). This trend is most likely to continue. From the point of view of conducting state policy, it is considerably more complicated to handle the problems of a couple hundred thousand Russian citizens residing in Estonia than the same number of Russian-speaking Estonian citizens. This idea has also been emphasised by several Western analysts (Made 1996). The formation of a large community of Russian citizens within the Estonian state is the result of an ethno-policy conducted largely under the principles of restitution, and adopted as the primary line in the Estonian policy at large. However, the pro-Soviet and anti-Estonian behaviour of the Russian-speaking minority in Estonia is steadily transforming into a more positive bearing to the independent status of Estonia (Kirch and Kirch 1995). There are manifold reasons for this change in attitudes; the main ones are connected to the relatively good economic conditions in Estonia compared to those in Russia and the level of stability and security in Estonia compared with the turmoil in Russia. Therefore, it

---

3. For more details see *The Baltic Times*, 6-12 June 1996.

may be estimated that ethnic conflicts of violent character can happen in Estonia only in the event of the influence of a concrete external factor. Russia's policy on defending her compatriots in the "near abroad" does not entirely rule out the possibility of such a scenario. Fearing the "fifth column" is a distinct part of Estonia's threat perception. This also reveals itself through the open question as to the conscription of the male non-citizens residing permanently or temporarily in Estonia and falling into the conscripts' age-group. The initiative of the Estonian Ministry of Defence from the end of 1995 to establish an alternative service for these people to train them for rescue operations as well as provide them with additional Estonian languages courses was assessed by several MPs as leading to "fifth columns" within the Estonian state at large and in the Estonian Army directly. This sensitive problem remains unsolved.

Given the prevailing fears and the fact that defence in the Estonian version is still primarily associated with defending the territory of the country, it is understandable that the main security political aim of Estonia since 1991 has been to get out of the Russian "sphere of influence" and acquire at least some political distance from the most obvious source of danger to the independent statehood. The real obstacle to achieving this goal comes from the purely geographical proximity of Estonia to Russia.

PHASES IN ESTONIAN SECURITY POLICY

*The phase from 1988 through August 1991.* By the end of 1988 the activities of the popular movements to support national liberation in Estonia had matured to the stage of open expression and on 16 November 1988, Estonia adopted the Declaration of Independence. Estonia was thus first among the Soviet republics to promulgate the supremacy of its own laws over the all-Union ones. The *de jure* restoration of independence was achieved three years later on 20 August 1991 and ended the pre-independence period. However, with Russia's numerous occupation forces still located on the territory of Estonia and a lack of international recognition this time-frame refers to the stage of *symbolic* independence.

The period is characterised by the creation of numerous political organisations (their number being between 40-50) and the predominance of popular movements. These organisations emerged, disappeared and re-established themselves largely in relation to the four different elections which took place between March 1989 and March 1991 for the representative bodies of the republic and in connection with the referendum on Estonia's independence on 3 March 1991.[4] Another characteristic of this period was Estonia's drift towards economic autonomy from the Soviet Union.[5] Further, it was a period when the primary decision as to the basic political line of Estonia's future policy was made. Although Estonia could opt between the policy of restitution and that of secession, the decision of the Supreme Council of Estonia concerning the status of the country, passed on 30 March 1990, explicitly indicated the preference to keep with the principle of historical continuity. This choice was of decisive importance to the whole state-building process. According to this decision the de jure existence of the Republic of Estonia did not end with the Soviet occupation of Estonia on 17 June 1940. The aspirations were to restore the 1918-1940 Republic of Estonia.

By and large, this period evolved with manifold activities to establish conditions for conducting the policy of Estonia independently from the central authorities of the USSR. Emphasis was placed on informing the international community of the peaceful aspiration of Estonia for independent statehood and on searching for international support for that process. It concerned both creating the structural bases for international relations as well as formulating the initial ideas for the country's independent foreign and security policies. Setting up the Baltic information bureaus and offices in Denmark, Sweden and Great Britain, enlarging the structure and staff of Estonia's own Foreign Ministry and educating qualified employees for the diplomatic service were the essential structural elements of this process. Looking for workable solutions in the sensitive sphere of an independent security policy–with foreign occupation forces and military bases continuing to exist on its territory–turned out to be the most complicated conjectural aspect of the process. In this context the notions of *neutrality and a demilitarised neutral Baltoscandia* entered the discussions.[6] Neutrality was estimated to be a feasible means for the

---

4. The respective elections took place to the Congress of the Peoples' Deputies of the USSR on 26 March 1989; to the Estonian Congress (the representative body established to counter the Soviet-period local Parliament) on 24 February to 1 March 1990; to the Supreme Soviet of the Republic of Estonia on 18 March 1990.
5. On 27 July 1989 the Congress of the Peoples' Deputies of the USSR adipted the law on the Estonian, Latvian and Lithuanian transition to economic independence starting from 1 January 1990.
6. For more details see: Reports of the Heritage Society of Estonia, 1989; *Vaba Maa*, May 1989; *Vaba Maa* special issue, October 1989.

gradual transition from the state of a Soviet Republic to an independent country. The emerging political parties referred to neutrality for two main reasons. First, since the basic factors shaping the political thinking and decision-making in Estonia in the period were the ideas of historical and legal continuity of the nation-state, neutrality was strongly bound to that particular outlook. Already by 24 January 1918, one month before the official proclamation of the Republic of Estonia, the then highest legislative body of Estonia, the Landtag, stated in the Memorandum on the Political Situation in Estonia that "the Republic of Estonia has to be declared a neutral state" (Warma 1946). And in 1938 neutrality was declared to be the official foreign policy line of the Republic (yet, these were also the historical counterarguments to neutrality, for it had not prevented Estonia from becoming occupied). Second, at the end of the 1980s neutrality was perceived by the new political elite as a way to mark Estonia as a state apart from what was called the Soviet Union and as a possible argument to be presented to the Soviet Union when demanding the withdrawal of its troops from the country.

Inputs from historical memory also urged the restoration of many of the pre-war security structures in facilitating the break-away from the Soviet Union and the return to civil society. The restoration of the National Guard-type organisations, components of the defence forces of the pre-war republic, was part of the national liberation movement. Thus, on 17 February 1990 the Defence League, the paramilitary organisation prohibited in June 1940, declared its restoration. The pro-independence voluntary police organisation–the Home Guard–was established in May 1990 since the loyalty of the Soviet background militia in Estonia was dubious as to the country's independence. At the very beginning of 1991, while still under Soviet regime, the Estonian government initiated its first steps to restore control through national means (via the Home Guard), called *economic control,* over Estonia's borders with Russia to the east and Latvia to the south. This initiative indicates the beginning of the formation of the Estonian border-guard.

Conclusively, the period of actively striving for independent statehood and searching for means to facilitate this search was marked by two main characteristics. First, the political rhetoric used was relatively cautious to avoid serious conflicts with the Soviet Union (later Russia). Second, the political practice was largely driven by the principle of restitution.

*The phase from 20 August 1991 through 31 August 1994.* The landmarks of this period are the de jure restoration of Estonia's independence on 20 August 1991 and the de facto achieving of her independence after the withdrawal of the Russian troops on 31 August 1994. This stage may be determined to be that of *re-establishing independent statehood*. In this period Estonia focused its political activities around three main goals: *first*, restoring and securing the internal basis for independent statehood; *second*, establishing the institutional bases for integration with the Western community; and *third*, aspiring for the withdrawal of the Soviet-Russian military forces from the territory of Estonia. It also reveals the stage of explicitly evident Western involvement in Estonian-Russian relations.

At the internal level of Estonia's policy-making, inputs from the historical memory continued to be predominant. This not only concerned the regulation of citizenship issues and ownership problems, but also the formation of Estonia's own Defence Forces which started in September 1991[7] and was pictured after the pre-War type Army. The re-establishment of the 1938 Citizenship Law by the Supreme Council of Estonia on 6 November 1991 was in accordance with the restitution-line policy. Although historically conditioned and justifiable, this was utterly unproductive for Estonian-Russian relations. The numerous Russian-speaking minority,[8] who suddenly found themselves facing totally new requirements in their relationship with the Estonian state, perceived the citizenship policy as being directed against their staying in Estonia and in violation of human rights. The argument became the political concern of Russia.

Historical continuity as the primary line of conducting the independent Estonian policy was further emphasised by the new Parliament elected by the Estonian citizens on 20 September 1992. The Parliament declared on 7 October 1992 that the present Republic of Estonia was identical to the Republic that had existed in 1918-1940. The aim was partly connected with the need to convince itself and the electorate to stick to the line of re-establishing the nation-state, but the most important purpose was to create as much political distance as possible to Russia and to attempt to escape the status of Russia "near abroad."

---

7.  The Estonian Parliament adopted the Law on Defence Forces on 3 September 1991 creating thus the legal bases for the establishment of the Estonian Defence sector.
8.  According to the 1989 popular census the Russian-speaking minority comprised of roughly 38.5 per cent of the total population and the figure can be estimated to be approximately the same in 1991. For more detailed information on ethnic composition of the Estonian population see i.e. Estonian Human Development Report 1995.

Russian-Estonian relations of the time were primarily determined by impacts of historical legacy. Estonia expected Russia to: *first,* condemn the 1940 aggression against Estonia and apologise for Stalinist mass repression against the Estonian people; *second,* acknowledge the 1920 Tartu Peace Treaty between Estonia and Russia;[9] and *third,* immediately withdraw all Russian troops from the territory of independent and sovereign Estonia. In response, Russia detached itself from the Soviet Union and bound all problems to the minority issues in Estonia. With both sides keeping to their demands, the relationship was a blind end. Hence, strong Western involvement was indeed needed to regulate matters between Estonia and Russia. To counter-balance Russia's accusations of human rights violations in Estonia, the Estonian laws were announced by the Estonian authorities to be subordinate to the opinions of foreign (meaning Western) experts.[10] In addition, mediation on the part of the United States was decisive in accomplishing the troop-withdrawal from the territory of Estonia.[11]

This period also reveals the beginning of Estonia's active aspiration towards Westward integration through, first and foremost, establishing the relevant institutional basis. Estonia joined the UN and the CSCE in September 1991, followed by membership in the Council of the Baltic Sea States in March 1992, the North Atlantic Co-operation Council in December 1992, and the Council of Europe in May 1993 as well as obtaining the Western European Union's Associated Partner Status in May 1994. NATO's PfP initiative of January 1994 was evaluated by Estonia as a concrete means to develop solid co-operation with the most credible "hard" security organisation and pave the way for future membership in the Atlantic Alliance.[12] Membership in NATO, the only efficient mechanism to provide Estonia with "hard" security guarantees, became openly advocated as the primary security-politcal goal of the country and estimated by the Estonian politicians to be achievable in the foreseeable future. The

---

9. The Treaty was one of the greatest successes of the early Estonian diplomacy. Russia signed it actually as a loser of the war and as such the treaty carries certain negative connotations to the Russia of the present day. Estonia, however, sees the treaty as a sacred principle of Estonian statehood. This principle is also included in Article 123 of the Estonian Constitution.

10. The relevant announcement was made by the Estonian Prime Minister at the Summit of the European Council on October 8-9, 1993.

11. A positive solution was reached as to the troop-withdrawal issue only when the US bound the problem to America's economic support to Russia.

12. Estonia signed the PfP framework document on 2 February 1994.

European Union and its defence component, the West European Union, were distinguished as structures most relevant to the states geographically and historically close to Western Europe to which Estonia pictures itself by both criteria.

*The Third Phase.* This phase started after the withdrawal of the Soviet-Russian troops from Estonia in August 1994 and should continue until the factual enlargement of NATO and/or the EU, or may be interrupted by some unexpected change altering the whole European integration process. The key-word of this period is *state-building*. Since the withdrawal of the Soviet-Russian troops from Estonia the importance of the national-line rhetoric has declined to a certain extent and become substituted with the prevailing liberal-democratic outlook advocated by the majority of political parties participating in the formulation of the main political trends. Liberalism is being estimated to be the only possible contributor to Estonia's Westward integration primarily in the direction of the European Union, marking Estonia's politico-economic goals.

Military alliance in the form of membership in NATO continued to be priority number one in the areas of security and defence. The official Estonian rhetoric focused on promoting the idea of a "security belt" to be created in the vicinity of Russian borders through memberstates of NATO (Estonia being one), in order to support Russia's co-operation with stable states and create favourable conditions for integration with Western Europe. The reason behind this was also the strategy of building up Estonia's own defence forces on contemporary standards by making further use of Western assistance and experience, exercised not on the level of ad hoc activities but through concrete short-, medium- and long-term projects. It is important that NATO-aspirations were also backed by strong support from the side of the general public. Neutrality came to be evaluated by all the Baltic States as a dangerous policy not to be pursued since it added to the vulnerability of the countries.[13]

Through more regular military co-operation with the Nordic States and especially with Denmark's supportive assistance as well as via participation in the PfP programme, concrete results were achieved by the Estonian defence forces in aquiring a certain (though not yet adequate) level of inter-operability and compatibility with contemporary standards. These

---

13. Neutrality to mean automatic danger to the Baltic States was mutually emphasised also by the top politicians of Latvia, Lithuania and Estonia at the 9th session of the Baltic assembly in Riga on 5-6 October 1996.

frameworks also contributed to the advancement of inter-Baltic military co-operation. The establishment of the Baltic Battalion in September 1994 and the preparation for the creation of the joint air surveillance and monitoring system as well as the common Baltic mine-sweepers squadron assure this argument.

Since the Autumn of 1994 a certain relaxation was expressed by the Estonian Government as to the border problem vis-à-vis Russia and the Tartu Peace Treaty. Estonia showed first signs of a willingness to compromise with Russia and agree to the existing border, if Russia acknowledged the existence of the 1920 Peace Treaty as historically (and psychologically) important to Estonia. This "flexibility" was determined by Estonia's aspirations towards EU and NATO membership, both pointing to the unsolved border-problems as solid obstacles for further integration with these organisations. However, the national line still dominated the political decision-making with regard to the minority and citizenship questions. The new Citizenship Law (from 19 January 1995) and the new Language Law (from 21 February 1995) were much in keeping with the standards of the early-independence as judged by the Russian-speaking community in Estonia. Estonian authorities backed the policy with support from international expert commissions who evaluated the laws and regulations to be in correspondence with international standards. Also, the fact that since the 1995 March national elections the Russian community in Estonia had acquired the possibility to voice their concerns in Parliament via the six seats gained by the Russian electoral union, was used to encounter criticism. Yet, the number of Russian citizens residing in Estonia predictably began to grow.[14] Estonia's relations with the Russian Federation were approached from the side of Estonia by a policy of positive engagement.[15] Still, driven by historical prejudices and uncertainty as to the nature of post-Soviet Russia, Estonia's policy towards Russia remained reserved and occasionally provocative.[16]

---

14. By the end of 1996 the number of Russian citizens in Estonia had grown to approximately 100,000 compared to the 35,000 in 1994. (Source: *Citizenship and Migration Board of Estonia,* October 1996).
15. For more information on the policy of positive engagement see i.e. *Estonia Today,* Press Release of the Estonian Ministry of Foreign Affairson Estonia and the EU. Tallinn 1995.
16. Estonia's rigid oposition to Russia's membership to the Council of Europe in 1995 and the statement of support for Chechnya by a group of MP's in Spring 1996 have predictably been perceived by the Russian authorities as hostile policy towards Russia.

POSSIBILITIES FOR REGIONAL CO-OPERATION

In the wake of the 1997 Madrid summit, Estonia's longterm security and defence prospects linked to NATO looked less achievable than in 1991. The manifold political and functional obstacles for Estonia to obtain hard security against the still hazardous large neighbour became extensively discussed on both the international political and academic levels (e.g. Asmus and Nurick 1996). Also, Russia's decisive role in determining the process has become increasingly apparent.

It is within this context that regional security and defence co-operation are being again put on the political agenda of Estonia. As in the early days of independence, however, the reconsidered regional and sub-regional alliance options have remained limited in scope. Also, Estonia continues to be selective. *First,* co-operative defence arrangements even with democratic and non-imperialistic Russia are excluded from consideration. The genuine belief is that neither of these two characteristics will solidly materialise in Russia. The force- and threat-line tactics favoured by Russia with respect to her smaller neighbours, especially Estonia, gives the Estonian politicians reason to assume that secure distance from Russia can be maintained only by keeping Russia out from wherever the strategy of Estonia is designed. *Second,* the Belarus initiative from the Spring of 1995, to establish a nuclear-weapon-free zone "between the Black Sea and the Baltic Sea," including among others also Estonia, is beyond the current interests of Estonia. The once so popular idea has now lost its attraction, meaning and necessity for an Estonia avoiding any close security or defence arrangement with a group of countries, some of which are members of the Commonwealth of Independent States. *Third,* the Nordic States are seen from the Estonian prism to have developed into an even more diverse group of countries than in 1991. This is explicitly shown in their security policy attitudes and roles towards the Baltic states (e.g. Mouritzen 1998: 64-79). Denmark is being most persistent in supporting full Baltic membership in both NATO and the EU. Denmark is also contributing most extensively to setting up military co-operation and carrying it into practice. The other Nordic NATO-state, Norway, is not aspiring for high profile in the Nordic-Baltic security relations. Accepting the idea of the importance of the Baltic region to the security of Europe, Norway strongly emphasises the essential role of Russia in this respect.[17]

---

17. For more details see i.e. *The Baltic Times,* 6-12 June 1996.

Finland and Sweden are both stressing their deep respect for the choice of each country to make its security arrangements and expect others to do the same. In practical terms both are promoting security co-operation, helping the Balts in training their military and delivering material support. However, mixed signals on the part of the Nordic neutrals concerning the creation of closer forms of co-operation between the non-Alliance states and NATO are due to the still-missing commonly shared picture within the Nordic community as to the process of Alliance enlargement vis-à-vis Estonia and the other Baltic States. In addition, as perceived from the Estonian perspective, the majority of the Nordic states are not aiming at too close an involvement with Baltic security and defence matters because they are currently not able to extend any formal security guarantees to any of the Baltic countries. *Finally*, this makes the inter-Baltic security and defence co-operation an important component of Estonia's security strategy. Co-operation on the sub-regional Baltic level is being interpreted in Estonia as providing "...examples of broader European co-operation, covering local needs and indicating means of integration into Euro-American system" (Öövel 1995).

Joint defence efforts are estimated in Estonia to be one more means of making Estonia, Latvia and Lithuania credible partners for co-operation with NATO. The nineteen joint participation activities of 1996 between the three Baltic states focused on the acceleration of the development of the common air surveillance system in the region; the training of the BALTBAT; the creation of a naval training group and developing the command, control and communication system. However, despite the comparatively broad scope of interaction, it is most likely that the political proposition of the Baltic Assembly from December 2, 1995, declaring that " [...] the threat posed to the one of the three States shall be regarded as the threat to all three [...]" [18] is obviously more an expression of political solidarity than an indication of a common military response to possible aggression against any of the three countries. Insufficient military capability is considered by the Estonian side to be the main argument for not creating any Baltic military alliance or pact. With the Estonian side still as the strongest supporter and Lithuania as the main opponent, the idea has not yet acquired high profile among all three Baltic states. Rather, Estonia aspires to participation in the preparation of the *Combined Joint Task*

---

18. For the text of the resolution see *The Monthly Survey of Baltic and Post-Soviet Politics*, December 1995.

*Forces* (CJTF) and in this sense makes best use of the inter-Baltic co-operation. In Estonia the Baltic military co-operation is as a rule ranked as third in importance when the defence policy priorities of Estonia for the year 2000 are considered. Given that co-operation with NATO countries is top priority and relations with the Baltic Sea States second, it is obvious that inter-Baltic co-operation will also be considered as a subject of broader international frameworks in the coming years. However, the enlargement policy of NATO and especially the Baltic States' own recognition that they will be excluded from any rapid entry to the Atlantic Alliance most likely means that Estonian officials will recognise the growing importance of other security aspects besides the military one and consider more seriously "soft security" options.

SOFT SECURITY AND THE EUROPEAN UNION

In terms of military security, the EU is not seen as a means to offer sufficient assistance in the event of a major crisis. Nonetheless, it is crucial for Estonia as it ties the country economically and politically to Europe.

Direct relations between Estonia and the European Union go back to August 1991, when the European Community recognised the restoration of the Republic of Estonia. The Agreement on Trade and Economic and Commercial Co-operation between Estonia and the European Community, which came into force on 1 March 1993, marked a considerable shift towards the EC (later EU) since it contained a provision for Estonia to become an associated member at a later date. The Free Trade Agreement between Estonia and the EU from 1 January 1995, the European Stability Pact signed by Estonia on 20 March 1995, the Association Agreement from 12 June 1995 and submission of the official application for EU membership at the end of 1995 indicate for Estonian authorities realistic prospects of joining the Union. Both the Free Trade Agreement and the Association Agreement between Estonia and the EU include no transition period. The Estonian side perceives this as a strong vote of confidence that the Union is within reach. This was exacerbated by the 1997 selection of Estonia by the EU Commission for the first wave of enlargement (excluding Latvia and Lithuania, e.g.)

Opinion polls show still a slight and steady decline of the positive EU image among the general public in Estonia. According to the data presented by the *Central and Eastern Eurobarometer* (1996, Survey No 6), the number of those to whom the EU held a positive image in 1991 was 38 per cent, whereas by 1996 the figure had declined to 30 per cent. The negative image of the EU shows a slowly increasing tendency during the same period: in 1991 it was 1 per cent and in 1996 8 per cent. To some extent this drift can be explained by the fact that people are getting more familiarised with EU matters: there is more information on both the negative and positive sides of this Union. The same Eurobarometer also displays that 76 per cent of those who say they have the right to vote in Estonia, would vote FOR joining the European Union in case, as asked in the question, "there were a referendum tomorrow on the question of European Union membership." Positive views are primarily based on economic reasons. Yet, political reasons like "the EU helps to maintain peace in Europe" or "law will be more democratic" are also of relatively high importance to Estonians.[19] Consequently, in Estonia the EU is definitely regarded as part of the security political dimension. Therefore, within the European framework this policy could be further implemented as a possibility to resolve the security dilemma facing Russia. The political rhetoric in Estonia around the EU has been comparatively lower in tone and more restricted in scope than that concerning NATO. Also, the activities of the local politicians dealing directly with Estonia's EU matters have a very short history. Since the parliamentary elections in April 1995 and the formation of the new Cabinet, the Estonian Government has established the post of a Minister without portfolio for Euro-reforms. Besides, on 17 October 1995 the Translation and Legislative Support Centre was opened in Tallinn to make officially sanctioned English translations of all Estonian legal acts and Estonian translations of the EU legislation. In addition in 1996 the European Integration Bureau was established under the Euro-reform Minister's jurisdiction, and the European Integration Council was founded and headed by the Prime Minister. These structures function as the initial institutional instruments to work for Estonia's membership of the European Union. Given the better economic conditions and more rapid progress of economic and political reforms, Estonia will most probably strive for earlier inclusion into the EU over emphasising the Baltic unity within this context. Interpretation of the mixed signals from the West is the basis for the belief that Estonia's earlier EU-membership than that of Latvia and Lithuania is not entirely ruled out at the EU level.

---

19. The Central and Eastern Eurobarometer study on Estonia was carried out by the Social- and Market Research Ltd. SAAR POLL.

However, it should be noted that Estonia is still at the very beginning of the Euro-process and just creating essential broader and tighter contacts. These bases include, first and foremost, the harmonisation of the activities of life, laws and regulations affecting the political, economic, and social spheres. A further intersection with the EU can be achieved only through reaching compatibility with EU standards. The manifold and diverse aspects of EU membership is still a relatively abstract notion to the general public who primarily associate it with Western economic stability and prosperity. The number of local experts and people who feel confident enough to discuss the subject of the EU at the level of the general public is limited since the notion itself, the European Union, is a comparatively new one and in the process of development. Given the diverse views among the EU core-states as to the perspectives and nature of the Union in the future, the European identity–and prosperity-bound positive image of the Union is most likely to be sustained in Estonia, since it allows for the most positive scenarios. Further aspirations towards EU-membership should eventually produce some political anti-EU movements and pressure-groups, who will exploit national feelings by referring to the manifold dangers to the Estonian national identity and to the additional complex bureaucracy. Euro-scepticism is presumably going to be only one part of the political platform of such groups.[20] However, for the upcoming years the number and influence of these groups will remain marginal. First, on the general level European identity is not perceived as contradictory but rather as complementary to Estonian identity. Second, open markets are on the level of average people/consumers associated with a broad range of products and free choice of which they have been deprived for the extensive period of Soviet planned economy. And third, the EU and the West are evaluated as being modern, hence marking development.

It is most likely that in this respect Estonia is going to concentrate more intensively on implementing the EU-direction policy in the foreseeable future. However, a political unwillingness from the "core" of the Western world to recognise the concerns of the "edges" could serve to ruin the prevailing positive understanding of contemporary Western values among

---

20. These groups will most probably represent the national-radicals disillusioned in the restored Estonian Republic either due to the implementation of the citizenship-policy which they consider to be not strickt enough or because the political, economic and military elites of the reestablished republic include also previous nomenclatura.

the average people of the country, who have undergone the most painful stages of the reform policy.


THE HISTORICAL HERITAGE AND THE PRESENT

The policy of the restored Republic of Estonia is marked by strong influences from an historical memory which rests on the recollections of the period of independence between the two world wars. It was in the comparatively short period from 1918 to 1940 that Estonia developed its first traditions of an Estonian state ruled by Estonian-speaking locals. These traditions–the evolving formulation of legislation, the creation of state institutions and the formation of policy making mechanisms designed to serve the power structures of the. inter-war period of independent statehood–have been estimated by Estonians to be the unique models to be followed also at the beginning of the 1990s when the second chance of independence was gained. Earlier the territory "between East and West" had been governed in turn by the Germans, Swedes, Danes and Russians. Secession of Estonia from Russia became possible in 1917 with the outbreak of revolution in the Russian Empire. The local national elite aspired first for the status of autonomous Estonia within the Russian Federation.[21] This soon was followed by requests for full independence, if necessary also trough the intermediary form of the United Scandinavian States (Laar and Vahtre 1989). However, for Estonia the realistic possibility to declare independence already appeared the following year on 24 February. A Provisional government was nominated and neutrality was declared in the Russian-German war. Although Germany refused to recognise the new state and came to occupy Estonia, the Estonian delegations abroad succeeded in getting de facto recognition for independence from Great Britain, France and Italy in May 1918. After the outburst of the revolution in Germany in the beginning of November 1918, the Estonian Provisional government assumed power although the situation remained tense; already by the end of the month Soviet Russia tried by way of military conquest to establish Soviet republics in the Baltic area. On 29

---

21. After the 1917 February Revolution in Russia the Provisional Givernment accepted the proposal of the Estonian politicians on self-government and the respective law took effect on March 1917. As a result the first Estonian self-government, the Land Council, was elected.

November 1918 an Estonian Workers' Commune was proclaimed in Narva, North-east Estonia. Moscow recognised it on 7 December as the government of Soviet Estonia. By the beginning of 1919, two-thirds of Estonia was under Soviet control. Still, the Estonian defence forces, led by General Johannes Laidoner, performed successful counter-attacks. Assistance was provided by a British fleet and volunteers from Finland and Scandinavia. The Estonian War of Independence came to an end in 1920 when the Tartu Peace Treaty was concluded by the governments of Estonia and Soviet Russia on 2 February. The Treaty included recognition of Estonia's independence and sovereignty by Russia and came to serve as the basis for relations between the two states.

In the beginning of the 1920s, the main direction of Estonia's security policy was focused on the West. Within the period 1921-1922 the major powers of the Entente granted de jure recognition to the Republic of Estonia and in September 1921, Estonia was accepted to the League of Nations. Estonia also joined all the international conventions and agreements which aimed at non-aggression in inter-state relations. At the same time Estonia's security policy was also aimed at the creation of the Regional Baltic League stretching from Finland to Poland. However, this striving was never realised due to differing interests of the countries within the region.[22] The regional dimension shrunk to the agreement between Estonia and Latvia concluded in 1923. Political co-operation with Soviet Russia was, by and large, avoided until the end of the 1920s when the USSR finally adopted the doctrine of the "construction of socialism in one separate country" and signed with Estonia the bilateral Agreement on Non-Aggression and Peaceful Settlement of Disputes in 1932. The agreement was extended in 1934, and the same year the Treaty of Peace and Co-operation between Estonia, Latvia and Lithuania was signed. The latter remained, however, a relatively loose form of co-operation. By the mid-1930s the change in the international situation, connected with the strengthening of fascist Germany and internationally recognised Soviet Union, became apparent. The security policy of Estonia, not too successful in pursuing the regional alliance policy, focused on the policy of neutrality which became finalised in the Neutrality Law adopted in December 1938. The USSR first approved of those initiatives, yet soon labelled the Estonian

---

22. On the one hand the creation of the regional league was hampered by the Polish-Lithuanian conflict over Vilnius. On the other hand Finland was inclined to closer ties with the neutral Scandinavia.

neutrality "illusory" and proposed to provide the Baltic States with security guarantees to their independence and neutrality. This proposal was under discussion at the British-French-Soviet talks in Moscow in the summer of 1939. The Baltic States did not agree to that and in June 1939 Estonia and Latvia signed non-aggression agreements with Germany. However, in reality, the Baltic States had been captured between the totalitarian USSR and totalitarian Germany, which became evident through the German-Soviet Non-Aggression Pact, signed on 23 August 1939, and the secret protocol attached to the document. Under the secret protocol Estonia became part of the Soviet Union's sphere of interest. On 28 September 1939 Estonia was compelled to conclude with the USSR the Treaty on Mutual Assistance which permitted the location of Soviet military bases and troops (25,000) on the territory of Estonia. The Soviet pressure on Estonia increased and on 16 June 1940 the USSR presented a note to the Estonian government with an ultimatum demanding a new government, loyal to the USSR, to be appointed and additional Red Army troops be stationed in Estonia. The Estonian government resigned and on 17 June Estonia became de facto occupied. Most of the Estonian leaders, including president Konstantin Päts, were arrested and deported to the USSR. In July the Soviet-controlled government in violation with Estonian electoral laws staged new elections to the State Assembly (Parliament), which voted on 21 July for the proclamation of an Estonian Soviet Socialist Republic. On 6 August 1940 the Estonian SSR was incorporated into the USSR. The red terror, which followed, took the lives of thousands of Estonians and an estimated 10,000 were sent to Siberia during the mass deportations carried out in the period July 1940–June 1941. This was followed by years of genocide (in March 1949 an estimated 20, 700 Estonians were deported to Siberia) and sovietization since the end of World War II until the regaining of independence in 1991.

The inter-war experiences along with the knowledge of the post–World War II Soviet occupation serve as the major factors as well as account for the prejudices in determining the security policy understandings and strivings of the re-established Estonian Republic. It is indeed the capability of self-defence that has been acknowledged as an extremely important precondition for implementing a successful security policy. The fact that Estonia performed no resistance to the Soviet occupation is often compared with the different strategy used by Finland (cf. chapter 4) and the retrospective contrast admittedly gives advantage to the Finnish way. In the contemporary Estonian vision, credible self-defence requires defence forces of the size, level of preparedness and degree of mobility that allow them first and foremost to carry out preventive counter-aggression activities. But also, in the event of aggression and threat to the vital interests of Estonia (i.e. sovereignty, territorial integrity and independence), to be able to exercise independent defence until the arrival of help and support from military allies.[23] The latter are being actively looked for in the West and much more cautiously within the Baltic sub-region. Here it is presumably the hard experiences under Soviet occupation that increase the strivings towards amd the trust in the West, overshadowing the inter-war experiences which could arguably provide for more uncertainty as to the credibility of the West in guaranteeing security. The concrete historic heritage thus forbids Estonia to accept classic finlandization (e.g. Mouritzen 1988) as a model for security and defence. Historical memories of the unsuccessful attempts of creating regional alliances in the inter-war period have not entirely been evaded when formulating the contemporary Estonian security policy. However, developing regional networks is increasingly becoming acknowledged as an important element in providing for both state and international stability and security. Yet, mistrust and suspicion towards Russia's role in regional security arrangements cannot quickly nor easily fade in Estonia.

## HOW ABOUT THE FINNISH MODEL?

The overall international developments and the evolution in Estonia suggest that for the upcoming decade, the security of Estonia will consist of mixed security regimes. It is evident that Estonia can achieve comprehensive Western support and assistance, only if it has explicitly made clear that NATO or any other Western military organisation is not being dragged into a potential military conflict on her territory. Accordingly, further improvement of the individual defence capability and enhancement of the inter-Baltic as well as Baltic-Nordic and Baltic Sea regional co-operation should be taken for granted when looking for security guarantees outside the Baltic sub-region. The increasingly interdependent international community suggests the enhancing importance of "soft"

---

23. The principle is formulated also in the document The Bases of the Estonian Defence Policy, approved by the State Assembly (Parliament) of Estonia in May 1996.

security guarantees to both young and mature democracies in the coming years.

The Finnish model of state defence and security in the post-war period, although suggested increasingly by both Euro-American and Russian strategic analysts, has not become popular among Estonian politicians who would like to "escape" the geographic reality–the neighbourhood of Russia–through purely westward alliance policy. However, the *contemporary* Finnish (Swedish) model (cf. chapter 4) is indeed more than worthwhile for a small state located between Russia and the West. If unravelled, this modern version of the Finnish model implies: full membership in the EU, partial membership in the WEU, and extensive co-operation with NATO in the framework of PfP. For Estonia, to adopt this model would mean marking herself with a concrete and credible security identity which does not ignore the highly important geopolitical factors. Yet, "if Estonia could within ten years become only Finlandized then it would be a great achievement. I hope that Estonia will by then be still alive, but there is no reason to count on a happy future" (Made 1996). It is obvious that a key to success in Estonia's security policy is future Russian policy; above all, however, it is the capability of Estonia to cope with this policy. In the last section of chapter 7, environment scenarios for Estonia covering the upcoming decade are formulated and discussed.

# 6  Latvia

ZANETA OZOLINA

The recent debates over the EU and NATO enlargement put it bluntly: three Baltic states will not be included in the first group of candidates. But what solutions correspond with Latvia's national interests? Latvia's geostrategical position between East and West offers three options for national security policy: integration into Western security structures; participation in security arrangements offered by Russia and CIS; and neutrality. Latvia has made its choice giving priority to the West. But a question remains: Why is this foreign and security policy option most appropriate for "the fragile Latvian security situation" of the upcoming decade? We will try to find answers by exploring the formation of a Latvian security policy which could be characterised as a process of identification of possible threats and search for instruments of their prevention. In the final section of chapter 7, a set of Baltic scenarios will be formulated.

## LATVIA'S SECURITY ENVIRONMENT

Considering that countries have opportunities to decide their destiny independently, the theory of international relations provides researchers with a wide variety of solutions. The specifics place us in a certain limited framework which has been defined in the first chapter of the book. The main point of departure is a famous saying among politicians: "where you stand depends on the chair you sit in." In the international system policy options of countries depend on their geographical location and distribution of power. From a regional polarity perspective, Latvia has been placed between two poles and, in this sense, there is not much difference from the Cold War systemic and European bipolarity. The two poles are Russia, which is looking for its place in a new European and world order, and traditional Western democracies, also adjusting their structures to new realities. In this specific polarity, there is not much space left for Latvia to influence the redistribution of power process. But speaking in terms of an environment perspective, the regional polarity looks different from Latvia's in that a small country's perspective could be used as an instrument for achieving its short and long term security goals. But before defining its goals, let us decide what the salient environment of Latvia is.

*Russia.* Latvia's security environment is asymmetrical because of Russia, which is the main actor directly influencing security policy options not only in Latvia, but in the other pole, namely, Western Europe as well. Therefore, Latvia's search for security always has been and will be dependent on Russia's particular place in the international system as well as its foreign policy goals towards Latvia. But what is making Russia the main factor of Latvian security and stability? The basic point of departure is the historical background. Latvia has been conquered by the Russian Empire for 200 years and after a short period of independence from 1918 till 1940, was occupied again. Russia was perceived–and to some extent is still perceived–as a country which twice gave freedom to Latvia, and twice acted as an occupying country. Therefore, their relation building process has been overshadowed by these historical legacies. From the Latvian side it is difficult and painful to get rid of historical memories and injustices but, at the same time, Russia is still behaving like a superpower trying to protect its sphere of interests by different means and, thus, hindering the process of creating a new European security arrangement. Although, Russia was the first country to internationally recognise Latvia's independence in August 1991, early on during the process of its self-identification as a new political actor it pretended to be democratic and a modern state while at the same time, through official documents on foreign and security directives, it obviously demonstrated its willingness to restore dominance in ex-Soviet territories including Latvia (Stranga 1997: 141-185). Even now Russian Minister of Foreign Affairs Yevgenij Primakov is pursuing a strategy of regional hegemony in the space of the ex-Soviet Union (Stranga 1997: 187-188). As a consequence, Latvian reaction to Russia's patterns of behaviour followed a counter-reaction that Russia is a country still keeping its interests in Latvia alive. But it would be unfair to ignore either the dynamic changes in Latvian-Russian relations, or the threat perception in Latvia.

In spring 1994 a sociological survey was done by Talavs Jundzis in co-operation with the Latvian Academy of Sciences. This survey proved the cleavages in security thinking in Latvia in favour of internal vulnerabilities and the presence of Russian troops in what, of course, was interpreted differently by citizens and non-citizens. Respondents had to answer the question of which factors were the most threatening to Latvian security and independence. *Citizens* of Latvia put the factors in the following order:

> *Weak economy: 21.2 %*
> *Presence of Russian troops: 19.9 %*
> *Implemented Russian foreign policy: 18.5 %*
> *Unsolved social problems: 15.4 %*
> *Crime: 9.1 %*
> *Unclear national relations: 6.3 %*
> *Uncontrolled spread of weapons: 5.0 %*
> *People unloyal to Latvia: 2.2 %*

Answers of *non-citizens* differed from previous ones:

> *Weak economy: 26.3 %*
> *Unsolved social problems: 24.4 %*
> *Unclear national relations: 17.5 %*
> *Crime: 10.6 %*
> *Implemented Russian foreign policy: 8.8 %*
> *Uncontrolled spread of weapons: 5.5 %*
> *People unloyal to Latvia: 1.8 %*
> *Presence of Russian troops: 1.4 %*

(Jundzis 1995: 243)

The latest sociological survey investigating threat perception in Latvia was done in the end of 1995 by the Latvian Shipping Company. The results obviously demonstrate changes in public opinion with respect to possible sources of threats in comparison with the data collected in 1994. The most important shift takes place in the assessment of internal and external dangers. Russia as a potential jeopardy to Latvian security has been put in fifth place (29.8 per cent citizens and 1.7 per cent non-citizens).

The most significant source of threats in Latvia from the point of view of respondents were: *Crime and drug smuggling:* 53.4 % citizens, 18.4 % non-citizens; *corruption:* 44.9 % citizens, 16.3 % non-citizens; *pollution:* 40.9 % citizens, 14.6 per cent non-citizens; *terrorism:* 38.7 % citizens, 12.8 % non-citizens; *loss of ethnic identity:* 18.6 % of citizens, 4.2 % non-citizens; *refugees and immigrants:* 10 % citizens, 1.5 % non-citizens; *ethnic minorities:* 3.8 % citizens, 0.4 % non-citizens (Rodin & Strupiss 1995: 2-5). The above mentioned cleavages in Latvia's political and security thinking on the level of the public and political elite reveal the existence of serious concerns regarding the creation of a stable state and civic society more than the potential danger eminating from Russia.

The current state of Latvian-Russian relations could be characterised as duel ones. In developing their state identification process, they both have come to the conclusion that it is in their mutual best interests to have good economic contacts. The statement that "Latvian-Russian relations have never been better than they are now" would not be an exaggeration in so far as economics are concerned. For instance, Latvia imports 93 per cent of its heating resources, 90 per cent of its non-ferrous metals and 50 per cent of its electricity from Russia (*Diena* 3 January 1996). In 1995, foodexport to Russia increased five-fold in comparison with 1994. Already these facts are a good affirmation that unipolar dependence is moving slowly to interdependence. Hence, all demagogical statements regarding the use of economic sanctions in the case of Latvia (in July 1996, September 1996 and December 1996) would not hold true itself. Correspondingly, Russia's standards have never been implemented because it would have feedback on Russia's own economy. Even when the Russian Ministry of Transportation in August 1996 decided to cancel tariff discounts on rail freight travelling through Latvian and Estonian ports, the increase in transportation costs was 30 per cent. The initiator in this case was the Russian Ministry of Foreign Affairs' explanation that it as a way to facilitate increased freight transportation through the Russian port at Kaliningrad. The practical implementation of the decision led to losses for both sides, but Russia was a bigger loser than Latvia (Stranga 1997: 208-209).

But with respect to political relations, the situation is more problematic. Until Russian troops were withdrawn in 1994, the establishment of normal political relations was hindered by the permanent threat of Russia's use of military force or provocation in order to destabilise the vulnerable process of state building in Latvia. The shadow of Russian troops, along with the unsuccessful negotiation process, left an impact on Latvia's security policy when all efforts were pooled into European security structures. When the EU and NATO enlargement processes became more or less clear, and one of the pre-requisites for admittance was good neighbourly relations with Russia. Subsequently, dialogue between Latvia and Russia started from a new stage. But several topics are left for dispute.

1) Border agreements have not been reached yet between Latvia and Russia (this topic has been discussed accurately in chapter 2). The reason could be Latvia's full devotion to the issue of Russian troops withdrawal in

that it had no timeframe or wider vision of when troops would be out of the country. It should be taken into account that there is no consensus within Latvian society on the Abrenes district (which at the moment is Russia's territory). Among politicians there is an unwritten agreement that it was in the interest of Latvia's foreign and security policy that Abrene be out of debates with Russia, in order to settle more important issues and avoid making obstacles for integration into European institutions–which is much more significant than the restoration of historical justice. But while Latvian society has not defined its position on Abrene, for politicians it is almost impossible to come to a final decision that would not provoke controversies threatening the vulnerable and fragile political stability in the country. But without any doubts, a border agreement with Russia is one of the first rank priorities and, at the same time, a pre-requisite for admittance to the EU and NATO.

2) "Russian speakers" in Latvia are one of the central dilemmas in Latvian-Russian relations. It is not so much a matter of social guarantees and preservation of national identity as it is a political issue and means for implementing Russian foreign policy goals in Latvia. Ethnic composition in Latvia, in comparison with Estonia and Lithuania, is the most peculiar one. In 1996 there were 55.1 per cent Latvians, 32.6 Russians, 4.0 per cent Belorussians, 2.9 per cent Ukrainians, 2.2 per cent Poles and 1.3 per cent Lithuanians (*Latvia* 1996: 16). In the year 1997 we can conclude that the Law on Citizenship (adopted in 1994), along with the naturalisation process and several other programmes provided a necessary background for overcoming possible sources of contradictions within the society and helped to integrate rather diverse ethnic groups in Latvian society. But one aspect is the status and level of integration of ethnic groups in Latvia, while quite another is Russia's devotion to exploiting minority issues in the pursuit of its interests in neighbouring countries.

One such approach is their declaration of the necessity to defend the rights of ethnic Russians in the CIS and Baltic countries. A part of this statement is to support Russian culture, language, education. However, so far the Russian Embassy in Latvia has not demonstrated very active participation in such kinds of activities. Russia's financial assistance of less than two million dollars for supporting Russian communities outside Russia is not nearly sufficient enough. Perhaps the preservation of national culture is too limited in comparison with their real devotion: political interests.

It should be noted that there have been several periods in Russia's official policy with respect to minorities problems in Latvia and the Baltic states. Usually they bring it to the surface when it is necessary to gain benefit from big political bargainings. When the EU and NATO enlargement issues were activated in the second half of 1996, in June Boris Yeltsin approved a new national policy conception for Russia. A substantial part of the concept was devoted to support for "ethnic Russian-landers in the Baltic states." Some months later, in September, a newly established Foreign Policy Operations Council, in defining its goals, mentioned the possibility of using the "severest sanctions" if need be (see Stranga 1997: 203).

It is rather evident that Russia, in real terms, does not care about Russian speakers in Latvia or their rights. Rather, they are using them as a stick in their foreign policy strategy, especially when it comes to NATO enlargement.

Therefore, in order to overcome these stacked issues and move a frozen relations with Russia forward, it is necessary to get the dialogue with Russia on track. But it requires both sides, otherwise it will become a monologue. We can fully agree with the Latvian Minister of Foreign Affairs Valdis Birkavs, a man very concerned about increasing dynamics between both countries, when he says:

> Latvia's and Russia's dialogue will successfully progress only if, and when, both sides will leave behind historical experiences, and their consequent baggage, and go on to build their relationships like two equal subjects of international law. This means that Latvian security questions, and the solving of them, cannot be rearranged due to special relationships that would form between Russia and the Euroatlantic structures. I think that Latvia has a right to desire that its opinion be taken into account in the forming of these relationships (Birkavs 1997: 11).

*Estonia* is Latvia's northern neighbouring country and has the same historical heritage. Correspondingly, it is on its way to achieving a democratic society as are the rest of the Baltic nations. The common history and common current problems put Latvia and Estonia on the same path to Western structures. Estonia, on the one hand, has always been a good partner sharing similar values with Latvia. But, on the other hand, being alike the other Baltic nations, it was rather active in competing for better and faster reforms with Latvia. We can fully agree that at the very beginning of independence, Estonia had an advantage because of close links with Finland during the Soviet occupation, and because psychologically, it was more open to Western ways of thinking. To illustrate, Estonia was the first Baltic country to start the economic reforms under Gorbachev's years of rule, creating grounds for economic independence in the process. Feeling their Finnish links, Estonia from time to time started to play up the fact that it had left Latvia behind. For instance, the statement by the Estonian Association Agreement that the EU does not include a transitional period is nothing more than political bluffing. The reason is that these texts are identical with Latvian ones–except that Latvia uses the term "transitional period" *ending in 1999*, while the Estonian agreement uses *only* the year 1999. A Latvian–Estonian sea border dispute in 1995, which sometimes took rather sharp turns in using armed forces to board and chase Latvian fishing boats away from Estonian waters, was solved successfully in 1996. In economic terms, Estonia is not a very active partner with Latvia–which is understandable because of their very similar economic structures. For instance, in January-August 1995, only 2.8 per cent of Latvia's export went to Estonia, while imports from Estonia made up only a slightly higher 4.9 per cent. In political terms, Estonia is a reliable partner because of identical foreign and security policy goals.

*Lithuania* is very much like Estonia from the point of view of history and future desires. But Lithuania always has been a very peculiar neighbour, not so much from an economic perspective–the scale of mutual trade stands in January-August 1995 at a relatively low level: Latvia's export to Lithuania was 5.2 per cent and its import was 5.9 per cent (*Monthly Bulletin* 1995: 123) – but mostly for political reasons. What is the substance of the political reasons? From time to time Russia is using Lithuania in order to split the Baltic region and, in one way or another, it is succeeding. For instance, in different international forums Lithuania has: been portrayed as the good guy while Estonians and Latvians are seen as the violators of the rights of minorities; been mentioned as a country without any territorial claims; and one cannot forget that Russian troops were withdrawn from Lithuania one year earlier. This does not imply that there are such radical differences in policies of Lithuania and Latvia that Russia's treatment of the ex-Soviet republics should be so different. In comparison with Estonia, Latvia has not solved its oil dispute. Taking into account that oil is a more important commodity than fish, it will definitely take a longer time to resolve. Since Lithuania has recently improved its relations with Poland, it appears that Lithuania is slowly moving away from Latvia. If Lithuania favoured Baltic unity as the prerequisite for joining the

EU and NATO a year ago, now the Polish link has been chosen as the more credible and reliable way, especially after signals that Poland will be the first country accepted into NATO. From Latvia's perspective, this is a period where Lithuania's search for security options in looking for the best ways to realise its national interests should not be regarded as an abandonment or splitting action but merely an ordinary political step. However, the geographical and political logic dictates that no country can escape its place in the international system and, therefore, the structure will bring Lithuania to the Baltic track.

PHASES IN LATVIAN SECURITY POLICY

*The first phase* of Latvian security policy covers the period from 1988 to the end of 1990. During this period, security issues did not command any significant position in Latvian political thinking and activity, because all possible processes were aimed at recovering state independence. At the same time the first considerations with respect to Latvian security were put forward. The dominating factor influencing security matters was the necessity to predict possible reactions from the Soviet political and military elite. The first expressions were made in 1988 and 1989 when Latvian politicians and its public advocated the idea of the necessity to serve in the armed forces of Latvian Socialist Republic. On the 18 December 1988, the Latvian Popular Front (LPF) issued an official document "Attitudes to the Armed Forces of the USSR" (Latvijas Tautas Fronte 1989: 246), which generalised public discussion on this topic. Although it was almost impossible to establish national armed forces at that time, the idea was already there. One year later, during the Second Congress of the LPF, many important issues concerning security were put forward which had a unanimous impact on the future of Latvia. At the Congress, the programme was adopted and an entire chapter titled, "On Demilitarisation" (Latvijas Tautas Fronte 1990: 19) was fully devoted to security. Despite the fact that Latvia was still far from political independence, it was clear that an independent state and its security are indivisible matters. In this programme we can find the continuity of ideas concerning territorial armed forces.

A very popular proposal in the Scandinavian countries regarding the nuclear free zone in the Baltic Sea was welcomed, and demilitarisation of Latvia was discussed as part of deténte. The LPF congress discussed many other topics which helped prepare the political elite and society in general for real political dialogue with the USSR. Among them were: to establish a commission in order to control the armed forces and their relation to Latvian laws; to stop flows of retired Soviet officers to Latvia; to stop the creation of new military bases in Latvia; to take control over territories belonging to the Soviet army which had not been used for military purposes; the defence ministry of the USSR should pay rent for used Latvian soil; to work out principles for alternative service; to stop military training at schools and universities; and to remove military educational establishments from Latvia (Latvijas Tautas Fronte 1990: 19). After initial considerations, the unrealistic demands of the LPF later became a background for negotiations between Latvia and Russia regarding the withdrawal of Russian troops.

After the election of a new Supreme Council in 1990, a second *transitional period* of independence was declared; it subsequently ended in August 1991. In this regard, Latvia took a different route than Lithuania, which had already declared itself to be a sovereign object of international policy. The stated goal of the nation therefore determined the chief political priorities. Foremost among these was a gradual reduction of the state's dependence on the Soviet Union. The political and tactical resources used to achieve this end touched largely on the economic sphere. But this was a period when the Soviet Union's reaction towards the independence was not predictable and therefore different security options were on the agenda. One of the most popular was the idea of neutrality and demilitarisation. To some extent, it corresponded to systematic changes within the international environment, accepting the dissolution of bipolarity and the belief in launching a new world order, as well as means to restrain the Soviet Union from possible provocation.

The level of attention paid to security issues increased after the events of January 1991, when the first defence structures began to form in a fairly haphazard way in opposition to the aggressive Soviet policies in the Baltics. At that time, Russia's military threats to Latvian independence became not only a future fantasy, but a reality. Latvian security and defence problems were associated with direct signs from the Soviet Union that Moscow did not wish to let go of the three occupied Baltic republics. Subsequently, the country's security debate was given a strict and limited context: Latvian security meant the ability to defend the state against possible threats, provoked conflicts, or direct armed actions by the Soviet Union.

*The third phase* of Latvian security policy encompasses the time between August 1991 and the end of 1994. After the Moscow coup, Latvia enjoyed an unwanted "parade of international recognition" (or, to paraphrase Mikhail Gorbachev's term, "parade of sovereignty"). Thus, Russia was the first country to recognise the independence of Estonia, Latvia and Lithuania. At that time, changes in public opinion with respect to potential threats were rather evident. The accent shifted from direct military intervention to the internal situation, mostly in the context of possible conflicts provoked by the communists in order to destabilise the security situation in the Baltic countries. But the most important issue in the public debates around possible threats was, of course, the presence of the Russian troops in the three states, heightened by Russian diplomats who were hindering the process by different means.

The first attempts of threat analysis proved that the main concern for Latvian security was Russia and the issues related with its transitional difficulties. In 1991 a conception of the "Self-defence of the Republic of Latvia" was worked out. In the document, we can find the list of possible threats to Latvian security (further developed with unimportant changes in 1994). The following dominating threats in Latvia were mentioned: the presence of occupational armed forces; the presence and unhampered activity of foreign espionage and counter-espionage units; the presence and extremist activities of various communist, imperialist, or otherwise anti-state groupings; the tense crime situation, including the presence of armed, international and organised criminal groups; economic instability and the state's dependence on foreign energy resources providers; and the demographic situation, which could be manipulated by either anti-state elements or their own purposes (Latvian Ministry of Defence 1994).

The existing threat perception at that time determined the chosen foreign and security options. This process of actively searching for the most efficient means for preserving Latvia's independence and survival was overshadowed by a lack of experience, resources and a difficult geopolitical situation. Almost all problems–especially security in nature–were closely related with the presence of Russian troops. It was nearly impossible to predict the content, pace and results of the negotiation process between Latvia and Russia. Vagueness in the Latvian position, to a large extent, was dependent on political processes in Russia and systemic changes in the international environment. Many western countries internationally recognised Latvian independence but hesitated to express their support by practical economic and political activities. Therefore, Latvian politicians, after evaluating internal resources and external support, started the security building process with its nearest neighbours, Estonia and Lithuania, establishing the Baltic Parliamentary Assembly and the Baltic Council.

Once again, the crucial integrating factor was the presence of Russian troops in the Baltic States. In view of the fact that this was an important–if not most important–national security issue for these states, the concentration of political efforts on this issue strengthened co-operation between Estonia, Latvia and Lithuania. In October 1991 in Vilnius, all three states released a number of important statements concerning the withdrawal of Russian troops. The nature of the national security issue made certain that the Baltic states co-ordinated the raising of this issue to an international level. Unfortunately, an exaggerated concentration on the most pressing aspects of national survival overshadowed other important areas of co-operation.

The crucial security option for Latvia in this period was the active involvement in international and European structures. Immediately upon recognition from the Soviet Union, such international organisations as CSCE and the UN welcomed the three newly established countries to join the international community. From a Latvian security perspective, it was a significant step towards the West and one which could open opportunities for the internationalisation of complex national security problems; particularly the presence of Russian troops on the Latvian territory. In addition, paths to Western security organisations counter-balancing Russia's influence in the Baltics could be available. At the end of 1993 and the beginning of 1994, it was clear that neither the UN nor CSCE would be the organisations providing security guarantees for Latvia and the Baltic states.

The processes in Latvia and the international environment proved two basic preconditions for strengthening Latvian security. The first was linked to the possibility of military threat. In such a case, the state would be able with its internal resources to only detain wide range military actions for short period of time. The conclusion followed that a full membership in an alliance with hard security guarantees could help to deter military operations; Thus, NATO became a goal of Latvian security policy. The second offered rather clear acceptance of the fact that Latvian security was directly dependent on its internal situation: The successful implementation of the transitional period from totalitarianism to democracy i.e., the management of possible transitional contradictions was a basic guarantee for stability and security. But a realisation of this process can hardly be imagined by a portfolio of limited domestic resources and a peculiar geopolitical location. Full involvement into the EU was chosen as a necessary foreign policy goal. In the process of moving closer to the EU, Latvia would be able to simultaneously cope with two tasks: overcome the legacies left after the dissolution of the Soviet regime by civilised means; and integrate into Europe to become an integral part of European economic and security community.

The withdrawal of Russian troops from Latvia in August 1994 put an end to the third period of Latvian security policy. *From August 1994* the state was able to define its foreign and security policy directions within new circumstances. The main concern of Latvian security–Russia's presence on its territory–disappeared. The official position claiming Latvia's movement towards the EU and NATO was already stated in 1993/1994, but only in 1995 did it turn into a formulated and approved policy.

The result of political discussions held on 7 April 1995 was that Parliament accepted a foreign policy conception for Latvia. Later, on 12 June 1995, the Cabinet of Ministers accepted a national security conception. Both documents contain definitions of Latvia's national interests, among them the desire for full integration into the European Union and NATO (*Diena,* 8 March 1995). Latvia's security concept clearly defines its aim, which is basically made up of national independence, territorial integrity, the preservation and development of language, national identity and a parliamentary democracy regulated by the Constitution, and the guaranteed protection of its inhabitants and society as a whole. In creating its security, Latvia does not threaten any other country or national minority within its own territory (*Latvijas Vestnesis* 20 July 1995). In comparison with previous security documents of national significance, this is a remarkable step forward in Latvia's political thinking and perception of security, since a shift is taking place from narrow questions of state defence to an accent on aspects of societal security. In this sense Latvia's interpretation of security does not differ from that of other Western countries. Unfortunately, it must be noted that the Latvian document does not link national security to international security. The weakness of this official document is that national security issues are not discussed within a wider regional and international context, especially in view of the fact that Latvia, isolated from the general international environment, as well as in modes and forms of implementation of international relations and trends in global development, cannot guarantee its survival as a small state on its own (this is noted in the Concept). One may justifiably ask why Latvia wishes to integrate into European structures if it only wants to resolve national security issues by internally available means. On the other hand, however, Latvia's national security concept demonstrates a commitment to more actively resolving those internal factors that are slowing down integration into European and trans-Atlantic structures. This entails: stabilising the domestic, economic and social situation; guaranteeing stable social security; developing a state system and structure based on the rule of law; developing small but effective military structures; and respecting international and human rights norms. The ability of the state to resolve its internal problems and prevent instability from spreading to the international system and its neighbouring states can be viewed as a positive achievement in the state-building process.

The essence of the national security conception accepted by the Cabinet of Ministers in June 1995 is a statement of the main threats which face Latvia and the mechanisms which could be used to avert such threats. In Latvia's view, the most likely threat is not military action, but rather efforts by other countries to destabilise Latvia's domestic situation. For this reason, Latvia does not clearly separate internal threats from external threats. This means that resources to avert threats must also be sought both inside the country, and in co-operation with other countries and international organisations. The list of major threats (economic, political, military) includes a range of issues which are of interest not only to Latvia, but also to the international community–and particularly Latvia's neighbouring states. One issue to which considerable attention has been devoted is crime in all of its manifestations: organised crime, corruption, economic crime, narcotics trafficking, illegal migration, etc. Latvia has become more active in battling these problems, especially during the last year, but many initiatives have remained unfulfilled because of unsettled relations with neighbouring countries. The major route for illegal migrants, for example, passes through Russia, but Russia has no interest to sign any intergovernmental agreements in this area. Ecological threats are also a matter of common interest.

Naturally, the foreign policy and security conceptions play a significant role in establishing the country's security system, as well as in facilitating the country's self-identification process and in helping to prioritise international activities. The adoption of the two documents, however, does not in and of itself guarantee successful policies and rapid results. This is particularly clear with respect to the national security conception.

This initiative, which was very promising at its start, has not been brought to a successful end largely because of institutional disorder. While the document is theoretically well-written and practical in nature, it has for several reasons, become virtually irrelevant. First of all, the document was prepared without the input of broad swathes of the political elite. Second, there was virtually no public discussion of the document after its preparation. Third, the very process by which the conception was adopted was illustrative of the fact that Latvia still has not developed adequate systems for taking major decisions.

On 29 June 1995, Prime Minister Maris Gailis ordered all ministries, the Bank of Latvia and the national prosecutor's office to develop security plans for their respective sectors on the basis that a national security plan could be established. Although the work was supposed to be done by 28 July, at year's end only a few ministries had complied. To this very day there is no national security plan in Latvia, and the entire process has been subjected to the consequences of Latvia's change in government.

The valuable part of the Latvian foreign and security concepts is correspondence to national interests. The analysis of international processes and internal situation proves that a new stage in security policy is on its way.

The development processes of Latvian foreign and security policy are oriented towards Europe and its basic components–EU and NATO. The changes in these institutions stated clearly that it is almost impossible to join NATO security structures in the near future but there have been several invitations to search for other security arrangements corresponding to national, regional and international interests. But the question remains open as to whether Latvia's quest for EU and NATO has a deeper motivation, or whether it is only a political statement corresponding to wishes of some political forces.

NATO STRIVINGS

NATO as an important instrument of Latvian security was chosen because of several objective reasons. First of all, historical experience of the country and the contemporary interdependent international environment taught the political elite and public of Latvia that for a small country with a peculiar geopolitical location and limited resources, there were not many security options left. One thing is clear: that a self-help policy can help for a short period of time but could not protect a country in the case of real military danger. A policy of alignment would be most appropriate in corresponding to the state's national security interests. Therefore, in building up its security policy, Latvia was looking for several solutions–especially taking into account that the NATO option was not available until 1993. The concepts of "small entente" (three Baltic states) and "large entente" (three Baltic nations plus Northern and Eastern partners) were reconsidered but not accepted as sufficient or corresponding to the post-Cold War era. Secondly, NATO began to adopt to challenges provoked by the dismantling of the bipolar division of international structures. One of the proposed alliance strategies initiated by the American side in order to cope with transforming European security architecture was the idea of enlargement.

From the very beginning Latvia was very much in favour of NATO, supporting all initiatives proposed by the alliance. Latvia joined the NACC in December 1991, the Partnership for Peace in January 1994, signed an individual co-operation programme with NATO in February 1995 and most recently, participated in IFOR activities in Bosnia.

But the proposed enlargement strategy was met by objections–even the threat of military action from the Russian side in the case if NATO is going eastwards. Certain cautiousness was also expressed by the Western partners because of a lack of awareness that enlargement would bring stability and peace to the most vulnerable regions of Europe–Central and Eastern Europe including Latvia. The growth of pessimistic feelings (or perhaps realistic ones) was rather obvious after US Secretary of Defence William Perry's famous statement in September 1996 that the Baltic states were not ready for NATO membership. Reasonable fare to be left outside the future security arrangements in Europe motivated Latvian security and foreign policy makers to look for arguments why the NATO enlargement should expand to Latvia too.

Generalising the main arguments drawn from the current debates we can conclude that it is almost impossible to calculate the consequences of a NATO enlargement ignoring Latvia and the other Baltic states. Those countries weakest and most exposed to salient environments desire NATO membership most of all. But as it was stated at the end of 1996, those countries enjoying more or less secure international environments will be included in the first tranche, namely: Poland, Hungary and the Czech Republic. Leaving Latvia outside or, simultaneously, not offering it some kind of security arrangements will not be a solution for a stable and secure Western Europe. Rather, it will create new problems for Europe, European-Russian relations, and European-American-Russian relations. It would mean that Latvia will become more exposed to potential threats and dangers of counter-reactions from Moscow coming in the form of steps to halt further expansion, restore its sphere of influence by filling the created security vacuum in Latvia; and even provoke instability in the region with the purpose of stopping the further process of enlargement. Latvia is extremely vulnerable and unprotected against different kinds of Russian activities. Russia can use economic means, exploit the resident ethnic Russian population, threaten use of military force to protect Russian "interests," use weak points in economic and political developments to increase tensions and radicalise political views on both sides. All could have the effect of increasing the possibility of confrontation. If Latvia were left outside the Trans-Atlantic security arrangements, it would affect stability in Europe as well. For instance, Latvia is increasingly integrated economically and politically in Western structures. A conflict situation between Latvia and Russia could produce refugee flights into neighbouring countries and create tensions. At the same time, international organisations where Latvia is a full member e.g., OCSE, Council of Europe, UN, NACC, CBSS could be drawn into the conflict area. Therefore, the rationale for NATO enlargement is to include Latvia in the first wave. However, in Madrid NATO countries decided to postpone a decision on Latvia. It was extremely important from a Latvian perspective to keep the enlargement process open and on-going. This would give time for Latvia and the Balts to prepare themselves for participation in future European security arrangements, intensify bilateral and multilateral relations, and most importantly avoid new dividing lines in Europe.

In terms of calculating the best policy means for approaching NATO, the years 1996 and 1997 were instructive for Latvia. It does not mean, however, that they have always been successful and achieved expected results. Nevertheless, they were rather fruitful in making forecasts for the next decade. The first lesson–more or less an achieved agreement among political elite–was that only an alliance can help to improve the security situation in Latvia and guarantee the stability of utmost importance for a country building a democratic society. As an OMRI survey displays, 26 per cent of political elite think that Latvia should become a member of NATO now, 32 per cent in 5 years and 8 per cent in 10 years (*Transition* 1995: 43.). The question asked by Eurobarometer regarding a referendum on NATO membership ("if it took place tomorrow"), 31 per cent with the right to vote would say "yes" (*European Dialogue* (3) 1997). But the calculations on Latvia's future in the context of ongoing debates over

NATO enlargement led to the second lesson: that much should be done in shaping public opinion on NATO and its principles. For instance, an investigation conducted by the Latvian researchers showed that there is less understanding of what NATO is about in Latvian society; only 5.3 per cent of respondents affiliated themselves with NATO, while only 27.5 per cent were even interested in NATO affairs (Rodin & Strupiss 1995: 2-5). The unsatisfactory situation concerning the publicity of NATO issues was partly associated with the security policy-making process. Because of a lack of experience, it was held in a very closed environment without any wider public debates (the situation changed in 1996 when the mass media was overflowing with articles on the issue). Partly at the very beginning (1991–1994), NATO affairs were mostly elaborated at the Ministry of Defence level, which is not very active in public debates. Subsequently, NATO as an organisation dealt with military issues only. During the past, however, two years there have been significant cleavages accepting that NATO is not only a military alliance, but an instrument securing democracy and monitoring peaceful developments in the Trans-Atlantic area. A positive result has been the growth of NGO's in informing society on NATO matters by informative publications on the alliance and its prospects. The third lesson has been educative for foreign and security policy makers. The official announcement that NATO is not going to accept Latvia in the first tranche was perceived as a failure by Latvian diplomatic circles. Suddenly, it has become a rather different task to explain a failure which, in many aspects, was a success. As a consequence, Minister of Foreign Affairs Valdis Birkavs was blamed not only because of NATO non-expansion, but for pursuing unwise and unrealistic Latvian foreign and security policy. The fourth lesson has been not to rely only on the best option. Without a doubt, NATO is the best security policy choice for Latvia. However, it must calculate some other additional and supplementary security alternatives as well. It is worth mentioning such channels as the intensified dialogue with NATO countries having special interest in the region. Two good examples are Denmark and the United States, through bilateral co-operation and participation in the Partnership for Peace programme.

## EU STRIVINGS

The EU is an essential component of Latvian foreign and security policies.

Since the Madrid summit it is clear that Latvia will not be able to enjoy full NATO membership in the next decade, so the EU has become more important than ever. From the very early stages of Latvian independence, Western Europe and integration into its structures was an ultimate goal of Latvian international activities. The EU represented an organisation of broad scope and democracy, to which Latvia wanted to belong not only for geographical reasons, but for political and economic reasons as well.

With the European Community's recognition of Latvian independence on 27 August 1991, the first channels of mutual interaction were open. As an outcome of growing co-operation, the Free Trade Agreement with the EU was signed on 12 May 1992 and took effect in January 1995.

The growing interest in EU affairs became official in April 1995 when the Saeima (parliament)–by an overwhelming vote (with only few against and several abstentions)–adopted the foreign policy concept of Latvia: "The Fundamental Goals of Latvia's Foreign Policy" and "The Basic Directions of Latvia's Foreign Affairs." In its introduction, the role of the EU was clearly defined. It stated that "the EU is essential to the likelihood of the survival of the Latvian people and the preservation of the Latvian state" (*Diena,* 8 March 1995). "The final strategic goal of the Republic of Latvia is joining the EU" (ibid.). On the basis of this official document, the process of accession became more active: the already established European Integration Bureau was forced to change its profile from informative to more practical programmes harmonising EU laws with those of Latvia, and co-ordinating and developing new structural policies. It observes the activities of 23 EU working groups acting in the field of the harmonisation process with the EU. A *Latvia and European Union* quarterly journal was established. Latvia, as all Baltic states, signed the Association agreement on 12 June 1995.

The increasing movement towards the EU was overshadowed by unexpected results of the parliamentary elections in Autumn 1995. The pre-election campaign demonstrated that almost all parties had identical foreign and security policy orientations. They stated that the EU and NATO were the priorities, except in the non-influential, pro-Communist Socialist Party and the Party of Unity, which consisted of ex-directors of the Soviet times collective farms who proposed the already abandoned concept of neutrality (based on traditional reluctance to EU agricultural policy, it got farmers votes by promising them protection from rude EU regulations). But the results of the elections shook politicians and the public alike. The third place went to the populist party, The Movement for Latvia, lead by right-wing German businessman Joachim Zigerist. Meanwhile, the Party of Unity got 8 seats, bringing their combined total to 24 out of 100 seats in parliament. The participation of both political parties in the government coalition would undermine Latvia's pro-European policy. As a reaction to the brief political confusion, on October 13 1995, President of Latvia Mr. Guntis Ulmanis used his power to call for an extraordinary meeting of the Cabinet of Ministers with only one point on the agenda–the formal application to join the EU. The ministers unanimously supported the application and on October 27 a letter of application was submitted to the government of Spain, at that time becoming the first Baltic country applying for full membership in the EU (on February 1996, Latvia's application had been ratified by the European parliament as well as by the Danish, Swedish, Spanish and Italian parliaments).

In order to support the President's initiative and demonstrate Latvia's continuity in its policy towards the EU, leaders of the 11 political parties represented in the new Saeima signed a declaration at the behest of the Latvian president expressing their positive attitude toward application for EU membership. Even the Socialist Party signed with the understanding that, when it comes to that point, there will be a national referendum on joining the EU. Some additional initiatives followed after the Saeima elections were over: a new Committee of European Affairs was established in the Saeima; and a new post of Minister of EU Affairs was created in order to mobilise national intellectual resources for preparing necessary accession procedures. The first test for the newly created structures was the preparation of 25 volumes of replies to the 2500 questions given by the European Commission with respect to Latvia's readiness to join the EU. The national programme of integration into the EU was worked out and approved by the government in 1996. As Latvian Minister of Foreign Affairs Mr. Valdis Birkavs stated clearly that the programme is "an important and carefully planned step in order to bring Latvia closer to the standards of Europe, but the political developments of the past few months motivate us to increase the speed of the integration process and simultaneously revise the completion terms of various specific assignments" (Birkavs 1997: 4).

There is no doubt that among political elite, the EU has been approved as a way not only to the irreversibility of Latvia's independence, but mostly as a guarantee for the state's economic development, political stability and ideological symbol showing that Latvia belongs to Europe. It can be verified by a series of national surveys conducted by OMRI's Audience and

Opinion Research office (AOR) in co-operation with regional research institutions regarding the general population (April 1995), and the elite (Autumn 1994). The survey's main goal was to examine the attitudes of political elite and the public to Western Europe, Russia and the United States. The results demonstrated the significant differences of opinion among the decision–makers and population in general. The political elite are more inclined towards Europe, the EU and NATO. Asked how often people think of themselves as Europeans in addition to their own national identification, 57 per cent of political elites and 32 per cent of the general public strongly agree, 27 per cent and 32 per cent agree somewhat respectively (*Transition* 1995: 43). A similar survey on the EU's image in applicant countries conducted by the *Central and Eastern Eurobarometer* (1996, Survey No. 6: 47) testified that the public's opinion in Latvia does not coincide with elite's. In a comparative perspective, the positive image of the EU has declined from 45 per cent in 1991 to 35 per cent in 1995 and to 26 per cent in 1996 (*European Dialogue* (3) 1997). It can partly be explained by the predominant security concerns in 1991 when the EU was mainly perceived as a "soft" security guarantee for Europe, and partly by the unipolar dependence on Russia, partly by limited knowledge about the EU. Consequently, the negative image of the EU increased from 1 per cent in 1991 to 11 per cent in 1995 (*Eurobarometer* 1996: 47). This drastic increase can be ascribed to being more informed about the positive and negative sides of the EU. However, it would be worth mentioning that it also shows cleavages within a Latvian society where different social groups began to reassess their future prospects in various fields of economics, social sphere and national self-identification. Responsibility for the future of the country is also an explanation for growing cautiousness. On the basis of this group having a negative image about the EU, the favourable background for euro-sceptics could be spread out. Although there is no such movement for the time being, there are some voices which argue that some years ago Latvia got rid of one union, and today it urges to join a new one which differs only in its ideological principles. Nevertheless, the Eurobarometer gives very optimistic forecasts in 1996 stating that 80 per cent of the population of Latvia will vote for the EU if the referendum would take place tomorrow (*Eurobarometer* 1996: 59). But one year later only 34 per cent of population will vote for the EU (*European Dialogue* (3) 1997). When it comes to certain decisions, however, the local situation is more complicated than either "yes" or "no." Some of the domestic sociological surveys displace different dates and conclusions. For instance, the investigation of Rodin & Strupiss (1995), along with the national identity in Latvia contracted by the Latvian Shipping Company and the Institute of Social and Economic Studies "Latvia" (held in August–December 1995) indicated that only 13.3 per cent of the population affiliated themselves with the European Union and only 28.5 per cent with Europe. One-third of respondents expect the EU to be a danger for national identification (Rodin & Strupiss 1995: 2-5).

In the context of Latvia's future in the coming decade, issues related to the EU and its enlargement could be looked upon from the following angle. First of all, for applicant countries it is very important to be familiar with the EU's institutional reforms and discussions around this topic. While consensus on EU reforms and their implementation has not been reached, the enlargement strategy is more or less a concept rather than a real political process. So far, the EU has not been able to provide the applicant countries of Central and Eastern Europe a clear perspective on membership. Despite the fact that the enlargement strategy was announced in 1993 in Copenhagen, there have been so many unclear statements and interpretations concerning the future of the EU made by EU officials after that. On the one hand, it has demonstrated a lack of agreement on enlargement strategy, while on the other hand, it has caused different kinds of political consequences in Latvia ranging from disappointment over not being invited for direct participation in the EU's Intergovernmental Conference, to the discord in Baltic unity stating that Estonia could be the first Baltic country accepted as a full EU member.

Secondly, the domestic debates on full EU membership status and ways leading to it must be considered. Latvia is only in the very beginning of the process of movement towards the EU. As it was mentioned before, since the signing of the Association Agreement, there are signs of a more realistic approach to what the EU is all about. The EU is still very much interpreted as a "soft" security component of a rather vulnerable security situation in Latvia, but it is based on an understanding that Latvia's security interests can not be covered by purely military means. The comprehensive international environment tends to search for comprehensive means. In Latvia's case, the EU is an instrument providing a full range of opportunities for compromising internal and external interests. Therefore, the state-building process which started in the early 1990s as a rather chaotic process, is now taking a more organised shape partly because of necessity to bring economic reforms, political institutions, social arrangements and legislation in accordance with EU standards and regulations. The introduction of EU standards into Latvian society is a significant shift closer to the company of Western democracies in which welfare is the necessary pre-requisite for internal stability. The real process of integration ensures Latvia's involvement into European affairs. The statistical date obviously displays that the country is making radical changes from East to West in its trade turnover: in the first five months of 1996, 48.7 per cent of goods were imported to Latvia from the EU countries and 25.8 per cent from the CIS countries. Latvia's exports to the EU in the same period were 41.9 per cent and exports to the CIS countries were 39.4 per cent. However, with 25.6 per cent of all Latvian exports, Russia remained the most significant trading partner. Meanwhile, 13.4 per cent of exports went to Germany, 10.5 per cent to Great Britain and 7.2 per cent to Lithuania. Latvia imported 20.2 per cent of total volume of imported goods from Russia, 13.7 per cent from Germany, 9.4 per cent from Finland, 8.2 per cent from Sweden and 6.2 per cent from Lithuania (*Current Latvia* (29) 1996).

Thirdly, taking into account that Russia is not simply a bordering country but a power very much influencing Latvia's future, it is important to note that there is no pressure from the political elite so strong against EU enlargement as with respect to its NATO future. Even more, there have been several statements made by politicians and experts close to Russia's foreign policy-makers that it is in Russia's interest to have a stable and economically-developed country next to its border providing new markets and trade opportunities. As a member of Russia's presidents Advisory Board on Foreign Affairs, Andrei Karaganov commented that prosperity on Russia's borders means prosperity for the country. Latvia would thus be a gateway to the EU for Russia, especially taking into account the highly developed transportation system in Latvia which is widely used by Russia for its transit to Europe (Karaganov 1996: 28-38). Russia could become an indirect factor in Latvia's successful integration into the EU and Latvia's prosperity. It is well known that the growth of GDP in 1996 is because of the expanding exploration of Latvia's transit facilities. When the Latvian president Mr. Guntis Ulmanis visited Germany and the EU summit in the end of 1995, he received a confirmation that the Western European nations would choose to form a "tenth multimodal transport corridor" through Latvia for the transport of goods from the West to the East and vice versa. It would mean that Latvia would be a quick transportation route to Russia for goods requiring simple documentation, simultaneously drawing in foreign investments; the one "but" is the necessity to acquire Russia's approval of the "corridor project."

It should be stressed that from Latvia's point of view, the EU is not the only solution for its security concerns. Rather, it goes hand in hand with NATO as two complimentary organisations providing favourable background and a means for democracy and its preservation.

REGIONAL SECURITY ARRANGEMENTS

Regional security arrangements have been adopted as a very important instrument for achieving the final goals of Latvian foreign and security policies, namely: integration into the EU and NATO.

Naturally, the first is connected with the already established co-operation framework among *the Baltic countries*. In 1995 the dual nature of Baltic co-operation was becoming increasingly apparent, with the realisation that co-operation was a precondition for the survival of the three Baltic States. However, at the same time separate efforts and independent tactics were developed for reaching the foreign policy goals of membership into the EU and NATO. Estonia decided to rely more on Finland's wide-ranging assistance and support, while Lithuania moved toward the CEFTA, and especially Poland. The question of where Latvia was going to find its bastion still remained. Being sandwiched between Estonia and Lithuania, Latvia does not have any other options to rely on. Therefore, the country began pursuing a policy of intensive co-operation within the Baltic region. The Baltic co-operation could be characterised as a permanent process of interaction of centrifugal and centripetal forces. From the logic of a states' national interests and the protection of its physical existence–especially in small countries–they are looking for more powerful partners (as it is in case of Estonia and Lithuania). But the political reality is that it is not a solution for all problems of their weakness. Therefore, after pressure from the outside/international environment which wishes to deal with organised and stable partners, there is tendency to co-operate with like partners and strengthen their welfare and political stability. Estonia's urge to be the first on line to the EU and NATO through public statements about a lack of a transition period to the EU and incredible achievements in reforming economic and societal structures, of course irritated its neighbours. However, after the realisation that advantages from Baltic co-operation could be obtained on the way to Europe, it started its way back to Latvia intensifying a wide range of activities. The visit of Estonian Minister of Foreign Affairs Ilves to Latvia in February 1997 came as a surprise after some years of exceptionalist policies, when he offered to establish an Estonian-Latvian common market as a first step towards a Baltic Customs Union.

Nevertheless, despite differences and even unsettled points of contention e.g., the Lithuanian-Latvian dispute over oil exploration in the Baltic Sea, the efforts of Baltic politicians to maintain Baltic co-operation deserves appreciation. On 7 February 1996 a meeting of the three Baltic foreign ministers took place in Vilnius. In contrast to previous occasions, this time issues of importance to the Baltic states and the international community were discussed. The resolutions were evidence by the three countries trying to integrate into European structures as equal partners, proving that Baltic co-operation, too, was moving forward. All three states again reaffirmed their unity on the road to the EU and NATO, discussing the possibility of establishing a common information infrastructure and transit procedure and relaxing the border regime between the Baltic States. The ministers deemed it necessary to start discussions on a crisis management concept for the Baltics. The establishing of a joint Estonian, Latvian and Lithuanian working group was proposed. This was the first attempt on a regional level to begin work on such a programme in the absence of relevant concepts and firm guidelines from the viewpoint of national interests. In one sense it could be a disturbing factor, but in another sense, in view of the similarities between the Baltic states in the areas of national, regional and international security, it could be more rational and help evade restricting national interests. Such an initiative would further Baltic co-operation and integration into European and global security structures as equal partners who speak the same "language" and share the same concerns.

The highest achievements have been reached in the field of military and security. In September 1993 the three ministers of defence signed a declaration on closer co-operation in the field of security and defence following recommendations by the UN Charter and Security Council. The declaration called for the creation of a joint defence system with swift exchange of information between states, joint manoeuvres and seminars on security issues, as well as training for possible inclusion in UN peace-keeping forces. On 28 April 1994 a working group was established in Copenhagen to help with the establishment of BaltBat. On 27 February 1995 the three Baltic ministers of defence signed an agreement on co-operation in the field of defence and military relations. In accordance with the new agreement, the signatories have agreed to exchange information, jointly recruit and train armed forces, create an air space control system, expand BaltBat and strengthen ties with the UN and NATO. This agreement can in no way be viewed as the basis of a military alliance.

The interaction between the Baltic States is solid evidence that the process of integration has begun and the first positive results have been achieved. However, at present it is difficult to predict its future development and principal contradictions. For now, it is clear that the Baltic States themselves are unsure of what type of regional framework would be optimal. Therefore, interpretations vary among unions, alliances, or Benelux or Nordic co-operation models to the view that mutual co-operation should not overtake the emphasis on moving towards the EU and NATO. It must be noted, though, that there is a dominant view–the recognition that common guarantees for security problems should be sought since there is a common potential source of threat. In the case of the Baltic States, the stimulus for security co-operation has not come from national political actors but from outside pressure: first as a reaction to Soviet ambitions for a renewed empire; and then international pressure to come forth as a united regional actor. Unfortunately, the process of internal, regional self-identification has dragged on. The most important aim of integration for the Baltic States is preservation of independence; mutual integration as a stimulus and precondition for integration into Europe has not been fully accepted equally in all countries. But Latvia is the most active force trying to develop co-operative policies in the region. Even the Movement for Baltic Unity was established in 1997.

*Latvian/Baltic-Nordic co-operation* has been treated as a very important catalyst for integration into the EU and NATO. Since 1990 the relationship among these countries has developed increasingly and led to the Latvian side taking the interaction of "5+3" as a promise for indirect security guarantees (see also Ozolina 1996). This issue became especially topical in 1996 when Sweden and Denmark initiated different forms of security co-operation. But when leading US politicians (including Bill Clinton) invited Sweden and Finland to take more responsibility over the Baltic's security in presumably establishing a new security community in the Baltic sea region, the Scandinavian partners turned hesitant (see: Ozolina 1997: 117-122). Despite the already existing wide range of interactions among northern and southern countries of the Baltic Sea, it is difficult to imagine that five countries will protect the Balts in the event of military action. Widened and deepened co-operation around the Baltic sea is extremely important from "soft" security perspective but will not be able to fulfil NATO's role. The euphoria that the northern partners would serve as security providers for Latvia disappeared. But some other aspects of the importance of this co-operation became rather important. First of all, since the Copenhagen Summit in 1993, Denmark–and later Sweden and Finland– became advocates for Latvia's admittance to the EU. Through the PHARE programme, there are several projects led by the Northern neighbours helping to harmonise the process of Latvia's integration into the EU. Secondly, the Scandinavian countries are not against Latvia's membership in NATO. Thirdly, taking into account that Latvia is not going to be a full member of NATO in the next decade, geographically Latvia, together with its northern partners, will be inevitably involved in security co-operation in order to preserve stability in the Baltic Sea region. Fourthly, there are well-functioning channels of co-operation already established and, thus, a fruitful base for "soft" security guarantees. Fifthly, there is an already established forum for fostering integrationist tendencies in the Baltic Sea region, namely: the Council of Baltic Sea States. "Soft" security issues make up a substantial part of the regional agenda.

HISTORICAL LESSONS FOR THE PRESENT?

There are several parallels between Latvia's situation in the inter-war period and the situation of the 1990s:

1) Latvia gained its independence as a consequence of big historical events–the end of the First World War and the dissolution of the Russian Empire. In 1991 the same story was repeated with the dissolution of the Soviet Union in what would be characterised to some extent as an event of similar importance for the international community. For the independent and internationally recognised country "the window of opportunities was opened" and Latvia took its chance.

2) We can draw a parallel in Latvia's present international status to that in the first half of 1920s. Latvia was recognised internationally and was looking to its place into the European political structure. Europe of the 1920s was pretty much busy with security arrangements representing the whole spectrum of options starting from neutrality to alliances and collective security model proposed by the League of Nations. The same

spectrum of security policy choices are on the menu of the current international system.

3) The main power dictating the rules of the security game at that time was Russia which, as the first to recognise Latvian independence, at very early stages also tended toward democratic reforms. However, in a very peculiar way it participated in the forming of Europe's security structures. The main difference was that in the first half of the century, Germany was the other power having equal impact on Latvia's security choices. Today the situation is pretty much the same. It is almost impossible to define Latvia's security policy goals and means ignoring Russia's attitude and reaction.

4) We could also draw parallels with the inter-war period when neutrality was a very topical issue. In January 1920, the conference which brought together countries neighbouring Russia discussed the idea of Baltic Sea neutrality. Different approaches were represented there: the Poles refused to accept neutrality; and the Swedish side could not come to a decision. Theoretically, the idea was both acceptable and not acceptable to the Swedes. The reason for hesitation was Russia's support for neutralisation of the Baltic Sea. If Britain and France would agree to that then Sweden would lose the protection from its western partners (Andersons 1982: 202-3). Domestic political debates about Latvian neutrality were alive during almost all the years of independence. In the early 1920s, different politicians represented divergent positions on neutrality. In a 1922 discussion regarding the budget of Latvia, Minister of Foreign Affairs, Feliks Cielens (the Latvian Social Democratic party) stated that Latvia had to persue a politically neutral foreign policy. His fellow parisan Fridrich Vesmanis backed the necessity to overcome Latvia's dependence on Russia. While social democrats tried to prove that if neutrality would not be accepted by the great powers, it would not protect the country in case of war. The Minister of Foreign Affairs at that time, Zigfrids Meierovics, had doubts about the sufficiency of neutrality from two perspectives: Latvia was already a member of the League of Nations which demonstrated its involvement in international affairs; and neutrality would work as a security enhancing factor only if it would be supplemented by guarantees from such countries as Russia or Germany (Andersons 1982: 32-3). Positive shift in favour of neutrality took place in September 1938 when the collective security idea of LN failed. On 13 December 1938 the Latvian government adopted the "Law on Neutrality" declaring that Latvia is accepting a policy of full neutrality emphasising that neutrality is the best

policy option for preserving states' independence in case of war. The publicly declared peaceful foreign policy orientation of Latvia neither helped nor worked in the end of the 1930s. Latvian neutrality was not respected by Germany or the USSR and did not prevent occupation. This historical experience was put on the discussion table in Latvia only during the first days of independence as one of many foreign and security policy options. The negative and dramatic outcome of Latvian neutrality in the inter-war period stroked it off from the tentative list of choices.

5) Within the political elite of all three states was used the argument that Baltic co-operation was impossible because it failed during 1920-1940. History teaches us rather sad stories of the Baltic's willingness to establish well-functioning Baltic Entente and failures of this initiative.

Within the inter-war period, there were three basic ideas that helped to find solutions to cope with security and defence matters. These proposals revealed the periods of development of Baltic co-operation at that time. The first idea which was put forward for consideration was that of the Entente Cordiale. In fact, it was nothing more than the launching of the so-called "cordon sanitaire" based on co-operation among the states geographically located between Germany and Russia. This idea was acceptable and politically suitable to the Western European and participating countries, but fully unacceptable to Russia. From Russia's perspective such an arrangement would hinder its expansionist interests. The Latvian diplomats were planning to involve in the implementation processes Finland, Estonia, Latvia, Lithuania, Poland, Ukraine and Belarus. The same idea was proposed in 1992-1993 in order to establish the Baltic-Black Sea region with the same participating countries except for Finland. But the failure of such activities in the past overshadowed political discussions and the initiative died in the early stages. History testifies that at that time, it was more of a theoretical construction in the minds of politicians. All the potential participants were too different politically and economically, with rather specific geopolitical location and meaning. The difference became increasingly visible and fundamental as it moved from the North to the South, which is also the case today. We could find many similar features between Finland and Estonia, but it would take much more effort to state like characteristics among, for instance, Finland, Ukraine and Belarus. An obstacle for security co-operation was the permanently growing misunderstandings over territorial disputes, especially between Lithuania and Poland with respect to Vilnius (which led to political confrontation, cf. chapter 7). Finland, acknowledging the heavy complex of contradictions, moved away from the idea of Entente Cordiale. Attempts of the states to establish a security region was overlapped by each state's national security concerns, despite the clear realisation that these concerns could not be solved individually. During the period of 1919-1926, political leaders of the seven mentioned countries met in ten conferences to try and come to an agreement, but the international processes buried the idea of the Entente Cordiale, however. Ukraine and Belarus joined the Soviet Union, and Poland went through political regime changes under Pilsudsky's leadership. The Baltic States were left alone in a position of new political exploration. It was rather evident that there was no interest from the Scandinavian countries in security co-operation at that time, or from other European states for that matter. Therefore, in the beginning of the 1920s, Estonia, Latvia and Lithuania started to elaborate on the establishment of the Baltic Union. Their starting point was a geopolitical location but, unfortunately, the national interests prevailed and the Baltic diplomats were not able to reach any agreements in this respect. After several years of searching for the best solutions, Estonia and Latvia signed an agreement on 1 November 1923 which laid the groundwork for further co-operation in politics and security. Lithuania also expressed its willingness to join the agreement but ongoing disputes with Poland made this process slow and later impossible. The relations between Latvia and Lithuania, and Estonia and Lithuania, started to worsen. Meanwhile, Lithuania withdrew itself from the Baltic Union's project. In the mid-20s, it became clear that the Baltic States were more competitors than partners. This conclusion would be tested in current political situations, too. But the history of Baltic security co-operation brings us back to the third parallel. When politicians of all three Baltic States took the first steps in the big political games, they had to face the unpleasant reality: they were small states with limited resources and limited means of political influence and, as such, they became objects of manipulation in the interests of bigger powers. The historical irony was that the political behaviour of big powers in Europe forced the Baltic States to set up an alliance. Germany was already on the way to a fascist regime, Poland moved closer to Germany, and the Soviet Union offered not any hopeful promises, but threats. Lithuanian diplomacy with respect to Poland collapsed, putting Lithuania in an isolationist position the only way out of which was to join the treaty signed by Estonia and Latvia in 1923. In May 1934, Lithuania officially stated this fact. On September 12, 1934 in Geneva, the agreement "On Understanding and Co-operation" was signed by all three Baltic countries. The establishment of the Baltic Entente should be assessed as a significant outcome of the early years of Baltic co-operation. At the same time, however, it should be mentioned that this political act was not only implemented too late, but the alliance was considered too small and weak and, thus, did not receive enough recognition from the general public and international community. But the basic point was that in terms of potential military threats, the Baltic Entente would not be able to avert military attack. The changes in political regimes in the Baltic countries toward authoritarianism nullified the achieved results of the Baltic co-operation. Consequently, the Baltic Entente was never tested. But the historical experience left from the inter-war period gives us good comparative material which is very useful in assessing the current processes of security co-operation among the Baltic States.

But the situation in Europe between the World Wars was rather different from the political atmosphere today. The direct extrapolation of historical lessons can falsify the solutions. Baltic co-operation at that time did not have enough background for mutual initiatives and activities. Latvian historians Inesis Feldmanis and Aivars Stranga are right when analysing the failure of the Baltic Entente; they explore pre-requisites of a strong and effective union among nations. The authors are using a concept that if nations feel threatened by a single entity, they work together (this is not the only reason). In the Baltic case, there was not a unified conception of threats and enemies (Feldmanis & Stranga 1994: 97). Latvia had an opinion that possible threats could come from two countries–Germany and the USSR. Estonia felt threatened only from one side–the USSR–and did not consider Germany a significant danger. Meanwhile, Lithuania took a different stand from Latvia and Estonia. From Lithuania's perspective the largest enemy was Poland and, to lesser extent, Germany (cf. fig. 7.1). The Soviet Union was a friend and ally. The idea of the BE was not developed among political elite and societies. All three countries did not accept unified actions and solutions for strengthening their national securities. Instead, they searched for security guarantees among big powers choosing bilateral solutions, though this unfortunately did not correspond to political realities. Among other hindering factors we could mention: undeveloped economic ties, the high level of mutual competition, and the lack of regional self-identification. The common historical identity developed only after 1940.

6) Actually, the Baltic States have faced similar political choices in the 1990s as they experienced in an inter-war period where they enjoyed the status of being independent states and acceptance by the international

community as political participants in world affairs. It should be mentioned that after the first successful results of the international recognition, Latvia and its neighbours were overwhelmed by "Wilsonian" images of the future prospects of the inter-state system in Europe. Latvia became a member of The League of Nations and was involved in the business of creating a system of common security, as well as making plans regarding common justice and a new world order free from wars and conflicts. Due to the slow pace of security developments in Europe, the three Baltic countries began to consider the most appropriate security arrangements for stability in the region and the counterbalance of growing German and Russian ambitions.

7) The idea of Baltic unity was a backbone of Latvian foreign policy before the Second World War. In the pre-war period, Latvia was an initiator of many political projects in trying to bring together the three Baltic nations. Perhaps it was provoked at that time by idealistic feelings and sentiments to give birth to the forgotten Hanseatic League. Today, the situation is pretty much the same when Latvia is taking responsibility for Baltic co-operation and pushing for co-ordination in all the most important activities like customs union, free economic zone, military co-operation and joint efforts on the path to the EU and NATO.

8) Latvia's recent and not so recent historical experience shows that since 1935, the Latvian society lived under authoritarian rule. There is no doubt that the authoritarian regime in the country in the late 1930s differs from the Soviet occupation rule. However, there are some ideological similarities having impact on the contemporary understanding of processes taking place in Europe. During both regimes the interpretation of Latvia's place in the world economy was rather similar. The economic independence from the external influence was greatly appreciated. Almost all changes and dynamics taking place outside the country were assessed as potential danger, especially if it had any impact on the national economy. Simultaneously, isolationism and the ability to rely on its own resources was also evaluated highly. Therefore, contemporary Latvian arguments against EU membership can find very fertile soil. The above mentioned stereotypes of conservatism came to the surface in debates over the regulations of selling landed property. Even in the Saeima, the historical heritage based on the slogan "we will not sell out an inch of Latvian land" was brought on the discussion table as the object of a long and controversial political fight concerning adoption of a law allowing non-citizens to buy land.

Reaching the conclusion of the paragraph, it would be worthwhile to remember that history never repeats itself in identical patterns. As Latvia's Minister of Foreign Affairs Mr. Birkavs reminds:

> ..it is good to remember that history has no identical situations–the Europe of today is unlike the Europe of the beginning of the 1920s. We have every reason to believe that the integration process will not be set back to form a new 'Versailles System' and generated instability. (Birkavs 1997: 30)

But history teaches us a logic of developments in the inter-state relations, especially in the context of geopolitics when small countries border big powers. Latvia twice experienced Soviet occupation, which excluded it from democratic developments taking place in Europe. Therefore, the Latvian state is looking for policy options leading away from unipolar dependence on Russia, toward integration into the current international system. Correspondingly, they are looking toward the dominating international institutions as providers of stability and welfare. This explains why Latvia is so in favour of being integrated into the EU and NATO. Once upon a time it was left on its own while the great powers shaped Europe corresponding to their political interests. Subsequently, such small nations as the Balts were left outside and ultimately became passive objects of the distribution of power. History is offering another opportunity for Europe to create a co-operative, inclusive security system. Organisations established in correspondence to Cold War structures–the EU and NATO are trying to cope with the new realities and attempting to correct the historical injustices by offering enlargement strategies.

The first steps in the independent definition of Latvia's security policy goals, and the means for implementation, are obviously displayed in Latvia's changed status from being a scared, nervous and irritated small state to a country planting future visions in deep acknowledgement of its history, and the contemporary environment of the international system. Latvian security concerns, initially relating mainly to Russia, have been transformed to a wider understanding: the stability of each country is conditioned by both external and internal factors. As a small country, Latvia cannot be absolutely free in choosing opportunities offered by the international system. But the country can create a democratic society with all the necessary attributes to make itself an interesting and favourable partner in interstate relations. The important lesson offered by history and post-Cold War cleavages is that a country cannot rely on only one policy option. Therefore, Latvia's security has been looked upon as a minimum three-fold process: the EU dimension; the NATO enlargement process; and regional co-operation. Latvia is fully devoted to all three directions. Unfortunately, it is not only in Latvia's power to implement all three policy options. To a large extent, Latvia's future will be dependent on developments in Russia and the implementation of the enlargement strategies offered by the EU and NATO. These possible scenarios will be elaborated in the final section of chapter 7. However, despite the fact that external factors of Latvia's future are stronger than internal ones, strategic perspectives by Mr. Birkavs illustrates the basic principles of the state's foreign and security policy:

> Latvia's future in a changing Europe is largely dependent on the international situation, and global level solutions, more so than on our desires or subjective activities. However, this does not mean that Latvian foreign policy should slip into a passive mode, rather, exactly the opposite is true–positive tendencies in world politics could materialise in a way acceptable to us only if we have an active foreign policy and if we are able to utilise every opportunity. (Birkavs 1997: 7)

# 7 Lithuania

GRAZINA MINIOTAITE

Lithuania's security situation and security policy are closely linked to the processes and challenges that have accompanied the emergence of the new European security environment. For the purposes of our analysis here, the "two worlds" view (Keohane and Nye 1977; Goldgeier and McFaul 1992) will be used to provide a context for understanding Lithuania's challenges.

Under this "two worlds view," the international system is considered to be made up of two different worlds, each with a different set of rules of the game: the first world, the "zone of peace," comprises the powerful and advanced industrial democracies; and the second, or "zone of conflict," includes the less developed countries on their different stages of transition towards democracy. The interaction between the two worlds consists of a continuous trade-off between the balance of power logic and the security community logic. This is a simplified view of the international system, to be sure, yet it is helpful at grasping some of the basic features of Lithuania's situation with respect to security. The specific plight of Lithuania's security is brought about by her being situated between the two worlds (the East and the West). According to some criteria, she belongs to the conflict zone ("an outpost of the East"), while according to other criteria, she is rather in the zone of peace ("a Western bridge builder eastwards"). This is why in her security policy and, particularly, in the rhetorics of security, an oscillation between the two kinds of logic can be easily discerned.

The present chapter does not aim at tackling the question of how the two zones can be expected to relate to each other. Its is a more modest one, namely to explore the peculiarities of the security situation and security policies of a country finding itself on the meeting ground of the two worlds. The analysis of recent Lithuanian security policy begins with March 11, 1990, when the Supreme Soviet of Lithuania[1] (with Lithuania still part of

---

1. In 1996 the newly elected Seimas of Lithuania retroactively renamed it as the Lithuanian Restoration Seimas, inciting a discussion on the limits to history's politicization.

the USSR) declared the restoration of the independent state of Lithuania. This was the day when a new actor of international relations was born, eager to obtain full membership in the international community. From those very first days, Lithuania faced the problems of the preservation and international recognition of her sovereignty. Accordingly, the main concerns of the chapter deal with the political and military aspects of the country's security. Of the various factors that may be considered relevant, we are mainly interested here in the geopolitical situation of Lithuania, the risks relating to this situation, the main trends in the development of security policy of the country and the historical continuity of security policies. Finally, six common Baltic scenarios will be delineated (with co-authors).

## LITHUANIA'S SECURITY ENVIRONMENT

In the 1990s Lithuania entered its new stage of state formation in a much better geopolitical situation than compared with 1918. By contrast with the inter-war period, the country both increased its territory and for the first time in the 20th century, brought both the Vilnius and Klaipeda regions under its sovereignty. Neither Lithuania nor its neighbours have any territorial claims on each other (at least on the official level). Bilateral agreements of co-operation have been signed with the neighbouring states: with Russia in 1991, with Poland in 1994, with Belarus in 1995. Because of a greater demographic homogeneity as compared with Estonia and Latvia (80% of the population are Lithuanians), the country has no internationally recognised problems with its national minorities.

The end of the Cold War seemed to promise that Lithuania's strategic position in the confrontation between East and West would no longer be of relevance. However, subsequent developments have shown that the optimism was somewhat premature. Lithuania is part of the emerging European security complex[2] and its security inevitably rests on the specific interdependencies within the system. With the European security system losing its bipolarity, the cultural watershed between East and West has nevertheless remained and still holds the potential of becoming transformed into a political and even military confrontation. As a small nation,

---

2. See Buzan 1991. On the application of the security complex theory to the Post-Cold war Europe see Buzan, Wæver & de Wilde 1997.

Lithuania does not exert a significant influence on the security dynamics in the region; yet because of its geopolitical situation,[3] she has the possibility of choosing either the Eastern or the Western alignment. It should be noticed that the concepts of East and West are highly value-laden: the West being associated with prosperity, security and democracy; and the East with poverty, totalitarianism and insecurity. From the point of view of Lithuania's national security, the West is not identified with any particular country but rather with their different alliances, in particular, with the EU and NATO being the most important ones. After regaining her independence, Lithuania became unwavering in its choice of integration with the West. The choice was even sanctioned by a constitutional amendment: "On the Non-Alignment of the Republic of Lithuania with Post-Soviet Eastern Alliances" (1992). As the first and present Minister for Foreign Affairs, Algirdas Saudargas observed: "The pro-Western choice is due to the lack of alternatives. By choosing non-alignment with the East, the only alternative to integration with the West would be total isolation" (*Atgimimas* 20 December 1995: 171).

Lithuania has no direct borders with any Western state. It has land borders with Russia, Belarus, Latvia and Poland, and a marine border with Russia and Latvia (cf. fig. 1.1). Like Lithuania, Latvia and Poland seek a wide-ranging integration with the West, while Russia and Belarus, politically the domain of the CIS, are embodiments of the East.

*Latvia.* Traditionally, Latvia has been a dependable neighbour of Lithuania. The two countries' present relations, impelled as they are by the common endeavour of integration with the West, can be described as close co-operation. This has found its expression in the free trade agreement signed and ratified in 1996 as well as in co-operation in international organizations and the military domain. Other common undertakings such as joint border controls, a unified customs system, a customs union and the harmonization of laws are also under way. However, there have also been "neighbourly" squabbles characteristic of relations between sovereign states with national interests sometimes overshadowing common goals. The typical case in this respect is the protracted dispute over the sea border delimitation. In the disputed area of the Baltic Sea shelf, there is a promising oil deposit claimed by both Latvia and Lithuania. Within the

---

3. Lithuania straddles the cultural watershed between Eastern and Western Christianity, as well as that between Catholicism and Protestantism; with some qualifications one could even speak about the ideological watershed between communism and capitalism.

conceptual framework of territorial sovereignty, the chances of reaching a mutually advantageous agreement are rather small. As the Latvia's Prime Minister Andris Skele put it, in the situation "the two countries intending as they are to join the European Union appear somewhat ridiculous" (*Lietuvos Rytas* 2 December 1996). The solution of the problems relating to the sea border delimitation moved from the deadlock only in 1997, when the two countries agreed to separate the problems of the sea border delimitation from the problems relating to common economic interests. However, the final solution of these problems may still take some time.

*Poland.* Lithuania and Poland have old historical links. One can point to a common history beginning with the Lublin Union 1569 which brought the Polish-Lithuanian Commonwealth into existence. The common history includes both their joint uprisings against the Russian empire in the 18th and 19th centuries, and also the Polish occupation of Vilnius in 1920. It is hardly surprising that in the dynamics of Polish-Lithuanian relations, historical arguments played a prominent role from 1990-1997. One can distinguish three stages in the dynamics of this short period.

The first stage was the period from the declaration of Lithuania's independence on March 11, 1990 until the August putsch (1991) in Moscow. It was characterized by Poland's unqualified support for the Lithuanian case (with the exception of official recognition). At the time, though critical of the way minorities were treated in Lithuania, Poland did not support the autonomy demands of the Polish ethnic minority (See Burant 1993, 1996; Miniotaite 1993).

After the August putsch, when Lithuania achieved international recognition, the relations between the two countries deteriorated. At the end of 1991, Lithuania's Defence Minister Audrius Butkevicius pronounced Poland the greatest threat for Lithuania, while Poland's president Lech Walesa in his letter to Vytautas Landsbergis, chairman of Lithuania's Supreme Council, described the two countries' relations as "near-crisis" (Lopata & Zalys 1995: 19-20). The events could only turn this way due to Lithuania's status as an independent agent of international relations faced with the challenge of its political identity. By taking inter-war Lithuania as the model, the image of Poland as Lithuania's malicious enemy was also naturally embraced. The image was also operative in shaping early

Lithuanian policies towards the Polish ethnic minority.[4] However, a gradual improvement in Lithuanian-Polish relations began in 1992. The Declaration of Friendship and Good-Neighbourly Co-operation was signed in 1992 although the signing of the main document, a Treaty of Friendship and Co-operation, was delayed until 1994. The delay was mostly due to the opposition's demand in Lithuania that the treaty included a clause condemning the occupation of Vilnius in 1920; this, however, was not acceptable to Poland.

The year 1994 was the turning point in Polish-Lithuanian relations. The change was related to the rise of the movement in Central European states towards closer association with NATO. Poland was becoming "a bridge linking Lithuania with the EU and NATO" (Purlys & Vilkelis 1995: 29). During President Kwasniewski's visit to Lithuania in 1996 it was agreed upon to prioritize military co-operation. The two countries endorsed common projects on airspace control, joint military exercises, peacekeeping (the establishment of a joint Lithuanian-Polish peacekeeping unit, LITPOLBAT, is under consideration). The right wing coalition that came to power in Lithuania in Autumn 1996 is intent on a simultaneous progress of Lithuania and Poland towards an association with NATO. It even seems that an attempt is made on the part of some politicians is being made at changing Lithuania's identity from that of a Baltic state to that of a Central European state. In July 1997 a joint Lithuanian-Polish Parliamentary Assembly was created. The seven years' dynamics of Polish-Lithuanian relations have made it clear that the nationalist security policy is being supplanted by a more pragmatic one.

*Russia and Belarus.* In the inter-war period, threats were coming from both East and West. In the 1990s external threats are only associated with the East. As already noted, the concept of the East is not only a geographical, but also a normative concept, so that its component parts are subject to change. Under current security conditions, the East is identified with Russia and Belarus (a country, which in signing a Union Treaty with Russia in 1996, closely linked its security policy with that of Russia's).

In the beginning, Russia's security policy was intent on a resolute integration with Western economic, political and security structures. Gorbachev's rhetoric of "our common European home" and of "returning

---

4. Even if the dominant public opinion in Lithuania is right in maintaining that the problem of the Polish ethnic minority was largely fomented by Moscow, certain political moves in Lithuania were hardly conducive to its solution (see Burant 1993: 403).

to Europe" was still quite alive. However, since the middle of 1993 and, in particular, since the Russian elections of December 1993 which culminated in the phenomenon of Zhirinovsky, there has been a noticeable nationalist turn in Russia's foreign and security policies. Since the beginning of 1994 Russia has made quite an effort at restoring its image of strong power pursuing nationalist policies. The newly coined concepts of the "near abroad" and "defender of Russian minority rights" have been used to justify the extension of Russia's national interests to the Baltic States. Additionally, Russia has also persistently opposed the Baltic countries' closer association with NATO.

Russia has been a potential threat for Lithuania primarily because of the nature of processes within Russia after the collapse of the Soviet Union. One can distinguish several component parts of the threat: (1) Russia's political instability, the precariousness of its democracy, the strengthening of nationalist and pro-imperialist elements within it; (2) ethnic, regional, nationalist-religious and social conflicts within Russia itself and within the sphere of its influence (Commonwealth of Independent States); (3) the giant military forces and the huge stock of mass destruction weapons, the control over which is under serious doubt; and (4) the continuing social and economic crisis that has adversely affected the balance of political powers within Russia (*Atgimimas* 2 August 1995). As Covington concludes: "Russia's insecurity will be a dominant factor for the next several years as Russia forms new relationships with the nations of the CIS, Central and East Europe, and the West" (Covington 1995: 446).

Since 1994 Russia has been treating its relations with Lithuania within the concept of Russia's strategic interests. Lithuania is important for Russia primarily because of its providing the shortest route to the Kaliningrad region. Russia's military transit, while vitally important for Russia, has been a source of tensions between Russia and Lithuania (Joenniemi 1996b; Nekrasas 1996; Wellmann 1996). The high militarization of the Kaliningrad area and the consequent threat of ecological pollution for the surrounding area is also of importance. In 1994 the Baltic Assembly (the common forum for Lithuanian, Latvian and Estonian parliamentarians) adopted a resolution calling for the demilitarization of the Kaliningrad region. The joint effort of Lithuanian politicians and American Lithuanians succeeded in making the problem of Kaliningrad region an international one. In September 1996 the U.S. Congress adopted a resolution urging a gradual demilitarization of the region and closer attention to its ecological problems.

The delimitation of the border between Russia and Lithuania is expected to be completed by 1997. Agreement has been reached for 90% of the land border; however, problems have emerged with the sea border. Negotiations have been hampered by the presence of an oil deposit situated in an area in the Baltic Sea shelf still not assigned to any of the two countries. In 1995 four Russian and German companies signed an agreement to establish a consortium, KANT, for the exploitation of the disputed oil deposit.

Russia's threat for Lithuania is not constant in magnitude. Thus, it undergoes changes depending upon the vicissitudes of the political and economic processes in Russia, as well as on the country's changing international situation, its relations with Western powers and also on Lithuania's own ability to maintain friendly relations with Russia without giving in on matters of political independence.

Lithuania's relations with her neighbours indicate that at present, the country finds itself in a relatively stabile geopolitical position. Relations with Latvia and Poland are shaped by the common goal of integration with the West. To be sure, this does not preclude the possibility of tensions. However, these are mostly brought about by the economic and political competition on the way to the Western world and are not really threats to their security. With respect to security, their relations have been developing according to the logic of a "security community." In Lithuania's relations with Russia and Belarus, common goals and interests have also been prominent. However, a measure of unpredictability in the economic and political development of the latter two countries, as well as their military power, have prompted Lithuania's distrust of bilateral agreements and led her in search for more reliable guarantees of security. The search has shaped the main tendency of Lithuania's security policy.

THE LITHUANIAN SECURITY POLICY: THE MAIN LANDMARKS

One can discern three stages in Lithuanian security policies: (1) From March 11, 1990 to September 17, 1991–the period from Lithuania's declaration of independence to Lithuania's joining the United Nations; (2) from September 1991 to September 1993–the period from international recognition of Lithuania's independence to the withdrawal of Russian troops; (3) from September 1993 to the present–the period of intensified integration with Western security and defence arrangements, and extension of regional co-operation.

1) When the Supreme Council of Lithuania passed the Declaration of independence, there were few people either in the Soviet Union or in other countries who took it in earnest. The act looked like just another political manifestation of which there was the veritable explosion with "perestroika's" beginning. The session of the Supreme Soviet of the USSR resolved that the declaration was invalid and thus, the issue seemed to closed. According to international criteria, sovereignty can only belong to a state that has control over its territory and whose territorial integrity is recognised by the international community. The deputies had hoped that Western governments–which in the past had repeatedly denounced Lithuania's annexation[5]–would immediately recognise the undoing of one of the consequences of the Molotov-Ribbentrop Pact. The government expected that the Soviet Union would have to yield to international pressure and "let loose" Lithuania, as well as Latvia and Estonia. This was, indeed, what eventually happened, but only after 18 months of dedicated and bitter struggle by the Lithuanian people.

The reaction on the part of international community to the Lithuanian declaration was lukewarm, strictly confined to the "no harm to Gorbachev" frame of mind.[6] It was becoming obvious that the "road to freedom" led through (cleared-up relations with) Moscow. Moscow rejected outright all forms of negotiations suggested by Lithuania. Under these circumstances, a twofold strategy was adopted by Lithuania: first, to prove to the world that it was not Moscow but rather the Lithuanian government which had control over the situation on Lithuania's territory; and second, to maximally exploit the growing disintegration tendencies in the USSR and the political struggle between Gorbachev and Yeltsin (Gerner and Hedlund 1993).

The first of these strategies was based on the premise that the state could only survive because of the concord between the citizenry and the

---

5. Officially the annexation of the Baltic states was only recognized by Germany (on 10 January, 1941) and by Sweden (on 30 May, 1941).

6. The first to congratulate the Lithuanian people with a "return to the family of free nations" were the deputies of Poland's parliament. US President George Bush stated on March 23 that his country supported the Lithuanians' right to self-determination and urged the Soviet Union to enter into immediate negotiations with the Lithuanian government. Czechoslovakia's president Vaclav Havel, in a letter to Vytautas Landsbergis, called for a political dialogue between Lithuania and the USSR and offered his country and good offices for the negotiations. The European Parliament in Strasbourg adopted a resolution on the issue of Lithuania. Although it did not recognize Lithuanian independence, the resolution treated the USSR and Lithuania as two different states that had to resolve their disagreements by constructive dialogue.

government, not simply because of military power. The earliest practical result of the Declaration of Independence was defiance of the Soviet rule and the gradual introduction of the country's own legal order. This was first practised on the law concerning military conscription. Lithuanian youth refused to serve in the Soviet army. From the Soviet point of view, this amounted to criminal civil disobedience to be smashed by repressive measures. Lithuanian government institutions emerged and began functioning in parallel with Soviet governmental institutions. Soon after the Declaration of Independence the Department of National Defence was created. Mass media were almost unanimous in the support for Lithuania's independence. In an attempt to crush Lithuania's resistance, the Soviet Union imposed an economic blockade. The measure failed to achieve its goals. The ten weeks of the blockade consolidated the concord between Lithuania's population and government as well as created conditions for the release of private initiatives in economy and again attracted the world's attention to Lithuania' case. Lithuania's independence was becoming ever more real and the military putsch attempted in January 1991 further strenghtened these aspirations. The putsch failed because first, there was mass resistance by the Lithuanian population in using diverse forms of non-violent action,[7] and second, because of the pro-Lithuanian stance of Russia's leadership.[8] "Moreover, the West finally became aware that Baltic independence was an international problem and not just an internal domestic affair of the Soviet Union" (Vardys and Sedaitis 1997: 182).[9]

---

7. On the relation between nonviolent action and civilian defence see: Sharp 1991; Ackerman and Kruegler 1994; Burrowes 1996; Miniotaite 1996.

8. Of decisive importance was the stance taken by the Chairman of the Russian Supreme Soviet, Boris Yeltsin. Yeltsin, formally appealed to Russian soldiers not to obey thoughtlessly those "who are inclined to solve political problems with the help of military troops." The appeal continued: "before attacking civil objects on Baltic soil, remember your native land, think about your own republic and the present and future of your own nation. Violence against justice and the Baltic nations will cause new and serious crises in Russia itself, and will worsen the status of Russians, residing in other republics" (Saja 1992: 356).

9. Strong protest against Soviet aggression and support for Lithuanian independence was voiced by most Western governments, political parties, and international organizations. On January 14 the prime ministers of Sweden, Iceland, Norway, Denmark, and Finland protested to Gorbachev about the behavior of Soviet troops in Lithuania. The European Community issued a statement on January 14 that read: "The Community and its member states demand that the current actions of the Soviet Union towards Lithuania not be continued or carried over to the other Baltic states. Otherwise, they will have to react accordingly to this situation and break off relations with the Soviet Union" (Saja 1992:

Russia's recognition of the independence of Lithuania's as well as independence the other Baltic states in July of the same year spurred several Western states to follow suit. Subsequently, in September, Lithuania, Latvia and Estonia gained the UN membership. Eighteen months of struggle for international recognition strengthened Lithuania's self-confidence and reinforced the country's orientation to co-operation with the other Baltic states. The experiences accumulated during that period also proved Russia's significance for Lithuania's security.

2) After achieving international recognition, Lithuania's priorities in security policy largely coincided with the build-up of political identity. Domestic and foreign policies hence became closely linked. The most important factors influencing security policy were Russia's military presence on Lithuania's territory, the social problems which appeared in the transition from a centralized to market economy, and the displacement of nationalist pro-Western political elite by the more cosmopolitan left (after the elections to Seimas at the end of 1992).

The major events of the period can be identified as follows: the withdrawal of Soviet troops from Lithuania (31 August, 1993); the establishment of diplomatic relations with a growing number of foreign countries, gaining membership into the main international organizations (UN, CSCE, NACC, Council of Europe, World Bank, International Monetary Fund); starting the delimitation of the border with neighbouring states and the passing of a constitutional amendment banning Lithuania's participation in any economic, political and military alliances or associations with the former Soviet Union republics (1992).

Lithuania's struggle for independence played out against the general background of the dissolution of the Soviet Union. Beginning as a struggle against totalitarianism it became part of the general tendency that undermined the Soviet Union. Before the Declaration of Independence, the struggle was mostly guided by universal values, and by the Kantian idea of the human being "as primarily the bearer of reason and morality, and only secondly as the representative of a nation or separate culture." After the

---

344). The Foreign Minister of Denmark, Ellemann-Jensen, offered refuge to the Lithuanian government in case it would have to operate in exile. Denmark also offered shelter to prospective refugees from the Baltics. A radical resolution was adopted by the Alting of Iceland: "There is no more appropriate way to solve the problems of the Baltic states than to fully and unconditionally recognize their independence" (Saja 1992: 349). Iceland was the first to officially recognize Lithuania's independence (11 February, 1991). Numerous rallies and pickets at the embassies of the Soviet Union took place all over the world.

Declaration of Independence and, in particular, after the country's international recognition, nationalist motives grew in strength (Jurgaitiene 1993). This had an imprint both on domestic policies and on the basic assumptions of foreign policy.

The single-minded orientation to the West could be channelled either in a southern or northern direction. The southern direction via Poland led to Central Europe; the northern one led to Scandinavia. Because of the history of inter-war relations between Poland and Lithuania as well as the present day recurring tensions with the Polish minority (some 7% of the population), Lithuania's policies were pushed in the northern direction. This was, in fact, in accordance with the orientation preferred by the Lithuanian population.[10] Security policy of the North European states served as the earliest model for Lithuania's security policy. Lithuania had the option of choosing either "finlandization" (Finland), "neutrality" (Sweden) or an "alliance policy" (Denmark, Norway). At first, the policy of neutrality, often presented in the picturesque image of a bridge between West and East, seemed the most cogent one for Lithuania.

At the beginning of the period, pro-Western policies dominated; however, when the left came to power, active policies towards the East became more prominent. In 1993 Lithuania expanded her relations with all CIS states. Free trade agreements were signed with the Ukraine, Belarus and Kazakhstan. Improvement of relations with Russia became a major goal; however, because of frictions related to Russian troops' withdrawal, the results remained rather modest. Attempting to hasten the withdrawal of the troops, Lithuania co-operated closely with the Baltic states and with international organizations. Resolutions favourable to the Lithuanian case were adopted by conferences of the CSCE and UN.[11] The security policy of the period can be characterized as that of laying the foundations for the transition from a policy of neutrality to an alliance policy.

3) After the withdrawal of Russian troops from Lithuania, a pro-Western policy became conspicuous. The aim of integration with the West was extended to also include integration with Western security and defence structures. In January 1994 Lithuania made an official application for

---

10. Surveys on the geopolitical orientation of the population have been carried out since 1989, showing the general preference of the West to the East, with the most attractive from among the Western nations being Germany and Sweden (Gaidys 1994: 113).

11. As a matter of fact, Russian troops were withdrawn from Lithuania one year earlier than they were withdrawn from Latvia and Estonia and earlier than from Germany and Poland.

membership into NATO.[12] In the same year, Lithuania became an active participant in the Partnership for Peace Programme. In May 1994 Lithuania became Associate Partner of the WEU and signed a free trade agreement with the EU. In June 1995 Lithuania signed the European Agreement together with Latvia and Estonia. In December 1996 the Baltic governments signed the announcement of the three countries' determination to join the Organization for Economic Co-operation and Development (OECD).

The common goal of achieving membership in the EU and NATO brought about a closer co-operation of the three Baltic states. However, with the exception of such collective institutions as regular meetings of the Presidents, the Baltic Council of Ministers, the Baltic Assembly and the Baltic Council, the co-operation is not premised on the goal of political integration. Considerable efforts have been made in establishing the Baltic states' co-operation in matters of defence. The co-operation was formalized in an Agreement on Co-operation in the Fields of Defence and Military Relations, signed on 27 February 1995. It is also implemented by the formation and training of the joint Baltic Peacekeeping Battalion (BALTBAT). In addition, a joint Baltic regional air surveillance system is under way along with the soon-to-be formed Baltic naval training group. The possibility of creating a military alliance of the Baltic States is permanently on the political agenda.[13]

Lithuania's relations with the North European countries have expanded. After the withdrawal of Russian troops, their relations developed in accordance with the formula "5 plus 3." There are regular meetings of foreign affairs, defence ministers and heads of governments in considering issues related to the Baltic States' integration with the EU, WEU and NATO. Correspondingly, military co-operation has linked Lithuania to

---

12. Contacts of Lithuania's Defence Ministry with NATO began as early as 1991, with the first NATO seminar held in Vilnius in December 1991.

13. The issue of building the Baltic Defence Union was raised at the 6th session of the Baltic Assembly (Riga, April 1995). In August 1996 a group of Estonian politicians issued a joint statement calling for a Baltic Security Pact that would help maintain the security of the Baltic states till their admission to NATO (*The Baltic Independent* 27 January–2 February 1995). According to the data of the "Baltijos tyrimai" (Baltic Survey) of January 1996 more than half of the population of the Baltic countries would support the creation of military alliance among Lithuania, Latvia and Estonia; the percentage in Lithuania was 69%, in Latvia 67%, in Estonia 64% of those surveyed (*Lietuvos Rytas* 9 February 1996).

Denmark, Sweden and Norway.[14] Lithuania is also a participant in the collective institutions of the Baltic Sea countries, the Council of Baltic Sea States and the Baltic Round Table.

This should suffice as illustration of Lithuania's integration with the West. The process of integration is obviously broadening and deepening. Lithuania's politicians have made it clear that the main gravitational centers for current Lithuanian foreign and security policy, the European Union and NATO, are not in themselves an ends but only the means for the ultimate end–Lithuania's prosperity and security within the framework of state sovereignty. A major question that could be a topic of concern for politicians, scholars and the public at large is whether Lithuania's membership in the EU and NATO is actually the means what is aspired for. However, it seems that there have been no serious studies of the issue despite the fact that the European Union is a major experiment of the 20th century (the prospects of which are far from evident even for its authors). It has been simply assumed here that membership in the EU is both beneficial and essential as there are no alternatives (this might be warranted in view of the experience of integration with the East).[15] Sociological surveys have confirmed the fact. According to statistics from "Eurobarometer," at the beginning of 1996, 86% of Lithuania's voting population was in favour or undecided of Lithuania's membership in EU.[16] In 1996, practical preparatory work strenghthened. In June 1996 the Seimas passed the amendment to Article 47 of the Constitution allowing the sale of land to foreigners and also ratified the European Agreement. Parliamentary groups were created for supervising work on the harmonization of laws in the

---

14. Lithuania signed agreements on military cooperation with Denmark (1994) and Norway (1995).

15. In an otherwise valuable study on "Lithuania's Integration into the European Union" (Maniokas & Vitkus 1997) published by the European Integration Studies Centre, the question of the reasonableness of the integration is not even raised. The only issue attended to is that of how far Lithuania meets the criteria for membership in the EU. However, a dispute between the integrationists and the "Eurosceptics" might develop since the creation of the National Democratic Movement for the Independent Lithuania in 1997.

16. See *Central and Eastern Eurobarometer*, 1996, No 6: 59. It might be of interest that at the beginning of 1995, according to the survey done by the Friedrich Naumann foundation and the Institute of International Relations and Politics (Vilnius), only 40% of the Lithuanian population were in favour of joining the EU. See *Atgimimas*, 1995, No 26. According to the data of *Central and Eastern Eurobarometer*, 1997, No. 7, during the year 1996 the percentage of those supporting Lithuania's membership in EU dropped by 7 %.

different domains of legal regulation as preparations were made for a free trade agreement. In 1996 the Ministry of European Affairs was created for the co-ordination of preparatory work on Lithuania's joining the EU. In Summer 1997 a Parliamentary Committee for European Affairs was instituted with the explicit aim of promoting the European idea in the society.

Lithuania's membership in the EU has been treated favourably both in the West and in the East. The situation is much different concerning its intention of joining NATO. An active and unswerving Baltic quest for membership in NATO is perceived in Russia as a challenge to her national interests. It has been countered by the Russia Federal Council's statement against the expansion of NATO (March, 1996), by the Russia parliament's vote in favour of restoring the Soviet Union (March, 1996) and by the increased attempts at strengthening ties between CIS member states. All these measures have caused tensions in the region and made the issue of the Baltic countries more acute. This, in turn, has created the "Baltic dilemma" for the West, namely, "how to reconcile legitimate security interests of Russia and the CEE states and a unique opportunity to influence internal processes in those states by promoting stability in the transitional period" (Rotfeld 1996: 26).[17] The manner in which the dilemma will be solved is bound to have profound impact on the whole European security climate, with consequences directly relevant for Scandinavia, continental Europe, the EU and Russia.

From Lithuania's point of view, the dilemma has been solved to date by giving preference to Russia's interests ('Russia first') while postponing indefinitely the Baltic States' acceptance into NATO. The approach has been met both in the Baltic States and sometimes in the West with allusions to the realities of the Second World War. The "Munich complex," "New Yalta," "Danzig corridor" (relating to Lithuania's geopolitical situation after Poland's joining NATO), these have been the epithets often employed.[18] The assumption underlying these allusions is that similar to the eve of the Second World War, the Baltic States have again become the

---

17. The dilemma has also been discussed in the RAND study on NATO enlargement and the Baltic States (Asmus and Nurick 1996). See also: Asmus and Larrabee 1996; Asmus 1997; Hunter 1997.

18. See *Lietuvos Aidas* 11 May 1996. The results achieved during the meeting in Helsinki (March 1997) of the Presidents of Russia and the USA gave no reasons for this interpretation of the events. It seems that the fears of the Baltic states that Helsinki would become another Yalta have not come true, for no secret agreements were signed.

object of a deal between big powers. However, this kind of superficial juxtaposition of different historical realities does not take into account the specific nature of the new political situation. The security architecture that is emerging in the wake of the Cold War is proceeding on the paradigm of mutual dependence and integration rather than on a platform of national sovereignty and autarchy. In this paradigm, the "Russia first" solution can be interpreted not as a concession to Russia, but rather as an incipient attempt at creating a common security space involving both Russia and the Baltic States.

It seems that the efforts of the NATO countries at persuading the Balts to acquiesce in the scheme were not successful.[19] In response to the official declaration made in September 1996 by the US Secretary of Defence William Perry that the Baltic states were not yet ready for NATO membership, presidents of the three states reacted with a joint declaration: "We do not want to see new lines drawn in Europe and we do not want to see any grey areas created where conflicts may arise as the result of misunderstandings" (Carrol 1996). The Baltic States have their existence not in the hypothetical space of common security but rather "in the here and now" and that means, in the neighbourhood of the potentially dangerous Russia. Therefore, their disappointment in being "left behind the door" can be understood. The Western security offer to the Baltic states–membership in the EU, close political and military ties with NATO and regional co-operation–do not guarantee security in the event of a military aggression (even if it makes the probability of such an aggression less likely).

None of the three Baltic states considers any alternative to membership in NATO. They do accept "pillows" (Asmus &Nurick 1996) offered by the West. However, they seek membership in NATO both jointly and separately.[20] After the official visits by the Foreign Affairs Minister

---

19. Lithuania took a reserved and even critical attitude towards the U.S. Deputy Secretary of State Strobe Talbot's proposal of the Baltic Action Plan at the end of August 1996. The plan urged the Baltic countries to improve relations with Russia, to sign "Co-operation Charter" dealing with political, security and economic cooperation between the US and the Baltic States. Lithuania's politicians were apprehensive of the possibility that signing of such a charter could be interpreted as a recognition by Lithuania's security policy of the option of not joining NATO and as a default on the intention of seeking membership in NATO separately from the other Baltic states. However, after the NATO summit in Madrid, that has dampened Lithuania's ambitions of exclusivity, the Baltic Action Plan was treated more favourably. The USA-Baltic Charter is planned for signing in 1997.

20. According to the statistics of Eurobarometer, at the beginning of 1996 Lithuania's membership in NATO was supported by 83% of Lithuania's voter population (*Central*

Algirdas Saudargas to Germany and Poland, and after the Seimas' speaker Vytautas Landsbergis' address to the Polish parliament at the beginning of 1997, some significant changes in Lithuania's security and foreign policy have become evident. The idea has been circulated that during the first stage of NATO, expansion to the East for at least one of the Baltic countries should be accepted by the organization and that that country might as well be Lithuania. The strategy of moving toward NATO simultaneously with Poland has been embraced and actively supported by Poland. However, the policy turn is an outright challenge to the common Baltic approach expressed in the joint declaration of the presidents of Estonia, Latvia and Lithuania, "On Partnership for Integration" (April 1996), namely: "that in moving to the European Union and NATO the countries were intent to co-operate, not to compete" (Atgimimas 1996:1).

In justifying the new turn of Lithuania's politics, the image of Lithuania as a Baltic state has been subjected to a gradual erosion; correspondingly, attempts have been made at creating the identity of the country as one "belonging to Central Europe" (*Atgimimas* 20 December 1996) or to "Central Baltic Europe" (*Lietuvos Aidas* 25 February 1997). Have Lithuania's chances in joining NATO with the first group of countries, while simultaneously leaving Latvia and Estonia behind the door, increased?[21]

This is rather doubtful, as the results of the Madrid summit meeting in July 1997 demonstrated. In the final declaration that left Lithuania some hopes of joining NATO at some time, no one particular Baltic state was specifically mentioned. They were all referred to as "the countries of the Baltic regions seeking membership in NATO." Theoretically, Lithuania's chances may become more real if certain federal ties are established with Poland; practically, however, the scenario is premature. Post-Cold War Europe is still very much in the grip of the tendencies towards fragmentation rather than integration.

*Concluding remarks.* Basing ourselves on a survey of the past seven years of Lithuania's security policy allows a glimpse into some of its situational dynamics. Lithuania's pre-eminent goal for its security policy as

---

and Eastern Eurobarometer 1996: 60). During year 1996 the number of those supporting Lithuania's membership in NATO dropped by 10% (*Central and Eastern Eurobarometer* 1997, No.7).

21. In an interview for newspaper *Atgimimas* Algirdas Saudargas, Lithuanian Minister of Foreign Affairs, called the unity of the Baltic states a mere fiction that only exists in Western politicians minds' (Saudargas 1996).

well as its politics in general has been the build-up of the nation state and the preservation of its territorial integrity. Lithuania's security policy has been closely linked to the processes of state-building and the search for political identity.

The main goal of the first stage in Lithuania's security policy i.e., attaining international recognition, was favourably affected by an international climate propitious for liberation movements and a politically-adopted strategy of concord between the political elite and the population.

The second stage can best be described by the testing of the "binding idea" (Buzan 1991: 64) of the state. The history of relations with neighbouring states (tensions in dealings with Poland) along with the presence of Russian troops on Lithuania's territory were the most important factors for security policy of that period. This inclined leadership towards a policy of neutrality.

The third stage can be characterised by a turn towards the alliance policy of security. The period has been marked by an active security policy which may end up leading to either a hard security or a hard "insecurity." The nature of the relations between Russia and NATO here has been of cardinal importance. A certain misunderstanding concerning Lithuania's position has arisen because of two different interpretations of Russia's potential threat to European security. One is led by the logic of the security community, and the other by the logic of the balance of power. Both Lithuania's application for membership in NATO and Russia's subsequent negative reaction are rather based on a balance of power logic.[22] Lithuania's political identity formation "has not yet taken the shape of a security community including Russia" (Knudsen & Neumann 1995: 1).

Since the beginning of 1997 the emerging oscillation in Lithuania's security and foreign policy between orientation to Central Europe and orientation to the Baltic and Nordic states is an evidence of attempts towards a more active policy. The "new policy" is still at the formative stage, thus it is no wonder that it blends elements both of nationalism and pragmatism in being coloured by the history of Lithuania's statehood. In this sense, a survey of the lessons of Lithuania's past for contemporary politics is relevant.

---

22. In characterizing the security and foreign policies of Eastern European countries Paul Goble made a penetrating remark that these countries are oriented to the "old NATO and its guarantees against Russian revisionism in future" rather than to a "new NATO that will closely co-operate with Russia" (Made 1996).

## THE LESSONS OF HISTORY FOR THE PRESENT

In distinction from Latvia and Estonia who date their independence by the year 1918, Lithuania's history of statehood reaches as far back as the 13th century. The history comprises the period of the prosperous Great Dukedom of Lithuania in the 15th–16th centuries, the Commonwealth of Lithuania and Poland, the loss of statehood at the end of the 18th century, the period of national revival in the 19th century and the inter-war period of 1918–1940. Judging by its territory, geopolitical situation as well as the size and composition of its population, Lithuania now resembles the inter-war Lithuania much more than did the Great Dukedom of Lithuania. Thus, it is only natural that the features of contemporary Lithuania's politics are modelled mainly on those of inter-war Lithuania. However, a certain influence cast by the centuries old story of the splendour and fall of Lithuania also has its role. Accordingly, Baltic-Scandinavian trend in politics can be related to the inter-war interpretations of history, while the turn toward Central Europe has found inspiration in the older layers of Lithuania's history.

The inter-war Lithuanian state is an important source for the justification of the contemporary foreign and security policies (cf. also Jurgaitiene & Wæver 1996). An analysis of the story of its successes and failures is an urgent task for contemporary politicians and historians. Even if history is never written in the conditional mood, they have tried again and again to answer the question of whether it could have run a different course, to what extent the situation was dependent on Lithuania itself, and to the character of its foreign and defence policies. And in addition, there is the question of what can be learnt from the experience for the formation of contemporary policy. Their attempts at finding the answers to the questions have shown that at least four lessons for today, positive or negative, have been extracted from the history of inter-war Lithuania. They centre around four separate issues.

*Issue 1: Lithuania and the Baltic States, allied or separate?* The three Baltic states declared their independence in 1918 in the aftermath of the war and revolutions that led to the collapse of the Russian and German empires. Their main goal at that time was to define and secure international recognition of their territorial borders. At the time Lithuania had borders with Latvia, Poland and Germany (cf. fig. 7.1). Despite the common goal of the three countries, by the Paris Peace Conference of 1919 the Lithuanian Prime Minister and Minister for Foreign Affairs, Augustinas Voldemaras, had already claimed that Lithuania's exceptionable and preferable geopolitical situation, as compared with Latvia and Estonia was, allegedly, due to both Lithuania's lack of direct borders with Russia, and her lack of sea ports, like those of Riga and Tallinn which were important for Russia. Moreover, Lithuania was claimed to have the privilege of being able to appeal to international law because of its former history of statehood. The attitude in question had a strong influence on Lithuania's policy of security and on its foreign policy in the inter-war period.

In Autumn 1919 in Tartu, prime ministers of the Baltic states and Finland earnestly considered the possibility of creating a Baltic alliance which would also involve Poland. Because of Lithuania's territorial disputes with Poland, the Lithuanian delegation lent no support to the idea. Again at the Paris Peace Conference in November, Estonia came up with the idea of a regional security system involving Scandinavian and Baltic countries, and Poland. The negative attitude of Lithuania was once again prominent however. All later attempts at creating a Baltic security alliance without the participation of Lithuania (and also Finland) ended in failure.

It now seems that the creation of this kind of alliance in the 1920s, when the architecture of post-war European security was still in the making, could have had far reaching effects on the subsequent course of events. However, the propitious moment was missed. A return to the idea in 1934, coupled with the signing in Riga of the Agreement of the Entente Co-operation was already an overdue effort which bore no tangible impact on the power configuration already settled. Germany and the Soviet Union rapidly gaining in strength now dictating the rules of the game and held the destiny of the Baltic States in their hands. Subsequently, by 1940, the Baltic States were incorporated into the Soviet Union. Even though the incorporation was recognised "de jure" only by Germany and Sweden, the fact of the matter was that for Lithuania, Latvia and Estonia, they immediately became cut off from the West and were turned into "Soviet socialist republics" devastated by pre- and post-war deportations, collectivization, industrialization and "Russification."

### Fig. 7.1: Lithuania: Historically Disputed Territories

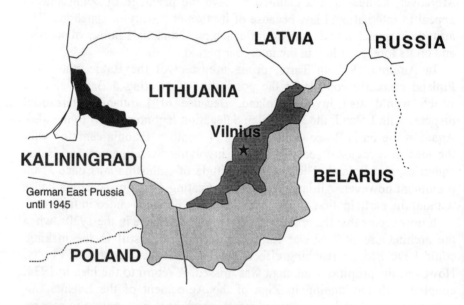

Polish territory in the interwar period. Then claimed by Lithuania, but not Lithuanian today.

Polish territory in the interwar period. Claimed by Lithuania and annexed in 1945.

Kleipeda/Memel-region. German territory until1919. Administered 1919-1923 by the League of Nations after peace-agreement in Versailles. Annexed by Lithuania in 1923, and recognized as such in 1924. Occupied by German troops in 1939. Re-annexed by Lithuania (Soviet) in 1945.

——— Current borders

·········· Polish-Russian interwar border

·············· Polish-German interwar border

Common experience with the Soviet occupation and joint efforts during the liberation movement have laid the foundations for the Baltic States' post-independence co-operation. The co-operation was also encouraged by the attitude of the West in treating the Baltic countries as a single region on all issues of importance. Against this background Lithuania's endeavours at finding a separate path to the West seem to be rather dubious. Present Minister for Foreign Affairs Algirdas Saudargas has reverted to the ideas of Lithuania's distinctive status as formulated in 1919 by the then-Foreign Minister Augustinas Voldemaras. Therefore, history in this case has played the role of "generator of ideas" rather than teacher.

*Issue 2: relations with Poland, past and future.* The territorial conflict between Lithuania and Poland was the "leitmotif" of the foreign and security policy of inter-war Lithuania. In a book published in 1938 commemorating the 20th anniversary of Lithuania's independence, Lithuania was characterized as the country "struggling for Vilnius" (Zaunius 1990: 30). The problems relating to Vilnius were raised at the Paris Peace Conference. The goal of Lithuanian political leaders was the restoration of independent Lithuania in its ethnic boundaries, with Vilnius as capital, and the area of Smaller Lithuania (Königsberg region) included within its boundaries.[23] The goal clashed with Poland's interests in its endeavour to re-establish Poland within the boundaries of 1793. Thus, it claimed the same territories as did Lithuania, the Vilnius and the Klaipeda (Memel) region. In an attempt to strengthen its position in the negotiations with Lithuania, Poland seized Vilnius on October 9, 1920. In 1923 the League of Nations resolved to cede Vilnius to Poland while recognising Lithuania's claims to the Klaipeda (Memel) region. Despite the resolution of the League of Nations, Lithuania refused to establish any relations with Poland until Vilnius remained in its hands.[24] In its efforts to regain Vilnius, Lithuanian security policy as defined by Voldemaras–fighting Poland with

---

23. The Smaller Lithuania, the south-western part of ethnic Lithuania was conquered by the Livonian order in the XIII century. The many attempts of Lithuania at regaining the strip of coast line including the port of Klaipeda were not successful. Until the Versailles Treaty of 1919 the territory in question was part of the German Empire. It should be noted that despite the centuries' long attempts at assimilation, after World War I an overwhelming majority of the original population was still Lithuanian; the Klaipeda region had the Lithuanian population of 48,9 % (Zostautaite 1992:13).

24. Internationally, the Polish occupation of Vilnius was qualified as such only in 1931, when the international court in the Hague decided that in seizing Vilnius Poland violated international law. Diplomatic relations with Poland were established in 1938.

the help of Germany and Soviet Union–turned towards an isolation from the other neighbouring states. Lithuania's policy was fitting for Soviet Union and Germany, which were both intent in preventing Poland from gaining dominance over the region. Even at the end of the 1930s when Germany and the Soviet Union became an imminent threat to the Baltic States, Lithuanian politicians saw Poland as the chief enemy.

It can be claimed, accordingly,that the conflict with Poland led to both Lithuania's isolation from the other Baltic states, and to a rapprochement with the Soviet Union; indirectly, this encouraged the "Polanization" of a Vilnius region occupied by Poland. As shown above, the tangled history of the relations with Poland has also been reflected on recent policies of Lithuania. The reconciliation with Poland stimulated by the expansion of NATO is a clear indication that a critical re-evaluation of the past has taken place.

*Issue 3: anti-defeatism.* The most painful page of Lithuania's history in the inter-war period was the loss of its independence in 1939-40. When analyzing the events of the time, it is difficult either to understand or justify the defeatist attitude of the governments of the three Baltic states.[25]As the British historian David Kirby wrote, "The governments of Pats, Ulmanis and Smetona need not have collaborated to the extent which they did. By agreeing to mutual assistance pacts in the autumn of 1939, they clearly compromised their countries' future existence" (Kirby 1994: 80-81). The defeatist stance of the Lithuanian government can be explained in part by the dictatorial character of the regime established since 1926. During nearly the whole inter-war period the country was under martial law. The formation of an independent civil society was thus greatly hindered which led to the political passivity of the population. At a critical juncture, having severed the vital ties with the societies, the governments found themselves lacking the political will.

---

25. "Our resistance would enrage Moscow and it would devastate our country;" "resistance would not only require considerable loss of life of our people, but would also destroy our whole economic life without giving any countervailing advantage." These were the reasons given by the Lithuanian Cabinet of Ministers in 1940 for the unconditional acceptance of the Soviet ultimatum (Truska 1996: 372). Judging from the long-term perspective it is evident that non-resistance did not save Lithuania from loss of life, did not prevent the devastation of the country. At a critical juncture it even contributed to internal division within the society and thus helped create an air of legitimacy for Soviet actions.

Contemporary security policy of Lithuania has explicitly faced the negative experience of 1939-40. In particular, this expression can be found in the document that is definitive of Lithuania's security policy "The Basics of National Security of Lithuania" (adopted by the Seimas at the end of 1996). The document stresses that the alliance policy in no way excludes the necessity of organising a self-reliant defence in the case of an aggression. Alongside the traditional military defence, an important role is accorded to civilian defence based on "non-violent resistance, disobedience and non-collaboration with the unlawful administration" (p. 9). National defence is based on the principle of a total and unconditional defence while "unconditional defence" refers to that defence of Lithuania which "shall not be tied to any preconditions and by which no one may restrict the right of the nation and each citizen to resist the aggressor" (p. 6). This reads as an outright polemic with the defeatist policy of 1939-40.

*Issue 4: neutrality or alliance policy?* In the beginning of 1939 when the danger to peace in Europe was beyond anyone's doubt, Lithuania opted for a policy of neutrality (the neutrality act was passed in January 1939). After the German seizure of the Klaipeda area, a non-aggression treaty was signed with Germany in March 1939 (an analogous treaty with the Soviet Union was in effect since 1926). The policy impeded the co-operation of the Baltic States in matters of defence. It also made the more active and flexible policy of the earlier period unfeasible. For instance, had Lithuania renounced the policy of neutrality and recaptured the Vilnius region in the first fortnight of September, it "might also have opened up a rather different scenario in which the Baltic countries could have played a more active role in the defence of their own interests" (Kirby 1994: 81).

Recent Lithuanian security policy, after the withdrawal of Russia's troops in 1993, has unambiguously turned to an alliance policy. This turn was definitely influenced by the painful lessons of the policies of neutrality on the eve of the Second World War.


BALTIC SCENARIOS FOR THE UPCOMING DECADE*

As the scenarios relevant for Estonia, Latvia, and Lithuania turned out to resemble each other a good deal, we have integrated them in order to save

---

* The present section has been co-authored by Mare Haab, Grazina Miniotaite, Hans Mouritzen, and Zaneta Ozolina.

the reader from unnecessary repetition. However, it is not being assumed that all three countries are necessarily sharing scenario at a given point in time; one may be first into the EU, while another is NATO avantguard. Special modifications for any of the three countries have been added, wherever that has been necessary. Using basically the same format as in the Finland chapter, but adding a dimension of neither EU- nor NATO-memberships, it is relevant to discuss the Baltic countries' situations and options during the scenarios depicted in fig. 7.2.

*Baltic grey zone security*

This scenario is in essence a continuation of the status quo; the Balts have been excluded from at least the first round of NATO enlargement, and living up to the requirements of EU membership, even for Estonia, has turned out to be a much more cumbersome process than expected. A delaying tactic in major Western capitals prevails in relation to the Baltic countries. At the same time Russia reluctantly, but clearly, accepts the geopolitical status quo in the region; there are no revisionist ambitions.

**Fig. 7.2: The Relevant Environment Scenarios for Estonia, Latvia, and Lithuania**

| West Enlargement | Russia | Status Quo Orientation | Revisionist Orientation |
|---|---|---|---|
| *Baltic Status Quo* | | Grey zone security | Grey zone insecurity |
| *Baltic EU Memberships* | | Soft security | Soft insecurity |
| *Baltic EU+NATO Memberships* | | Hard security | Hard insecurity |

In accordance with the uncertainty avoidance of major Western powers (cf. chapter 3), their strategy is one of delaying in relation to the Baltic countries; locking them out would be a far too drastic and dangerous step.

So since the EU as well as the NATO doors are still kept ajar, discussion on these would-be memberships continues. Baltic impatience with their double waiting room status is likely to reach new heights, but the countries' lack of desirable alternatives (cf. chapters 5, 6, 7) implies that they simply have to acquiesce in waiting and continue to perform as well as possible in PfP and in adapting to likely EU preferences.

Assuming that a NATO enlargement with Poland (and possibly others as well) has taken place, Russia will in accordance with its general orientation try to restore the status quo by converting the Baltic countries to a Russian sphere of influence. This will be attempted even by a reasonably democratic Russia. However, it will not succeed. Not only have the Balts been offered US "firm commitments" as a substitute for membership; given their anti-Soviet heritages, they are generally intransigent to Russian influence atttempts, probably even to co-operation that could be to their own economic advantage (with the exception of Lithuania that in view of its favourable demographic composition can take a more relaxed attitude eastwards). The Balts have no "Russian card" to play vis à vis the West, because the West would actually prefer Baltic-Russian co-operation and "good neighbourly relations".

A status quo oriented Russia has probably spent its scarce resources on other purposes than military ones; hence, the current capability of the Russian military forces (cf. chapter 2) has probably declined further. In spite of some Baltic perceptions, there exists no real threat to Baltic basic security in this scenario; the label for it, therefore, is "grey zone security".

Denmark, Sweden, and Finland–the Nordic countries that have included the Baltic countries in their task environments–are likely to play the largest (high politics) role during the present scenario. The efforts of these countries make the most difference to the Balts in the absence of EU and NATO memberships, and they also function as advocates within the EU and NATO for such memberships.

Estonia being attracted to Finland and Lithuania to Poland, Latvia fears relative isolation in the middle. Latvia is, therefore, the staunchest advocate not only of the link to Sweden and Denmark, but also of inter-Baltic co-operation. The latter will hardly be successful, however, since there is no unambiguous common enemy to the Balts in this scenario.

*Baltic soft security*

In this scenario the Baltic countries have acquired EU memberships, be they full ones or "political" ones exempting them from certain economic performance criteria (an interim period with Estonian membership and Latvia and Lithuania still in the waiting room is likely, cf. Asmus & Nurick 1996). NATO memberships being only possibilities in the horizon and the WEU-NATO backdoor being locked, the Balts are left with EU "soft security" as previously described.

However, this is actually a quite favourable situation–perhaps the best that the Balts can realistically achieve. With a continued Russian status quo orientation, there is no real challenge to their soft security. Russia wants to compensate for Polish NATO membership as in the above scenario, but with Baltic EU memberships Russia has no incentive (let alone possibility) of "bullying" the Balts. Russia is dependent on EU goodwill, and the Baltic countries have become important transit areas for East-West trade. With increased Baltic feeling of security, a certain cultivation of Russo-Baltic mutual advantages is allowed to take place (most markedly regarding Lithuania, cf. the previous scenario). With the Baltic heritage, though, it will never reach Finnish-Russian heights as described in the corresponding Finnish scenario.

*Baltic hard security*

In this scenario we presuppose that the Baltic countries have attained their ultimate objective, encompassing both EU and NATO memberships. Lithuanua may have entered NATO first in the wake of Polish membership, but one can also imagine all three joining simultaneously. It is unlikely that this should have happened in the face of resistance from a reasonably democratic Russia; either, Russia has accepted Baltic memberships in return for considerable concessions in one or the other area, or NATO has been transformed into a collective security organization, with Russia as a likely future member.

None of these preconditions are very likely to be fulfilled, of course. Should this scenario materialize, however, it would mean a favourable situation in the form of "hard security" for the Balts. This would entail a more relaxed Baltic attitude to co-operation with Russia in the form of an abandonment of the prevailing zero-sum assumption ("what you win we lose, and vice versa"). As in the previous scenario, though, co-operation will never reach Finnish-Russian heights, given the Baltic heritage.

*Baltic grey zone insecurity*

This is the most dangerous scenario of all to the Baltic countries: a revisionist rule in Moscow, probably a military dictatorship with a nationalist or communist orientation, with no significant Western counterweight (EU, NATO) to lean on for the Balts. A revisionist orientation in Moscow, if sufficiently ambiguous as seen from the West, does not lead to immediate Baltic NATO memberships, but instead to vague "guarantees". However, with Western influence in Moscow disappearing the Baltic countries would be faced with Russian threats to their basic securities. It is certain that a revisionist regime in Moscow would spend significantly more resources on military purposes than a status quo regime, thereby gradually improving its military capability.

It is likely that a revisionist Russia would take a tough attitude to disputed border issues and try to use Russian populations in the Baltic countries as more or less Trojan horses. If these populations have not been reasonably integrated in their societies at the time in question, such Russian strategy might be efficient (vis à vis Estonia and Latvia, notably). The Russian populated Narva district in North-East Estonia might become an area of contention and in any case a "hot spot". Russian attempts to "divide and rule" among the three countries would be exacerbated during these circumstances; probably, Lithuania would be treated as the "good guy," given its more favourable demographic situation. Even this country, however, might get trouble with Russia over the Kaliningrad transit arrangement. Also issues regarding territories acquired by Lithuania when ruled by the Soviet Union might come to the fore, such as the Klaipeda region that was turned over to the Lithuanian administration in 1950.

The counter-strategy to "divide and rule" is of course cohesion, if possible (Mouritzen 1997c: ch. 1). Inter-Baltic co-operation would be strongest during this scenario, since a common potential enemy in the form of Russia would be clearly discernible. In this particular respect, the situation would resemble the one preceding the Baltic independences (unless, of course, Lithuania managed to "escape" by entering a federation with Poland, a NATO member). Nordic contributions to Baltic independent statehood would be more in need than ever, but at least Finland with her own exposed geopolitical position would act more cautiously than during a status quo orientation in Moscow.

All three countries would be exposed to pressure due to their continued Russia dependence regarding energy ressources. This dependence will probably be somewhat exploited during all scenarios, but markedly so in this "worst case" situation.

## Baltic soft insecurity

In this scenario, the countries (or only one of them) have acquired EU membership, while the Russian challenge is supposed to be as in the preceding scenario. In other words: "soft security" will be put to its real test in the face of a revisionist Russia. The West has practically no influence on the Russian regime, and Russia's re-isolation from the West means that the Baltic role as transit area between East and West has vanished. The border disputes and the Trojan horses mentioned in the previous scenario would probably also be problematic for the Baltic countries in this scenario; the European Common Foreign and Security Policy would hardly prevent them from popping up.

Still, it is likely that the very membership of the EU with its prestige and reputation as the European "good company" will significantly heighten the threshold of military attack for any outside power. It would take not only a reckless regime in Moscow to try such an enterprise; it would also require that it had improved the current Russian military capability significantly. Nonetheless, "soft security" would probably be felt more like "soft insecurity" by the Balts under the circumstances.

## Baltic hard insecurity

This scenario implies a new Iron Curtain in Europe, at the eastern border of Estonia, Latvia, and Lithuania (Beylo-Russia being more or less incorporated in Russia). The Baltic countries are members not only of the EU, but also of NATO; this latter membership may have been provoked by developments in Russia, or the other way round: Baltic NATO memberships were at least part of the background making the soil fertile for revanchist forces in Russia.

Even though the Baltic countries will be front-line states in this scenario, it will not entail an altogether unpleasant situation for these countries. It will correspond exactly with the prevailing Baltic moods based on their anti-Soviet heritages: "we are West, and the West stops here". It will be more clear than ever what is "white" and what is "black," who is "friend" and who is "enemy".

# 8   Poland

WOJCIECH KOSTECKI

## INVERSION IN THE POLISH SALIENT ENVIRONMENT

Poland neatly illustrates the differences between the "eagle" and "frog" perspectives on polarity (cf. chapter 1). Of course, having the "iron curtain" close to its western border for 45 years has made Poland particularly sensitive to changes in the systemic power structure. The situation was quite simple: the bipolar order directly influenced the Polish position in international relations. Poland was an essential part of the "socialist camp"[1] and, as such, also experienced regional bipolarity: patterns of amity were clearly located in the East; conversely, the West constituted the main Polish enemy. The German desire of "revenge" and American "imperialism" symbolised hostility of the latter. However, as viewed from Poland the situation was originally characterised by Soviet unipolarity. It was the Soviet Union who possessed a monopoly on the (mostly negative) sanctions that could be imposed on Poland. The Soviet Union was able to use its ideological and political domination as well as the economic dependencies it forced upon Poland and, of course, its crushing military superiority to control Polish behaviour (environment unipolarity).

One should note, however, that behind the clear "friend-enemy" distinction in high politics, there were attempts to make use of the opportunities created by successive phases of détente. Since the 1950s Poland was, to quote the popular metaphor, "the most funny barrack in the whole camp" (cf. note 1). This was related to the changes in the communist doctrine made by the 20th Congress of the Communist Party of the Soviet Union. In Poland, the so-called post-October (1956) thaw introduced by Wladyslaw Gomulka brought some liberalisation in domestic policy. Later,

---

1. "Socialist camp" or the Soviet block: the grouping of states belonging simultaneously to the Warsaw Treaty Organization (WTO) and to the Council of Mutual Economic Assistance (CMEA)–both organizations fully subordinated to Moscow. They were based on co-operation of communist parties, that held hegemonic power in these states.

the Polish specificity also consisted of an opening to the West–especially in the economic domain–made by Edward Gierek.

After the Cold War ended, the systemic bipolarity became replaced by a more complex yet still rather fluid structure consisting of three main components: the first was constituted by the only superpower, the United States, which retained (and enhanced) its leadership role in world politics; the second one was created by the continuous bipolar pattern regarding the strength of nuclear potential (re: the USA – Russia); and the third was a multipolar political-economic formation which consisted of a "global democratic-capitalist triangle" (re: the USA–Western Europe–Japan [Buzan *at al.* 1990: 59]) and several regional powers. But from the viewpoint of the Polish environment polarity, the unipolar pattern has continued, although in *reverse form.*

This is because the end of the Cold War in Europe–as seen from Warsaw–was marked by: (1) the collapse of communist governments in East-Central Europe and the subsequent initiation of democratic and free market-oriented reforms; (2) the reunification of Germany–or, in some interpretations, the incorporation of the GDR by the FRG on the conditions of the latter; (3) the dissolution of the CMEA and the Warsaw Pact, and a corresponding rejection of inclusion of security commitments into the new treaties between the Soviet Union and Visegrad countries; and (4) the liquidation of the Soviet Union itself and the consequent withdrawal of Soviet/Russian troops from former Warsaw Pact countries. All of this amounts to principal change in the amity-enmity patterns in which Poland was a part of. It was the West that won the "grand rivalry" and established a model for civilizational development. Simultaneously, the main security risks now were perceived as coming from the East.

Thus, the West arose as the only legitimate and stable partner, able to provide military capability, political standards and economic assistance. Meanwhile the East appeared as the area of instability and "de-frozen" conflicts with little, if anything, to offer. In other words, now it was the West who had all the (mostly positive) sanctions which could be implemented to influence Polish politics in various domains. Therefore, in the Polish salient environment, the unipolar arrangement did not cease to exist. What indeed changed, however, was the location of the pole. Accordingly to the environment polarity concept, the salient pole of power– as viewed from a Polish perspective–shifted West. As a consequence, the Polish alliance policy has also made the necessary U-turn.

THE 1989-91 CHANGES AND AFTERWARDS

Being the first among the countries that enjoyed the "Autumn of Nations,"[2] Poland has experienced rather gradual transformations from its communist past to the democratic present. It took almost three years to eliminate the most visible remnants of the previous regime and to see the Soviet imperium collapsed. In fact, the processes of regaining Polish sovereignty lasted until late 1993 and were crowned by the symbolic date "the 17th of September,"[3] the day when the last Russian soldier left Polish territory. The processes themselves had two clear dimensions: one internal and the other external. Both contributed directly to the threat perceptions and alliance policy of Poland during the post-Cold War era. The internal dimension consisted of democracy building and redefinition of the regime values (Kostecki and Wiberg 1996: 157-165). The external dimension relied on a step-by-step loosening of the former ties with the Soviet Union and, ultimately, exploitation of the disappearance of the USSR itself, thereby adding to Polish autonomy in international relations.

*Internal dimension*

As a result of the agreement between the communist government and democratic opposition signed in April 1989, the mechanism of recovering sovereignty in the internal domain was put in motion. However, by the end of 1991, crucial elements of the old political system were also maintained. The June 1989 parliamentary election formed the so-called contracted parliament with only one-third of the seats available for representatives of the opposition. Several key posts in the government headed by the non-communist Prime Minister Tadeusz Mazowiecki, including the Defence Ministry and the Ministry of Internal Affairs, were still kept by ministers who were members of the Polish United Workers Party.[4] This situation changed only in October 1991, when the first free election took place. President Wojciech Jaruzelski, designated by the parliament with a

---

2. This is hardly an adequate expression though well established in the political jargon. The very term "Autumn" suggests decline and fall rather than revival of the East European nations, which was the case in 1989.
3. On 17 September 1939 the Soviet Union invaded Poland.
4. Polish United Workers Party–PUWP (Polska Zjednoczona Partia Robotnicza–PZPR), the communist party that wielded hegemonic power in Poland 1948-89.

guaranteed communist majority in July 1989, continued in office until December 1990 when he was succeeded by Lech Walesa, winner of the first free presidential election.

The essential deficiency of the Polish political system "in the making" has been constituted by the lack of a new constitution (which has only been passed by the National Assembly in April 1997). The fundamental principles of the post-communist regime are indicated in a document entitled *Constitutional Provisions* which, according to the Constitutional Act of 17 October 1992, repeals the old communist constitution of 1952 and contains the remaining rules that enumerate its most essential changes and amendments. The 1992 act itself was devoted solely to the mutual relations between legislative and executive institutions of the Republic of Poland, and relations between the local and central government. As far as the question of responsibility for foreign policy was concerned, it announced: "The President shall exercise general supervision in the field of international relations" (article 32, § 1); "Relations with foreign States, as well as with Polish diplomatic representatives abroad, shall be maintained through the appropriate minister dealing with foreign affairs" (article 32, § 3); and "The Prime Minister shall lay a motion to appoint the minister of foreign affairs, of national defence and of internal affairs after consultation with the President" (article 61) (*Materials and Documents* 2 [2] 1993: 18, 23).

It should be noted that the process by which the anti-communist opposition obtained power in Poland occurred under conditions of deep crisis in the state structures. "Inherited" from communism, this crisis was soon overlapped by another one–the transformation crisis. As a result, new threats to the process of democracy building, indicated by unruliness and instability, arose with consequences for the Polish international position as well. Warnings against the transformation crisis were sounded at the highest political level and considered so serious that they found reflection in a document known as *Guidelines for Polish Security Policy* adopted by the Committee for Defence of the Country in November 1992. The relevant fragment reads: "The great transformations of the political system now under way in Poland inevitably cause domestic threats to grow temporarily. These are non-military threats of political, social and economic nature. They weaken the State structure and *make it more vulnerable to external pressure*" (*Materials and Documents* [1] 1992: 18, emphasis added). The last point, that is, the possible vulnerability to external pressures, was, however, the principal concern of the new Polish regime from the very beginning.

*External dimension*

Attempts to achieve and strengthen the external dimension of Polish sovereignty took several directions. One course was bilateral in nature and concerned primarily with relations with the neighbours. In 1989 Poland had three neighbours: the USSR, Czechoslovakia, and the GDR. Shortly after, *none of them* existed anymore. Instead, there were seven *new states* along Polish borders: Russia, Lithuania, Belarus, Ukraine, Slovakia, the Czech Republic and (a reunited) Germany. Consequently, Polish bilateral relations had to be rearranged almost from scratch. Success was dependent upon persistent Polish effort to lay a solid legal foundation for those relations– and Foreign Minister Krzysztof Skubiszewski deserved the credit for it. Moreover, negotiations on relevant treaties not only had to be aimed at standard formulas for good-neighbouring and mutual co-operation, but also at solving the real problems: confirmation of the Polish western border, withdrawal of Soviet/Russian troops, and protection of Polish minorities.

Another direction was subregional, and translated into the establishment of new multilateral links. Its goal, as perceived in Poland, involved consolidation of the Central European countries' positions in the new geopolitical situation. Last but not least, there was the European direction i.e., aspirations to move closer–and finally to join–West European integration structures. Paying attention to the whole complexity of all those developments, one could, however, reduce them to one (and only one) behaviour: the search for the protection of freedom of choice in foreign policy vis-à-vis the declining power of the former "big brother," the Soviet Union.

The shadow of the former Polish-Soviet "indissoluble alliance" constituted the major point of reference for most of the post-1989 Polish foreign policy undertakings. The rapprochement between Poland and Germany was to ensure that international treaties based on equal rights and obligations–and *not* support of the Red Army–would guarantee the Polish western border. The collaboration among the Visegrad countries was aimed, in its essence, *against* the former ties with the USSR. Co-operation with the European Community/Union, *rather than* counting on "brother's help", was the desired method of gaining access to the resources for civilizational development. And the search for NATO membership served *to avert* the danger of a renewed Soviet/Russian domination.

In the period before the official liquidation of the USSR, the Polish approach to its eastern neighbour(s) was composed of three elements. As a point of departure, one was the elimination of the ideological factor from mutual relations and its replacement by a policy founded on the Polish raison d'etat and national interests. Next, Poland rejected the Ribbentrop-Molotov pacts of 1939 and stated that they were invalid "from their very inception," and condemned the "Yalta dictate" of 1945. Finally, Poland worked out and adopted the so-called two-track policy, which expressed the Polish response to the independence ambitions of the Soviet republics and was based on the dual desires of maintaining restructured relations with Moscow (the "USSR's centre") and on making efforts to establish and promote relations with the separate republics (Skubiszewski 1993a: 6-7).

The two-track policy had already begun by the Summer of 1990–in the wake of the declaration of sovereignty by Russia, Ukraine and Belarus. During the preparatory work all Polish partners received drafts of the political declarations on good neighbourly relations. After talks with representatives of the central government in Moscow concerning a new *non-satellite* treaty, Foreign Minister Skubiszewski travelled to Kiev where the *Declaration of the Principles and Main Directions of Development of Polish-Ukrainian Relations* was signed. Within a few days, another one was also approved: the *Declaration on Friendship and Co-operation* between Poland and the Russian Federation.[5] The third declaration, that with Belarus, was due to an internal debate on possible territorial claims in this republic and signed only a year later–in October 1991 in Warsaw. After the unsuccessful August coup, Poland, as Skubiszewski described it, "adopted a new approach: that of the East's opening to Europe." As he explained, Poland "worked out and carried into effect a policy of supporting the international and European aspirations of individual nations and their republic beyond [Polish] Eastern borders in a way that would bring their processes of independent government under the rules and mechanisms of the United Nations, the CSCE, and the Council of Europe" (1993a: 8).

The next step was taken when formal liquidation of the USSR took place in December 1991. Poland's eastern policy envisaged the following

---

5. One might mention here that it was the very first inter-state document signed by Russia following its proclamation of sovereignty.

alternative scenarios: continue its two-track approach and treat Russia separately from the other Republics on the assumption that it was successor to the Soviet state; or abandon it for the sake of equal treatment among all republics making up the CIS. With the latter option chosen as early as January 1992, it was suggested to each CIS republic–especially Poland's neighbours–to conclude a set of agreements with a draft proposal of a good neighbourhood treaty at the top of the list. The point, again, was to eliminate from relations with new states the elements of *dependence* characteristic of former relations with the Soviet Union.

There were no problems with such agreements with the Ukraine and Belarus (treaties with Latvia and Estonia were concluded as well). Only the relations with Lithuania have been strained, focusing on the Polish minority rights in that country and different interpretations of recent conflicts between the two nations i.e., in the 1918-1945 period until the beginning of 1994. But the prospects for a major Polish-Russian treaty remained uncertain for several months. From the very beginning, negotiations in this treaty were linked with the question of the Soviet troops in Poland. It was the personal decision of Prime Minister Tadeusz Mazowiecki to put the question on the agenda of talks with the Soviet (Russian) part as early as August-September 1990 (President Wojciech Jaruzelski was not asked for his opinion). Since then, his successor Lech Walesa's visit to Moscow and the signing of the treaty were strictly tied with success of the negotiations on troops withdrawal.

Not until early 1992 did Russia send a signal that it was ready to make some concessions and welcome a visit by President Walesa. During the visit held in May, Walesa and Boris Yeltsin settled the final texts of the documents in unprecedented face-to-face talks. As a result, the fundamental Polish-Russian *Treaty on Friendly and Good Neighbourly Co-operation* was signed along with a package of arrangements concerning the withdrawal of Russian troops,[6] among them the crucial agreement which set the deadlines: 15 November 1992 for combat forces; and 31 December 1993 for auxiliary units.

---

6. Among other things: the so-called zero option–solution of the conflict over financial questions: payment for environmental damage to Polish territory and unpaid bills for supplies vs. the value of installations being left by Russians.

THE EURO-ATLANTIC OPTION

As a result of the inversion in its salient environment and changes in threat perceptions, the main consequence of Poland's turn to the West was the so-called Euro-Atlantic option for its alliance policy. Understood as a "grand strategy" for an independent Poland, the option actually consists of several elements.

## The "Return to Europe" component

Apart from the obvious political and economic reasons, the Euro-Atlantic option assisted in *identity-building* for the Polish regime. The new regime presented its predecessor as the one that had looked eastward and therefore had been alienated from the Polish nation. In contrast, the post-1989 regime demonstratively showed its attachment to Western civilization. Hanna Suchocka (the then Prime Minister) declared: "With its culture and desires, Poland belongs to the West" (1992a: 1). Using another opportunity, she added that Poland aimed at "the family of democratic Western European countries, supported by the trans-Atlantic partnership," and explained: "Not because we need some umbrella, but because we all share the same values and objectives" (1993: 64).

In the further course of events, these axiological motives softened in the benefit of policy rationales. For instance, Krzysztof Skubiszewski was rather pragmatic when he appealed: "...in keeping with our reason of state and our strategic orientation towards Western civilization, in view of a possible dangerous course of evolution over there [in the East–W.K.]," Poland must consolidate its institutional ties with the Western structures, and give priority to its links with the Euro-Atlantic system of security (Skubiszewski 1993c: 136).

## "All forces West!"

The first condition for Poland for practical implementation of the Euro-Atlantic option was the necessity to re-establish relations with its western neighbour and principal "gateway" to Europe, Germany. In this regard, Polish diplomacy made several efforts to ensure that the question of confirmation of the Polish western border would be included on the agenda of international disputes concerning the prospects for the German state(s).

Following successful negotiations on German unification, the conclusion of the Polish-German Border Treaty became possible. The treaty was already signed by November 1990 and also contained a mutual obligation of unreserved respect for sovereignty–the clause that was lacking in People's Poland-RFG treaty from 1970.

As a result of the next round of bargaining–with German minority problems as the topical issue–another major treaty was concluded in June 1991, "On Good Neighbourhood, Friendship and Co-operation." The main sections of the latter treaty covered guarantees for territorial integrity, border inviolability, political independence, economic development and equal minority rights for citizens living in each other's countries. For Poland, the treaty had a special *European* context. It was perceived as a basic link in the whole chain of bilateral agreements aimed at strengthening Polish political and economic security in the transitional period, that is, until Poland would join the European integration structures.

The conclusion of the negotiations and successful development of bilateral relations made room for disclosing a far-reaching Polish aspiration. In October 1992 Hanna Suchocka announced that "Germany today is, first of all, our major ally in the quest for understanding and respecting the Polish interests in European institutions" (Suchocka 1992a: 4).

Another consequence of the post-1989 Polish alliance policy consisted of a new vision of the international role played by the United States. Identified by the previous regime as the primary cause for world disorder and a major source of power politics, the US was now portrayed as a principal guardian of democracy and security. By the same token, the attitude presented by the US was perceived as the "last instance" guarantee of Polish autonomy. Therefore, Poland formally declared its support for the United States' instrumental approach to the North Atlantic Treaty Organization.

In this concept, the preservation of NATO was to permit and legitimize the continued participation of the US in European affairs. This goal found its strongest confirmation in the above mentioned *Guidelines of the Polish Security Policy*, which stated: "Recognising that NATO remains a decisive factor of political stability and peace in Europe, Poland highly appreciates the Euro-Atlantic character of the alliance and supports the United States' military presence in Europe" (*Materials and Documents* [1] 1992: 16).

One can notice that such a formulation bears resemblance to ideas contained in the document entitled "Defense Planning Guidance in Fiscal

Year 1994-1999" prepared in consultation with the President by Washington officials in Spring 1992. The relevant fragment reads: "It is of fundamental importance to preserve NATO as the primary instrument of Western defence and security, as well as *the channel for US influence and participation in European security affairs"* (quoted after Petras & Vieux 1992: 14, emphasis added).

The subordination of all security policy undertakings to the principal West European strategy also constituted the main conceptual assumption of Polish eastern policy. The idea was based on the growing understanding that one of the conditions for successful Polish integration with Western structures was proper arrangement of the relationship with Russia. Thus, in the face of the recurrent public critique that Poland had not at all a deliberated and far-sighted eastern policy, Minister Skubiszewski responded: "The establishment of relations with the neighbours in the East is an integral part of our European policies with all the special ramifications of these relations" (Skubiszewski 1993a: 5). One of his officials was more precise: "Making our eastern policy we are guided by the chief directions of Polish foreign policy. And so, the main priority of this policy is integration with Western structures" (Jakub Wolasiewicz's opinion expressed in *Polska w Europie* [9] 1992: 73).

One more consequence of Poland's drift to the West was constituted by its positional changes inside the framework of the CFE treaty. For Poland, there was of course no doubt that the treaty, which had been initiated in the period of the East-West rivalry, later operated in a transformed international environment; therefore, proposals that concerned its modernisation were fully justified. However, the re-establishing of an equilibrium acceptable for all i.e, NATO members, Russia and NATO would-be members (do not mention the Ukraine security needs) could be done in different ways. In particular, one could imagine both increase of forces on the Russian side–to balance NATO and NATO would-be members potential–or alternatively, decrease of forces on the NATO side– to eliminate the preponderance gained after the dissolution of the Warsaw Pact. In practice, the Russian approach to the coming NATO enlargement, with unwillingness of some states like Poland or Germany to accept lowering of their national limits, brought in the former option on the agenda.

Therefore, one could expect that in the course of negotiations starting in 1996, Poland would demand the following: first, the establishment of a new concept of conventional arms control in Europe on the non-offensive defence principle i.e., in limitation of the number, structure and deployment of military forces levels which would not arouse feelings of threat among other states; second, on the basis of recognised security interests of a given state by other signatories–and not in the framework of a group context (NATO/"Europe" *versus* Russia)–a definition of the ceilings concerning a country's volume of arms; and third, maintenance and even broadening in the CFE treaty of additional zone limits (geographical) concerning the volume of arms, preventing too high a concentration of military forces in some geographical regions. This proposal gained particular gravity because of Russia's warnings that it would consider strengthening its military presence in the Kaliningrad region in the event of NATO's enlargement.[7]

### *The "end of banishment" syndrome*

The "Go West" attitudes described above reveal the core of the first phase of the debates taking place in Poland both on East-Central European security in general, and on Polish specific concerns. The main issue, which emerged during these discussions, referred to the strategies needed for establishment of mature arrangements for Polish security. Here the specific "end of banishment" syndrome influenced the Polish alliance policy to a great extent. The syndrome was reflected in the behaviour: "Leave every Eastern institution, join every Western one" (Keohane, Nye & Hoffmann 1993: 173-195, 342-380; Blank and Young 1992).

It is true that in the beginning *subregional* collaboration was perceived with great approval by the new Polish regime. The old ideas of Central European rapprochement or even integration were voiced with enthusiasm. In the early 1990s after the revolution and changeover of political regimes, Poland, Czechoslovakia and Hungary found themselves in similar circumstances: they were *against* former ties with the Soviet Union and *for* close relations with, and future membership of, the West European institutions. Co-operation among them seemed to be a natural and logical way of responding to the problems they were facing. The question of the dissolution of the CMEA and the WTO was first on the list of priorities.

---

7. Moreover, it has been noted in Poland that the region could become even a base for the nuclear weapons. Such a threat appeared in various statements made by Russian politicians and military in 1996 and–according to Western press–in recommendations prepared by Yeltsin's advisers (see Biuletyn 1996b: 22).

Soviet pressure for the inclusion of security commitments into the new friendship and co-operation treaties under negotiation with Poland, Czechoslovakia and Hungary was the most important issue. Next, association agreements with the EC, and treaties with Germany were the subjects of consultations.

But soon most of the premises for such co-operation disappeared and the existence of many obstacles became clear. First, the institutional links with Moscow, symbolized by the WTO and the CMEA, were broken and the process of withdrawal of Soviet/Russian troops was put in motion. Second, the social attitudes in all three countries were full of stereotypes. Third, the real premises of economic collaboration appeared rather weak, despite the introduction of a free trade zone.[8] Fourth (and of great significance) were differences in the importance attached to the possible Central European co-operation by particular states. For Poland, it was first of all the search for change of its geopolitical position; Czechoslovakia and Hungary counted on a much easier and faster "return to Europe" than in Poland's case. In sum, signs of competition and a "race" to the Western institutions occurred.

At the same time, the Polish desire to become a member of the West European structures grew. The first public declarations of Polish regime representatives regarding the intention to join the Western economic structures were made as early as in 1989. The "shock" reforms that were introduced by Leszek Balcerowicz (Deputy Prime Minister) since the beginning of 1990 authenticated the declarations. Formal negotiations on an association with the EC started in December of that year. Finally, the agreement establishing the association of Poland and the European Community (the so-called Europe Agreement) was signed in Brussels on 16 December 1991. The part of the agreement regarding trade arrangements became operative on 1 March 1992; the whole agreement came into force only by 1 February 1994–with delay caused by protraction of the ratification procedures in the majority of parliaments of the Community member states. Two months later, Poland submitted its formal application for full membership.

---

8. The Central European Free Trade Agreement (CEFTA) was signed in Polish town of Cracow, by the Ministers of Foreign Economic Relations from Poland, Hungary, the Czech Republic, and the Slovak Republic on 21 December 1992. Duty free exchange started on 1 March 1993.

The Polish aspirations sprang from the conviction that the community constituted the most effective response to the challenges of the future: medium-sized nations in terms of area, population, natural resources and armed forces–like Poland–do not have the capabilities to face up political, economic, social and environmental challenges of the 21st century. That is why the Polish motivation behind the ambition to join the EC had a rather *complex* character, including not only material well-being, economic and social growth, "but likewise and above all with the preservation and radiance of our national and state existence" (Skubiszewski 1993b: 67).

The above declaration confirmed that, in fact, the issue of the comprehensiveness of Polish security was at stake. But the subsequent course of events was far from Polish expectations. The decisions made by the Copenhagen Summit of the EU in June 1993 raised serious doubts. It is true that in Copenhagen, the member-states expressed their readiness to admit into the Union the associated countries from East-Central Europe. But the formulation of the conditions to be met by countries wishing access–especially "the capacity to cope with competitive pressure and market forces within the Union," and "the ability to take on the obligations of membership, including adherence to the aims of political, economic and monetary union" (Royal Danish Embassy 1993)–offered rather limited prospect for *full* membership in the *near* future. And pointing at the Union's capability for further enlargement–which has not been proved to be without its own difficulties–as another indispensable condition, made the fulfilment of Polish aspirations even more uncertain.

The subsequent developments were not especially encouraging, either. Of course, it is undeniable that some progress has been achieved. For instance, the Polish government decided in 1994 that all projects of the new regulations had to be in accordance with the rules adopted by the European Union (Resolution 1994). By this Poland anticipated the next move of the Union, namely, publication of the so-called "White Papers" in 1995 indicating the necessary changes in legal and administrative structures, which Poland–as well as other East-Central European states–had still to introduce. In the Autumn of 1996 the Polish side announced that about 400–or 50 per cent–of the EU's recommendations were already implemented.

At the same time, neither a detailed schedule nor even a clear concept for the further accession process was worked out. Despite the adoption of the document titled "Strategy for Preparing the Associated Central and Eastern European Countries for Future Accession to the EU" by the Essen

Summit in 1994, there were, in fact, no recommendations concerning steps towards full membership (Altmann 1996: 247). Three years later it was still to be decided how the EU would arrange its decision-making procedures, and implement its common agriculture and regional policies if it consisted of not 15, as today, but some 25 members. It was obvious, then, that the chances for Polish accession depended on the success of the EU's Intergovernmental Conference that started in March 1996 (von Ow 1995: 251-262).

The first step in this direction has been made during the meeting of the EU members and its associated partners in December 1996. The associated states were informed that the Union obliged itself to start negotiations on accession six months after the "successful conclusion" of the Intergovernmental Conference. "The Union will keep the time-table"– the Polish Prime Minister Cimoszewicz had no doubt after the meeting (*Gazeta Wyborcza* 16 December 1996). In June 1997, after approving the so-called Amsterdam Treaty, the leaders of the EU member states confirmed their promise, and a month later Poland was named an "almost certain" candidate to be invited to begin the negotiation process (*Gazeta Wyborcza* 8 July 1997).

However, a public report prepared by the Bertelsmann Foundation warned that "none of these states [of Central and Eastern Europe–W.K.] has fully met the necessary economic and legal requirements for EU membership" (Weidenfeld 1996: 7). Among the countries that noted several failures in their preparation to the Union's membership, Poland was criticised for its internal power struggle, delay in economic reform and obscuring the process of transformation by the network of old *nomenclatura* and new interest groups. Nevertheless, concluded the authors, under certain conditions Poland may enter the European Union by the beginning of the 21st century (Bingen, Czachór & Machowski 1996: 155-76).

The same assumption constituted the core of the "National Strategy for Integration," a document that had been asked for by the Polish Parliament in March 1996 and approved by the government in January 1997. It covered both general programmes of integration, and all three pillars of the European Union: economy,[9] common foreign and security policy, and

---

9. The public declarations of that time, made for instance by President Aleksander Kwasniewski, pointed to the most ambitious goal: Poland's wish to join also the European Monetary Union.

justice and home affairs. Furthermore, it also took into account requests for adaptation periods and temporary exclusions made by particular ministries (in fact, even some interest groups and lobbies). The *Strategy* addressed the concerns of the Polish society which, according to a variety of opinion polls, supported integration with the EU by a clear majority of 75-85 per cent but simultaneously expressed certain reservations.[10] These centred around: threats for agriculture and other weak sectors of the Polish economy–voiced mainly by the peasants' party; expansion of foreign cultural patterns–by the Roman-Catholic Church[11] (among others); and risk of "invasion" by Western capital, subsequently to be followed by political influence–by different groupings of nationalists.

Such fears, desired not to hurt any of the possible allies, contributed to Poland's approach towards the EU's dilemmas of "different speed," "concentric circles" and the like. The well-phrased formula, "Neither a loose free-trade zone nor an artificial European super-state should be the ultimate objective [of the pan-European integration – WK]," explained the most recent Polish position (Kwasniewski 1996a: 1295).

## Poland on the verge of NATO membership

Contrary to the quest for EC/EU membership which appeared at the very early stage of the Polish transformation, there were no public declarations by representatives of the new regime regarding the will to gain access to NATO until the Soviet's unsuccessful coup and disintegration in 1991. On the contrary, the quite sophisticated and far-looking concept of the "all-European security system" was elaborated. Consequently in his address to the parliamentary session of the North Atlantic Assembly in November 1990, Minister Skubiszewski saw no rivalry between NATO and the establishment of a security system in the framework of CSCE. Paying a visit to Brussels in July 1991, President Walesa announced that although political and military co-operation with the Atlantic Alliance was desired, Poland would not immediately seek to join NATO, and underlined the

---

10. At the beginning of 1997 even 88 per cent, but asked whether they would vote for the membership if a referendum is held, 62 per cent say "yes", 9 per cent–"no"; the rest do not know their own mind (see *Gazeta Wyborcza* 14 February 1997).

11. For instance, the representatives of the Church warned against the danger of lost of essential part of the Polish independence, namely: "the spiritual potential" (see *Gazeta Wyborcza* 16 August 1995).

importance of the CSCE process for the security of all of Europe. Even in the Autumn of 1992 Skubiszewski presented the Polish security concept as "a many-tier structure of institutional solutions that supplement each other" (Skubiszewski 1992b: 13ff.)

Moreover, the Soviet (and then Russian) pressure to keep the NATO political and military machinery as far away as possible brought about temporary softening of the Polish approach. Ironically, the most cautious position was taken by Defence Minister Janusz Onyszkiewicz. Using an informal forum, he considered a settlement by compromise, and had in mind an official declaration that Poland would not conduct a policy which could create a base for aggression on any country whatsoever (Janusz Onyszkiewicz's opinion in *Polska w Europie* [6] 1991: 48). He was also persuasive that the Polish need for NATO guarantees had to be understood as a Polish fear of great risks rather than of local conflicts, since it would not be to the Alliance's advantage to have a partner which would be unable to cope with minor instabilities. But any argument about great risks was at the same time contradictory to the Polish efforts to establish good neighbourly relations with other states (Onyszkiewicz 1992: 33-34; also his opinion expressed in *Polska w Europie* [9] 1992: 48). Lech Walesa suggested the re-establishment of a subregional security system in Eastern Europe. During an official visit to Germany in 1992 he presented a concept of "NATO-b"–a transitional organisation of states seeking Atlantic Alliance membership–endowed with joint military forces capable of counteracting local conflicts. And Hanna Suchocka warned that Polish association with NATO could not by any means replace safe relations with its neighbours (Suchocka 1992a: 4).

On the other hand, despite all dissimilarities, the very idea of rapprochement between Poland and NATO was not questioned. The association with (and ultimately membership of) NATO was perceived in three perspectives. The first referred to the assumption that NATO was the only existing structure in post-Cold War Europe that could guarantee security and stability to its members (Stefanowicz 1996). From the Polish point of view, NATO was capable of both providing the necessary means for national defence and could serve as a crisis-management tool.

The second perspective consisted in a kind of test of the real meaning of autonomy in Polish foreign policy. The intent to attain rapprochement with NATO and later to achieve membership was confronted by efforts from the Soviet Union/Russia to maintain its sphere of influence in East-Central Europe. From the very beginning, the question of Soviet/Russian recognition of Polish sovereign right to choose its allies became the inseparable thread of the diplomatic negotiations and political relations of the two states. At the same time, the moderate approach of Western countries towards NATO enlargement in the benefit of relations with Russia was understood as a warning against a renewed power politics and disrespect for Polish interests.

The third aspect was related to the above-mentioned change in Polish amity-enmity patterns. In the new circumstances Skubiszewski announced (1992a): "We count upon NATO co-operation and assistance in solving specific political, military, civil defence, economic and other problems." Furthermore, "Poland's membership in NATO would, thus, be the final confirmation of the irreversible nature of our country's incorporation in the system of Western states"–argued a leading expert in Ministry for Foreign Affairs (Kuzniar 1993:19).

Moreover, Russian pressure impacted the end of the hesitation of the Polish left-wing parties (which won the general elections in September 1993). While in opposition, they expressed several reservations concerning the Polish drift towards NATO. In particular, their representatives noticed that before joining the Atlantic Alliance, Poland should put its relations with Russia in order, and that some reforms of the Alliance were desired. But returning to power they issued a document stating: "Looking for credible guarantees of security we declare the will to join NATO as soon as possible" (*Gazeta Wyborcza* 11 October 1993). The declaration also constituted a response to the events taking place in Polish-Russian relations in the second half of 1993.

In August of that year, President Yeltsin came to Warsaw and signed the "Joint Polish-Russian Declaration." A crucial point of the declaration read: "The Presidents discussed the issue of Poland's intention to accede to NATO. President Lech Walesa explained Poland's well-known position on the issue, which was received with understanding by President Boris Yeltsin." But in exactly the next sentence the passage was more cautious: *"In perspective, a decision of this kind by sovereign Poland aiming at pan-European integration* is not contrary to the interest of other states, including also Russia" (*Materials and Documents* 2 [7-8] 1993: 210-211, emphasis added). The latter indicated that, in fact, the Russian side had in mind more comprehensive security arrangements than unqualified NATO expansion eastward. This was confirmed by later occurrences. In October Boris Yeltsin–in a special letter to several Western governments–stressed Russian concerns over developments leading to the eventual enlargement of the Atlantic Alliance, even if this enlarged Alliance would "not be antagonistic" towards Russia. Instead, Yeltsin proposed closer co-operation between Russia and the Alliance.

Subsequently, Poland did not hesitate long: in February 1994 it accepted a "Partnership for Peace" programme originally announced by the USA in October 1993–despite initially criticising it for having too low a profile. A month earlier, announcements about opening NATO to new countries were included in the Brussels Declaration, and President Clinton stated: "The question is no longer whether NATO will take on new members, but when and how" (International 1994). Since that time, Poland has been following the established pattern and waiting for the answer, namely: urging the West to rid itself of its caution and persuade Russia that it should not be afraid. In April 1996 Poland delivered the so-called Individual Discussion Paper, expressing the Polish desire to soon become a full member of NATO. The document also presented the steps previously taken by Poland in the political-military domain, such as: reform of the Ministry of Defence and plans for the restructuring of the Polish army in a view of future co-operation with NATO units.

Simultaneously, NATO has focused on developing a conceptual framework rather than practical moves–the activity that has found its most extensive expression in the document entitled *Study on NATO Enlargement* (NATO 1995). Particularly noteworthy, this approach for a long time has been accompanied by a lack of political groundwork for ratification procedure in NATO member states' parliaments, although the parallel study concerning parliamentary support for enlargement demonstrated a rather mild interest by some countries (Solomon 1995). Only recently has the interest for investigating the state of affairs in this domain grown (*NATO Review* 45 (1) 1995).

In 1996, the situation became clearer, though not fully satisfactory. Strong declarations by prominent NATO politicians appeared: "NATO enlargement will happen" (Solana 1996]); and by Western leaders: "In 1997, the process of Polish accession to NATO must become irreversible" (French president Jacques Chirac in Warsaw, quoted in *Gazeta Wyborcza* 13 September 1996). In several instances Poland was mentioned among the states that would be first to begin negotiations with. There were also signs of a path to a NATO-Russia agreement based on non-deployment of NATO's nuclear weapons and troops on the territories of Poland and other new members (e.g., Karsten Voigt, Warsaw, in *Gazeta Wyborcza* 31 May 1996). Finally, in December 1996 the foreign ministers of NATO recommended "to invite at next year's Summit meeting one or more countries which have participated in the intensified dialogue process, to start accession negotiations with the Alliance." They also announced: "Our goal is to welcome the new member(s) by the time of NATO's 50th anniversary in 1999" (*Ministerial Meeting of the North Atlantic Counsil* 1996).

But the most puzzling questions in Poland – "Will we be the first?" and "Can we really be sure?"–remained without an answer by the middle of 1997. During this period Polish anxiety was fanned by several games over NATO's enlargement including the French initiative of a five powers' summit meeting to set the conditions of enlargement; and different interpretations of settlements achieved by Clinton and Yeltsin in Helsinki (March 1997) and subsequent NATO-Russia Founding Act (May 1997). Threats made by Turkey that it would block NATO enlargement until the EU would accept its full membership, or the Italian approach of "Russia first" also contributed to Polish fears. It is obvious, then, that the decision made by Madrid Summit (8-9 July 1997)–the official invitation for Poland, the Czech Republic and Hungary to begin the negotiations–was welcomed in Warsaw with a relief.

It should be noted, however, that the fears mentioned above can be justified by a popular perception of the Western approach as a "waiting room strategy." It assumes: first, that Poland must have a prospect of an entrance to the Western structures in order to preserve an instrument of controlling Polish behaviour; second, that the final goal–membership with full rights–has to be successively moved away because its political, economical and military costs are in fact unacceptable. This is the reason why some doubts still exist over whether the process of negotiation and ratification, even when put in motion, can lead to a successful end.

At the same time, the Polish policy towards NATO enjoyed strong support from the public. At the beginning of 1997, 90 per cent of Poles proclaimed themselves in favour of NATO membership. However, only 45 per cent opted for entrance "as soon as possible" (*Gazeta Wyborcza* 14 February 1997). The results of polls in 1996 explained this divergence: more than half of the respondents preferred delay of entrance until the country's economic situation had improved while only one fourth of NATO's advocates were willing to pay money for membership (*Gazeta Wyborcza* 16 July 1996).

Thus, it was not a surprise that the most vigorous part of the public debate over joining NATO concerned the costs of membership. One should note, however, that this was a rather strange exercise. While in 1995 estimates by the Polish Ministry of Defence for money spent by 2010 ran into figures of 40-75 billion US dollars (Wieczorek & Zukrowska *forthcoming*), experts of the nongovernmental body, the Euro-Atlantic Association in the beginning of 1997 trimmed this amount to 1.5 billion! (*Gazeta Wyborcza* 21 January 1997). Different options taken into account ("complete equipment" *versus* minimal modernization) seem to be a partial explanation for this revised projection (Firlej 1996), while the political need to calm the public opinion also matters.

## HISTORICAL LESSONS FOR THE PRESENT

For a long timeframe, historical experience has exerted a major influence on Polish security policy (Karkoszka 1993: 89ff). The following section outlines motives of a Polish behaviour derived from the past and briefly elaborates on lessons that Poland drew from its history and which are important for the present, among them: *great sensitivity regarding sovereignty issues and equality of states' rights; the necessity of searching for political alliances; multilateral guarantees of security and comprehensive solutions; and the need to make the most of its geopolitical position–assuming it was not possible to change it* (cf. chapter 1).

Poland's geopolitical position always caused its relationships with Germany and Russia to be the most important factors in its politics. During the whole historical development Poland had to resist Germany's expansion eastward, the so-called *Drang nach Osten*. At the same time on the eastern border, Poland had to cope with Russian expansion westwards. In this context, the Polish political thinking was always based on an approach to two main neighbours. The question of which one was perceived as an enemy and which one as an ally defined the basic assumptions of Polish foreign policy. As a result, Polish attitudes toward other states were shaped in principle by its relations with Germany and Russia. Such a situation also existed in the twenty years of Poland's independence following World War I.

When the Second Polish Republic was born in 1918, there were three main political orientations: the federalists wanted to link all nations of old Poland into one powerful structure based on Jagiellonian ideas which, by their very essence, were hostile to Russia/the Soviet Union; the incorporationists fought for a single nation state whereby Germany was–

and would remain–the dominant Polish enemy; and the communists waited for a "world revolution" to solve all national and foreign policy problems.

In the early 1920s the international situation of Poland was rather favourable. The German threat was reduced by French-German confrontation and the Riga Treaty (1921) ensured peace on the eastern border. However, the concept of "two enemies" was supported by all political groupings (except communists of course). Several political alliances were proposed to secure Poland against both Germany and the USSR, and the concept of building a bloc of states between the Baltic and Black Seas was introduced.

Changes in European political relations marked by The League of Nations activity, the Soviet-German Treaty at Rapallo (1922) and Locarno Agreements (1925) resulted in the fall of the latter concept. Former federalists were looking towards The League of Nations as they hoped for co-operation with England and an aim towards an anti-Soviet direction. Former incorporationists criticised the politics symbolised by Geneva, Rapallo and Locarno as based on "paper guarantees" and, therefore, did not trust disarmament and pacifist slogans, nonetheless they were against any form of collaboration with the USSR as well.

With Hitler's accession to power and the subsequent successes of Nazism in Germany, the situation changed again. Under the new circumstances, the two most influential groupings, the "sanacja" (Pilsudski's[12] followers after 1926) and "endecja" (National Democratic Party) stood for "balanced" politics i.e., politics that maintained an equal distance from Germany and the Soviet Union. As a consequence, Poland concluded two non-aggression treaties: with the Soviet Union in 1932; and with Germany in 1934. In practice, however, signs of rapprochement with Berlin became visible. Only in the face of approaching German aggression did all groups unite efforts and proclaim themselves against any concession.

---

12. Józef Pilsudski (1867-1935), active member of the Polish independence movement, 1919-22 Head of State in the reborn Poland, since 1920 Marshal of Poland, supported ideas of a Polish-Ukrainian-Belorussian federation. In 1923 Pilsudski withdrew from political life, three years later he made a coup d'état and limited rights of the parliament for the benefit of the executive body. After that he, in fact, held power in Poland.

The People's Poland[13] which emerged after World War II could then be interpreted as an historical experiment and an attempt to escape from the focal point of traditional German-Russian competition by strict alliance with one of the rivals, the Soviet Union.[14] This experiment failed *doubly*: firstly, the very alliance as well as the People's Poland itself ceased to exist; and secondly, contrary to initial expectations, the alliance contributed enormously to Polish animosity towards the Soviets.

The main confirmation of the latter phenomenon was constituted by a dramatic feeling that large segments of Polish society experienced for 45 years. The feeling was expressed after the 1989 changes by Hanna Suchocka in the following words: "A few years ago [...] as each and every Pole, like the whole of our society, I was still living on the other side of the Yalta Wall which had torn my homeland away from the mainstream of modern civilisation and had doomed it to a life of anticivilisation, misery and backwardness" (Suchocka 1992b: 6).

Based on a legacy that associates all harms and misfortunes of the Polish nation with the lack of autonomy and intrusions of foreign powers, the first historical lesson has been formulated: the critical value of the state's *sovereignty*.

What it means today has been best manifested in the problem of stationing Soviet troops in Poland. The Poles perceived the troops' presence as symbolic, but still a best evidence of the lack of state sovereignty. Correspondingly, for Poland the solution to this problem meant a necessary precondition for conclusion of the new Polish-Russian treaty on co-operation (Nowakowski 1993: 9). Back in December 1990, Polish negotiators facing difficulties and looking for means of pressure even decided against letting Russian armies from former East Germany pass through Polish territory unless the Russians soldiers had first been evacuated from Polish soil–a move which, in itself, implied the elimination of a valuable source of income for the country as well as risk of German dissatisfaction.

Poland's tough position during the negotiations reconfirmed the present-day sensitiveness and primary significance bound to the concept of

---

13. People's Poland–the shorter form of official name "People's Republic of Poland," wrote down in the communist constitution of 1952. In December 1989 it was changed back to the "Republic of Poland" by the parliament.
14. I leave aside the question how such an alliance was imposed on Poland and whether there were other options available.

sovereignty. However, in the perception of the new political elites, it took on several components. One was related to the country's communist past. It treated sovereignty as a rather dogmatic idea and did not mention the limitation of freedom of action as an inseparable attribute of modern politics; and served as an illustration of fundamental differences between the old and the new regime. Another component dealt with the present. It was much more flexible and consisted of an acknowledgement of the different levels (or aspects) of sovereignty. This was, first of all, evident in the new regime's approach to European integration and the resulting limitation of member-states' autonomy it caused.

But the most important component of the Polish concept of sovereignty was the one which referred to the fear of a revival of "power politics" in Europe i.e., new foreign domination over Poland. It was expressed in the demands concerning *equality*. After the changes in 1989, they became quite a motivational factor for a large part of Polish behaviour.

For example, this can be seen in the essence of a proposal made in early 1990s by the Polish delegation to the plenary meeting of the Special Committee of the Forum for Security Co-operation (the CSCE body) concerning the right to belong or not belong to international organisations, and whether to be or not be party to bilateral or multilateral treaties, including treaties of alliance. "Appropriate arrangements by them or among them will be concluded only on the basis of the principle of sovereign equality" (*Materials and Documents* [1] 1992: 21). This is also why in 1993 the Polish side immediately rejected President Yeltsin's proposition of common "security guarantees" that could be offered to the new democracies of Central and Eastern Europe by NATO and Moscow together (Atlantic 1993: 3). The anxiety regarding a repeated great powers' conspiracy acting over the heads of Poles was so great that even the left-wing parties–in pointing to the "bad experience of history"–declared themselves against this idea (*Gazeta Wyborcza* 11 October 1993). Another experience, the Russian post-World War II security guarantees offered to (in fact imposed on) Poland–which ultimately led to Russian dominance–made no room for acceptance of such an idea in the foreseeable future.

However, three years later the suggestion of Russian and NATO's "cross-guarantees" for Poland–instead of full membership in NATO–remained on the Russian agenda. They were mentioned by Foreign Minister Yevgenii Primakow during his March 1996 visit to Poland, though he was not able to raise this matter in the framework of official talks. This was mainly because at that time the Polish sensitiveness to any possible limitation of sovereignty had been seriously hurt by the issue of a "corridor" between Belarus and Kaliningrad District (cf. fig. 1.1).

In fact, the concept of a transport corridor and special facilities for Russian transit via Polish territory appeared already by 1993. But the issue became a matter of high politics in February 1996 when Yeltsin stated that he and the president of Belarus would seek a Polish accord for the building of "a small bit of motorway" on the Polish territory. This idea was loudly and unanimously opposed by Polish politicians. President Kwasniewski explained: "We will not accept such a solution since our history has demonstrated that it never brings good results" [interview for *Kaliningradskaja Prawda,* quoted after Biuletyn 1996a: 6]. What he apparently had in mind was the conviction that any concept of a "corridor" put forward by an external power would be felt in Poland as an infringement of its independence. Once again, the lesson of history was the reason, namely, associations with the inter-war periods and problems with German demands for an exterritorial corridor to Eastern Prussia.

Poland's aspirations in equality for *all* states has been so strong that in 1996 Prime Minister Cimoszewicz even objected to Western intentions of concluding a NATO-Russia treaty before NATO's opening to Central Europe since, this would "in practical terms mean acceptance of special rights for Russia" (Materials and Documents 5 [10] 1996: 1282). Such an attitude has appeared unforeseeing in light of the further course of events, but then he obviously copied the Russian position: "We know that we have no veto right but we are definitely against...." The Polish opposition to the 1997 French initiative aimed at establishing a new "concert" consisting of the US, France, Germany, Great Britain and Russia, which would decide on the all-European security issues, was also in line with the reasoning mentioned above.

In 1989 Poland faced a "super-challenge": both the possibility and the necessity to completely rearrange its foreign relations (Olechowski 1994). The response to this challenge consisted of three components.

Memories of bilateral treaties from the 1930s which only postponed (joint!) German and Russian aggression constituted the first. This was one more historical confirmation that Poland alone was capable of opposing neither German nor Russian might (the less so if the two acted in common). Therefore, the lesson Poland received was the necessity of searching for political *alliances.* The second component was of a similar nature: what Poland also had to keep in mind was a recollection of the failure of the then alliances with Great Britain and France. Despite the guarantees received from London and Paris, Poland had to fight in 1939 without any real assistance from its allies. Moreover, it signified that Poland was not able to organise security by itself. Here the lesson reads: bilateral arrangements are worthless and must be replaced by *multilateral guarantees* of security. The third component related to the growing awareness of the role of the country's own strength: a weak Poland could hardly expect to be granted any real guarantees in the framework of any multilateral arrangements. Therefore, the necessity to look for *comprehensive solutions* to add to its own capabilities was the next lesson.

In sum, integration into a complex of West European institutions has become viewed as the only reliable option for ensuring Polish security in the 1990s (Spero 1992; Stefanowicz 1995). However, in the beginning the anti-Soviet heritage prevented Poland from drawing another conclusion: these institutions must not isolate Russia and repeat what happened in the inter-war period. This approach changed in parallel to the evolution of relations between the West and Russia. Facing a clear Western design to have Russia become involved in solving all-European security questions, Polish representatives again began pointing at the complexity of a new security system for Europe. It was stressed, for instance, that such a system should "consist of a number of separable but not separate elements" (Kwasniewski 1996b: 1313). Moreover, Poland asked for and obtained a chairmanship of the OSCE in 1998–just in time for its expected entering into NATO. Thus, Poland declared its commitment to solutions where Russia already was a part–and not only to the political-military alliance, NATO, to which Russia was an opponent.

With the end of the "socialist empire" great new opportunities arose for the materialisation of one of Poland's main political ideas since the end of the 18th century–as well as for drawing a conclusion from one more major historical lesson: the idea of *reversing the unenviable geopolitical position* between powers of the East and the West, and ensuring that this position is to Poland's advantage. This issue was a key problem among many debates for the new Polish elites. One could hear that for many years in the past Poland's place in Europe had been a "forefront of Christianity." In the changed geopolitical situation Poland could either become a "forefront" of the integrated and stable West, which meant the risk of turning into the periphery, or a real "bridge" or "shop-window" to the East, making an input to the regional stabilisation and development (Garnett 1996).

However, the full understanding of what this lesson means today, prompts not only an East-West dimension in political thinking, but also calls for a deepening of subregional co-operation. In the early 1990s, the relative lack of success in this respect resulted from the fact that initially, the collaboration with Czechoslovakia and Hungary was seen as a tool for dismantling the communist system and breaking off the old "chains" to the Soviet Union. Only later, the leitmotif of the easier road to European integration was stressed. Polish diplomacy in the West received an order to create a vision of Poland as being a crucial element for Central European arrangements as well as a stabilising factor for relations in the subregion. Such a vision was seen as enabling the fulfilment of a role as an influential subregional power. And in facing the possibility for obtaining an invitation to Western structures, the Polish politicians (together with the Czech and Hungarian leaders) declared the will of mutual support on the road to NATO and the EU.

In addition, Polish interest in the Baltic Sea region grew as the existence for large potential bilateral and multilateral undertakings was admitted (Ognik 1996). This was particularly true when such undertakings were to prepare for, and confirm the ability for, co-operation with the EU and NATO member states. In this respect, Poland especially welcomed the shift in Lithuanian policy and its declarations concerning counting on Polish advocacy. On the other hand, the Polish experience was perceived as an example to follow for the Baltic States on their "road to Europe" (Bleiere 1996).

The possible conflicts of interests there were settled in accord with the basic assumption: do not harm the process of rapprochement to Western Europe. For instance, the role of the minority question in Polish-Lithuanian relations confirmed this attitude as certain bilateral problems did not appear on the agenda so as not to disturb Poland's road to Europe. The Polish approach to the Council of the Baltic Sea States revealed the tendency to institutionalise regional co-operation in the security domain. And the progress achieved in the joint military enterprises, especially those which were undertaken together with Germany, Denmark, and other Nordic countries, and Lithuania, confirmed Poland's desire to improve the co-operative dimension of its military relations.

## SCENARIOS FOR THE UPCOMING DECADE

The historical lesson Poland endured, together with the inversion in the Polish salient environment, prompt a slight rethinking in the Polish case of the assumptions of scenario analysis.

First of all, it is clear that the alternative developments in Russia should be examined more from the external outcomes' rather than internal characteristics' point of view. The status quo-revisionist dichotomy reflects such a perspective, indeed; nevertheless, it is a "weak" or "strong" Russian state that also matters (Kostecki 1996: 151-163). A weak (or rather weakened) Russia appears as a single unit in security constellations. It still yearns for (re)gaining a global power status, but having no other means at its disposal, it employs a "balance-of-power" policy to realize this strategy. A strong (or strengthened) Russia fulfils the function of the "core" within the CIS and aspires–like a "united Europe"–to the role of a pole in the international system. In this variant Russia exercises its strategy of attaining global power status through means of integration policy and attempts to re-create its external empire.

Second, the continuation of the status quo in the Western dimension is not relevant in the Polish case. Moreover, the recent course of events indicates that Poland will enter NATO before joining the EU. Even if the country achieves only the preparatory or "political" stages of membership,[15] it will nonetheless indicate the end of the status quo as established by the termination of the Cold War.

This is why the "matrix" of a scenario analysis for Poland looks as follows:

---

15. That is, when the decision concerning enlargement of NATO is already made and negotiations succeed but amendments to the Washington Treaty not yet ratified, or the formal time schedule for adjustment to the EU requirements is set but the process has not been concluded.

**Fig. 8.1: The Relevant Environment Scenarios for Poland**

| West Enlargement | Russia Status Quo Orientation | Revisionist Orientation |
|---|---|---|
| Polish NATO Membership | Hard security | Poland exposed |
| Polish NATO + EU Membership | Comprehensive security | Troubles for Poland? |

*Poland enjoys hard security*

This is a situation where integration processes in Europe get an essential impetus. NATO membership is granted to Poland as well as to at least some other Central European states. By this, the so-called European security architecture is being based on a single pillar: the political-military alliance. This is hardly seen as a positive development in Moscow, even if a NATO-Russia treaty has been concluded. However, a weak Russia has no means to prevent enlargement of NATO. In the worst case it could go back to the countermeasures announced previously, among them deploy additional troops close to the Polish border and aim nuclear missiles at Polish targets. Nevertheless, as the country obtains the Atlantic Treaty security guarantees, these countermeasures do not constitute a significant threat to Poland.

In a middle term perspective of ten years (as assumed in this analysis), this situation means setting the most favourable balance between the goals achieved and the resources allocated. Poland adds to its own capability crucially: it receives political and military deterrence, confirmation that is a real subject of international politics, and access to the major civilisational circle. At the same time, it pays a considerably low price: it only has to adjust to the demands of one–not two–Western structures. Though the main effort is of course focused on NATO, some patterns of adaptations to the EU–in view of the still desired membership–are also present. The economic costs of modernisation of the army and the assuming of new military responsibilities are reduced because of a weaker threat from the East. Finally, the social and political costs are acceptable for the same reason.

One should be aware, however, that the situation described above also triggers certain processes in Russia. As a party who lost the game (over NATO expansion), it inevitably feels confused and dissatisfied, despite its status quo orientation. This means that as a member of NATO and a neighbour of a weakened, less assertive Russia, Poland enjoys hard security. But the question is: For how long?

### Poland enjoys comprehensive security

Here one deals with the success of European integration along with the declining power of Russia. The European Union effectively accomplishes the objectives drafted in the Maastricht project (and re-drafted during the Intergovernmental Conference 1996-97). A common strategy has been worked out concerning the extension of the EU to the states of East-Central Europe. This strategy has been accepted by all interested parties–including countries wishing to accede–and has now been fruitfully applied. The reformed EU has found the sources for financing the admission of new members. The relations between the EU, the WEU and NATO–as well as with the OSCE and other international/European organisations–have been properly arranged, thus the European security architecture is based on several mutually reinforced institutions.

The developments in Russia have frozen its character as a state characterised by a lack of progress concerning democratisation of political life and reform of the economy, and by a low level of societal support for authorities. A weakened Russia constitutes neither an attractive partner nor a credible client for a "united Europe". This results in an increased firmness in Russian political rhetoric and an intensification of diplomatic activities (Zubok 1992). But the efforts of Russia to stop the process of European integration have no chance to succeed.

For Poland this is the most favourable situation. Its former (eastern) pole of power is still alive but not able to execute its might because of the new (western) one. Poland enjoys a comprehensive security based not only on international treaties and formal guarantees but, first and foremost, on a community of interests. The latter means that any threat to Polish autonomy now is also a threat to the functioning of a pan-European integration mechanism, and thus will be resisted by the common efforts in both the political-military and economic domains.

## *Poland exposed*

This is the scenario in which interdependency between NATO enlargement and a strengthening of Russia is assumed. It means that security in Europe is based on a political-military organisation vis-à-vis the revival of a Russian power stemming from first of all its military capabilities, followed by the political influence and more assertive foreign policy. The first consequence of such a conjunction of developments is the return of elements of a bipolar arrangement to Europe–in its regional as well as systemic dimension. Moreover, it is reminiscent of the early stage of the Cold War where the two opposing ideological and military machineries faced each other.

Polish security in such circumstances depends on the ability of both the West and Russia to adapt to the situation generated. One possibility is development of a new "coexistence" formula as envisaged by the advocates of NATO-Russia co-operation on both sides. Here the Polish contribution to the success of the NATO-Russia agreement may be of crucial significance. Such coexistence would move the areas of potential conflict away from the NATO-Russia border i.e., the eastern border of Poland (it is assumed that independent Belarus already ceased to exist).

Another possibility arises from ideas like those presented during the 1996 presidential campaign by the leader of the Russian Communist Party, Gennady Zyuganov. According to him, in a world deprived of Soviet-American global balance, several major conflicts could arise, including one between Atlanticism and Eurasia. Thus, Russia can and must engage in different patterns of rivalry as the guarantor of a global geopolitical equilibrium of power (Smith 1996). It means, among other things, that Poland (as other East-Central European states which have obtained or applied for NATO membership) could be seen as one of several areas for a new power game. Even if this would not be the most important area, Poland will then expose itself to potentially fatal threats to its autonomy.

## *Troubles for Poland?*

Within the framework of this scenario two parallel processes are taking place. The Maastricht project has been successfully executed and the

European Union strategy of opening to the East has been effectively implemented. Russia has got a strong power position or ability to attain external objectives and direct the behaviour of other states. Its foreign policy has become characterised by a revisionist orientation. Moreover, similarly to the (West) European endeavour, the integration of states on the former Soviet territory serves the purpose of merging Russia into the global security constellation as a uniform unit rather than as a divided area, thus helping it to approach the role of a single pole in international relations.

These developments produce systemic and European bipolarity all over again. This time, however, it is a competition of two centres of power, each constructed according to the centre-periphery pattern and each paying attention to the strengthening of its inner structure. Therefore, the emphasis is placed on the reinforcement of homogeneity of the EU. The eventual adjustment period for Poland and other newly-accepted countries is shortened. Similarly, the integration of the post-Soviet territory is accelerated. The degree of control imposed by Russia over the former republics–with an exception of the three Baltic states located on the influence orbit of the EU–is increased. The CIS is based on common defence as well as on common market.

Adding to its deterrence by both having NATO guarantees and EU membership, Poland gains quite a comfortable situation. However, it does not mean that Poland has rid itself of all its troubles. First, the European "grand rivalry" with Russia uses up the financial resources that otherwise might have been spent to assist in covering the costs of parallel adjustment to the demands of the two above-mentioned institutions Poland has to bear. Second, the move of several states east of Poland towards the Moscow centre means that Poland alone plays a role of the buffer between the two rivals. In other words, the restored systemic and regional bipolarity enter into the Polish salient environment with full strength, creating a difficult task for Polish security policy.

# 9   Foreign Military Assistance

Michael Clemmesen

## INTRODUCTION

This chapter reflects my personal analysis and conclusions concerning military assistance to the Baltic states. Its first part is a fairly detailed description of the elements of situation in Baltic States that are relevant to any such assistance.

The description and analysis here is based on seven years of monitoring the Baltic States and their security debate, the last three of which have been spent working in the region. Since June 1994 I have been responsible for the local development and implementation of the Danish military assistance to the three Baltic states.

The chapter does not attempt to mirror or represent the official Danish position. Some observing the region from the outside may find my description of conditions and hurdles to development too harsh. However, if the recommendations come close to present official thinking and policy, it is no mere coincidence.

The narrative and analysis is based on my firm opinion that the effort small countries make to develop their defence forces can enhance their chances to survive as independent states. It applies to the Baltic States today as it has applied to Finland, Switzerland, and Israel in the past. An earnest and substantial effort also increases the chances for small states to gain security guarantees from foreign states, in the case of the Baltic States: from the West.

This position is not as self-evident as some non-Danes might think. A significant group of Danes along with a number of foreign policy makers still believe that because a small state bordering a great power can't defend itself (for any length of time) without outside assistance, the logical thing to do is not to waste money on defence beyond the creation of a well promoted military symbol. It applied itself to Denmark in the past, when it was placed in the shade of a less than friendly great Germany and later USSR, and it is now guiding their thinking in relation to the Baltic States.

That position ignores the fact that defence forces create conventional deterrence and thereby influence the advice given by military professionals of bigger states, both of potential aggressors and of potential guarantors and reinforcers. It also overlooks that a people demonstrating a clear and tough willingness to defend itself, rather than more or less passively demanding that concerned outsiders carry the burden, is sending a very positive political signal. It has a strong appeal to politicians of states that consider support.

A Baltic strategy for an approach to the West that only aims at European Union membership preparations and neglects a continuous and consistent development of the ability to mobilise a territorial defence is unsound. Even "soft" security effectiveness depends on "hard" security elements.

One should also be aware that the deliberate development of the state self defence capability is a national project that both shows and reinforces self confidence, even if it has to be done slowly due to other high priority elements in state building.

It must be added that the Baltic States are justified in worrying about Russia's future policies and actions: they do need guarantees. Very few in Russia want to see the loss of presence in and/or control over the Baltic coast as permanent. They see that loss as one of the tragedies of the breaking-up of the Soviet Union.[1] Any disagreement is about which levels of control and/or presence and what means are legitimate or suitable. There are clear outward signs of that attitude. There are no signs of Russian political willingness to accept (and tell the Russian population) what happened in 1939-40: partial occupation of independent states in 1939 followed by full invasion in 1940 and then by rigged and terror controlled elections of a people who could be pressed to ask for admittance to the Soviet Union. Even after the Baltic States abandoned all conditions there has been Russian reluctance to accept the present borders as international and thus permanent.[2] The Russians would also benefit from Western security guarantees to the Baltic States. It would assist them in coming to

---

1. I have drawn this conclusion from monitoring Russian statements about the Baltic States since 1991, as well as from conversations with persons that have observed the Soviet/Russian scene the last 10 years. When I have tested the position with Russians (including Russian Balts), it was never contradicted.
2. The continued Russian delay in signing the border agreement with any of the Baltic States, after the Estonians gave up the link to the Tartu Treaty, can with good justification be seen as a deep reluctance to accept any border within the former Soviet Union territory as final.

terms with their past by ruling out regression and thereby guide them towards a better future.


## INTERNAL CONDITIONS: ADVANTAGES AND HURDLES

Understanding of the specific background is crucial to understanding why development of Nordic-Western type defence establishments in the Baltic States is rather complicated and why some parts of the force building is likely to take many years.[3]

There is, however, some areas where the Baltic States have real *advantages* over other Central and East European countries. Many of hurdles listed later in the chapter apply to all countries of the former "Eastern Bloc". They are not only related to the Baltic States, and in some of the areas where the Baltic problems are more serious initially, they are easier to handle in the medium term than the problems of the other states.

One such area is the development of a well functioning bureaucracy. Though is it hard to start from scratch, you are much more likely to maximise the effect of foreign support and succeed within a decade under this circumstance than if you have to contend with vast conservative structures and ill suited organisational cultures as in, for instance, Poland. This applies to both civilian and military bureaucracies in the defence area.

Another area is the relationship between the professional military and political structures. Weak and developing structures are much more likely to subordinate themselves to democratic control in their heart than strong established structures with contrary ethos like the militaries of the future NATO member Poland and the present NATO member Turkey.

The lack of well equipped military forces in the Baltic states has made the start very difficult. But it also means that they do not have to spend a couple decades wasting scarce resources trying to maintain large amounts of heavy equipment that is likely to be in less demand in the future more defensively oriented force structures.

Small in size, the Baltic States display a clear understanding and acceptance of the fact that their populations must learn to speak Western foreign languages in order to have a future in Europe. They also realise that

---

3. The description is a personal analysis, based on conversations and observation rather than on written sources. Baltic comments to early drafts of the Chapter have helped to enhance clarity and balance.

to develop English language skill in the military cadres is the most important objective on the way to interoperability with NATO. It is rather impossible to "get through" to persons who do not speak English (or German). The most important element in acceleration of reform is to make sure that the key persons know enough Western languages to get their own experience abroad. They must be able to follow briefings by active participation in discussions to gain the in depth understanding that is a necessary foundation for sound change.

This scenario could take hold within the next five years in the Baltic States. In states like Poland where people are much less likely to need foreign languages in their daily life and service, the situation is not likely to be much different–even in the distant future–than it is in France today.

If a country builds up forces and procedures from scratch, it is only a matter of controlling the instruction given in the military cadre schools and staffs to ensure that NATO communications as well as operational and logistic procedures are being used in the forces. In other already existing Central and Eastern European large forces the real absorption of new ways of doing things is likely to take a long time and much effort–if it is possible at all. The Baltic defence forces can become more Westernised, reformed, and flexible in much shorter timeframe than the forces of e.g. Poland. In just four to eight years their professional military cadre could acquire the necessary combination of English language skill and relevant knowledge and experience.

But even if all these advantages are important, they are not enough to ensure the presence of real military capability and improvement in the Baltic security policy situation. The three states have to make significant progress in other areas to convince sceptical professional military advisors and politicians that they are natural members of the Western alliance. The hurdles on the way to progress in these other, more general areas can be divided into three groups: *political, the cadre background and style,* and different types of more purely *military* conditions. Nearly all the hurdles are the result of the damage done by the Communist/Soviet period to man and society.

The first *political* factor is the *fairly widespread attitude that military defence is hopeless and therefore a waste of money and young men's time.* Because the Baltic States are so small in comparison to Russia, it is easier to hope for the best while declaring that the moral obligation of the West is not to let the Balts suffer again in demanding support and aid.

Such an attitude is clearly present among the population and politicians of all three states, even if it is very rarely presented openly–least of all to foreigners. It is not considered "in good political taste" to publicise ones defeatism. There is also some difference from country to country. In Lithuania (and increasingly in Estonia) the defeatist attitude is being balanced by a determination to ensure that any new invasion would hurt the aggressor for a long time. Even if defence might be hopeless, national honour and self respect demands that the unresisted rape of 1939-40 shall not be repeated. For Lithuania, this attitude of spite is linked to the pride in the great power history of the country.

However, it is only slowly being understood and accepted that even if a small state can't resist the great power aggressor forever, the ability to defend the territory for a period and make the invader pay dearly for the aggression could deter the attack and thus make such adventure much less likely. After the experiences of first, Afghanistan, and then Chechnya, no Russian military planner is likely to underestimate the problems of defeating a well armed and motivated territorial defence of the Baltic States. Defence endurance can also make it possible for military advisors of Western politicians to consider a supporting intervention and security guarantees. The fact that not all Western contacts understand this and give advice accordingly is delaying the realisation of the fact in the Baltic capitals.

The despondent attitude has been nurtured by the unspoken understanding that part of the large, non-citizen, ethnic Russian population could act as not only a pretext, but as a fifth column.[4] Discussing the building of an effective territorial, "total" defence structure thus opens the question of the objective need to integrate the resident Russians, something that the political system has not yet matured fully enough to face. In fact, not even volunteers among non-citizens are allowed to do national service.[5] Some amongst the small groups of politicians that work hard to push the

---

4. According to *New Baltic Barometer III, representative survey,* November 1996, 32% of Lithuanians, 41% of Latvians, and 67% of Estonians thought that conflicts between the majority nationality of Balts and the Russian residents in their country are a threat to the peace and security of their country.
5. It was seen in the changes in the draft defence policy guidelines made by the Estonian parliament in 1996 and the debate in Latvian parliament about the draft conscription law. The only non-citizens serving in the two countries are persons that joined the regular officer and NCO cadres when the forces were created.

development of the defence forces see this clearly, but they are frustrated by a majority of parliamentarians that refuse to face the issue.

Understanding the links between national security and the minority issue comes only gradually. It is only very slowly being realised how difficult it could be for the West to give full security guarantees to countries where any foreign threat is likely to be closely linked to a domestic situation. It makes it difficult to present the black-and-white picture that is necessary when popular and political will to honour security obligations must be mobilised.

The above described "what is the use" attitude to defence has been linked to a fairly widespread understanding that Russia is unlikely to invade so soon after withdrawing its troops. It is also linked to the public awareness of rising crime rate, deep and widespread corruption, and wild capitalism. These factors together have led to the *highlighting of internal threats* in the public debate and some national security concepts.[6]

Internal threats to the nation, the state, and the state building process, are nearer and hopefully more manageable than any more remote, military threat. Giving priority to meeting that threat is supported by the interior ministry bureaucracies. In all Baltic States, these are stronger and more influential than the defence bureaucracies.[7]

It is underlined that the state is being undermined by both its dependence on foreign energy supply from one source (Russia), and destabilisation through foreign (Russian) or organised (Russian) crime money getting control over significant other sectors of the economy. A big neighbour state is more likely to use (is using?) tools such as illegal immigration and other smuggling, corruption of politicians, and destabilisation of the economy rather than military means to destroy the newly regained independence.

The parliamentary committee in Latvia dealing with defence against external military threats is also explicitly responsible for legislation related to meeting these internal threats.[8] The Latvian volunteer defence

---

6. Of Latvia and Lithuania. Estonia started with the development of the guidelines for development of the defence.
7. This factor is reinforced by the higher priority of some supporting states given to the development of the Interior Ministry forces. That higher priority is often motivated by a mixture of "liberal" and optimistic–critical–attitude to all things military and of national self interest.
8. The committee is named "Defence and Interior Affairs Committee." In Lithuania the name is the "National Security Committee," and in Estonia "Defence Committee."

organisation Zemessardze ("Guardians of the Land," normally translated as "National Guard") has independent police authority to enable it to fight that threat as well.

This focus on the internal threat is mirroring the concerns of ordinary people. However, during conversations it becomes clear that it must also be seen as a defensive turning away from something that is subconsciously perceived to be hopeless.[9]

A key obstacle to all rebuilding of state institutions is the *political effect of the general destruction of inter-human relations* in the Communist/Soviet period. Most of the problems in this area are rather similar in other Central and Eastern European states.

The misuse of the natural feeling of solidarity for fellow human beings makes it very difficult to re-establish structures that depend on social cohesion. It applies to the development of an honest system for the collection and use of public revenues as well as to any type of compulsory state service. It is to a high degree, within few ethical limits, everyone for himself–survival of the fittest.

It is often very difficult to establish co-operation between human beings or organisations. "The others" are distrusted, their efforts sabotaged, and formal agreements entered without any intention of implementing your own part of the deal. Negotiations about necessary co-operation between two organisations can take place without co-operation even being discussed: the side that needs support may be too proud to ask for it, and the other side will not offer it without being asked.[10] All want to build an independent empire without the need to co-operate with anyone.

Few are willing to take responsibility for decisions that can be or have proven to be unpopular. People that ought to lend support to necessary projects wait to show their hand in the hope that someone else may take the blame for failure.

One result of this is that it has become very difficult to get projects started and implemented. Nobody takes the initiative to create the necessary formal co-operation, and even if this happens and some plan is made "on

---

9. My feeling the the internal security emphasis is somewhat driven by opportunism is supported by answers to the *New Baltic Barometer III, representative survey,* November 1996: 72% of Lithuanians, 68% of Latvians, and 81% of Estonians listed the Russian state as a threat to the peace and security of their country.

10. One clear example was the discussion in 1996 about the amalgamation of the Estonian Border Guard navy and the Defence Force navy.

paper," there is no natural drive to implement, to get things done. The maximum one can hope for is that somebody with a formal responsibility starts pushing. If no such person shows initiative, nobody else will.

For too many politicians and officials, public and political office is viewed as an access to privileges, a path to power to do favours for "clients" or friends and, in some cases even a road to personal enrichment. The way in which the former Soviet state property has been privatised is one example.[11]

There are significant differences between the Baltic nations in relation to how they have reacted to Soviet pressure and destruction. Some have been hit much harder in some fields than others. Their survival "strategies" were different. Some nations had been closer to extinction than others. The more collectively minded Lithuanians have withstood the pressure in large "family" groups, the Estonians as individuals under siege, and the Latvians were pressed most, and often reduced to the mere sabotage of central decisions.[12] However, part of the above mentioned problems are present in all the three societies.

As mentioned above, there is a widespread and strong *negative attitude to personal contributions to the common good, including conscription for the national armed forces.*

However, small front-line states with low population density can only hope to build a conventional deterrent force through a "Nordic type" conscription-mobilisation system. If the terrain favours defence, as it does in the Baltic States (with woods, swamps, and a weak infrastructure in the border regions), then the defence forces can be relatively lightly equipped (and thus inexpensive). For some politicians in the three states, however, this fact is very difficult to accept, as small contract-recruited armed forces

---

11. One of the times where political misuse of office became exposed to daylight was at the late 1995 Lithuanian banking crisis that led to the resignation of the Prime and Interior Ministers. Another was the 1997 Tallinn apartment privatisation scandal, but it is clearly visible elsewhere, and common knowledge. There is a difference between the three states as to which style and how few limitations corrupt politicians and officials show. As in most other former socialist states "nomenclature-privatisation" has taken place. I wonder about how a lot of former Soviet military and other state equipment can remain outside the reach of the armed forces that need it. One example is the ten MI-8 ex-Soviet Air Force/Aeroflot helicopters rotting "without owner" in Vilnius Airport.

12. Partly based on own observations, tested on Baltic friends. I first had the Latvian "sabotage"-reaction described to me by Janis Jurkans, Foreign Minister in the transition government. As a member of the Parliaments of independent Latvia he had realised how difficult it had been to move to a more positive approach.

would be more popular (and if military defence is hopeless anyway, why support an unpopular policy). Also, short service conscript units are not very useful as auxiliary police in countering the other, high priority interior threats mentioned above.

Conscription to the Soviet army was very unpopular in the Baltic republics, especially in Estonia and Latvia. Treatment of the servicemen was often brutal. The non-Slavic conscripts were pressed extra hard. The system was often just a way of levying cheap, nearly "slave" labour; training was limited, the waste of servicemen's time unlimited.

It has been rather difficult to make the Baltic peoples realise that service in the new independent armies is very different. In too many cases this scepticism is partly justified: in many respects the armies are still rather unreformed–and in some units service is unnecessary rough–as mindless waste of young mens' time still goes on.[13] More about this later.

The memory of Soviet conscription comes together with a fairly widespread, uncritical copy-cat attitude to all things American. In the military field this means that a modern army must be professional, hi-tech, and (thus) small to be efficient.

The sum of these factors means that it has been very difficult for the small group of active pro-defence politicians to get the parliaments to pass new laws abolishing the exemptions to service that have characterised the laws made in reaction to Soviet conscription and, thus, expose even students to an equal service burden. Only new laws could form the basis of the reserve mobilisation system necessary for creating a proper territorial defence system.

*The state lacks money* for any public spending, including defence. The public and political will to create an efficient state revenue system and enforced collection system is only slowly developing. It is also important that Western economic advice asks for a minimal state sector. Only Estonia has introduced a fairly efficient direct taxation system. Among the public there is widespread suspicion that too little of any additional collected

---

13. However, it is only the young, those who have to serve, that are rather unhappy. According to *New Baltic Barometer III, representative survey,* November 1996, 66% of Lithuanians, 65% of Latvians, and 60% of Estonians think that military service, when young, is one thing that you always owe to your country. The negative attitude to service in the age group 18-29, however, is nearly twice more widespread than in the age group 30-59, and three times more widespread than in the age group 60-74.

revenue would be honestly spent for the public good. As a result, the state–including the defence forces–must be kept small.

In both Latvia and Lithuania there have been years where insufficient state finances has meant that the already inadequate funds have arrived too late for regular payments of salaries etc., and that the defence budget has not been made fully available at the end of the year.

Due to the limited financial resources it becomes crucial that available funds are used well. However, this has not necessarily been the case, particularly in relation to weapon and other military equipment procurement where naïve buyers are easy targets in the hard world of arms sales.

*The three Baltic states find it difficult to enter a real co-operation.* In the inter-war period, and both before and after the three states regained independence, the Soviet and Russian leadership used the fact that the three states found it very difficult to co-ordinate policies to divide and control them.

The three states regard themselves as competitors rather than partners, and are aware of their very considerable differences. However, as they are viewed and treated by both East and West as one region, their ability to develop co-operation and co-ordination can be crucial for their security.

Until now, full success in military co-operation has been limited to two projects. the Baltic Peacekeeping Battalion (BALTBAT) and the much less known formal co-operation between the volunteer defence organisations. Elsewhere Baltic differences and the Soviet tendency to sign and celebrate rather than implement fine sounding declarations have hindered the development of co-operation. In the opinion of this author an unsupported Baltic military co-operation project is likely to end up as either "a pie in the sky" or a Potemkin Village.[14]

BALTBAT is being realised due to the foreign involvement and drive given to support the original Baltic idea. Only the volunteer forces' co-

---

14. The Baltic defence ministers have signed two broad co-operation agreements, the first on 2. June 1992, and the second on 27 February 1995. In both they agreed to co-operate closely in several important areas: e.g. a common crises management system, a common special communications system, weapon and equipment standardisation, common search and rescue system, common tactical manuals, co-ordinated use of training structures etc. The only two significant fields where progress has been made without the involvement of the supporting states, have been the co-operation between the volunteer defence forces (that had started already without permission) and the now formalised regular meetings between ministers, their head civil servants, the commanders, chiefs of staff, and service chiefs.

operation is a truly Baltic project, and it did not come about as a result of political initiative but rather as result of the growing friendship and contacts between the organisations themselves.

Three other Baltic defence co-operation projects–the Baltic Naval Squadron (BALTRON), the Baltic Air Surveillance System (BALTNET), and the Baltic Staff College (BALTDEFCOL)–are now on the way beyond the concept stage. As with BALTBAT this is the result of direct supporting state initiatives and involvement.

Another element in Baltic defence politics is the not uncommon *popular attitude that national defence is too serious a matter to be left to politicians that one can't trust.* This is a symptom of the fact that democratic traditions and attitudes are still being built, and this will not improve faster than the general political morale. There is a feeling on the part of the general public of estrangement from the parliamentarians, widespread support for the presidents, and some sympathy for the idea of a technocratic, apolitical, even autocratic government.[15] Thus, it is both important to stress the principle of political control with the armed forces and at the same time accept the fact that there are good reasons why some politicians maintain a too low standing in the general public and the military to command real respect and loyalty.

In all three states it is considered *crucial to develop generally accepted policy papers in the defence field,* and follow these up by creating a legal framework etc. for the development of the defence forces. In most other states the understanding of the implications of geography etc. has developed over the years, gradually leading to the formation of common understanding. In the Baltic States, the public and the politicians have had to start from scratch in the very difficult situation described above and below, with no common domestic understanding of what defence means, and without the benefit of a co-ordinated foreign advice built on understanding of local conditions.

The drafting and political acceptance of the first basic documents has not been a simple process. The Latvian "Concept on Security" came first,

---

15. According to *New Baltic Barometer III, representative survey,* November 1996, 62% of Lithuanians, 45% of Latvians, and 39% of Estonians thought that it would be "best to have a strong leader who can quickly decide things without bothering with Parliament and elections." In all three states the president was the most trusted of the political institutions: 54 % in Lithuania, 67% in Latvia, 72% in Estonia. The parliaments were trusted by: 33% in Lithuania, 32% in Latvia, 54% in Estonia.

in the summer of 1995. However, even if the concept thereafter has formed the de facto basis for the subsequent work on defence structures, it was never formally accepted by parliament.[16] After a very difficult process with conflicting concept proposals, Lithuania reached political agreement on the text of the "National Security Concept" in the autumn of 1995. It was then to be accepted by parliament within a framework law, but this never happened due to disagreement within the governing labour party. The law was only passed by the parliament in late December 1996, after the general election and change of government. Estonia followed with its "Guidelines of the National Defence Policy," that was passed unanimously by parliament in the late spring of 1996.

The hurdles in relation to the *cadre background and style* are in some ways easier to handle with respect to time and resources than with the political problems. It has been difficult to *build ministries of defence* using *a mix of people with very little formal training in or background knowledge* about resource management; for that matter in even running an office in an effective manner with lateral communication and formal decision levels. In these areas, it did not matter if one recruited people with a background in the Kafka-like Soviet bureaucracies, or merely young people without experience.

Only in Lithuania did the situation differ somewhat. Here, part of the ministry was built by dedicated and very capable people with a background of organising popular resistance in various fields during the last years of the Soviet period. Many of these key persons are still working in the ministry. Lithuania was also helped in this respect by her first defence minister, Audrius Butkevicius, who was an excellent judge of character and manager of men. The good start made it easier to recruit and keep very capable young people later.

In Latvia, the ministry was initially overloaded with Soviet style bureaucrats with good formal but very few real qualifications for leading the development of a ministry of defence of a small state. They were followed by a steady trickle of youngsters, too many of whom left in frustration after they had learned some English.

In Estonia, the ministry of defence was only created several months after the country regained independence at a time when the General Staff had already been established as a large, albeit Soviet-type organisation only

---

16. The new Latvian Minister of Defence, Talavs Jundzis, however, has indicated his will to try to have the concept passed late 1997.

with better defined fields of responsibility. The ministry of defence came late as a competitor for the smaller Estonian pool of talented young people who sought public careers; consequently other ministries got first pick.

For a long time is was fairly complicated to work with the Estonian and Latvian ministries. If one sent a fax or letter, one could not be sure where it ended up. It was necessary to distribute copies to the action addressees next time one met them (one might as well have sent a message to a black hole in the universe). The filing system of the ministries was at best rudimentary. It is only in the last one to two years that the situation at the Ministry of Defence level has really improved in these two countries. In each country, a small group of bright and hardworking, young people have succeeded in compensating for the difficult and late start.

However, the problems are not over. The three ministries face very difficult hurdles in stabilising the civil service. The officer and civil service salaries can't compete with the private sector, where a bright, hardworking, English-speaking youngster will be paid at least two to three times more money. In other state and local bureaucracies it is sometimes possible to supplement an insufficient salary by taking bribes. In the ministry of defence there are few services to sell. One only has the dedication to one's country and the importance of the work as a compensation for the low public salary.

The problem with irrelevant background and personality profiles is not limited to the manning of the ministries. Most *Baltic former Soviet officers were trained for the technical branches, e.g. as engineers for the air surveillance, air defence or rocket forces.* Relatively few were trained as infantry, field engineer or artillery officers, the most relevant backgrounds today. Those with staff training and experience are used to having a very limited area of responsibility, and are normally unable to act without detailed orders. In a Western type staff of a small country, officers will normally have wide responsibilities, and particularly in a building up/definition phase such as this, one has to show initiative and moral courage in the daily work. Many ex-Soviet staff officers who were trained to plan operations of divisions, field armies, and fronts according to strict rulebooks ("norms"), find it very difficult to understand and plan for the defence of a small state with limited, only slowly expanding forces, and without access to unlimited resources. Some do, but very few. Most try to recreate small versions–or sometimes even direct copies[17]–of what they knew in the past, not understanding the irrelevance of what they are doing.

In Lithuania, development is facing an additional hurdle. The more senior members of the defence leadership are convinced that there is a scientifically correct solution to every military problem. This applies both to force and command structure development and defence operations. The "brain" at the centre has the most correct picture, orders mobilisation, makes the plan, issues orders, and controls the execution closely. There is very little acceptance of low level initiative and drive. Any present day Lithuanian military force is likely to be smart and tough. However, too many units are dominated by centralised, formal discipline, and are therefore likely to be in trouble should they meet any significant unforeseen problem with the need to improvise. As local initiative and ability to improvise is crucial to military effectiveness in the defence of Lithuania (because of her weak, thinly distributed forces, and need for local co-ordination with volunteer defence forces), this characteristic is most unfortunate. Perhaps too many leading Lithuanians are still coming to terms with how inadequate the Soviet pseudo-scientific, centralised, command approach is in relation to human affairs, including fighting. Was their struggle only for national freedom, and not against Leninism and its elitist centralism? The centralism is strange when one considers the guerrilla "forest brothers" traditions and the demands of the National Security Concept.

In Estonia, the combination of far too few qualified military professionals and the often poisoned political climate has been (and still is) a major obstacle in the development of the defence forces. There may be some understanding among politicians of the fact that you can't build the army without using military professionals. But there has been little ability or willingness to support the few available, good experts, most of whom were involved in pioneering work in the first few years of independence. Their continued work has been hampered or hindered by slander campaigns: "There must be some black spot in their past–probably working for some military intelligence organisation"; or they actually showed

---

17. One such example was/is the Lithuanian Military Academy until reforms that may be initiated by the new government in 1997. In the civilian Tartu Aviation College in Estonia I was introduced to a scaled down copy of a Soviet Aviation University; they planned to be able to do all types of aviation engineer training in the college, ignoring that it would be highly cost ineffective with the very limited number of students.

initiative during the first years, so they must have made mistakes in administration, broken some rules that should be evident today. Many parliamentarians seem willing to listen and participate in the gossip. Some army builders have hurt the self-esteem of these politicians in their impatience to get results; and with their lack of familiarity with courtesy. In the less than clean political world of Estonia, one favourite pastime has been to search for–and broadcast by an uncritical press–possible mistakes of the military cadre, thereby slowing and setting back development

*All organisations* are seeking independence in the sense that they *want to minimise dependence on other organisations* and influences in carrying out their core mission. But in the Baltic States, as probably elsewhere in the former Soviet Union, it is worse than normal. This is due to the interplay of at least two factors: firstly, the general problem of creating and maintaining good and trustful relations with people that one does not know; secondly, the fact that the waste of resources was the natural state of affairs, thus making it quite normal for all organisations that needed helicopters, communications, armoured vehicles, ships, etc. to have their own instead of co-operating about the use of common resources.[18]

The obstacles in the more purely *military field* are partly the result of post-independence decisions made in the Baltic States where their new armed forces were formed as a strange *mix of border guards, clubs, and armed volunteers from the resistance.* But other obstacles are inherited from the Soviet forces.

Even before independence ever became a reality, the Baltic republics tried to show their determination to gain it by setting up structures to mark the borders in a symbolic way. When independence came, it became a high priority to use the first armed forces to achieve control of the borders.

In Estonia, where it took a long time to establish a ministry of defence, the Border Guard, "Piirivalve," was set up under the "Ministry of State," later it came under the Interior Affairs Ministry. In Latvia, the Border Guard Brigade formed the main part of the regular armed forces. In Lithuania, the Border Service became one of two main components of the regular army. It is only gradually realised–if at all–that border policing is a

---

18. It has proven very difficult to understand that it is a good idea to use military helicopters for Search-and-Rescue or police work, and the same thing applies when one is trying to sell the idea that the ships of the defence force navy can carry out the policing of the territorial waters.

demanding speciality that can't be combined with a capability to defend the border acting as a well trained, light infantry force.

However, there was international pressure to transfer the border forces from the Ministry of Defence (adding to the already rather bloated armed forces of the Ministry of Interior). In Lithuania, the Border Service was transferred to the Interior Ministry mid-1994; in Latvia, it was only happening at the beginning of 1997, leaving the hitherto lowly prioritised rump of the regular army to develop with the rest of the limited money available.

The only other regular force beyond the border protection force that was given equal high priority was the establishment of national honour guard sub-units.

In all three countries, the regular defence forces became small (2,000–4,000 men), limited by the need for (cheap) conscripted personnel for the Border Guard forces, a Soviet type paramilitary police unit, and prison guard duty–as well as by the general low level of efficiency and equality of the conscription system.

In Latvia, the low political interest in the rest of the regular forces meant that it was up to the officers that had joined, to create what was more of less naval, air force, and airborne "clubs" of interested specialists. The success of these clubs depended on the drive and professionalism of the officers involved. The "naval club" succeeded in building the nucleus of the future navy/coast guard on the basis of vessels donated mainly by Germany and Sweden.

Even in Lithuania with its dynamic first defence minister, the element of club-building was strong. When one has limited money, one has to build on professionalism linked to the enthusiasm of individuals. The units of the regular army–the "Iron Wolf Brigade" units–were modelled on the best they knew, the Soviet Airborne Regiments (scaled down to one-third size). That made the units and subunits much too small to be able to fight as the light infantry the country needed, and the garrison support structures used about half of the available man-power. The small, very professional navy was built on the basis of the two frigates the minister got in a bargain with Russia. The air force kept and flew what it could lay its hands on.

Only in Estonia did the army-building take place guided by a strong professional hand. The first Chief of the Estonian General Staff and acting commander, Colonel Ants Laaneots, realised that the only force with effective defence, and, therefore, deterrent capability, his country could afford was a territorial defence force more or less inspired by the Finnish model. The regular units were, therefore, organised as Western type and size infantry battalion groups. The defence force navies and airforces came later, in 1994, as an extra-parliamentary initiative by the then commander, Major General Alexander Einseln.

In all three states these regular forces were built from the top. From the winter of 1991, however, the volunteer defence forces had started to expand. In Estonia, the process took the shape of the re-establishment of the inter-war period Defence League ("Kaitseliit"). In the two other states, new organisations, in Latvia the Guardians of the Land, ("Zemessardze") and in Lithuania the Volunteer National Defence Organisation ("SKAT") were formed. It took a couple of years to establish an accepted system of political/defence leadership control over these organisations. In Latvia, where the regular structures are weakest, it is still an on-going process. These volunteer defence organisations still form the largest part of the national defence forces (Estonia 7,500, Lithuania 11,000, Latvia 17,000). In both Lithuania and Latvia these forces were much more ready and able to absorb and use Western ideas than most of the regular units. In Estonia, both regular and volunteer forces were eager to learn and use non-Soviet models.

In all three countries the first couple of years of enthusiastic force building were followed by a couple of years of near stalemate. Some of the reasons for this stalemate were specific to the three states: (Estonia–involved personalities; Latvia–general doubt about the usefulness; and Lithuania–disagreement within the governing party). However, other reasons were common to all: the lack of basic documents; no reform of the conscription system; and an insufficiency of funds. In Estonia and Lithuania, the stalemate has now been broken: specific problems have been solved; additional funds allocated;[19] credits for procurement guaranteed; and basic documents passed by the parliaments. In Latvia the only positive development has been the passing of a better conscription law. Otherwise the situation is becoming critical because of insufficient funding.

What strikes any Western military professional who visits most Baltic states military units is the *continued presence of some of the inherited Soviet army ways*. In all three states the percentage of soldiers on different work detachments is too high, even if the situation is better in Estonia than

---

19. The 1997 defence budgets are as follows: Estonia 52.2 million US $ (equals 1.22 % of the GDP), Lithuania about 80 million US $ (equals 0.92 % of the GDP), Latvia 35.4 million US $ (equals 0.68 % of the GDP).

in Latvia and Lithuania. In the latter two countries the number of soldiers on guard duty is also much in excess of what is considered necessary in the West. To some extent it can be explained by the low level of funding, the situation with the societies generally, and the low level of manning of the units. However, some of the explanation can certainly be attributed to the difficulty of moving too far away from the Soviet ways, even if these undermine the effective implementation of any training schemes.

Specifically in Estonia and Latvia, it has proven very difficult to stop or even limit the harassment and collective punishment of soldiers. This again has lead to a far too high level of suicide incidents and accidents during training. As underlined by the military authorities of the two countries, one part of the problem is the indifferent conscription system that sends too many soldiers of low quality to the defence force units.

The training is not aimed at developing "brain" and the ability of independent action among the soldiers. The typical physical activity is body building and athletics rather than orienteering and team games. Training is anachronistic in underlining drill and learning rules by heart. This is not what one needs to outfox a stronger invader as an infantry or later guerrilla force.

Some of these problems are related to cadre limitations. The number, quality, attitude, and type of non-commissioned officers is not adequate. The young officers that are trained in the Baltic States officer academies are not particularly well prepared. The reason is that these academies either mirror the Soviet type mixture of basic and theoretical military training (Lithuania and to some extent Latvia) or a blend of basic and civilian academic training (Estonia). In Estonia, however, most of the new officers did not come via the officer academy but rather were trained on practical officers courses of some months' duration.[20] Some problems are a natural result of the fact that the armies are still too "revolutionary" to accept the authority of formal rank. Officers have to be respected by their juniors to be effective. Natural authority is always important, but in peace time formal rank is normally accepted in a military unit. The Baltic States militaries have not yet reached that point.

The *military infrastructure has to be rebuilt more or less completely*. The best military barracks, bases, etc., of the Baltic States were built by the

---

20. The first normal basic course for regular officers of two years' duration started, however, in September 1997. One month later started the first three years advanced course.

Imperial Russian Army around the end of last century and have not been repaired or maintained properly for 50 years. The rest were built by a combination of unskilled military labour and engineer units after the Second World War, with the newer being worst. They were left to rot during the last years of Soviet rule and, in most cases, the Russian troops smashed what they could not tear out of the walls to take with them when they departed. What they left, the local population took as fire wood and scrap metal.

In order to create a sound military infrastructure, the Baltic militaries have to use very significant resources for reconstruction. In order to keep the good cadre, they have to find and repair military flats in the vicinity of the units. The armed forces' families can't afford civilian accommodation.

The *condition in relation to weapons and other military equipment is very difficult*. The only new or fairly new equipment in the three countries are: Israeli weapons and radios bought by Estonia; some Russian produced trucks and later some heavy mortars bought by the same country; a small number of light weapons purchased by the Latvian Zemessardze; the Russian AK-74 family weapons, some trucks, as well as the arriving Swedish produced Carl Gustav anti-tank weapons bought by Lithuania; a handful of light 4 wheel drive vehicles bought by each state; and the foreign donated equipment for the Baltic Peacekeeping Battalion. Even this limited procurement has represented a significant economic and sometimes political burden. Of the equipment, only the weapons from Israel have arrived in a quantity significant enough for the defence capability of the country in question.

Otherwise, the countries have had to make do with a mixture of well used, light weapons, some (of Eastern manufacture) purchased, others donated. A varied bazaar of trucks and other vehicles as well as signals equipment have come from a number of donors.[21] Most of the donated equipment has arrived without manuals or spare parts.

The Baltic States have so far not been able to implement any common policy in the matériel field, neither in relation to their own purchase or to new donated equipment. Thus, the future donations, e.g. to BALTBAT,

---

21. To give an example: The Estonian army Auto Transport company's 100 odd vehicles are of more than 40 different types. Most states, including Denmark, has only donated equipment that the Baltic States have specifically asked for. But as their situation was desperate, they accepted most offers, and the logistic conditions got still more complex.

could worsen rather than alleviate the situation by increasing the number of types of matériel, if no agreement on standardisation is reached.[22]

The *conclusions* from this description of the internal conditions can be listed as follows:

*A comprehensive change in the fundamental political conditions* will take at least a couple of decades, as it will depend on changes in the society, political system, and wider security policy areas (e.g. minority politics).

With *the right focus of advice and assistance,* however, a lot can be accomplished in the defence forces during next few years. The emphasis should be on improving the quality of the Baltic States cadres. Western types of training for the military (officers and NCOs) and civil service cadres (including English language training), and the establishment of more attractive service conditions (careers, contracts, salaries, housing) are first priority areas.

*A proper conscription-reserve system* must be implemented very soon. This must include the introduction of modern leadership and training principles, along with much better use of conscripts' time. It must also introduce reserve cadre training and contracts, refresher training system, general and limited mobilisation systems etc. To achieve real progress here it may be necessary to give very friendly but candid advice to one or two of the Baltic states.

*A Baltic system for standardisation,* procurement, and maintenance of weapons and other equipment should be established as soon as possible. They should be advised strongly against acting alone on the temptation of weapon producing firms.

Real Baltic co-operation should be encouraged in a very direct way, normally involving supporting nations directly to initiate and implement individual projects.

---

22. There may be some hope for improvement in this field. During the meeting of the Baltic vice-ministers of Defence on 11-12 February 1997 they agreed to establish a Baltic Standardisation Working Group to co-ordinate and supervise the implementation of NATO standards in the Baltic defence establishments. This group may also be tasked with the more immediate need to increase the level of vehicle standardisation etc. But in the Baltic states one thing is a forum and meetings, another implementation.

THE PARTNERSHIP FOR PEACE SUPPORT AND THE BALTIC STATES

Some of the support for the Baltic States takes place within the limitation of the PfP framework.

Seen from the Baltic states' perspective, the Partnership for Peace programme was what NATO offered when what they needed was Article V guarantees. All three states realised that they should use the programme to the maximum to get closer to NATO and to those guarantees. They did all they could do within their very limited resources to be amongst those countries performing best according to implicit criteria of the programme. In the words of the US Secretary of Defence "They have maintained model participation in Partnership for Peace, not only in exercises, but in the real work of peacekeeping in Bosnia and other places around the globe. They have made impressive commitments and have shown that we can count on them to do their part".[23]

The fact is, however, that the programme has been a somewhat mixed blessing for the Baltic States due to its limitations and focus.

The purpose of the programme was not to prepare the partner states for NATO membership. Consequently, emphasis has not been placed on what the states needed to do to become eligible for membership of a NATO where one not only has to contribute to non-Article V operations, but where one must also maintain a certain capability for initial self defence, an ability to receive and co-operate with NATO reinforcements, and–if possible–a capability to reinforce other member states for crisis management or defence.

In some respects the PfP activities support the development of a capability for military co-operation in Article V operations; in other ways, however, it undermines such a development.

The priority given to the English language training of officers and civil servants in preparing them for co-operation with NATO countries and their armed forces within the PfP framework is crucial for the development of the ability to operate in any type of mission. The same can be said about the adoption and integration of NATO standard operational and technical procedures. In the Baltic States, the army and air surveillance/air space control areas are of special relevance. The integration of NATO SOPs in the naval field can be of significance in crisis management situations.

---

23. From Secretary Perry's letters of 3rd. October to the three Baltic states Defence Ministers.

But in other areas the emphasis of PfP activities has been detracting from the Baltic States' attempt to develop a minimum self defence capability. This is due to the focus of PfP, which implicitly accepts that there is no need for the development of self defence capabilities in the partner states. The truly important issues are to get transparency in planning and budgeting as well as proper democratic control of the defence forces, and to develop a part of the partner forces so it can participate in "soft" operations such as peace-keeping, humanitarian support, and search and rescue.[24]

A substantial number of exercises have been held and are still being arranged outside the region in order to practice the accepted types of operations. In addition, a planning process has been established in order to identify the important inter-operability objectives to further the capability for "soft" operations. Seminars and courses—of varied quality and relevance to the Baltic States—are arranged by NATO schools and commands as well as NATO member states. Eager to score as many points as possible for good PfP behaviour, the Baltic states show up, having to pay expenses that seem trivial to most outsiders, but are heavy in relation to the Baltic defence budgets.

That focus of the PfP programme could be seen as proper by other partner states applying for NATO membership as for instance, Poland, which does have a very significant self defence capability and for whom the emphasis on democratic control of the armed forces is not an irrelevant issue. For Poland, spending money on symbolic participation in exercises where the main purpose is presentation of the NATO command, host-nation and partner flags was a painful, but still relevant investment in the future.

For the Baltic States, however, the situation is rather different. The exercise participation has tied up too large a part of the very limited defence budget needed for the building up of a self defence capability from scratch (unlike the reform and maintenance of that capability in Poland). One aim of the programme seems to be the creation of a company of 100-150 men within the armed forces with full NATO inter-operability, ready to show the flag in soft operations and exercises practising those soft operations. This NATO-compatible sub-unit in each Baltic state is to be manned by regulars, equipped with American donated equipment, and

---

24. My analysis of the *Annex to the NATO Communiqué M-1(94)2: Partnership for Peace: Framework Document.*

trained to speak English to be ready for external operations. However, it might be more relevant to use the same pay sum and English training effort differently. It could build and maintain the cadre of an infantry brigade-size mobilisation formation that would be able to co-operate with NATO forces in national self defence.

Secretary Perry stated in his letter to the Baltic ministers that his "judgement ... (that the Baltic states) are not yet ready to take on the Article V responsibilities of NATO membership has been reached in the context of (his) view that there are certain basic membership requirements in terms of military capability".[25] The "soft" operations focus of the PfP programme has contributed a little to that situation.

A limited change of focus of the PfP activities, e.g. in the direction of the more demanding Peace Enforcement operations, will not change much. These activities would still aim at the symbolic rather than the substance in relation to preparation for NATO membership. Thus, Baltic attempts to perform well would not assist them in diminishing Western military concern about their lack of ability to carry out an efficient initial defence.

The PfP-programme cannot support the development of mobilisation and reserve structures or the development of e.g. signals training centres that could further general instead of specific inter-operability. This is not the fault of the PfP organisation: it can't ignore the purpose and framework of PfP agreed upon by the NATO member states. The programme can only assist in the removal of the above listed hurdles in a few areas.

It is, therefore, better that the Baltic States rather than trying to over-accomplish in the PfP-activities field, should use their resources to develop those bilateral programmes with NATO and other supporting states that more clearly enhance the development of self defence capabilities.


THE BILATERAL SUPPORT PROGRAMMES

The bilateral programmes to assist the Baltic States in the recreation of armed forces started early, and cautiously. The first significant support given more or less equally to all Baltic States came from Sweden and Germany, who donated different types of old equipment and took students

---

25. From Secretary Perry's letters of 3rd. October to the three Baltic states Defence Ministers.

for training in the supporting country. Sweden supplemented this by establishing major programmes to support the policing of the borders.

The US concentrated on the development of the initial contacts, allowing the three states' national guards to establish Military Liaison Teams in the Baltic capitals.[26] This support concentrated on giving support to the volunteer defence organisations and was limited to familiarisation with US methods in "non-lethal" (non-combat) fields.

Finland started very early giving substantial, high profile support to the Estonian Border Guard, and more discrete, but still very effective training support to the Estonian army. The key programme was from the start the offer of full officer and NCO training at the Finnish army schools. By early 1997, about 30 officers and three times that number of NCOs have been trained. This cadre training programme is in its combination of quantity and quality the best given by any supporting country to a Baltic state. The other parts of the Finnish support[27] to Estonia withered away in the two years that followed the appointment of the retired US officer Alexander Einseln as Estonian defence force commander. He did not see the Finnish defence model as relevant for Estonia. This may be one reason why he did not make sure that the officers trained in Finland were employed properly for the good of the Estonian army.

Initial UK support focused on Latvia, whereas Denmark began its support in Lithuania. The first support was entirely bilateral. Co-ordination began in 1994 when the Nordic states and the UK agreed to support the establishment of a Baltic Peacekeeping battalion. The idea was born during a 1993 meeting of the Baltic defence commanders. The US and Germany later supported the idea by allowing part of their national support go through that project. For the US it became a very substantial part of the support. Later on, other supporting states joined. Denmark accepted the role of lead nation, responsible for the co-ordination. To make the co-ordination effective, a steering committee was established, with representatives from the supporting and the Baltic States' defence ministries. The committee became supported by a "Military Working Group" with staff officers from the involved supporting military headquarters.

---

26. Maryland National Guard in Estonia, Michigan National Guard in Latvia, Pennsylvania National Guard in Lithuania.
27. Finnish reserve officers of different seniority volunteered and were approved to work as advisors to the Kaitseliit and other Estonian authorities.

As mentioned, the bilateral support was very cautious initially. No supporting states wanted to donate or even sell weapons, and several states limited the training assistance in the Baltic States to non-combat subjects. The presence of Russian troops in the Baltic States until the end of August 1994 prompted this conservatism.

However, by 1995 and 1996 these reservations had been lifted. The East European states had no reservations about selling weapons, and Poland and the Czech Republic were the first to donate heavy infantry weapons to the Baltic States.[28] In 1996 the Western policy changed gradually. The first opening was the donation of weapons to BALTBAT from the supporting states. Later followed limited sales, and substantial donations of weapons and equipment have taken place in 1997 from the US, Sweden, and Germany.[29] The limitations in relations to training have also disappeared gradually.

Not only has the character of support changed, but at the same time its volume has increased. Danish support has grown from of couple of events in 1992, to 30 in 1994, 70 in 1995, about 150 in 1996, to 250 in 1997. The programme now covers all of the following areas: full officer training in Denmark; a large number of short courses for different levels of officers in the army, navy, air force, and volunteer defence organisation in all three states; specialist courses; naval NCO training, on the job training for civil servants, advisory missions; seminars; and training of units for (and service in) peacekeeping missions. Some activities are recurring year after year. New activities have been developed as a result of the experience of former contacts as well as from the concrete wishes of the Balts themselves; additionally, they are taking place, sometimes in very short notice, due to a suddenly realised demand.

Denmark decided in 1994 that it could accomplish at least two important things with one effort by including troops from the Baltic States in Danish army units involved in peacekeeping operations Croatia (and later Bosnia). The Baltic and Danish militaries would get the clear picture of each other necessary for deepening future co-operation and assistance; additionally, the Baltic States would gain both an opportunity to heighten

---

28. Heavy mortars and anti tank guns.
29. Two mine sweepers with all equipment has been donated to Estonia by Germany. The USA has donated pistols and M-16 rifles to all three states and BALTBAT as well as M-14 rifles to Latvia. Sweden is donating very substantial packets of weapons and equipment made available by defence cuts.

their international profile, and experience in co-operation with international organisations. By the end of 1997 more than 600 Balts have served six months' tours in 11 platoons (five Lithuanian, four Estonian, two Latvian), and one company (Lithuanian) formed part of a Danish battalion. In number of man-days away from the Baltic States, this has been by far the biggest Western and professional education project by any supporting state.

Other states are increasing their assistance at the same time. The Czech and especially Polish support for Lithuania is now substantial. Sweden is likely to increase its support after the lull that followed the country's pioneering contribution. The German programme is growing in the number of activities, as is the Danish. Finland has resumed its very comprehensive support programme for the Estonian land forces. US and UK programmes are stable and substantial. The Norwegian and Dutch support is likely to increase.

The *future Danish policy of support to the Baltic States* has a clear purpose: to work to facilitate NATO membership for the Baltic States. Baltic membership in the alliance is not seen as directed against Russia in any way. As expressed elsewhere: there is no reason for Russia "to feel threatened by moving the no-invasion line eastward".[30] As the three states are not among the first new members allowed in at the opening of the alliance, they should be given a clear perspective for membership, and until they are allowed in, they should be linked politically and militarily as closely as possible to the alliance. To remove any obstacles for membership, Denmark is to support the Baltic States through both bilateral and multilateral assistance projects. We are to support both their ability to participate in PfP and their capacity to develop their national defence.[31]

The total amount of support is impressive, and the different programmes are addressing most of the above listed obstacles. But *the results would be better with a higher degree of co-ordination.* All the good will is sometimes threatens to swamp the Baltic States because of their limited ability to finance their end of the programmes and because they have to little qualified manpower to absorb it. However, the supporting states have not been very good at co-ordinating their assistance, as each want his flag

---

30. Quoted from William Safire's essay "NATO: Bigger is Better" in *New York Times* 16th. December 1996.
31. The latest official wording of the Danish policy can be found in the pamphlet *Danish Security Policy. MFA Issues in Focus.* November 1996.

and prestige visible. There is a fair amount of jealousy and competition involved.

Different models have been tried or suggested to improve the co-ordination of the effort. There is general agreement that the best way of co-ordinating a multinational project such as BALTBAT is by the use of the leading nation/steering committee model. This has led to the adoption of similar structures for the next projects, with Germany as the lead nation for the Baltic Naval Squadron (BALTRON) project, Norway for the Baltic Air Surveillance system (BALTNET) project, and Sweden for the Baltic Defence College (BALTDEFCOL) project.

Finland has suggested that it became co-ordinating nation in relation to all support to Estonia. However, this has neither been seen as acceptable by Estonia or other supporting states. A compromise would be to more clearly identify limited projects where the major contributor could assist the receiving nation in co-ordinating the assistance.

The UK and Sweden have tried to improve co-ordination of the support in the field of Defence Management without much succes.

The local defence attachés of the supporting states are meeting regularly to exchange information about the planned co-operation programmes. This has made it possible to some degree to avert unwanted overlap, but very different planning and budgeting procedures (including different budget years) together with differences in openness has made it difficult to make significant progress beyond that. The only small successes have been in the local co-operation between Denmark and the UK in relation to infantry officer training and in the co-operation between Denmark and Sweden in updating the Lithuanian surveillance of the sea border. In these two cases national projects have been tailored to be mutually reinforcing rather than competing.

The next attempt to improve co-ordination will be the creation of a support project database in the Baltic capitals by Norway and the UK. However, as a more ambitious initiative, the Nordic States have now established a political and military co-ordination "umbrella" for all the major projects and other support.

It is not only in relation to actual support that the bilateral assistance has been less than perfect. All the supporting states, as well as the involved NATO agencies, have offered advice. However, too much of the advice has been given without the necessary understanding or analysis of the local conditions and needs. As the Baltic States have not yet developed the necessary professional knowledge, internal consensus, and diplomatic astuteness to identify and reject bad advice, this has been a difficult problem. However, the creation of the International Defence Advisory Board (IDAB)[32] chaired by the British general Sir Garry Johnson has helped a great deal by focusing and co-ordinating advice. The board, however, is limited by the little time it can spend in the three capitals to monitor and listen.


## THE WAY AHEAD

Though many of the obstacles listed above have been addressed by the combination of PfP and bilateral programmes, not all have, and not in the most effective way.

The need for a balanced economic development of the three states limits the resources that can be allocated to defence over the next ten years. Therefore, force development models and supporting advice must be cheap and relevant for the Baltic States.

Some investment has to be made to improve the military infrastructure. More is needed in the next years. However, the absence of politically accepted long term defence structure plans makes it more than likely that some of the invested money has been (and will be) wasted. In order to avoid such waste, foreign supporters should assist the Balts more in developing such plans and in convincing the politicians to commit themselves.

As already mentioned, all procurement of weapons and other equipment must be much better managed by the Balts than has happened so far. The Baltic States need assistance in living up to the decision in principle to procure and maintain equipment together, with states like Denmark, which does not produce weapons or trucks itself assisting during project planning, negotiations, etc. Because the Balts cannot afford to purchase more that the absolute minimum, any contract is likely to be a heavy burden in the coming years; therefore it is crucial that they get the best deal possible.

The donation of equipment must become much better controlled than today. As it stands now, many of the gifts only add to the logistical problems of the small armies, increasing the unit running cost. This

---

32. The board has members from the main supporting Western and Nordic states. It is in principle independent of the government structures of the supporting states.

situation could be helped by assisting the Balts in making their equipment plans become part of the force development plans.

The pressure on the Baltic defence forces, not the least from their own ministries of foreign relations, to participate in a very large number of rather symbolic PfP exercises needs to be relaxed. The main mission for the Baltic states is to build up main defences forces that can work according to the NATO-procedures that are relevant to their chosen self defence plan. The peace time force is likely to consist of relatively small mobile reaction units that can only be augmented through mobilisation of reserve elements. That small standing force should be the "main school" of the armed forces, and PfP–and "In the Spirit of" PfP exercises should aim at improving the whole of the force, not only a part of it.

The conventional deterrent of the Baltic States, the main defence, is planned to consist of territorial defence forces potentially much larger than the standing elements. In theory, a significant group of trained personnel can be mobilised not only to beef up the mobile units, but to back up or replace the volunteer defence organisation units to create a rather strong territorial defence structure. However, it will take time before such forces can move from the concept stage to exist as cohesive, well trained and equipped units.

The Baltic States first must develop a proper reserve system; thus far, only Estonia has started. As the economic situation makes it possible, the equipment standard of these larger forces must reach a credible level. The regular and the reserve cadre for the reserve units must be available and trained through a system of call up for refresher training. The only place where the Baltic States can pick up relevant and updated experience in this area is in the Nordic supporting states. However, even the reserve cadres should be trained according to relevant NATO standards to ensure that the deterrent value is at a maximum and that determination to integrate in the Western structures is evident. Therefore, NATO memberstate instructors must get involved.

To prove that the Baltic States are willing to go on carrying their burden in international operations, the BALTBAT project should be continued as now planned. The project should not, however, be the main tool in developing the defence co-operation between the states. That should be attained by the gradual integration of the cadres of all Baltic defence forces.

The basic education of army officers, civil servants, and army NCOs must remain a Baltic state national responsibility. To make effective training and education possible, the present schools and academies should be reformed and developed. The supporting states should contribute significant resources to accelerate that development. So far, only Finland seems ready to take on the burden of helping one of the states (Estonia) by seconding the necessary number of assistant instructors for a substantial period. No state has come forward to offer similar support to the two other states.

The Baltic States have agreed in principle to establish common schools for advanced and specialist training. The first step to implement that agreement has been taken with the decison to establish a common staff officer school (BALTDEFCOL). This could lead to the establishment of other schools for signals training, combat engineer training, indirect fire support training, pilot training, naval officer education, naval mine warfare training, etc. If such a common school structure becomes reality, it would mean that the Baltic States would have reached a higher level of integration and inter-operability than forces of any other group of nations in the world. As the common language would have to be English, it would also mean a uniquely high level of integration with NATO, with all the resulting benefits in security policy profile. It is, however, unlikely that the good idea will be realised without one supporting state–or rather a group of these states–coming forward for each of these education/training projects to take the lead, pay some supplementary infrastructure, second some personnel, and assist the Baltic States in the definition of the project.

In order to make the support from the different states become more co-ordinated and focused, a structure with greater formal power in relation to the main supporting states must be involved. The present system is simply not good enough.

The only organisation with enough prestige is NATO. However, the central NATO authorities are unlikely to have enough local knowledge and flexibility to be effective. Therefore, the main co-ordination should take place at two levels: in the partners' capitals, and via Baltic presence in "Partner Staff Elements" at the sub-regional headquarters.

A NATO-PfP office with representation from the main supporting states could be a clearing house for bilateral projects and assist the host nation in managing incoming offers. It could also ensure that the NATO structure was informed about the situation.

The sub-regional headquarters will, by being in the area, have a more relevant and updated knowledge about the situation and defence structure needs in the Baltic region than any higher level command. The NATO-members (and other PfP-partners) involved in the sub-regional headquarters will be countries that are already heavily involved in bilateral support for the Baltic States.

*A final remark*

For the Baltic States, a realistic hope of EU- and NATO-membership is the key element in creating the necessary belief in the future that must be developed for the state building process to proceed. Particularly in Latvia, the rather widespread "get rich quick, there may not be a tomorrow" mentality is undermining political and public service moral as well as the development of a sound economical structure. Only by setting up a framework and foundation for the future can the supporting states press for the necessary substantial changes. Proper border control and an effective fight against organised crime will not happen without reforms in the attitudes to public service; and that will not take place without a well-founded belief in a guaranteed independent future. Therefore, guarantees must be given, but only on the condition of quick, visible, and real reforms in behaviour.

# 10 Prospects for Europe's Baltic Rim

CLIVE ARCHER

This study has focused on Europe's Baltic rim area in the post-Cold War period, placing it within the context of the relationship between Russia and the West as institutionalised in the EU and NATO. It is accepted that the countries in the area, can themselves have important inputs into the development of the Baltic Sea area, but the key factor will be stability or instability of the Russian Federation. The questions posed by the chapters in this book are "how has this space between the West and Russia developed politically and in security terms and how might it develop?" This leads on to a subsidiary enquiry as to how each of the states covered might evolve. This chapter will provide a synthesis of how the rim area–and the countries that compose it–has developed in security terms, and of the scenarios for medium-term security, with special reference to relations with the West and with Russia. Will the area develop into a region; will it become a bridge to Russia from the West; will it form a new buffer with a more hostile Russia; or will it constitute a grey zone?

These are the themes that will be examined in this chapter. Before embarking on this examination, it is worth outlining the security environment of the Baltic rim.

## THE SECURITY ENVIRONMENT IN THE BALTIC RIM

What has changed since 1989 in the environment of the states in the Baltic rim area? Clearly the overall strategic balance both in Europe and more generally has changed from one of bipolar ideological contest with a nuclear stand-off to a situation where the United States is seen as the only remaining superpower, where the old ideological battle of communism versus capitalism has ended and where the stress is more on the dangers of proliferation of nuclear weapons rather than on their deterrent value.

As pointed out in chapter 1, the effect of the global configuration of power is felt differently in particular regions. So how has the security environment in Europe's Baltic rim changed from 1989? A broad overview might show how the Cold War divisions between East and West in the Baltic has been replaced by two localised regional powers–Russia and Germany, an intrusive world power–the United States, and a number of smaller powers ranging from Sweden and Poland to the three Baltic states. However, it should be remembered that in the Cold War period, there was a zone of neutral states–Finland and Sweden–in the area and the Nordic states maintained policies that meant their part of Europe was, on the whole, one of low tension. The unification of Germany has strengthened the reasons for involvement of the Federal Republic in the security of the Baltic rim, just as the break-up of the Warsaw Treaty Organization and of the Soviet Union has severely depleted Russian capability in the area. The independence of the three Baltic states brought a new source of tension to the eastern end of the rim, and a social and economic division between East and West endures. Despite the opportunities for conflict that have existed in the area, it has in reality been remarkably free of all forms of armed conflict since the collapse of the Soviet Union in 1991. This reflects a number of factors, including restraints from outside placed on potential parties to conflict, the institutionalisation of co-operation and the active peace agenda of the Nordic governments.

It is worth looking at the response of the states in the area to the changed security environment since 1989. The approaches of Russia and of the West will be examined first as providing the security context of the Baltic rim space, then the Baltic rim states will be considered.


THE RESPONSES OF THE TWO MAIN ACTORS

The security policy of Russia in Europe's Baltic rim can be seen as "fundamentally different from the former policy of the Soviet Union" (Baranovsky 1996: 164) and the difficulty that Moscow has had in defining its post-Cold War security policy is well documented in the chapter on "The Russia Dimension" in this book. In that chapter, Alexander Sergounin points out that the Baltic lands have always been "a zone of interaction" between Russia and the outside world, both in peaceful and warlike ways. In the new security situation in which Russian policy-makers find themselves, the main sources of insecurity are to the south and east and, anyhow, the country is no longer able to dominate the Baltic rim and has an ambiguous attitude towards the area. However, Sergounin also points out a number of factors that still lead to a continued Russian security interest in the region. The geopolitical changes may have pushed Russia's presence in the Baltic back to Kaliningrad and St Petersburg, but the country has a continued strategic military standing there of some importance, making the Baltic rim "still a field of NATO-Russian military confrontation", though–as pointed out above–not one of military conflict. Furthermore, Russia still has its political influence in the area–not least that of "protecting" the Russian-speaking minorities–to consider and the region is one of economic potential for Russia. Often intertwined with this last issue are the elements of humanitarian and human rights issues.

What is also demonstrated in the chapter by Sergounin is the development of Russian policy over time from that in 1990, when Russia and the Baltic republics were still part of the Soviet Union and looked to each other for support, through the 1993-4 disagreements between Russia, Estonia, Latvia and Lithuania, to the compromise agreements reached on most issues between these parties in 1995-6. This latter period has seen two strands in Russian policy–that of co-operating with the other states in the Baltic rim on either a bilateral or multilateral basis, and that of expressing concern about the eventual extension of NATO membership to the three Baltic states. The ambiguities, dichotomies and uncertainties of Russia's policy in the region have resulted mainly from domestic sources, though they have often been triggered by external stimuli.

In particular, policy statements about the protection of Russian minorities abroad represent a consensus of sorts between the Communists, the nationalists and some disillusioned liberals, with the Russian State Duma obliging the President to show more consideration for the Russian minorities in the Baltic states and to link the issue with Russian troop withdrawals. However, while these aspects of Russian policy have caused frustration and bitterness in the Baltic states and annoyance in some Western countries, actual Russian governmental dealings with the Baltic states have been moderate–compared with the voices from the Duma–though scarcely friendly (see chapter 2). This could possibly be explained in terms of the Russian government not wanting to be seen to act against international norms and standards in Europe and thereby risk some sort of sanctions by the West. (It should be remembered that Mr Gorbachev's government suffered this response after troop action in the Baltic states in early 1991). Also the Russian government may have its own reasons for not pushing conflict too far in the Baltic rim. As well as endangering the sort of economic and political reforms associated with the Yeltsin government, action there may not be successful. Russian armed forces have not managed to pacify Chechen rebels within the Russian Federation and there is no certainty that even some form of covert action against one or more of the Baltic states would be successful in terms of, for example, guaranteeing the rights of the Slavic minorities there. Furthermore, Moscow must calculate that the main security threat will be from the south and east, as Sergounin mentions.

Having seemingly decided not to use the threat of force over the minorities and troop placement issues, will Moscow rule out this option for good, one of the pre-conditions for a security community (Joenniemi & Stålvant 1995: 36)? One commentator has written in this context that "the risk of returning to the strategy of pressure does exist–prompted by the gradual erosion of democracy in Russia and increasing salience of "great-power" and even nationalistic arguments" but that this trend is "restrained by serious incentives not to undermine the post-Cold War pattern" (Baranovsky 1996: 182).

Thus, it would seem to be the wider strategic consideration of relations with the West that is forcing "the strategy of pressure" (let alone coercion) against the Baltic states off Moscow's agenda. Are there factors that might drag it back on? The suggestion is that one significant external factor–the extension of NATO membership to the three Baltic states–and the possibility of internal changes within Russia may provide the incentive to change from being a more passive "status quo" power to one having revisionist ambitions.

The latter possibility has been a subject for speculation in the West and chapter 2 outlines the constellation of political forces that have so far contributed to the Russian debate on its Baltic security policy. It could be that with the rise of the statist "derzhavniki", a suitable compromise has been reached–a more hard-line verbal approach tempered with pragmatism in negotiations. Sergounin asserts that internal changes in the government of Russia to a more authoritarian or Communist regime would have adverse effects on the country's relations in the Baltic rim, but that the present policy of "muddling through" is likely to continue. One element that is seen as possibly changing either the policy of the present government or the chances of the nationalists and Communists coming closer to power, is that of the Baltic states joining NATO (Lieven 1996: 175-9). Such a move can be seen as "bandwagoning" in alliance theory terms (see chapter 11), and will be perceived by Russia as rewarding the West with "extra benefits" (new alliance members) over and above those already gained by the collapse of the Soviet Union. This is clearly a factor that can influence the security configuration in the Baltic rim, over which the Baltic states and the West have some considerable control.

Chapter 3 reminds the reader how the developments in Western Europe in the early 1990s–the Maastricht process in particular–were themselves partly determined by the end of the Cold War and the collapse of communism in Eastern Europe. The resultant unification of Germany bolstered the internal developments that had taken place within the European Communities since the "relance" of the mid-1980s with a Franco-German deal that formed the core of the Maastricht Treaty of 1992. Thus, the planned European Union became a pole of attraction–part of the bandwagon to join–for the newly liberated states of East and Central Europe. With the membership of the former-EFTA states in 1995, this pole became even more attractive to those left outside, despite all the negative elements–its seeming failure in former Yugoslavia, referenda results in France and Denmark, the collapse of the Exchange Rate Mechanism and the wrangling about European Monetary Union–that undermined the integration process from 1992.

The EU presents certain problems for would-be members in the Baltic rim. Not only is its success as an effective Union in doubt after the turbulence of the early 1990s, there is the question of how to approach the organization. As Hans Mouritzen points out in chapter 3, it is hard to get a handle on the nature of the EU. Its innovative structure makes it an uneasy negotiating partner for any state, let alone those–like the Baltic states– which are emerging into the world after some years forced hibernation and with scarce foreign policy resources. Furthermore, the decision-making structure of the EU has meant that its "foreign policy" has tended to favour the lowest common denominator. The exception can be in those areas where a majority of the member states have only a weak interest whereas some members have strong and overlapping concerns. This has been the case in the Baltic rim where the Nordic EU members–backed by Germany and the United Kingdom–have been able to steer EU policy towards the Baltic states and Baltic co-operation as a whole very much in the direction that they desire.

In carrying out such a policy, these countries–and, implicitly, the EU– have generally been backed by the United States. They represent the "wideners" within the EU as described by Mouritzen, although Germany's commitment to extended EU membership is perhaps the most conditional. Though the Baltic states are relatively poor and have a sizeable Russophone population, their candidature for EU membership has been pressed by the above Western countries, partly to provide them with "soft" security[1] in the absence of NATO membership in the immediate future. However, the EU's Amsterdam summit in June 1997 showed that EU membership was unlikely to come any sooner, with 2002 being seen by observers as the earliest entry date for even the lead candidates such as Poland (Jenkins 1997: 5).

The West's approach towards the extension of NATO membership eastwards has been one of confused motives and policies. The original disagreement between the United States and certain European members over NATO enlargement led to the interim arrangements of the North Atlantic Cooperation Council and the Partnership for Peace programme. However, once the United States, supported by Germany, had got its way over enlargement, the "who, when and how?" questions had to be asked. The answers to each of these have been neither clear nor always consistent. As Mouritzen points out, NATO has a sort of check-list for potential candidates and clearly those scoring the highest marks will be at the top of the list for entry, though that does not prevent the "failures" from trying again. The "when" of enlargement will be politically determined and is not open to the sort of negotiating delays that EU membership must inevitably bring. The "how" is a little more complicated. The signing of the Washington Treaty and ratification by the existing members provide only the formal elements, leaving questions about stationing of troops, membership of the military command structure and the use of territory for exercises still open.

The difficulties of having the Baltic states as early new members of NATO are covered in chapter 3. Can NATO expansion take place without these countries feeling that they have been placed in a "grey zone" or that Russia has been given a "velvet veto" over their membership? Given what has been said about the issue of Baltic membership of NATO and Russian attitudes, perhaps the West should use the period after a NATO extension as a period of positive action in the Baltic rim.

---

1. The idea of "soft security" is one that encompasses the non-military, civic aspects of security, such as those relating to the environment, or to crime (Helveg Petersen 1996: 1, 8).

THE RESPONSE OF THE COUNTRIES IN BETWEEN

What of the response of the Baltic rim countries to the post-1989 security situation in their part of the world? While the main focus of this book has been on the Baltic rim states, especially their relations with Russia and the West, it is well to give some consideration to the role in the area of the Nordic states–not just Finland. As can be seen, these countries have been particularly active in supporting Baltic rim institutions.

The early reflexes to the changes in Eastern Europe in late 1989 showed a caution on behalf of most of the *Nordic countries*. In official assessments, there seemed to be an emphasis on the dangers of the new developments which were seen either as being not so significant (see chapter 4) or as offering a threat to progress in arms control and as affecting Northern Europe less than the central region (Archer 1994a). As the Baltic states moved to independence, some Nordic states–though not Denmark and Iceland–also showed characteristic reticence in recognising the new governments (Mouritzen 1994: 162-3; Ellemann-Jensen 1996: 136-142). Once done, however, these governments turned their mind to the wider question of the security future of the Baltic rim.

The Nordic states–with the behind-the-scenes (and sometimes overt) support of the United States, Germany and the United Kingdom–set about socialising the three Baltic countries and the Russian Federation in its behaviour in the Baltic region. This consisted of preaching to both sides the virtues of political compromise in Russian-Baltic state relations, and, in some cases, providing the means by which such a compromise could be reached. For example, seeing that the question of living accommodation was a stumbling block in settling the issue of the repatriation of Russian troops in the Baltic states, the Nordic states provided aid to house those troops in Russia. The Nordic governments were also instrumental in persuading the Baltic governments to establish a Baltic Council–modelled on the Nordic Council–and then in creating a Council of Baltic Sea States to include all the littoral governments (plus, of course, Norway and Iceland). Furthermore, they have been eager to apply the instruments of the Organization for Security and Cooperation in Europe (OSCE) to the Baltic region, especially in the use of a Baltic Regional Table of the European Stability Pact, of OSCE monitors to oversee the withdrawal of Russian troops, and of its High Commission on National Minorities (Archer 1997b: 84-91).

The Nordic countries have also been involved in promoting more direct security co-operation in the Baltic rim. In particular they have supported the idea of a Baltic peacekeeping force by training officers and NCOs for a Baltic battalion (BALTBAT, see chapter 6). Baltic platoons were trained by Denmark and integrated into the Danish peacekeeping battalion in Croatia and in the Danish battalion in the IFOR Nordic-Polish brigade deployed near Tuzla (Hækkerup 1996: 11-13). The Nordic states have themselves been co-operating over defence matters, and not just in their assistance to Baltic peacekeepers. The end of the Cold War has made the differences between the security policies of the Nordic states less significant and this has allowed greater co-ordination of action between the five countries. However, the impression should not be given that, since 1989, all has been sweetness and light between the Nordic states. There has also been a certain amount of competition between the countries and a lack of agreed leadership in their Baltic policies. Not least Danish, Finnish and Swedish politicians have sometimes been less than complementary about each others' efforts (Ellemann-Jensen 1996: 136-7; Mouritzen 1997b: 37-47).

The shift of emphasis away from "hard" to "soft" security after the end of the Cold War has allowed the Nordic countries to co-operate more intensively over security than during the Cold war period. However, on the question of "hard" security–the defence of the national territory–the five countries still follow different courses: Denmark, Iceland and Norway rely on the security guarantees of NATO to bolster their national efforts, while Finland and Sweden are so far content to rest on their own defences. There has been an increased willingness by the Nordic states to work together on such matters as the creation of the Nordic Battalion, which saw service in former Yugoslavia (Archer 1994b). As mentioned in chapter 4, Swedish and Finnish defence and security policies had become more parallel by the mid-1990s, to such an extent that the two countries submitted a joint memorandum in this area to the IGC (Archer 1997a).

Membership of the European Union has completed the Finnish move westward that began with their membership of the Nordic Council in 1954, and it has also meant an end to dealing with its eastern neighbour on a bilateral basis. While the message of the post-war years was that Finland could manage alone even when faced by a super-power as its direct neighbour, it should be remembered that the country was not entirely on its own. Its growing co-operation with the other Nordic states tied it ever more closely economically and socially to those states, and the working of what became known as the "Nordic balance" associated the security destiny of Finland with that of its Nordic neighbours. So even if the turn to Europe in

1991 represented a break with the main theme of post-war Finnish policy, it did allow a minor theme–that of close co-operation with the Nordic states– to come to the fore in the security field. Taking up this option may have provided another factor to add to those that explain the moderated bandwagoning seen in Finnish policy since 1991 (see chapter 11).

An early new member of NATO will be Poland, a state that has already increased its military relations with Germany and Denmark (Danish Ministry of Defence 1996; Krohn 1995: 596-7). This has importance in the Baltic region as it would bring NATO's frontier up to the territory of the Russian Federation–in the shape of the Kaliningrad Oblast–in continental Europe. Again, this *"inversion of the principal amity-enmity patterns"* (chapter 8) will matter little should the security agenda, and NATO's status, change significantly, as foreseen in the Paris agreement between NATO and the Russian Federation.[2] Poland itself has focused its attention more to its land frontiers and its relations with the other Visegrad states (the Czech Republic, Slovakia, and Hungary) than to the north and the Baltic, and has seen its regional efforts there subordinated to wider strategic goals (Ognik 1996: 129). As stressed in chapter 8, Polish governments since 1989 have sought links with the West as a way of averting domination by the Soviet Union, then by Russia. Thus, the emphasis on belonging to the West, and the priority given to the Euro-Atlantic link. This strategic move has necessitated Poland placing its relations with neighbouring countries– including Germany and Russia–in order, and Kostecki's chapter demonstrates that this process was not easy but that Polish decision-makers understood that integration into the West depended on their success in arranging their relations with Russia (ibid.: 9).

Poland's membership of the Council of Baltic Sea States (CBSS) hides the reality that Baltic co-operation has not had the priority given to relations with the EU, NATO and even the Visegrad states. To that extent and because of its greater distance from Russia, Poland is less affected by the salient environment of the Baltic rim than are the three Baltic states and even Finland. Though it has a Baltic coast, it is also a Central European state that will soon form the Central European flank of both NATO and the EU. However, the failure of the EU's Amsterdam summit to track a clear

---

2. The Founding Act on Mutual Relations, Co-operation and Security signed between Russia and NATO on 27 May 1997 represented a high point in bringing together the two main former adversaries of the Cold War and also created a NATO-Russia council, though it did not give Russia the right to veto NATO decisions (See EIU 1997: 15).

course for potential new members could mean that Poland has a few years yet during which other forums–such as the CBSS–might be used to advantage.

Poland's move to NATO membership augured by that organisation's Madrid summit in July 1997 is clearly one welcomed by the wide spectrum of Polish political opinion, as shown in Kostecki's chapter, but–as also demonstrated by that author–it is not without its pitfalls. The NATO-Russian Paris agreement is just the sort of deal that Poles fear, and they may be wondering whether the price paid to Russia for acceptance of NATO enlargement has not been too high. Certainly a more revisionist Russia could leave Poland more exposed, even if it had become part of NATO. There is, therefore, some incentive for any Polish government to ensure that the divide between Russia and NATO is not a stark one and instead involves a "grey zone" both in geographical and conceptual terms. This would mean looking favourable at the Baltic states, Finland and Sweden remaining outside NATO, but a continuation of PfP activities in the Baltic rim, involving Russia as a partner though not with any *droit de regard*.

The security of the three *Baltic states* is almost always seen as being bound together in the West, and this factor is recognised by the governments of the three countries. However, chapters 5 to 7 make it clear that these states have differences in their security background and the problems of defence co-operation are underlined in chapter 9. On the one hand, Estonia is seen as being the most advanced in terms of economic reform, whereas Lithuania has perhaps the closest defence links with the West. Finland has strong links with Estonia; Poland established a closer liaison with Lithuania after some initial problems (see chapter 7). Latvia seems the most exposed of the three, with its large non-Latvian population, its political divisions, and, as yet, comparatively weak institutional connections with the West. That being said, Estonia has its own problems with the Russian minority, especially those in the north-east of the country; and Lithuania has to deal with the thorny issue of Russian troop transits through to Kaliningrad. Each of the chapter authors for the three Baltic states have, however, charted the progress made by those countries in re-establishing their independence and in orienting themselves towards the West. In addition chapter 11 shows that the three states have tried to avoid being abandoned by the Western bandwagon and being left alone with their Russian neighbour.

In terms of relations with Russia and the former Soviet Union, all three states have gone through more or less the same phases: an initial period of friendship with the Russian leadership while the Soviet Union still existed, followed by increasing alienation from the Russian Federation, and then a period of negotiations leading to a *modus vivendi*. It is clear that the three countries still consider the major threat to their security to be from Russia and from the Russian minority within their states. However, the picture is by no means in such sharp relief. As set out in chapter 9, the very weakness of the Baltic states economic infrastructures and societies is a core element in their lack of security and provides a basis for further insecurity when connected to outside pressures and the ethnic question. Clemmesen stresses the "internal obstacles to change" within all the Baltic states defence forces and many of these reflect wider problems in the three countries' politics and in their society. Western states–not least the Nordic ones–have increased their defence assistance and sovereignty support to the Baltic states, but this will be of little use unless the Baltic states undertake many of the reforms mentioned by Clemmesen.

All three of the Baltic states have placed EU and NATO membership high on their agenda. This should be seen in the context of the perceived threat of entrapment by the Russian Federation, but the very factors that make these countries weak states–their weak economies and governmental structures, their minorities problems and their social divisions–are some of those that make them less attractive to institutions such as the EU and NATO. In considering the current security dilemmas of these states, the internal factors should not be forgotten or played down. The salient environment of the Baltic rim determines the main external security consideration of the three Baltic states. However, it is by no means the end of the story. Having considered the current situation of the Baltic rim states, the future of the region–especially the security scenarios of the rim countries in a wider context–will now be examined.


THE BALTIC RIM: DEALING WITH THE WEST

The shaping of Europe's Baltic rim into a region of its own depends on a number of factors. The very concept of a political-security region is a contested one (Neumann 1994). At least it would seem that the major actors in the area should perceive themselves as being the main providers of their own security with, perhaps, institutions exclusive to the area playing an important role. Since 1989, a tension has developed between what Poland, the Nordic countries and the Baltic states can do to provide for their own security and the security outcome imposed on the area by the Russian-NATO equation. While the context for the Baltic rim states is provided by that latter relationship, the policies of the individual states are important in taking up particular opportunities, as can be seen in Michael Clemmesen's chapter. This section will trace the possible future security development of Europe's Baltic rim, examining those contradictory elements of integration and fragmentation.

The main thrust of this book has been the contextual security of Europe's Baltic rim, in particular the states there bordering Russia. Their future security is contingent on whether the Russian Federation will accept, albeit reluctantly, the status quo or whether it will try to revise the post-1991 (let alone the post-1989) settlement in the area (see next section). To an important extent this depends on the internal forces within Russia, but what the Russian government can do, will depend on the state of their armed forces (and covert services) as well as the capability of their diplomacy.

In what may be a mutual action-reaction relationship, the West can both respond to and promote uncertainty in Russia. Accepting the East and Central European states into NATO without changing the basic collective defence core of the Organization, was perceived by the West as at least an irritant to the Russian leadership, thus the 1997 Paris agreement was signed between NATO and Russia. Eventual admission of one or more of the Baltic states into NATO could provide the political provocation for more revisionist approaches by Russia. On the other hand, Baltic membership might be provoked by changes within Russia, and might then be seen as a stabilising measure by confirming that the 1991 settlement–that saw the Baltic states regain their independence–is not open to revision. This stabilising element has been bolstered by the signing of the Paris agreement with the Russian Federation and could be followed by the revision of arms control agreements more in line with Moscow's needs.

What other factors may determine the security shape of the Baltic rim in the medium-term future? The nature of the wider European security architecture will decide what is on offer for the Baltic rim states. The institutions of European security will be affected by developments within Russia, but in the end the main formulations will be decided by the United States and the major West European powers–Germany, France and the United Kingdom, with an input from the other EU and NATO members.

The Organization for Security and Cooperation in Europe (OSCE)–and, to a lesser extent, the Council of Europe–will remain as the major depositories of values and norms and will provide some institutional underpinning of "soft" European security, for example in the case of human rights and minorities. The European Union will provide other elements of soft security for its members, especially in the form of the Common Foreign and Security Policy, and will also give some underpinning to states with Europe Agreements through trade and aid arrangements and institutional links.

The "harder" aspects of security–such as collective defence, peace enforcement and "peacekeeping plus"–will still come mainly from NATO with its extended membership. Non-members will not be entirely left out, as the PfP and EAPC will provide some points of contact between NATO and other states. The Western European Union will continue to act as a link between the EU and NATO, while at the same time being a forum within which the EU states can develop their common defence. However, the EU's Treaty of Amsterdam suggested that this will continue to be a convoy-like procession, advancing at the rate determined by the most reluctant but with certain EU members in the vanguard.

Another major contribution to the security development of the Baltic rim will be the security policies and provisions of the countries in the area. Their conduct within the constraints of arms control and disarmament arrangements (such as the Conventional Forces in Europe agreements) and the major European institutions such as the OSCE, the EU and NATO, will bring a level of trust and certainty. The security policies of the states in the area will also be open to internal pressures. It is likely that this pressure will be for a reduction in spending on defence, though this may change should a more revisionist or militaristic government come to power in Russia.

What are the security options facing the states in the area? As suggested, one major option will be whether to spend more on defence or not. Should the Russian Federation start to increase the resources devoted to defence–as a response to internal demands, newly defined fears and partly to rebuild its collapsed armed forces–the Baltic rim states will be under greater pressure to increase their defence expenditure. The three Baltic states may anyhow find their defence spending rising for the same reasons as those posited for Russia. Poland will find its defence expenditure increasing as a result of NATO membership and coming in line with requirements of the Atlantic Alliance. The Nordic states, whose defence expenditure has fallen during the 1990s will see a stabilisation in this spending, with difficult decisions being made about large replacement projects.

With the extension of NATO to include Poland, the two non-aligned states of Finland and Sweden will be faced with the question of their possible membership. Mouritzen deals in chapter 4 with the conditions under which Finland might join NATO and speculates whether Swedish membership might be the "triggering event." Assuming that NATO remains as primarily a collective defence organization which may also take on some "peacekeeping plus" operations, and given that the first round of new members is limited to the Visegrad states (except Slovakia), there seems little incentive for Sweden–or Finland–to consider membership.

Indeed, if the two countries' main security concern in their region is that of the Russian-Baltic states' relationship, then there is some purpose in remaining outside NATO, at least as long as the Baltic states are excluded. They can provide for those three states a model of countries that are EU members, participate fully in the Union's Common Foreign and Security Policy, are active in peacekeeping operations, including those under NATO command, and are still not NATO members. However, the major variance from this model by the Baltic states is their inability to defend their national territory to any significant extent (see, for example, chapter 6). Thus, their situation is closer to that of Finland in the early post-war years and Finland's response–that of adapting to Moscow's will (see chapter 4)–is scarcely politically acceptable in the Baltic states, nor would it be guaranteed to work as well as it did for Finland. Thus, the three states feel that only NATO membership can help underwrite the defence of their national territory.

This scramble for NATO membership could possibly undermine the wider "liberal institutionalist" security menu which, it has been suggested, the Nordic states are following in their region.[3] At least it could be interpreted as a vote of no-confidence in such an approach as it would be clear that the collective defence sought through NATO by the Baltic states would be directed against the Russian Federation, and thus could negate the concept of a non-zero-sum approach to security. It certainly could be a move away from the sort of common and comprehensive security advocated by the OSCE.

---

3. This approach places an emphasis on developing international society, especially through a range of international institutions. (See Archer 1997b: 83-4).

However, this need not be the case: NATO membership by the Baltic states could be seen as being compatible with a more "liberal institutionalist" approach given certain conditions. One would be a change in the nature of NATO so that it would become much more a common security organization. The Danish government–the most fervent NATO advocate of NATO membership for the Baltic states–is positive about the creation of "a new and different NATO" and closer links between NATO and Russia (Helveg Petersen 1996), and the Paris agreement between NATO and Russia suggests that this view has met with some success. The second condition–which would be associated with such a change in NATO–would be for Russia to accept that the Baltic states entering NATO is not aimed at it. Short of a revision of NATO's nature, this might be brought about by a number of promises concerning limits on NATO exercises, weapons and troops on the Baltic states' soil–a version of Norway and Denmark's restrictions–as a follow-on to the Paris agreement between NATO and Russia. However, such moves seem to negate the main point of NATO membership as understood by the three Baltic states: the Article V collective defence element and integration into the military command structure and activities of an American-led alliance. There is, thus, a gap between the expectations of the Baltic states of NATO membership and what is on offer. Now that it is clear that the Baltic states will not be among the first entrants to NATO, there is a breathing space during which this gap might be narrowed. This could be done by making the Baltic states more prepared for collective defence by an extensive arms and military assistance programme, a move that would no doubt bring a reaction from Moscow. More effective–and more likely–would be an effort to moderate Baltic expectations of NATO and prepare them for membership of an organization vastly different from NATO Mark I which existed up to 1991. This would be assisted if one of the Baltic states–Lithuania is the most likely candidate–became a NATO member in the proposed second round of expansion. Not only would this reassure the other two states that the prospect of membership could be achieved, but it might allay some Russian fears that NATO was somehow anxious to pull the Baltic states within its borders at one go.

The option of EU membership by Poland and the Baltic states is one that presents fewer problems in the security field, partly because Russian politicians do not view it as being so threatening and partly because Russians may hope to gain more directly through such extensions. It has also been seen as providing soft security for the new members, as it would seem unlikely that other states would make threats against an EU member and it would allow the new members to build up the economic and political bases of their societies. The first contention can be challenged, as Greek membership of the EU has not prevented disputes with Turkey, though it may be argued that having both states in NATO has allowed the United States to exercise a hegemonic brake on any drift into conflict by the two.

The options open to the Baltic rim states mean that, in the medium term, they could all end up in both NATO and the EU, or–at the opposite end of the spectrum–only Finland would be in the EU and only Poland in NATO. The intermediate alternatives would allow for a combination of memberships of western institutions, with the most likely one being Poland in both the EU and NATO, Finland in the EU and one or more of the Baltic states joining the EU while remaining hopeful candidates for membership of NATO (see chapter 1). Membership of the two major institutions by all the Baltic rim states will provide a greater chance of integration in the area. It would allow for regional activities, such as those based on the EU's Interreg scheme, and may encourage further Baltic-based exercises within the NATO context, but the states within the area will have shown by their choices that they wish to stress their links with countries outside the Baltic rim, namely the major EU powers and the United States. The area is thus less likely to develop a *strong* regional identity.

Regional institutions are more likely to be valued if it is known that a number of the Baltic rim states will not be joining either the EU or NATO for some years. Baltic Sea co-operation–as well as providing some functional benefits–could be used to demonstrate that the states involved are worthy partners. Should one Baltic state–Estonia in the case of the EU and Lithuania in the case of NATO–join before the other two, regional institutions such as the Council for Baltic Sea States, those existing between the Baltic states and those of Nordic-Baltic co-operation, will assist in preventing any differentiation from becoming permanent. Baltic Sea co-operation may also help to build bridges to Russia that–if maintained–will soften the effect on Russia of eventual Baltic rim states' membership of the EU and NATO. Whether there is a successful development of a Baltic region in the interim period will depend not just on the rim states but on Russia, to which attention will now be given.

## THE BALTIC RIM: RESPONDING TO RUSSIA

In the country chapters 4 to 8, the various options of countries joining or remaining outside of the EC and/or NATO were considered in the case of two Russian scenarios: one whereby Russia accepts the status quo, and one where it tries to revise the post-1989 and post-1991 settlements. What are the likely outcomes for the Baltic rim space as a whole of these options?

From the viewpoint of creating a new security system within Europe, the optimum solution would be a full extension of both NATO and EU membership to all states in Europe's Baltic rim with special arrangements along the lines of the May 1997 Paris agreement being made for Russia. In this scenario, Russia remains not just a *status quo power*, but an accepting one. It allows NATO and EU membership by its Baltic neighbours mainly because it also receives benefits from the EU and reassurance from a changed NATO. NATO membership would not only promise hard security for its new neighbours, but it would have also contributed considerably to their feeling of security by bringing Russia into a closer relationship with the expanded organisations.

This seems an optimistic scenario, and hard security for the Baltic states and Poland–and possibly Finland–is more likely to be achieved at the expense of a new dividing line in Europe. On one side will be the three Baltic states, anxious about the attitude of a riled Russia but satisfied with their "insider" status; Finland, perhaps pulled into NATO membership by a Swedish move in that direction; and Poland, with anxieties about the status of Kaliningrad and of Belarus. On the other side will be Russia, including the militarised exclave of Kaliningrad, and Belarus, perhaps with a closer relationship with Moscow. In this case Russia would have reluctantly accepted the NATO expansion–at least to the extent that no forceful action is seriously contemplated–but a Cold Peace would have broken out in Europe.

A more *revisionist government* in Moscow faced with such an expansion of Western institutions up to its borders may decide to take firm action. This would certainly involve an even closer link with Belarus and perhaps put some pressure on Ukraine to join in defence arrangements. In the Baltic rim, Kalinigrad might be strengthened militarily, though there must be some doubt as to the defence logic of building up such an outpost. The calculation by the West–and the Baltic states–would be that their inclusion into NATO and the EU would so affect Russia's perception about the utility of any direct military action against those states, that they would then be safe against retaliatory action. This may be a correct estimation, but Russia could also take diplomatic and economic action against the Baltic states, and Moscow may decide to treat the West as its adversary, thereby introducing a "Small Ice Age" in east-west relations. Russia could seek allies in China or to its south, possibly with Iraq, or even a discontented Turkey, and it might decide that arms control and disarmament treaties were no longer valid. The security of the Baltic states would have been bought at a high cost.

Considering the scenario of EU membership being extended along the south coast of the Baltic Sea (though not to include Russia), but NATO expansion in the north stopping with Poland, the outcome could be one acceptable by all sides as an interim stage. This would particularly be the case with a *status quo government* in Moscow, which would not feel so pressured if neither the Baltic states nor Sweden and Finland had been included in the NATO fold. EU membership could be perceived by the Russians as an opportunity, especially should the formal relationship between Brussels and Moscow be improved at the same time. Trade possibilities between the EU and Russia could be enhanced by Baltic states' EU membership, and there would be an insistence by the Union that border issues should be solved previous to membership by the three states.

The Nordic countries, especially Finland, would be content with this situation, especially as it would relieve them of the pressure to consider NATO membership. Finland would continue to be on the right side of the economic fault-line in Europe, but would have the Baltic states by its side. Economic assistance to these countries–and to Russia–would be a more urgent matter and one that would receive more attention within the EU than at present. However, it would be doubtful that, with EU membership by the Visegrad states–there would be any extra spare resources. The Nordic states may become the advocates within the EU for action to assist Russia, but they also may have to content themselves with something like the present level of aid.

Should a *revisionist government* in Moscow be faced by EU membership by one or all of the Baltic states, on top of that of Poland, a different reaction might be expected. Such a government may calculate that the EU membership by the Baltic states forebodes their joining NATO, but non-NATO membership for the time-being also allows Moscow some freedom of action. The Russian minority such as that in Narva in Estonia, might appeal to Moscow, especially should EU membership by Estonia lead to greater border controls between them and the Russian Federation.

Social and economic disruption that might accompany the Baltic states becoming part of the Single European Market could be exploited by the Russian authorities, thereby increasing the sense of insecurity. However, the calculation in Moscow could be that no direct action should be taken against the three states once they are part of the European Union as this could provoke retaliation–certainly in an economic form–by the major EU members.

The Nordic states could play an important role in such a situation in providing intermediaries in some of the disputes, in restraining the Baltic governments and also in impressing on the Russian Federation the cost of any hostile action. One possible counter-threat against Moscow could be that of Finland and Sweden applying for NATO membership in response to Russian action in the Baltic, providing a resonance of the old "Nordic balance" days. However, this is a threat that would have to be used sparingly against a government that was finely balanced in its calculations, and it would have to be credible.

A continuation of the present situation whereby Finland, Sweden and the Baltic states stay out of NATO and the Baltic states are not deemed ready for EU membership, though the doors of both organizations are opened for Poland, would not excite a *status quo government* in Moscow. Should Russia attempt a modest form of "balancing" in response to Poland's NATO and EU membership, this would be resisted by the Baltic and Nordic states especially if it involved bringing the Baltics closer into the Russian sphere of interest. Further co-operation with Belarus might be viewed with Western scepticism, but little else. However, in this situation of "grey zone security", Russia would have neither the resources nor the will-power to intervene militarily in the Baltic states.

In such a case the Nordic countries will continue to play an active role in the Baltic rim, attempting to heal the scars left after the Baltic states left the Soviet Union. They will be the most high-profile of the Western states in the Baltic area and their emphasis will be on building up the institutions of co-operation in the region so that they may survive the Baltic states joining the EU and provide effective bridges to Russia after such a move.

A *revisionist authority* in Moscow may not be content to leave the current situation as it is, especially after Poland joins NATO and the EU. As has been pointed out in this book, there are a number of issues that present themselves as sources of conflict between Russia and the Baltic states and any of these could be manipulated by a hostile government in Moscow or, indeed, by local power groups. Shorn of definite Western guarantees, the Baltic states could become attractive compensation for Poland's move.

In such a situation the response of the Nordic states could be vital. They will urge the Baltic states to stay united and to resist any "divide and rule" tactics by Moscow. They will continue with their low-level military assistance but will not want to provoke a response by selling arms to the Baltic states. They could hope to raise the cost of Russian hostile action both by strengthening the ability of the Baltic states to defend themselves–as outlined in chapter 9–and by organising the threat of Western sanctions against any precipitate Russian move. However, should an aggressive government be in power in Moscow, Finland–with its long border with Russia–may be cautious in its dealings with the power to its east which could then be the dominant military threat in its salient environment. Finland would have to consider the whole question of NATO membership: would this be an effective way of safeguarding itself against hostile Russian action or would membership provoke a Russian counter-move against the Baltic states? Fearing such a reaction could lead to Finnish inaction, although should Sweden join NATO, Finland's dilemma would become extremely acute. The cost of a "wrong" Finnish decision could be high for the Baltic states and peace in the area more generally.

The Nordic states have been identified here as key players in any process of region-building in the Baltic Sea area. However, the opportunities for such activities will, to a great extent, depend on the attitude of the government in Moscow–whether it is status quo or revisionist–and on the success or otherwise of the Baltic states' quest for EU and NATO membership. It seems that under the conditions of Poland entering NATO but no other institutional expansion for the time-being and a status-quo Russian government, the Nordic states have the greatest freedom of manoeuvre in the Baltic rim. Their contribution in the areas of both trade and security (widely defined) would continue and the various regional forums–such as the Council for Baltic Sea States–would try to tackle "low political" issues. They would still have an important role–as would regional plans–should the Baltic states join the EU but–together with Sweden and Finland–remain outside NATO for the time-being, though the level of Baltic-wide regional co-operation would depend on the attitude of Moscow. The more the Baltic rim states are drawn into NATO and the more revisionist the Russian government becomes, the less influence there will be for Baltic regional arrangements and their Nordic sponsors.

CONCLUSIONS

Russia has been identified as the major factor in determining the security future of Europe's Baltic rim, with either its acceptance of the status quo opening up opportunities for co-operation or its intention to revise the post-1989 and post1991 settlements acting as a source of insecurity. The scenarios outlined above have examined the response of the Baltic rim states in terms of EU and NATO membership. If the five Baltic rim states–Estonia, Latvia, Lithuania, Finland and Poland–are considered together, it can be seen that their interests and actions will be most confluent if all are NATO and EU members and Russia remains a status quo power. Failing the achievement of this scenario, a continuation of the status quo in both Moscow and among the Baltic Sea states (though with Poland joining NATO) will also see a good deal of common interest among the five rim countries. Baltic membership of the EU and Polish membership of the EU and NATO, with the status quo being maintained in Russia, would see some differentiation in the rim states policies, especially if Finland started to consider NATO membership in line with a Swedish move in that direction.

A revisionist government in Russia could see a unity of purpose and policy among the five rim countries with all joining NATO and the Baltic states starting the process of becoming part of the EU. Interest could become most fragmented should the Baltic states not be accepted for NATO membership after Poland has been allowed in. Finland could be pulled by a Swedish NATO application to follow suit, thereby leaving the Baltic states exposed. In such a situation, Baltic states' membership of the EU could ameliorate the divisions between the rim states, but there would still be the danger that increased Finnish "hard" security could be won at the expense of the Baltic states. There is also the problem under such conditions of a differentiation being made between the Baltic states themselves, with Lithuania perhaps being sheltered by a close relationship with Poland. In all these cases regional institutions could help to keep the Baltic rim states together, though a hostile Russia would trim the utility of Baltic-wide institutions.

Are the states covered in chapters 4 to 8 above, forming a bridge, a buffer or a grey-zone? At the moment, they have the potential for all three elements. The Baltic rim could represent a bridge between Russia and the West, especially if EU membership by all the states led to development of trade with the Kaliningrad and St Petersberg areas. The Baltic states–much against their will–could also form part of a buffer (including Belarus, Moldava and Ukraine) that would separate countries such as Poland, let alone Denmark and Germany, from any adverse security trends in Russia. Finally, they could represent a grey-zone of non-EU (except for Finland) and non-NATO states (except for Poland from the date of its joining NATO) that, nevertheless, are candidates for membership of both organisations. The present relationships of the EU and NATO with states in the Baltic rim are gradated rather than being just those of members/non-members, so the metaphor of a grey-zone is perhaps the most meaningful one.

The danger for the Baltic states is that, failing NATO and EU membership, they may become the buffers, not to mention a sphere of influence, of a revisionist regime in Moscow. Even with EU membership, the possibility of acting as a bridge with a hostile Russian government is small and if all the rim states become NATO members they will certainly resemble a new Western buffer against a revisionist Russia. At least a status quo government in Moscow will allow non-zero sum agreements with Russia to accompany EU and NATO membership, thereby allowing the rim states to become more links between East and West rather than part of a new division.

It should not, however, be imagined that the only salient factor affecting the future nature of the Baltic region is that of the nature of Russian foreign policy, neither should it be accepted that this nature cannot itself be affected by the action of the rim states. Indeed, it has been the contention of the Nordic states during the 1990s that a positive approach should be made to Russian decision makers in order to include them in the building of a Baltic region. The Nordic countries have also encouraged the Baltic states to deal diplomatically with the Russian authorities and with their own minorities and have assisted in the state-building process in the three countries.

The way that the shades of grey develop in the security area will to a certain extent affect the perception of the area as a region. The more security is black and white–and the more the economic divisions become more stark–the less chance there is of the Baltic rim being perceived as one region. To that extent, the failure of all the Baltic rim states to become both EU and NATO members before the end of the twentieth century holds out opportunities. It allows a greater space for dealing with the concerns of the Russian Federation and for preparing the Baltic states, in particular, for integration into Western institutions. As already seen, it is the internal policies, just as much as the external ones, that are of importance for the survival of these states. The existence of this space–in time and between Russia and the Western institutions–allows for positive action by the Nordic states to help build a Baltic Sea region. One of the tasks of region-building–especially as undertaken by the Nordic countries–is to reduce the element of polarity in the area and to increase the aspect of commonality. So far, they have had some relative success, but there remains much to be done.

# 11 Lessons for Alliance Theory

HANS MOURITZEN

The pre-theory in chapter 1 directed our attention towards factors in states' salient environment, including past salient environment, as we wish to account for their alliance policy. We did not commit ourselves to testing a proper theory, saying which specific alliance behaviour should occur under which circumstances and why. In this chapter, however, it will be discussed what lessons can be learnt from the recent history of Europe's Baltic rim regarding the viability of specific alliance theories. Which theoretical expectations are confirmed and which are disconfirmed, and what do these results teach us about the theories' underlying assumptions?

There are several hypotheses/theories that are relevant here. Baker Fox (1959) found in her study of small states during World War II that "anti-balance of power behaviour" was typical for them, and she suggested that such behaviour might characterize small-states generally (ibid.: 187). Instead of trying to restore the balance of power like the classical "holder of the balance" (e.g. Britain) would do, the small state's support is rendered to the probable winner. Through this form of bandwagoning, or "weathercock policy" as critics would say, a contribution–however modest–is made towards an even more askew balance of power. Top priority is given to safeguarding the small state's core values in the short run; otherwise, there may be no long run to bother about. It cannot afford the luxury of trying to safeguard its long-term interest in a more balanced polarity (ibid.: 181; cf. also Rothstein 1968: 11-12; Handel 1981: 29). Mouritzen (1988) found that Danish foreign policy in the 1930s and Swedish and Danish policy during World War II bandwagoned in neat correspondence with the balance of power in their salient environments. As vigorously expressed by Rothstein (1968: 11):

> Small Powers threatened by neighbouring Great Powers, or intent on securing benefits for themselves in the course of Great Power conflicts, were forced to play a perilous game: moving quickly from the lighter to the heavier side of the balance as soon as an apparent victor in any contest could be discerned.

He adds, normatively, "if power corrupts, so does the lack of it." Not specifically concerned with small states, there has been a debate on bandwagoning vs. balancing in alliance politics (Waltz 1979; Walt 1987; Labs 1992; Kaufman 1992; Walt 1992).

## THE BASIC LAW OF BANDWAGONING

Behind the disagreements on what is the typical form of behaviour can often be found different definitions of the central concepts at stake. Some specifications and comments to the bandwagoning (anti-balance of power) hypothesis should be made here. There are no aspirations to observe or measure any absolute balance whatsoever. Even if this might be meaningful, it would present considerable practical problems. What is possible, however, is the observation of clear-cut *trends* in this balance, including major turning-points. Correspondingly, it is possible to analyse trends, including major shifts, in (weak power) policies. In other words, the concept of bandwagoning is meaningful diachronically (cf. also Mouritzen 1994). "Supporting the winner" refers, hence, to the trend-winner–who may be the under-dog in absolute terms. And "support" may actually mean a less hostile attitude than previously.

With this trend-stipulation of "bandwagoning", I seem to differ from the literature that was referred to above (although certain formulations implicitly reveal a trend focus). A status instead of a trend focus prevails (e.g. Labs 1992: note 2). As formulated by Walt (1992: 471):

> Properly understood, bandwagoning means aligning with the strongest or most threatening state, thereby rendering it more powerful but also more benign (or so the bandwagoning state hopes).

By this definition, other ways of rendering the powerful more powerful and benign–such as making one's neutrality more "friendly"–are excluded from sight. Through Walt's narrow definitions of both bandwagoning and balancing, several in-between positions are neglected. As pointed out by Kaufman (1992: 437), referring to postures vis à vis the Nazi threat, neither the British policy of appeasement, nor French indecision, nor American aloofness, nor Polish neutrality, fall strictly into either category. By contrast, a trend distinction between bandwagoning and balancing is logically exhaustive: either one moves one way or the other or not at all. A status perspective makes the distinction non-exhaustive: there will be an arbitrary number of statuses in-between, as hinted by Kaufman's examples (cf. also Labs 1992: 392-4).

Let us now see how theoretically useful the trend perspective may be, as judged from the experiences of the present book, i.a. Since the Cold War, the Soviet Union/Russia was obviously the power loser and the US/the West consequently the power winner. Bench marks here were Soviet troop withdrawals from Eastern Europe from 1988, the fall of the Berlin Wall and the East European revolutions 1989 and, first and foremost, the dissolution of the Soviet Union 1991. The "losses" of the Baltic countries, Belarus, and the Ukraine, in particular, were geopolitical blows in relation to the West. To this should be added the gradual reduction in Russian military strength since then, due not least to general demoralisation in the armed forces (cf. chapter 2).

How have the rim states analysed in chapters 4-8 reacted to this revision of the balance of power in their salient environment? For *Finland,* we saw that its major re-orientation in the post-war period (declaring a wish for EU membership, recognition of the Baltic countries, laying a distance to neutrality and the FCMA Treaty) occured in September 1991, as the Soviet Union and its ideology disintegrated. It is noteworthy that the revolutions in East and Central Europe 1989-90 made little or no impression on Finnish policy; the crucial factor was the power structure in Finland's immediate neighbourhood that was not transformed until September 1991. Finland bandwagoned towards and eventually into the EU, but it stopped there. Even if all options were explicitly held open, Finland did not declare any specific aspiration to join NATO. Also in order not to provoke Russia, Finland was somewhat more cautious in military co-operation with the Baltic countries than were Sweden and Denmark.

*Estonia, Latvia,* and *Lithuania* went through strikingly parallel developments in their declaratory policies. During their rather symbolic independencies prior to international recognition in September 1991, they aimed for "neutrality" and a demilitarized status. The idea of a nuclear-free zone in the Baltic Sea area that had been debated in various forms in the Nordic countries was also supported. These declarations were attempts to signal a difference from the Soviet Union and were probably also thought to be instrumental in would-be negotiations concerning Soviet troop withdrawals. During the interim period between international recognitions and the Russian troop withdrawals (August 1993 in Lithuania, August 1994 in Estonia and Latvia), aspirations were heightened. Whereas "neutrality" had previously provided a symbolic link to the inter-war republics, the traumatic outcomes of these neutrality policies, inter alia, made "neutrality" an impossible option in the formulation of proper security policies. Among various Western international organizations, also NATO membership was openly mentioned as a possibility. Apart from getting the former Soviet troops out of the countries, the main Baltic priority in this period was to avoid being seen as Russian "near abroad", both by Russia and the West. It was vital not to be lumped together in any contexts with the CIS countries. After the troop withdrawals from the three countries, the EU and NATO membership strivings became more substantial (e.g. Europe agreements in June 1995, active participation in NATO's PfP). Lithuania even applied officially for NATO membership in January 1994.

Even though internal developments in *Poland* were to a large extent an ice-breaker in relation to Soviet domination of Eastern Europe, the new Polish democratic regime adapted to a large extent its foreign policy (alliance) orientation to trends in the Soviet power position. Even though the attitude seemed to be "leave every Eastern institution; join every Western one," Poland was anxious not to rock the boat too much: EC membership was high on the agenda in contrast to NATO membership that would have provoked the Soviet Union. Instead, the role of the CSCE for the future European security order was emphasized. With the revolution of Poland's salient environment through the proliferation of neighbours 1990-91, implying inter alia that Poland no longer bordered mainland Russia, NATO membership officially entered the agenda and eventually became priority no.1. Poland was welcomed into NATO at the NATO Madrid summit in July 1997.

The general pattern seems to be that the weaker the Soviet Union/Russia and thereby also the less threatening, the more the rim states turned away from it, paradoxically as it may sound at first sight. Thereby, they weakened its position further. In short, they bandwagoned.

## Boundary condition and theoretical justification

The empirical results reported above obviously support the bandwagon hypothesis, as here specified in a trend perspective. There is one further modification, however, that should be made in relation to Baker Fox's hypothesis. Bandwagoning is not necessarily characteristic of "small states"; the decisive boundary condition is that the unit in question is subject to unipolarity in its salient environment: that there is one power pole here that is paramount on positive/negative sanctions in relation to the unit in question. Bandwagoning may also occur somewhat beyond the unipole sphere, but that is less frequent.

The small state literature is rich on discussions concerning the proper definition of "small state."[1] The focus here on salient polarity instead of size makes it unnecessary to delve into the essence of "smallness." We can happily ignore the question, whether Finland, Estonia, Latvia, Lithuania or Poland are "really" small powers or not. The point is simply that they were all potentially subject to Russian paramount power during the period, or part of it (Finland and Poland, as part of the process, definitely slipped out of the Russian orbit with the dissolution of the Soviet Union).[2]

The underlying reasoning presupposed here is that during unipolarity, the weak is in a geopolitically highly dependent position vis à vis one power pole. This paramount power possesses significant negative sanctions that the weak anticipates (manifest threats are usually redundant). As the balance of power tips even more in favour of the paramount power, its negative sanctions also increase, and the assets of the weak are not requested to the same extent as before. Unilateral dependency has become more marked than before. In order to prevent the negative sanctions from materializing, i.e. in order to retain status quo, the weak will have to sweeten status quo to the paramount power more than before. In other words, in addition to a favourable balance of power development, the paramount power is rewarded with some extra benefits. This is bandwagoning as stipulated above. Conversely, if the balance tips to the disfavour of the paramount power, inverse tendencies will be found. The weak power may even be able to jump into an opposing alliance or, more often, to a roughly symmetric position between two power poles (one of them being the former paramount pole). Also this is bandwagoning: the strong power is "punished" for its weakened position, so that it may be further weakened.[3]

---

1. For a survey and discussion, cf. Christmas-Møller 1983.
2. Needless to say, Poland was subject to much stronger Moscow dependency than Finland during the Cold War (as also appears from chapters 4 and 8). Elsewhere, I have used the term "asymmetric constellation in bipolarity" instead of "weak unipolarity" about Finland's Cold War position (Mouritzen 1994).
3. It should be added that this bandwagon argument also applies to a "pole of attraction," a unipole with predominantly positive sanctions; cf. the self-reinforcing mechanisms in relation to EU enlargement. For empirical studies of bandwagoning among EU would-be insiders, cf. Mouritzen *et.al.* (1996).

A unipole with negative sanctions will always be dangerous in some sense to its environment, also when it reaches its low ebb; one can always make worst case scenarios for the future. The crucial question for the surrounding units therefore is not whether it is desirable to jump out of dependence; it is rather when it is *possible*. For pure power reasons, that is probably near to the low ebb of the continuum.[4]

A member of an *opposing alliance*, including a weak power, will not typically engage in bandwagoning. Its reason for joining the alliance in the first place was typically to borrow military or other counterweight from a strong power in the face of a perceived increasing threat (thereby reinforcing a bipolarity, probably). This balancing is the opposite of bandwagoning, in the sense that a contribution was offered towards balancing off the increased threat. In connection with periods of specific tension, allied powers will seek to balance again through, e.g., a rearmament effort or a specific alert. Correspondingly, should the other side become more friendly or even break down, they will lower their guard.

Weak front-line states, however, may be an exception from this general rule. For instance, Denmark displayed a marked front-line cautiousness (non-provocation) during the Cold War: no foreign bases or nuclear weapons on Danish territory, special exercise patterns near the island of Bornholm, e.g. As soon as the Red army had withdrawn from the vicinity of Lübeck to Kaliningrad, however, Denmark could shout her "real" opinion eastwards on several issues; the major example of this new attitude was the avantgarde position on Baltic independence. The Danish reaction to the introduction of Martial law in Poland 1981 was extremely cautious compared to its reactions to the violent events in Lithuania and Latvia in January 1991. The weaker the Soviet Union in Denmark's salient environment, the more anti-Soviet Denmark could act. In other words, Denmark bandwagoned: the Soviet Union was "punished" by Denmark for being a trend-loser.

---

4. As argued and corroborated empirically elsewhere (Mouritzen 1994; in particular: 159), states that are located roughly symmetrically between power poles will also (trend) bandwagon, although to a minor degree than those in the orbit of the dynamic unipole.

## HOW MUCH BANDWAGONING?

The universal trend in the sphere of a unipole–and a little bit beyond–is bandwagoning. However, powers do it to various extents, as illustrated by fig. 11.1. Some of them move from being part of the unipole to an opposing alliance (or wishing to join it), others move just a little bit: out of the unipole sphere, but not enough to enter an opposing alliance, or modestly within an opposing alliance (the weak front-line state). Whereas the Finnish re-orientation was almost a revolution measured with the yardstick of Finnish post-war policy, it was modest in comparison with those of the four other countries in chapters 4-8.

**Fig. 11.1: Degrees of Bandwagoning 1988-1998**

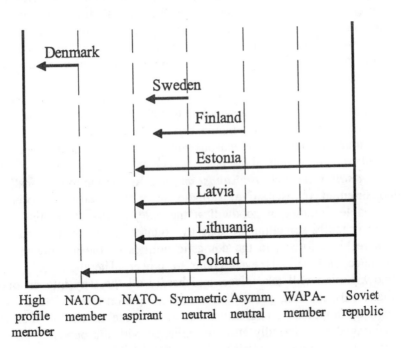

Note: Sweden and Denmark have been added as comparative background

Turning to a status instead of a trend perspective, the outcome so far is NATO membership for Poland, for others strong willingness to attain such (the Baltic countries), and for Finland an unprecedented "non-exclusion of any possibility"–even NATO membership (although it is far from the agenda). These provisional outcomes can be expressed in terms of the states handling of the "abandonment/entrapment" dilemma as presented by Snyder (1984). Two evils must somehow be mutually rated by any alliance candidate: what is feared the most, being left alone with the perceived danger (abandonment), or being drawn into war that could otherwise have been avoided (entrapment)? One main observation that we can summarize from chs. 4-8 is that none of the five countries seem to experience much of a dilemma. For Finland, whereas entrapment is an evil, abandonment is actually seen as a good thing. In other words, there is no dilemma at stake under the prevailing circumstances. The four other countries do not experience a dilemma, either, but for almost the opposite reason. Abandonment is an evil, but entrapment is an unavoidable evil (to be explained below). In other words, all energy should be mobilized to avoid abandonment. Again, there is no dilemma at stake, since the choice is so self-evident.

Why is it that Finland comes out so differently from the other four countries in making the abandonment/entrapment priority? Or to put it differently: why is it that Finland bandwagons so relatively little and the other four so much? The reasons are twofold, but intertwined. I shall formulate them in general terms:

*1) A status quo vs. a revisionist unipole.* In relation to a basically status quo oriented (conservative) unipole, it makes sense to safeguard a reasonable liquidity of goodwill at the pole, so that it remains satisfied. There is really something to lose by counter-balancing: the "hawks" (or even reckless forces) in the domestic politics of the unipole might gain influence and perhaps even come to power. Therefore, only cautious bandwagoning will take place, and hardly all the way into an opposing alliance. By contrast, goodwill is wasted in relation to a revisionist (or even reckless) unipole. Its aggression bound to come sooner or later will be encouraged by a friendly attitude. Alliance with the opposing pole is the only sensible option, if at all available. So should an opportunity arise, the unit will bandwagon as quickly as possible; it has nothing to lose.

One may ask why this factor has affected Finland differently from the four other countries? After all, the five countries were (are) dealing with the same unipole. Still, *differential impact* was clearly possible. Irrespective of decision-makers and their perceptions in each rim-state (cf. below), Finland and to some extent Poland faced a Russia that was different from that facing the Balts. Should Russian revisionism occur, the Baltic countries could be expected as its first targets, since they had recently been Soviet republics. Poland gradually became unlikely as target of would-be Russian/Soviet revisionism, although its status as former Warsaw Pact member and its geopolitical in-between position could not be ignored. Finland with its geopolitically remote location was safer, and any revisionism in that direction would have to be based on far-fetched pre-World War I inspiration.[5] In other words, one and the same unipole revisionism may apply differently to different countries. In this sense, salient environments that are similar at one level of abstraction (our criterion of case selection in chapter 1) turn out, on closer inspection, to be somewhat different and bear different implications.

*2) The foreign policy heritage.* The differential impact argument is based, i.a., on the countries' different historical positions in relation to the unipole. These have also entailed that forceful, but contradictory, foreign policy *lessons* have sedimented in the five countries, as described in the chapters. Finland learned from the inter-war years and World War II that alliances and alliance speculations are dangerous; if need be, Finland can manage on her own militarily. The post-war lesson was that Finland could manage on her own politically as well; it was actually possible to do business with a status quo oriented Eastern neighbour. So the two heritages amounted to one and the same lesson: "do it yourself"; being virtually abandoned is actually a good thing. The four other countries have made the opposite experience. Being dominated by the Soviet Union (Poland) or subject to occupation (the Baltic countries) after World War II have entailed perceptions of this unipole as being by nature aggressive and dominating, the "empire of evil," be its name the "Soviet Union" or "Russia." The current Russia is and will be revisionist, even if it may manage to conceal this to the West. Whereas entrapment will happen in any case when bordering such a power, abandonment is an evil that should be avoided almost at any price. With this perception, quick bandwagoning to the opposite camp is the sensible strategy, if and when the opportunity presents itself. As the experiences of 1939-40 showed, the Baltic countries could not stand on their own militarily, and Poland was caught between two enemies. NATO's and the EU's assets are not *only* their hard and soft

---

5. Finland was a Tsarist Grand-Duchy prior to 1917.

deterrences vis à vis a revisionist Russia, but also–notably for Poland–their multilateral diplomacy. This favours dependency spreading and "Einbindung" of Germany (the 1939 lesson).

Summing up, whereas it was natural for these countries to shun abandonment almost at any price (entrapment being unavoidable), for Finland abandonment was a good thing and entrapment an evil that could be avoided. So the choices were easy for all five, albeit they were made differently; none of them experienced a dilemma. We should remember, however, that the basic law of (trend) bandwagoning applied to all of them; the difference was that Poland and the Baltic countries bandwagoned much more than did Finland.

## NON-MOBILITY REVISITED

Let us return with these results in mind to some axioms of international politics that were discussed in chapter 1; in the process, we shall relate to some further authors as well. Kenneth Waltz's (1979) theory of international politics predicts that states will balance during anarchy. Even if it is primarily intended for the great powers that constitute the international system, it is claimed that "secondary states" will normally balance as well (ibid.: 127). The Soviet Union/Russia being the underdog here, Waltz's theory predicts that the rim states would join it so as to counterbalance the US superpower. Likewise, it postdicts that Western Europe after World War II would have allied with the Soviet Union against the US superpower, instead of the other way round as actually happened. These and similar prediction shortcomings are due to the theory's unstated assumption that nation-states are mutually mobile, finding its main inspiration in micro-economic theory with its mobile firms and consumers. As argued in chapter 1, this assumption entails that nation-states face one and the same "system," as their "average" environment will be roughly the same after some circling around in the system. Thereby, it is neglected that states actually face different and relatively stable salient environments. These have significant explanatory power in relation to their behaviour, since power and incentive wane with distance.

The graphical illustration of bandwagoning in fig. 11.1 (the arrows) should be interpreted as figurative mobility, at best; the implications of non-mobility were sought modified, but whether it will eventually succeed and to what extent is dubious, even in the case of a "success alliance" like

NATO. Joining an alliance was interpreted in chapter 1 as an attempt to modify an unfavourable environment polarity. This was tried actively by Poland and the Balts in the period considered here, but it led to a membership invitation to Poland, only. In spite of non-spatial rhetoric, major Western NATO powers obviously respected Russian sphere of interest thinking to some extent. Whereas three former Warsaw Pact members could be invited in spite of Russian objections, it was apparently seen as too provocative to accomodate the Balts likewise, given their locations on former Soviet territory. Moreover, Poland's declared intent not to deploy NATO forces or nuclear weapons on her territory (in line with classic Danish-Norwegian frontline cautiousness) seems to be an anticipation of Western wishes and, thereby, ultimately Russian ones. Again, this would never be admitted in public. The Baltic countries were compensated by being hinted in the final Madrid communiqué as possible future members, as well as by a US-Baltic charter. Still, a statement by the US Secretary of State Madeleine Albright in Vilnius on 13 July 1997 is quite telling regarding the parameter of non-mobility in international politics: NATO membership should make Lithuania or other would-be members face Russia with more self-confidence; it should not be an encouragement to turn their backs on Russia. In other words, even successful alliances do not change the map and provide new salient environments to newcomers; at best, they modify environment polarities somewhat.

Unknowingly, Stephen Walt's (1987) alliance theory respects the non-mobility axiom and its implications. Even though Walt credits much of his thinking to Waltz, his theory is nothing less than a revolution compared to his predecessor. States ally according to the "balance of threat" facing them; they will balance *against* the severest threat (rather than bandwagon with it). Balance of threat is an attribute of states' salient environment as here understood; there is no international system with significant explanatory power left in Walt's theory.

However, the balancing/bandwagoning debate in the wake of Walt's theory is somewhat incommensurate with the results reported here, since I use a trend rather than a status perspective in the definition of these concepts. Still, it should be obvious that Poland and the Baltic countries seek to ally as they "should" according to the Walt perspective, since they see themselves as more threatened from the East than from the West, to say the least. Finland, however, constitutes an anomaly for Walt's theory not only during the Paasikivi-Kekkonen era, but also after the 1991 watershed.[6] Seen in a trend perspective as here, however, the anomaly disappears.

Theory of alliance policy should be formulated relative to the polarity prevailing in states' salient environment, rather than their size; in the case of unipolarity and a little bit beyond as in this book, states will bandwagon in accordance with the power trend prevailing, be they "small" or not-so-small. This is the basic law. To which degree will depend not only on further geopolitical features, but also on lessons from past policy successes/failures and, thereby, past salient environments.

---

6. As clarified by Walt (1992: 472), his view is that weak states (like Finland, presumably) are more likely to bandwagon than strong states are, although both weak and strong states prefer to balance. Walt can choose, of course, to consider cases of weak power bandwagoning as non-deviant from his theory, but then the theory is hardly subject to falsification regarding weak states.

# Bibliography

Ackerman, P. & C. Kruegler (1994): *Strategic Non-violent Conflict: The Dynamics of People's Power in the Twentieth Century*. Westport, CT: Praeger

Adomeit, H. (1995): "Russia as a 'Great Power' in World Affairs: Images and Reality," *International Affairs* 71 (1): 35-69

Allison, G.T. (1971): *Essence of Decision: Explaining the Cuban Missile Crisis*. Boston: Little, Brown & Co.

Altmann, F.L. (1996): "The Accession of the Countries of Central and Eastern Europe into the European Union: Problems and Perspectives," in W. Weidenfeld (ed.): *Central and Eastern Europe on the Way into the European Union: Problems and Prospects of Integration in 1996*. Gütersloh: Bertelsmann Foundation Publishers (247-57)

Andersons, E. (1982): *Latvijas Vesture: 1920–1940. Arpolitika*. 1. sej. Stockholm: Daugava

Antola, E. (1991): "The End of Pragmatism: Political Foundations of the Finnish Integration Policy Under Stress" in *Yearbook of Finnish Foreign Policy 1991*. Helsinki: Finnish Ministry of Foreign Affairs (17-22)

Arbatov, A. (1992): "Imperiya ili Velikaya Derzhava?" [Empire or Great Power?], *Novoye Vremya* 49 & 50: 16-18; 20-23

Arbatov, A. (1993): "Russia's Foreign Policy Alternatives," *International Security* 18 (2): 5-43

Arbatov, A. (1994): "Russian National Interests," in R.D. Blackwill & S.A. Karaganov (eds.): *Limitation or Crisis? Russia and the Outside World*. Washington & London: Brassey's Inc. (55-76)

Arbatov, A. (1995): "NATO and Russia," *Security Dialogue* 26 (2): 135-146

Arbatov, A. (1996): "The Future of European Security: Split or Unity?" in The Olof Palme International Center: *Visions of European Security: Focal Point Sweden and Northern Europe*. Stockholm: The Olof Palme International Center (234-250)

Archer, Clive (1994a): "New Threat Perceptions: Danish and Norwegian Official Views," *European Security* 3 (4): 593-616

Archer, Clive (1994b): "Conflict Prevention in Europe," *Cooperation and Conflict* 29 (4): 367-86

Archer, Clive (1997a): *Finland, Sweden, the IGC and Defence.* ISIS Paper. Brussels: International Security Information Service

Archer, Clive (1997b): "Security considerations between the Nordic and Baltic states," in B. Heurlin & H. Mouritzen (eds.): *Danish Foreign Policy Yearbook 1997.* Copenhagen: Danish Institute of International Affairs (81-100)

Asmus, R.D. & F.S. Larrabee (1996): "NATO and the Have-Nots: Reassurance after Enlargement," *Foreign Affairs* 75 (6): 13-20

Asmus, R.D. & R.C. Nurick (1996): "NATO Enlargement and the Baltic States," *Survival* 38 (2): 121-142

Asmus, R.D. (1997): "NATO Enlargement and Baltic Security," in B. Huldt & U. Johannessen (eds.): *1st Annual Stockholm Conference on Baltic Sea Security and Cooperation.* Stockholm: The Swedish Institute of International Affairs (11-16)

Asmus, R.D.; R.C. Kugler & F. S. Larrabee (1995): "NATO Expansion: The Next Steps," *Survival* 37 (1): 7-23

Baker Fox, A. (1959): *The Power of Small States.* Chicago: University of Chicago Press

Baldwin, R. (1994): *Towards an Integrated Europe.* London: Centre for Economic Policy Research

Baranovsky, V. (1996): "Russia," in A. Krohn (ed.): *The Baltic Sea Area: National and International Security Perspectives.* Baden-Baden: Nomos Verlagsgesellschaft (164-182)

Bingen, D.; Z. Czachór & H. Machowski (1996): "Poland," in W. Weidenfeld (ed.): *Central and Eastern Europe on the Way into the European Union: Problems and Prospects of Integration in 1996.* Gütersloh: Bertelsmann Foundation Publishers (57-76)

Birkavs, V. (1997): "Latvia: A Baltic Region State in a Changing Europe." Speech at the University of Latvia (Riga, 24 January)

Blackwill, R.D. & S.A. Karaganov (eds.) (1994): *Damage Limitation or Crisis? Russia and the Outside World.* Washington & London: Brassey's, Inc.

Blanc-Noël, N. (1992): *Changement de Cap en Mer Baltique* [A change of direction on the Baltic Sea]. Paris: Foundation pour les Études de défense nationale

Blank, S. & T.-D. Young (1992): "Challenges to Eastern European Security in the 1990s," *European Security* 1 (3): 381-411

Bleiere, D. & A. Lejins (eds.) (1996): *The Baltic States: Search for Security*. Riga: Latvian Institute of International Affairs

Bleiere, D. (1996): *The Baltic States and Central Europe in the Context of Eastern Enlargement of the European Union*. Draft for the International Workshop "The Security of Small States in a Turbulent Environment: Baltic Perspectives." Riga, 30 November

Bogaturov, A.D.; M.M Kozhokin & K.V. Pleshakov (1992): "Vneshnyaa Politika Rossii" [Russia's Foreign Policy], *USA: Economics, Politics, Ideology*, 10: 28-37

Boulding, K. (1962): *Conflict and Defense*. New York: Harper & Brothers

Brecher, M. (1972): *The Foreign Policy System of Israel*. London: Oxford University Press

Burant, S.R. (1993): "International Relations in a Regional Context: Poland and its Eastern Neighbours: Lithuania, Belarus, Latvia," *Europe-Asia Studies* 45 (3): 395-418

Burant, S.R. (1996): "Overcoming the Past: Polish–Lithuanian Relations, 1990-1995," *Journal of Baltic Studies* XXVII (4): 309-329

Burrowes, R. (1996): *The Strategy of Nonviolent Defence: A Gandhian Approach*. New York: State University of New York,

Buzan, B. (1991): *People, States and Fear: An Agenda for International Security Studies in the Post-Cold War Era*. 2nd ed. London: Harvester Wheatsheaf

Buzan, B.; M. Kelstrup; P. Lemaitre; E. Tromer & O. Wæver (1990): *The European Security Order Recast: Scenarios for the Post-Cold War Era*. London & New York: Pinter Publishers

Buzan, B.; O. Wæver & J. de Wilde (1997): *Security: A New Framework for Analysis*. Boulder, CO: Lynne Rienner

Calabuig, E. (1991): "Quand les Allemands retournent à Kaliningrad-Königsberg" [When the Germans Return to Kalinigrad-Königsberg], *Le Monde Diplomatique* (August)

Carlgren, W.M. (1981): *Mellan Hitler och Stalin*. Stockholm: Militärhistoriska Förlaget

Carlsen, P. (1996): Speech at the conference "NATO and EU Enlargement: The Case of the Baltic States." Printed in *Conference Proceedings*. Riga: Latvian Institute of International Affairs (39-46)

Chernomyrdin, V.S. (1996): "Vystuplenie na Vstreche Glav Pravitelstv Stran-Chlenov Soveta Gosudarstv Baltiyskogo Morya" [Speech at the Meeting of the Heads of Governments of the Member States of the Council of the Baltic Sea States], *Diplomaticheskiy Vestnik* (August): 9–

13

Christiansen, T. (1996): "European Integration and Nordic Security: The Role of the European Union in the Baltic Sea Region" in A. Orrineus & L. Truedson (eds.): *Visions of European Security: Focal Point Sweden and Northern Europe*. Stockholm: The Oluf Palme International Center (278-295)

Christmas-Møller, W. (1983): "Some Thoughts on the Scientific Applicability of the Small State Concept: A Research History and a Discussion" in O. Höll (ed.): *Small States in Europe and Dependence*. Vienna: Braumüller (35-53)

Clemmesen, M. (1996): "Denmark" in A. Krohn (ed.): *The Baltic Sea Region*. Baden-Baden: Nomos Verlagsgesellschaft (72-85)

Connors, S.; D.G. Gibson & M. Rhodes (1995): "Caution and Ambivalence Over Joining NATO," *Transition* 11 August: 42-44

Covington, S. (1995): "Moscow's Insecurity and Eurasian Instability," *European Security* 4 (3): 438-456

Crow, S. (1993): *The Making of Foreign Policy in Russia under Yeltsin*. Munich & Washington, DC: Radio Free Europe/Radio Liberty Research Institute

Cyert R. & J. G. March (1963): *A Behavioral Theory of the Firm*. Englewood Cliffs, NJ: Prentice-Hall

Danish Ministry of Defence (1996): *Trilateral Defence Cooperation Denmark-Poland-Germany*. 2nd edition. Copenhagen: Ministry of Defence

Dawisha, K. & B. Parrott (1994): *Russia and the States of Eurasia: The Politics of Upheaval*. New York: Cambridge University Press

Dellenbrant, J. & M.–O. Olsson (eds.) (1994): *The Barents Region: Security and Economic Development in the European North*. Umeå: CERUM (Centre for Regional Science)

Dunlop, J.B. (1993): *The Rise of Russia and the Fall of the Soviet Empire*. Princeton: Princeton University Press

EIU (1997): *Country Forecast: Europe: Regional Overview*. London: Economist Intelligence Unit

Ellemann-Jensen, Uffe (1996): *Din egen dag er kort*, Copenhagen: Aschehoug

Fadeev, D.A. & V. Razuvayev (1994): "Russia and the Western post-Soviet Republics," in R.D. Blackwill & S.A. Karaganov (eds.): *Damage Limitation or Crisis? Russia and the Outside World*. Washington & London: Brassey's Inc. (106-122)

Fedotov, G.P. (1991): *Sudba i Grekhi Rossii* [Russia's Destiny and Sins]. 2 vols. St. Petersburg

Feldmanis, I. & A. Stranga (1994): *The Destiny of the Baltic Entente: 1934-1940*. Riga: Latvian Institute of International Affairs

Finnish Institute of International Affairs (1992): *Yearbook of Finnish Foreign Policy*. Helsinki: Finnish Institute of International Affairs

Finnish Ministry of Foreign Affairs (1996): *Finland's Statement*. Press Release, 29 May. Helsinki: Finnish Ministry of Foreign Affairs

Firlej, E. & P. Wieczorek (1996): "Integration of Poland with NATO," *The Polish Quarterly of International Affairs* 5 (1): 27-44

Foreign Affairs Committee of the Finnish Parliament (1995): "Security in a Changing World." Helsinki: Ministry for Foreign Affairs

Gaidys, V. (1994): "Lietuvos saugumo problemos ir viesoji nuomone," in V. Bagdonavicius (ed.): *Lietuvos nacionalinis saugumas: teorija ir realijos*. Vilnius: Filosofijos, Sociologijos ir Teises Institutas (110-113)

Garnett, S.W. (1996): "Poland: Bulwark or Bridge?" *Foreign Policy* 102 (Spring): 66-82

Gerner K. & S. Hedlund (1993): *The Baltic States and the End of the Soviet Empire*. London: Routledge.

Goldgeier, J. M. & M. McFaul (1992): "A Tale of Two Worlds: Core and Periphery in the Post-Cold War Era," *International Organization* 46 (2): 467-91

Goldman, K. (1982): "Change and Stability in Foreign Policy: Detente as a Problem of Stabilization," *World Politics* 14 (2): 230-66

Grieco, J. (1988): "Anarchy and the Limits of Cooperation: A Realist Critique of the Newest Liberal Institutionalism," *International Organization* 42 (3): 485-507

Gromov, F. (1995): "Znachenie Kaliningradskogo Osobogo Rayona dlya Oboronosposobnosti Rossiyskoi Federatsii" [The Role of the Kaliningard Special District for Russian Federation's Defence], *Voennaya Mysl* (July-August): 9-13

Handel, M. (1981): *Weak States in the International System*. London: Frank Cass

Heininen, L. & J. Käkönen (eds.) (1991): *Arctic Complexity: Essays on Arctic Independence*. Occasional Papers 44. Tampere: Tampere Peace Research Institute

Heise, V. (1996): "The North Atlantic Treaty Organization" in A. Krohn (ed.): *The Baltic Sea Region*. Baden-Baden: Nomos Verlagsgesellschaft (207-223)

Helveg Petersen, N. (1996): "The Role of the European Union: 'Soft' Security?" in *The Baltic Dimension of European Integration*. Riga: Latvian Institute of International Affairs & The Royal Danish Embassy (90-100)

Heurlin, B. (1995): "Security Problems in the Baltic Region in the 1990s: The Baltic Region and the New Security Dynamics and Challenges" in P. Joenniemi & C.–E. Stålvant (eds.): *Baltic Sea Politics: Achievements and Challenges*. Stockholm: The Nordic Council (55-77)

Heurlin, B. (1996): "The U.S. Impact on European Security as we Approach the Year 2000" in A. Orrineus & L. Truedson (eds.): *Visions of European Security: Focal Point Sweden and Northern Europe*. Stockholm: The Olof Palme International Center (118-135)

Hunter, R. (1996): Speech at the conference "NATO and EU Enlargement: The Case of the Baltic States." Printed in *Conference Proceedings*. Riga: Latvian Institute of International Affairs (13-27)

Hunter, R. (1997): "U.S. Views on European Security Challenges: NATO Enlargement, Russia and the Baltics," in B. Huldt & U. Johannessen (eds.): *1st Annual Stockholm Conference on Baltic Sea Security and Cooperation*. Stockholm: The Swedish Institute of International Affairs (53-57)

Hækkerup, H. (1996): "A multinational force culture," *Enjeux Atlantiques* 13 (June): 10-13.

Hækkerup, H. (1997): "From Adazi to Tuzla." Speech in St. Petersburg, 26 April 1996. Printed in B. Heurlin & H. Mouritzen (eds.): *Danish Foreign Policy Yearbook 1997*. Copenhagen: Danish Institute of International Affairs (135-139)

Institute of Europe (1995): *Geopoliticheskie Peremeny v Evrope: Politika Zapada i Alternativy dlya Rossii* [Geopolitical Changes in Europe: Western Policy and Alternatives for Russia]. Moscow: Institute of Europe

International Institute for Strategic Studies (1990): *The Military Balance 1990-1991*. London: International Institute for Strategic Studies

International Institute for Strategic Studies (1995): *The Military Balance 1995-1996*. London: International Institute for Strategic Studies

International Institute for Strategic Studies (1996): *The Military Balance 1996-1997*. London: International Institute for Strategic Studies

Jenkins, C. (ed.) (1997): *Country Forecast: Europe: Regional Overview*, 2nd quarter. London: Economist Intelligence Unit (5-14)

Jervis, R. (1976): *Perception and Misperception in International Politics*. Princeton, NJ: Princeton University Press

Joenniemi, P. & C.–E. Stålvant (1995): "Security Problems in the Baltic Region in the 1990s," in Pertti Joenniemi & C. – E. Stålvant (eds.): *Baltic Sea Politics: Achievements and Challenges*. Stockholm: The Nordic Council (9-53)

Joenniemi, P. & P. Vares (eds.) (1993): *New Actors on the International Arena: The Foreign Policies of the Baltic Countries*. Research Report 50. Tampere: Tampere Peace Research Institute

Joenniemi, P. (1991): "Regionalization in the Baltic Area: Actors and Policies," in P. Joenniemi (ed.): *Co-operation in the Baltic Sea Region: Needs and Prospects*. Research Report 42: Tampere: Tampere Peace Research Institute (147-65)

Joenniemi, P. (1993): *Finland söker sin plats i det nya Europa*. Mimeo. Tampere: Tampere Peace Research Institute

Joenniemi, P. (1996a): *Managing Border Disputes in Present-Day Europe: The Karelian Question. Copenhagen:* Copenhagen Peace Research Institute

Joenniemi, P. (1996b): *Kaliningrad: A Region in Search for a Past and a Future*. Background Paper Prepared for the International Colloquium "Kaliningrad. Future Prospects of the Region." Travemunde: Ostsee-Akademie, 3 – 5 November

Jonson, J. (1994): "In Search of a National Interest: the Foreign Policy Debate in Russia," *The Nationalities Papers*. 22 (1): 179-192

Jonson, L. (1992): "Russia in the Nordic Region in a Period of Change," in M. Kukk, S. Jervell & P. Joenniemi (eds.): *The Baltic Sea Area: A Region in the Making*. Oslo: Europa-programmet/Karlskrona: The Baltic Institute (79-106)

Jundzis, T. (1995): *Latvijas drosiba un aizsardziba*. Riga: Junda

Jurgaitiene, K & O. Wæver (1996): "Lithuania" in H. Mouritzen; O. Wæver & H. Wiberg (eds.): *European Integration and National Adaptions: A Theoretical Inquiry*. New York: Nova Science (185-229)

Jurgaitiene, K. (1993): "Romantic Nationalism and the Challenge of Europeanization: A Case of Lithuania," in P. Joenniemi & P. Vares (eds.): *New Actors on the International Arena: The Foreign Policies of the Baltic Countries*. Research Report 50. Tampere: Tampere Peace Research Institute (32-38)

Kalela, J. (1971): *Grannar på Skilda Vägar*. Borgå: Söderström

Kamp, K.-H. (1996): Speech at the conference "NATO and EU

Enlargement: The Case of the Baltic States." Printed in *Conference Proceedings*. Riga: Latvian Institute of International Affairs (47-55)

Karaganov, S. (1995): "Fifty Years After Victory," *International Affairs* (Moscow) 41 (4-5): 59-64

Karaganov, S. (1996): "Presentation at the Conference," in P. Apinis & A. Lejins (eds.): *NATO and EU Enlargement: The Case of the Baltic States*. Riga: Latvian Institute of International Affairs (28-38)

Karkoszka, A. (1993): "Poland's Security Policy," *The Polish Quarterly of International Affairs* 2 (1): 89-112

Kaufman, R. G. (1992): "To Balance or to Bandwagon? Alignment Decisions in 1930s Europe," *Security Studies* 1 (3): 417-447

Keohane, R.O, J.S. Nye & S. Hoffmann (eds.) (1993): *After the Cold War: International Institutions and State Strategies in Europe, 1989-1991*. Cambridge, MA: Harvard University Press

Keohane, R.O. & J.S. Nye (1977): *Power and Interdependence: World Politics in Transition*. Boston: Little, Brown & Co

Kirby, D. (1994): "Incorporation: The Molotov-Ribbentrop Pact," in G. Smith (ed.): *The Baltic States: The National Self-Determination of Estonia, Latvia and Lithuania*. London: Macmillan (69-85)

Kirch, M & A. Kirch (1995): "Search for Security in Estonia: New Identity Architecture," *Security Dialogue* 26 (4): 439-448

Kirch, M. & A. Kirch (1994): *Changing Identities in Estonia: Sociological Facta and Commentaries*. Tallinn: Institute of International and Social Studies/Estonian Academy of Sciences/Estonian Science Foundation

Knudsen, O.F. & I.B. Neumann (1995): *Subregional Security Cooperation in the Baltic Sea Area. An Exploratory Study*. Oslo: Norwegian Institute of International Affairs

Kolvisto, M. (1992): *Finland och Morgondagens Europa*. Helsinki: Tidens

Kostecki, W. & H. Wiberg (1996): "Poland." in H. Mouritzen; O. Wæver & H. Wiberg (eds.): *European Integration and National Adaptations: A Theoretical Inquiry*. New York: Nova Science (157-184)

Kostecki, W. (1996): *Europe after the Cold War. The Security Complex Theory*. Warshaw: Institute for Political Studies

Kozyrev, A. (1994): "Cooperation in the Barents Euro-Arctic Region: Promising Beginning," in O.S. Stokke & O. Tunander (eds.): *The Barents Region: Cooperation in Arctic Europe*. London: Sage Publications (25-30)

Krohn, A. (1995): "European Security in Transition: 'NATO going East,' the 'German Factor': Security in Northern Europe and the Baltic Sea Region," *European Security* 4 (4): 584-602

Kukk, M.; S. Jervell & P. Joenniemi, P. (eds.) (1992): *The Baltic Sea Area: A Region in the Making*. Oslo: Europa-programmet/Karlskrona: The Baltic Institute

Kupchan, C. A. (1988): "NATO and the Persian Gulf: Examining Intra-alliance Behavior," *International Organization* 42 (2): 317-346

Kuzniar, R. (1993): "The Geostrategic Factors Conditioning Poland's Security," *Polish Quarterly of International Affairs* 2 (1): 9-28

Kwasniewski, A. (1996a): "Statement by the President of the Republic of Poland at the Europa Forum. Berlin, 23 November," *Materials and Documents*, 5 (11): 1294-96

Kwasniewski, A. (1996b): "Statement by the President of the Republic of Poland, at the Assembly of the Western European Union, Paris, 4 December," *Materials and Documents*, 5 (12): 1313-16

Labs, E. J. (1992): "Do Weak States Bandwagon?" *Security Studies* 1 (3): 383-416

*Latvia* (1996): *Latvian Human Development Report*. Riga: UNDP

Latvian Ministry of Defence (1994): *The Latvian Defence System Concept*. Riga: Latvian Ministry of Defence

Latvijas Tautas Fronte (1989): *Gads pirmais*. Riga: LTF

Latvijas Tautas Fronte (1990): *2. kongress. Programma. Statuti. Rezolucijas*. Riga: LTF

Levy, J.S. (1994): "Learning and Foreign Policy: Sweeping a Conceptual Minefield," *International Organization* 48 (2): 279-312

Lieven, Anatol (1996): "Baltic iceberg dead ahead: NATO beware," *The World Today* (July): 175-9.

Lindberg, L. (1971): *The Political Dynamics of European Integration*. Princeton, NJ: Princeton University Press

Litera, B. (1994/95): "The Kozyrev Doctrine: a Russian Variation on the Monroe Doctrine," *Perspectives* (Winter): 45-52

Lopata, R. & Zalys, V. (1995): "Lietuvos geopolitinis kodas," *Politologija* (1): 13-21

Lukin, V.P. (1994): "Russia and Its Interests," in S. Sestanovich (ed.): *Rethinking Russia's National Interests*. Washington, DC: Center for Strategic and International Studies (106-115)

Maclay, M. (1992): *Multi-Speed Europe? The Community Beyond Maastricht*. London: Royal Institute of International Affairs

Made, Raimond (1996): "Interview with Paul Goble," *Luup* 7 (April): 16-17

Malcolm, N. & A. Pravda (1996): "Democratization and Russian Foreign Policy," *International Affairs* 72 (3): 537-552

Maniokas, K. & G. Vitkus (eds.) (1997): *Lithuania's Integration into the European Union: Summary of the Study on the Status, Perspectives and Impact.* Vilnius: European Integration Studies Centre

Matochkin, Y. (1995): "From Survival to Development," *International Affairs* (Moscow) 41 (6): 8-14

Medvedev, S. (1994): "Security Risks in Russia and the CIS: A Case Study," *The International Spectator* 24 (1): 53-87

Michalski, A. & H. Wallace (1992): *The European Community and the Challenge of Enlargement.* London: Royal Institute of International Affairs

Miniotaite, G. (1993): "Nonviolence as a New Model of Conflict Resolution: The Case of Lithuania," *Loccumer Protokolle* (7): 521-24

Miniotaite, G. (1996): "Lithuania: From Non-violent Liberation Towards Non-violent Defence?" *Peace Research: The Canadian Journal of Peace Studies* 28 (4): 19-36

*Ministerial Meeting of the North Atlantic Council held at NATO Headquarters* (1996): Final Communique, retrieved electronically, NATO gopher. Brussels, 10 December

Ministry of Foreign Affairs of the Russian Federation (1992): *Kontseptsiya Vneshney Politiki Rossiyskoy Federatsii* [The Foreign Policy Concept of the Russian Federation]. Moscow: Ministry of Foreign Affairs of the Russian Federation

Ministry of Foreign Affairs of the Russian Federation (1993): "Kontseptsiya Vneshney Politiki Rossiyskoy Federatsii" [The Foreign Policy Concept of the Russian Federation], *Diplomaticheskiy Vestnik,* Special Issue (January): 3-23

Morrison, J.W. (1994): *Vladimir Zhirinovskiy: An Assessment of a Russian Ultra-Nationalist.* Washington, DC: National Defense University

Mouritzen, H. (1980): "Selecting Explanatory Level in International Politics: Evaluating a Set of Criteria," *Cooperation and Conflict* 15 (3): 169-182

Mouritzen, H. (1988): *Finlandization: Towards a General Theory of Adaptive Politics.* Aldershot: Gower

Mouritzen, H. (1994): "Testing Weak-Power Theory: Three Nordic Reactions to the Soviet Disintegration" in W. Carlsnaes & S. Smith (eds.): *European Foreign Policy: The EC and Changing Perspectives in Europe*. London: SAGE (156-177)

Mouritzen, H. (1996): "Balance of Influence: The Weight of Brussels in High and Low Politics" in J. de Wilde & H. Wiberg (eds.): *Organized Anarchy in Europe: The Role of Intergovernmental Organizations*. London: Tauris Academic Studies (281-296)

Mouritzen, H. (1997a): "Kenneth Waltz: A Critical Rationalist Between International Politics and Foreign Policy" in I. B. Neumann & O. Wæver (eds.): *The Future of International Relations: Masters in the Making?* London: Routledge (66-89)

Mouritzen, H. (1997b): "Denmark in the Post-Cold War Era: The Salient Action Spheres" in B. Heurlin & H. Mouritzen (eds.): *Danish Foreign Policy Yearbook 1997*. Copenhagen: Danish Institue of International Affairs (33-51)

Mouritzen, H. (1997c): *External Danger and Democracy: Old Nordic Lessons and New European Challenges*. Aldershot: Dartmouth

Mouritzen, H. (1998): *Theory and Reality of International Politics*. Aldershot: Ashgate

Mouritzen, H.; O. Wæver & H. Wiberg (1996): *European Integration and National Adaptations: A Theoretical Inquiry*. New York: Nova Science

NATO (1995): *Study on NATO Enlargement*. Brussels: NATO

Nekrasas, E. (1996): "Lithuania's Security Concerns and Responses" in A. Lejins & D. Bleiere (eds.): *The Baltic States: Search for Security*. Riga: Latvian Institute of International Affairs (58-74)

Neumann, I.B. (1994): "A region-building approach to Northern Europe," *Review of International Studies* 20 (1): 53-74

Nordic Council (1992): *Co-operation in the Baltic Sea Area: Second Parliamentary Conference on Co-operation in the Baltic Sea Area*. Report from a conference arranged by the Nordic Council at the Storting, Oslo, Norway, 22-24 April 1992. Stockholm: Nordic Council

Norwegian Ministry of Foreign Affairs (1992): *Nordiske Lands Utenriks- og Sikkerhets-politikk i et Nytt Europa*. Oslo: Norwegian Ministry of Foreign Affairs

Nowakowski, J.M. (1993): "Polska pomiedzy Wschodem a Zachodem" [Poland between East and West], *Polska w Europie* 11 (April): 5-20.

Ognik, H. (1996): "Poland" in A. Krohn (ed.): *The Baltic Sea Region: National and International Security Perspectives*. Baden-Baden: Nomos (129-140)

Olechowski, A. (1994): "Poland and the Shaping of Europe's Future,"

*Polish Quarterly of International Affairs* 3 (3): 7-14

Onyszkiewicz, J. (1992): "Kilka uwag o bezpieczenstwie Polski" [Some Remarks on Polish Security], *Polska w Europie* 8 (April): 27-36

Osherenko, G. & O.R. Young (1989): *The Age of the Arctic: Hot Conflicts and Cold Realities.* Cambridge: Cambridge University Press

Ozolina, Z. (1996): "The Nordic and the Baltic Countries: A Sub-Region in the Making?" in A. Lejins & D. Bleiere (eds.): *Baltic States: Search for Security.* Riga: Latvian Institute of International Relations (93-112)

Ozolina, Z. (1997): "Baltic-Nordic Interaction, Cooperation and Integration," in A. Lejins & Z. Ozolina (eds.): *Small States in a Turbulent Environment: The Baltic Pespective.* Riga: Latvian Institute of International Relations (93-112)

Pedersen, T. (1993): "The Common Foreign and Security Policy and the Challenge of Enlargement" in O. Nørgaard, T. Pedersen & N. Petersen (eds.): *The European Community in World Politics.* London: Pinter (31-52)

Petlyuchenko, V. (1993): "The Orthodox Church and Foreign Policy," *International Affairs* (Moscow) 39 (3): 62-71

Petras, J & S. Vieux (1996): "Bosnia and the Revival of US Hegemony," *New Left Review* 218: 3-25

Pleshakov, K. (1993): "Russia's Mission: the Third Epoch," *International Affairs* (Moscow) 39 (1): 17-26

Podberezkin, A. (1996): "Geostrategicheskoe Polozhenie i Bezopasnost Rossii" [Russia's Geostrategic Position and Security], *Svobodnaya Mysl* vol. (7): 86–98

Porevo, M. (1989): "Finnish Neutrality and European Integration" in *Yearbook of Finnish Foreign Policy 1988-89.* Helsinki: Finnish Institute of International Affairs (18-23)

Posen, Barry (1984): *The Sources of Military Doctrine: France, Britain and Germany between the World Wars.* Ithaca & London: Cornell University Press

Pozdnyakov, E. (1993a): "Russia is a Great Power," *International Affairs* (Moscow) 39 (1): 3-13

Pozdnyakov, E. (1993b): "Russia Today and Tomorrow," *International Affairs* (Moscow) 39 (2): 22-31

Purlys, V. & G. Vilkelis (1995): "Cooperation between the Baltic States: a Lithuanian View," *NATO Review* 5 (September): 27-31

Razuvaev, V. (1993): *The Russian Federation and the Near Abroad: Geopolitical Problems.* Moscow: INION

Rodin, M. & Strupiss, A. (1995): *Euroidentity and National Identity: Latvia's International Tendencies*: Report for Latvian Shipping Company. Riga: Latvian Shipping Company

Rogov, S. (1993): "A National Security Policy for Russia," in J.E. Goodby & B. Morel (eds.): *The Limited Partnership: Building a Russian-US Security Community*. New York: Oxford University Press (73-82)

Rogov, S. (1995): "Russia and the United States: a Partnership or Another Disengagement," *International Affairs* (Moscow) 41 (7): 3-11

Rotfeld, A.D. (1996): *Europe: Towards New Security Arrangements*. Paper presented at the Seminar on "The Future of European Security Policy: Focal Point Sweden and Northern Europe." Stockholm: Olof Palme International Center, 8-10 March

Rothstein, R. (1968): *Alliances and Small Powers*. London: Columbia University Press

Royal Danish Embassy (1993): *Joint Statement of the Royal Danish Embassy and the Delegation of the Commission of the European Communities on the Results of the Copenhagen Summit on Central and Eastern Europe.* (Warsaw, 25 June). Duplicated material

Rutskoi, A. (1992): "Ya–Tsentrist, Derzhavnik i Liberal" [I am Centrist, Derzhavnik and Liberal], *Argumenty i Facty* 37 (October): 2

Rybkin, I. (1995): "The State Duma and Russia's External Interests," *International Affairs* (Moscow) 41 (11-12): 28-33

Saja, K., (ed.): (1992): *Lithuania, 1991.01.13: Documents, Testimonies, Comments, State.* Vilnius: The Publishing Center

Salovaara, J. (1993): "Finnish Integration Policy: From an Economic to a Security Motivation" in *Yearbook of Finnish Foreign Policy 1993.* Helsinki: Finnish Institute of International Affairs (16-24)

Saudargas, A. (1995): "Lietuvos uzsienio politikos prioritetai," in S. Mijonaitiene (ed.): *Lietuvos nacionaliniai interesai ir jos politine sistema.* Vilnius: Konferencijos Medziaga, 1994 gruodzio 16-17 (168-75)

Sergounin, A.A. (1993): *The Russian Dimension of Nordic Security: Challenges and Opportunities.* Working Paper. Copenhagen: Centre for Peace and Conflict Research

Sergounin, A.A. (1996): "The Russian Dimension of Nordic Security: Hard Choices and Opportunities" in The Olof Palme International Center (ed.): *Visions of European Security: Focal Point Sweden and Northern Europe.* Stockholm: The Olof Palme International Center (104-116)

Sharp, G. (1990): *Civilian-Based Defence.* Princeton, NJ.: Princeton

University Press

Shumeiko, V. (1995): "Kaliningrad Region: A Russian Outpost," *International Affairs* (Moscow) 41 (6): 6-9

Singh, A.I. (1995): "India's Relations with Russia and Central Asia," *International Affairs* 71 (1): 69-81

SIPRI (1994): *SIPRI Yearbook 1994*. New York: Oxford University Press

Sivonen, P. (1996): "Finland" in A. Krohn (ed.): *The Baltic Sea Region*. Baden-Baden: Nomos (86-95)

Skubiszewski, K. (1992a): Statement by Professor Krzysztof Skubiszewski, Minister of Foreign Affairs of the Republic of Poland, at the opening session of the seminar "Security in Central Europe: NATO and the Central European Perspective" (Warshaw 12 March). Duplicated material

Skubiszewski, K. (1992b): "Problems of Security in Central Europe." Lecture delivered by Professor Krzysztof Skubiszewski, Minister for Foreign Affairs of the Republic of Poland, at the Hebrew University in Jerusalem and the Israel Council of Foreign Relations. Jerusalem, 9th November 1992. In *Materials and Documents* (1): 10-15

Skubiszewski, K. (1993a): "The Eastern Policies of Poland." Address by Professor Krzysztof Skubiszewski, Minister for Foreign Affairs. (Warsaw 18 November). *Materials and Documents* 1 (1): 5-19

Skubiszewski, K. (1993b): "The Position of the Government towards Transfrontier and Border Region Co-operation." Address by Professor Krzysztof Skubiszewski, Minister for Foreign Affairs of the Republic of Poland, (Warsaw 3 March). *Materials and Documents* 2 (3): 66-70

Skubiszewski, K. (1993c): "Poland's Foreign Policy in 1993." Statement by Krzysztof Skubiszewski, Minister for Foreign Affairs of the Republic of Poland. (Warsaw 29 April). *Materials and Documents* 2 (5): 131-41

Smith, M. (1996): *The Geopolitics of Gennady Zyuganov*. NATO Integrated Data Service. NATO gopher: retrieved electronically

Snyder, G. H. (1984): "The Security Dilemma in Alliance Politics" in *World Politics* (July): 461-495

Solana, J. (1996): Address by Mr. Javier Solana, Secretary General of NATO, at the University of Warsaw, 18 April. NATO Press and Media Service: duplicated material

Solomon, G. (1995): Communication between the Chairman and Members Concerning Parliamentary Support for NATO Enlargement: Information Document. (North Atlantic Assembly, October). NATO gopher: retrieved electronically

Solonevich, I. (1991): *Narodnaya Monarchiya* [People's Monarchy]. Moscow

Spero, J. (1992): *"Deja Vu* All Over Again: Poland's Attempt to Avoid Entrapment Between Two Belligerents," *European Security* 1 (4): 92-117

Spykman, N. (1944): *The Geography of Peace*. New York: Harcourt

Stankevich, S. (1992): "Russia in Search of Itself," *The National Interest* (Summer): 47-51

Stankevich, S. (1994): "Toward a New 'National Idea'," in S. Sestanovich (ed.): *Rethinking Russia's National Interests*. Washington, DC: Center for Strategic and International Studies (24-32)

State Duma (1995): *Law on National Security of the Russian Federation* (Draft). Moscow: State Duma

Stefanowicz, J. (1995): "Central Europe between Germany and Russia: A View from Poland," *Security Dialogue* 26 (1): 55-64

Stefanowicz, J. (1996): "Poland," in R. Smoke (ed.): *Perceptions of Security: Public Opinion and Experts Assessments in Europe's New Democracies*. Manchester & New York: Manchester University Press (107-28)

Steinbruner J.D. (1974): *The Cybernetic Theory of Decision: New Dimensions of Political Analysis*. Princeton, NJ.: Princeton University Press

Stenelo, L.-G. (1981): "Prediction and Foreign Policy Heritage," *Cooperation and Conflict* XVI (1): 3-19

Stranga, A. (1997): "Baltic-Russian Relations: 1995–Beginning of 1997," in A. Lejins & Z. Ozolina (eds.): *Small States in a Turbulent Environment: The Baltic Pespective*. Riga: Latvian Institute of International Relations (11-59)

Stupavský, P. (1996): "Zahranicná politika Ruska v ére Jel'cina" [Russia's Foreign Policy in the Yeltsin's Era], *Mezinárodni vztahy* (3): 5-10

Suchocka, H. (1992a): "We Count on Understanding Not Only of Unity of Aims But Also of Unity of Interests." Address by Madam Hanna Suchocka, Chairman of the Council of Ministers of the Republic of Poland, at the inauguration of the academic year at the Lublin Catholic University 18th October, 1992. In *Materials and Documents* (1): 1-5

Suchocka, H. (1992b): "The Polish Government is Pursuing and is Determined to Pursue Friendly Policies towards Other Nations of the World." Address by Madam Hanna Suchocka, Chairman of the Council of Ministers of the Republic of Poland, to the Bundestag, Bonn,

Germany, 5th November, 1992. In *Materials and Documents* (1): 6-10

Suchocka, H. (1993): Address by Madam Hanna Suchocka, Chairman of the Council of Ministers of the Republic of Poland (London, 3 March). *Materials and Documents* 2 (3): 62-6

Sukianen, I. (1948): *Karel'skiy Vopros v Sovyetsko-finlyandskikh Otnosheniyakh v 1918–1920 Godakh* [The Karelia Issue in Soviet–Finnish Relations, 1918–1920]. Petrozavodsk

Sweedler, A. (1996): "Security in Northern Europe in the Context of European Integration: an American Perspective" in A. Orrineus & L. Truedson (eds.): *Visions of European Security: Focal Point Sweden and Northern Europe*. Stockholm: The Olof Palme International Center (252-264)

Szajkowski, B. (ed.) (1993): *Encyclopaedia of Conflicts, Disputes and Flashpoints in Eastern Europe Russia and the Successor States*. Harlow: Longman

Temirkhanov, I. (1994): "Gruppy Davleniya v Rossiyskoi Politike," [Interest Groups in Russian Politics], *Ukraina Segodnya* (7): 39-53

*The Baltic States: A Reference Book* (1991): Tallinn, Riga & Vilnius: Estonian Encyclopaedia Publishers/Latvian Encyclopaedia Publishers/Lithuanian Encyclopaedia Publishers

Thompson, J.D. (1967): *Organizations in Action*. New York: McGraw-Hill

Travkin, N. (1994): "Russia, Ukraine, and Eastern Europe," in S. Sestanovich (ed.): *Rethinking Russia's National Interests*. Washington, DC: Center for Strategic and International Studies (33-41)

Trenin, D. (1995): "NATO: How to Avoid Confrontation," *International Affairs* (Moscow) 41 (7): 20-26

Truska, L. (1996): *Antanas Smetona ir jo laikas*. Vilnius: Valstybinis Leidybos Centras

Trynkov, A. (1995): "O Nekotorykh Realiyakh Politiko-ekonomicheskoi Karty Evropy" [On Some Realities Following from the Politico-economic Map of Europe], in *Zapadnaya Evropa na Poroge Tretyego Tysyacheletiya* [Western Europe on the Threshhold of the Third Millenium]. Moscow: Russian Institute for Strategic Studies/Institute of World Economy and International Relations (65-68)

Trynkov, A. (1996): *A Regional Security Assessment: An Expert View From Moscow*. Mimeo. Moscow: Russian Institute for Strategic Studies

Turtola, M. (1987): *Från Torne Älv till Systerbäck: Hemligt Försvarssamarbete mellan Finland och Sverige 1923-1940*. Stockholm: Militärhistoriska Förlaget

Törnudd, K. (1993): *Den Nya Politiken*. Helsingfors: Schildts

US Department of State (1993): *Country Reports on Human Rights Practices for 1992*. Report Submitted to the Committee on Foreign Relations of the US Senate and the Committee on Foreign Affairs, US House of Representatives by the Department of State. Washington, DC.: US Government Printing Office

Uspensky, N. & Komissarov, S. (1993): "New Stage in Cooperation in the Baltic Region," *International Affairs* (Moscow) 39 (2): 79-85

van Buren, L. (1995): "Citizen Participation and the Environment in Russia," in J. DeBardeleben & J. Hannigan (eds.): *Environmental Security and Quality after Communism: Eastern Europe and the Soviet Successor States*. Boulder, CO.: Westview Press (127-137)

van Ham, P (ed.) (1995): *The Baltic States: Security and Defence After Independence*. Chaillot Papers, no. 19. Paris: Institute for Security Studies

Vardys, S. & J.B. Sedaitis (1997): *Lithuania: The Rebel Nation*. Boulder, CO: Westview Press

Viitasalo, M. & B. Österlund (1996): *The Baltic: Sea of Changes*. Helsinki: National Defence College

Vladislavlev, A. & S. Karaganov (1992): "The Idea of Russia," *International Affairs* (Moscow) 38 (12): 30-36

von Ow, B. (1995): "The Accession of the Countries of Central and Eastern Europe into the European Union: Problems and Perspectives" in W. Weidenfeld (ed.): *Central and Eastern Europe on the Way into the European Union: Problems and Prospects of Integration*. Gütersloh: Bertelsmann Foundation (251-62)

Väyrynen R. (1993): "Finland and the European Community: Changing Elite Bargains," *Cooperation and Conflict* 28 (1): 33-48

Vozgrin, V. (1992): "Sankt Petersburg: Russia's Northern Capital," in M. Kukk; S. Jervell & P. Joenniemi (eds.): *The Baltic Sea Area: A Region in the Making*. Olso & Karlskrona: Europa-programmet/The Baltic Institute (107-119)

Walt, S. (1987): *The Origins of Alliances*. Ithaca: Cornell University Press

Walt, S. (1992): "Alliance, Threats and the U.S Grand Strategy: A Reply to Kaufmann and Labs," *Security Studies* 1 (3): 448-482

Waltz, K.N. (1979): *Theory of International Politics*. New York: Random House

Warma, A. (1946): *The Foreign Policy of the Republic of Estonia*. Stockholm

Weidenfeld, W. (1996): "Preface" in W. Weidenfeld (ed.): *Central and Eastern Europe on the Way into the European Union: Problems and Prospects of Integration in 1996*. Gütersloh: Bertelsmann Foundation (7-8)

Wellman, C. (1996): "Russia's Kaliningrad Exclave at the Crossroads: The Interrelations between Economic Development and Security Politics," *Cooperation and Conflic* 31 (2): 161-183

Wiberg, H. (1994): *Europe: The Western Project and the Hesitant North*. Research Paper no. 7. Athens: Research Institute for European Studies

Wiberg, H. (1996): "Adaptive Patterns and their Deep Roots: A European Overview" in H. Mouritzen; O. Wæver & H. Wiberg: *European Integration and National Adaptations: A Theoretical Inquiry*. New York: Nova Science (43-64)

Wieczorek, P. & K. Zukrowska *(forthcoming)*: "Koszty integracji Polski z Unia Europejska i NATO" [The Costs of Membership in the European Union and NATO], in J. Stefanowicz (ed.): *Polska i Europa na przelomie wieków* [Poland and Europe on the Turn of 20th Century]. Warsaw: Institute for Political Studies

Wise, M. & R. Gibb (1993): *Single Market to Social Europe: The European Community in the 1990s*. Essex: Longman

Wolfers, A. (1962): *Discord and Collaboration*. Baltimore: The Johns Hopkins University Press

Wæver, O. (1990): "Three Competing Europes: German, French, Russian," *International Affairs* 66 (1): 153-170

Wæver, O. (1991): "Culture and Identity in the Baltic Sea Region" in P. Joenniemi (ed.): *Co-operation in the Baltic Sea Region: Needs and Prospects*. Research Report No.42. Tampere: Tampere Peace Research Institute (79-111)

Wæver, O. (1996): "Power(s) and Polarity in Europe: 1989-1994 Patterns" in H. Mouritzen; O. Wæver & H. Wiberg: *European Integration and National Adaptations: A Theoretical Inquiry*. New York: Nova Science (29-42)

Zaunius, D. (1938): "Du Lietuvos uzsienio politikos desimtmeciai" in V. Kemezys (ed.): *Lietuva 1918-1938*. Kaunas: Spaudos Fondas (30-43)

Zhirinovskiy, V. (1993): *Poslednyi Brosok na Yug* [Last Dash for the South]. Moscow: Liberal Democratic Party of Russia

Zhuryari, O. (1994): "The Baltic Countries and Russia, 1990–1993: Doomed to Good-Neighborliness?," in P. Joenniemi & J. Prikulis (eds.):

*The Foreign Policies of the Baltic Countries: Basic Issues.* Riga: Centre of Baltic-Nordic History and Political Studies (75-86)

Zostautaite, P. (1992): *Klaipedos krastas.* Vilnius: Mokslas

Zubok, V. (1992): "Tyranny of the Weak: Russia's New Foreign Policy," *World Policy Journal* 9 (2): 191-218

Zyuganov, G. (1995): *Za Gorizontom* [Over the Horizon]. Veshnie Vody: Orel

Øberg, J. (ed.) (1992): *Nordic Security in the 1990s: Options in the Changing Europe.* London: Pinter

Öövel, A. (1995): "Estonian Defence Policy, NATO and the European Union," *Security Dialogue* 27 (1): 93-111

# Index

References from Notes indicated by 'n' after page reference

abandonment/entrapment dilemma
    290
alliance policy 2, 7, 292-3
alliance theory 283-94
amity-enmity patterns 267
army-building, *see* force building
anarchy 4
anti-balance of power behaviour, *see*
    bandwagoning

balance of relevance,
    between NATO, the EU, and WEU
    76-9
BALTBAT 236, 237, 245, 250, 251,
    253, 255, 266
BALTDEFCOL 237, 253, 256
Baltic co-operation, *see* inter-Baltic
    co-operation *or* regional co-
    operation
Baltic Council 265
BALTNET 237, 253
BALTRON 237, 253
bandwagoning vs. balancing 283-94
    and "small states" 286-7
    and weak front-line states 288
    balance of threat theory 293-4
    degrees of bandwagoning 289-92
    Russia 277
    trend vs. status definition 284-5
    theoretical justification 286-8
Border Guard, Baltic states' 241-2

calculated amalgamation 77
CBSS 265, 267, 268, 274, 278
CFE treaty 271
civil service, Baltic states' 239

complexity reduction 12
conscription, Baltic states' 234, 235,
    243, 244, 246
conventional deterrence 228, 234
Council of Europe 271

defeatism 231
defence
    collective 272, 273
    spending 271, 272
dependency spreading 79
deterrent capability 242
differential impact 290-1

EAPC, see NATO
EFTA 263
environment polarity 4
    vs. systemic polarity 5
    World War II 5
    Gulf conflict 1990-91 5-6
Estonia
    Baltic co-operation, *see* inter-
        Baltic co-operation *or* regional
        co-operation
    bandwagoning 285-6, 291
    CFE treaty 111
    CJTF 121-22
    CSCE 117
    economic control 115
    EU 118, 119, 122-5, 129
        membership criteria 83
    European Stability Pact 122
    finlandization 128-9
    historical lessons 125-8
    inter-Baltic co-operation 118, 119,
        122, 128

NATO 111, 119, 120, 121, 123,
   128-9
   enlargement 111, 118
   membership criteria 88-9
   NACC 117
   PfP 117, 129
near abroad 112, 116
neutrality 114, 115, 118, 126, 127
Nordic states 120
nuclear deployment 111
regional co-operation 120-2, 128
   alliances 128
Russian speaking minorities 110,
   112, 116, 117, 119
scenarios 188-93
   Baltic grey zone insecurity 191-
   2
   Baltic grey zone security 188-
   90
   Baltic hard insecurity 192-3
   Baltic hard security 190-1
   Baltic soft insecurity 192
   Baltic soft security 190
security
   environment 109-13
   geopolitical factors 129
   hard 117
   identity 129
   policy 113-20, 127
   regional 120
   self-defence 127, 128
   soft 122-5, 128-9
state building 114, 116, 118
threat perception 109, 112, 113
troops withdrawal, Russian 115,
   116, 117, 118
UN 117
WEU 117, 129
EU 228, 257, 259, 264-80
   see also Estonia, Finland, Latvia,
      Lithuania or Poland
Amsterdam treaty 271
CFSP 271, 272

core-periphery Europe 82
EU as membership pole 74
EU membership criteria 82-3
EU multi-depth 80-2
Europe Agreements 271
Europe as a school class 75
low EU self-control 74-5, 79
US-Europe relationship 75-6
widening vs. deepening 79-82
European unipolarity 73-5

Finland
   abandonment as advantage 101,
      290
   and Baltic republics 92
   and disintegration of the Soviet
      Union 91-2
   as active bridge-builder 104
   as 'outpost of the rich' 103
   as 'outpost of the west' 99
   bandwagoning 285, 290
   'don't fix it, if it ain't broke' 102
   EC internal market, as challenge
      91
   entrapment as risk 101
   environment polarity, phases in 93
   EU and soft security 93-5, 103-7
   good neighbourly relations 102
   historical lessons 99-102
   low politics 91, 103, 105
   NATO 97-8, 104-5, 106-7
      popular and elite reluctance
         101
      if Sweden joins 104-5
   neutrality 96
   parallel action with Sweden 96-7,
      103
   power structure in salient
      environment, change of 91,
      100
   security challenges 95-7
   scenarios
      enjoying hard security 104-5

enjoying soft security 103-4
under hard insecurity 106-7
under soft insecurity 105-6
'trust only yourself' 100
watershed 1991 91-3
force
building 242, 243
structures 229
fragmentation, European 77

geopolitics 5, 261

inertia 8-9
inter-Baltic co-operation 236, 246
*see also* Estonia, Latvia *or*
Lithuania
international politics, axioms of 4-5,
292
international system 5
IR 5, 6n
IR realists 77

Kaliningrad (*and* KOR) 21, 22, 32,
44-7, 134, 170, 191, 205, 218,
261, 267, 268, 275, 279

Latvia
Baltic
co-operation, *see* inter-Baltic
co-operation *or* regional co-
operation
Council 141
Customs Union 154
Entente 160
Union 159
bandwagoning 285-6, 291
border agreements 135
CBSS 146, 156
CEFTA 153
Council of Europe 146
CSCE, *see* OSCE
demilitarisation 138, 139
distribution of power 131, 162

Estonia 136-37
Association Agreement 137
EU 135, 137, 138, 142, 144, 148-
53, 154, 155, 156, 161, 162,
163
Association Agreement, 148,
151
enlargement 134, 136
Free Trade Agreement 148
membership criteria 83
PHARE 156
good neighbourly relations 134
historical lessons 156
inter-Baltic co-operation 153, 154,
158, 160, 161
Kaliningrad 134
Lithuania 137-8
LPF 138, 139
National Guard 233
NATO 135, 138, 141, 142, 144-7,
148, 152, 153, 154, 155, 156,
161, 162
enlargement 134, 136, 147, 163
IFOR 145
membership criteria 88-9
NACC 145, 146
PfP 145, 147
neutrality 139, 148, 156, 157, 158
nuclear free zone 139
OSCE 141, 146
regional
co-operation 155, 163
polarity 131
security arrangements 153-6
Russian speaking minorities 135,
137
salient environment 132, 145
scenarios 188-93
Baltic grey zone insecurity 191-
2
Baltic grey zone security 188-
90
Baltic hard insecurity 192-3

Baltic hard security 190-1
Baltic soft insecurity 192
Baltic soft security 190
security
  collective 156, 157
  community 155
  environment 131-8
  guarantees 141
  hard 141
  national conception 143, 144
  policy phases 138-44
  societal 142
  soft 150, 151, 156
state building 134, 143, 151
threat
  analysis 140
  factors 133
  perception 132
troops withdrawal, Russian 134,
  135, 137, 139, 141, 142
UN 141, 146, 154, 155
unipolar dependence 150, 162
learning, of foreign policy lessons 8-
  9, 291-2
*see also* Estonia, Finland, Latvia,
  Lithuania *or* Poland (historical
  lessons)
liberal institutionalist approach 272-3
Lithuania
  alliance policy 175, 181, 187
  anti-defeatism 186
  BALTBAT 176
  Baltic
    alliance 183
    Assembly 170, 176
    co-operation, *see* inter-Baltic
      co-operation *or* regional co-
      operation
    Council 176
    military alliance 176
  bandwagoning 285-6, 291
  bilateral agreements 166, 171
  bipolarity 166

Council of Europe 174
CSCE, *see* OSCE
demilitarisation 170, 171
EU 167, 169, 177, 178, 179, 188-
  92
  CFSP 192
  Europe Agreement 176, 177
  free trade agreement 176, 178
  membership criteria 83
finlandization 175
Free Trade Agreements 175
geopolitics 166, 167, 171, 182,
  183, 189, 192
good neighbourly relations 189
historical lessons 182-8
inter-Baltic co-operation 174, 176,
  182, 185, 187, 190, 191
Kaliningrad 170, 191
Latvia 167-8
  free trade agreement 167
NATO 167, 169, 170, 176-81,
  186, 188-93
  enlargement 188
  membership criteria 88-9
  NACC 174
  PfP 176, 189
near abroad 170
neutrality 175, 181, 187
non-alignment 167
OSCE 174, 175
Poland 168-9, 185
  minority 175
political identity 174, 181
regional co-operation 172, 179,
  183
revisionist Russia 191
Russia and Belarus 169-71
Russian speaking minorities 170
scenarios 188-93
  Baltic grey zone insecurity 191-
  2
  Baltic grey zone security 188-
  90

Baltic hard insecurity 192-3
Baltic hard security 190-1
Baltic soft insecurity 192
Baltic soft security 190
security
    balance of power 165, 181
    collective 190
    common 179
    community 165, 171, 181
    grey zone 188, 189, 191
    hard 181, 190, 191, 192
    policy 171-82
    regional system 183
    soft 190, 192
state building 181
strategic interests 170
troops withdrawal, Russian 171,
    174, 175, 176, 187
WEU 176
UN 171, 174, 175

military, Baltic states'
    effectiveness 240
    infrastructure 244, 245, 254
ministries of defence, Baltic states'
    238, 239, 241

NACC, see NATO
National Guard, Latvia's 233
NATO 229-30, 247, 248, 249, 252,
    253, 255, 256, 259, 261, 262, 264,
    266, 267, 269, 270, 273-80
    see also  Estonia, Finland, Latvia,
        Lithuania or Poland
    article V 247, 273
    EAPC 84-5, 271
    enlargement 84-9, 268
        multi-depth as compromise 84-5
        membership criteria 86-9
    NACC 84-5, 264, 271
    non-article V operations 247
    PfP 84-6, 247-49, 252, 254, 255,
        256, 264, 268, 271

NATO-Russia Funding Act 268, 270,
    273, 275
non-mobility of nation-states 4, 292-3
Nordic balance 266-7, 277

OSCE 265, 271, 272

perception 9
PfP, see NATO
Poland
    alliance policy 196, 197, 203, 205,
        218
    amity-enmity patterns 196, 211
    balance of power policy 221
    bandwagoning 286, 291
    bilateral arrangements 219
    bipolarity 195, 224, 225
        systemic 196
    CBSS 220
    CFE treaty 204-5
    communist doctrine 195
    concert 218
    Council of Europe 200
    CSCE, see OSCE
    EC 206, 207
    EU 199, 207, 208, 209, 220, 221,
        222, 223
        Amsterdam treaty 208
        concentric circles 209
        Europe Agreement 206
        membership criteria 83
        White Papers 207
    Euro-Atlantic option 202-14
    free trade zone 206
    geopolitics 199, 206, 214, 219,
        224
    good neighbourly relations 199,
        200, 201, 203, 210
    historical lessons 214-20
    identity-building 202
    Kaliningrad 205, 218

NATO 200, 203, 204, 205, 209,
211, 212, 213, 217, 219, 220,
221, 222, 223, 225
Assembly 209
enlargement 205, 211, 213, 224
PfP 212
*Study on Enlargement* 212
NATO-Russia Funding Act 213,
224
non-offensive defence 204-5
nuclear weapons 212
OSCE 200, 209, 210, 217, 219,
223
regional
bipolarity 195
co-operation 205, 220
security system 210
salient environment 195-7, 202,
221, 225
scenarios 221-5
enjoying comprehensive
security 223-4
enjoying hard security 222-3
Poland exposed 224
troubles for Poland? 224-5
security 219
comprehensive 219, 223-4
multilateral guarantees 219
sovereignty 216-8
external dimension 199-202
internal dimension 197-9
status quo-revisionist dichotomy
221
threat perception 197, 202
troops withdrawal, Russian 196,
199, 201, 206, 216
two-track policy 200, 201
WEU 223
UN 200
unipolarity 195, 196
environment 195
pole vs. non-pole actors 6

power and incentives, waning with
distance 4
power projection 7
pre-theory 10, 283

regional
co-operation 278
*see also* Estonia, Latvia,
Lithuania *or* Poland
identity 274
revisionist power 275, 276, 277, 279,
280
revisionist vs. status quo orientation
10-11, 290-1
Russia
arms control 37, 38
Atlanticists, *see* debate on Baltic
security policies
Baltic area
and Baltic/Nordic security
doctrine 25-6
and bilateral security
agreements 37
and Military District (MD) 31
as buffer zone 18, 34
bordering Russia 1
CBMs 37, 38
CFE treaty 34, 36, 68
debate on Baltic security policies
58-68
Atlanticists 59-61
derzhavniki 65-8
Eurasianists 61-5
derzhavniki, *see* debate on Baltic
security policies
doctrinal background 16
economic dimension 23-4
enlightened post-imperialism,
concept of 27
ESC 35
EU enlargement, Moscow on 35
Eurasianists, *see* debate on Baltic
security policies

executive-legislative relationship
57-8
foreign policy doctrine 17, 24, 51,
63, 70
geopolitical and strategic
dimension 18-23
historical background 15
humanitarian dimension 24-5
interest groups 50-4
isolation from Europe 18
Kaliningrad, *see* KOR *or*
territorial disputes
KOR 21, 22, 32, 47
Kozyrev Doctrine 67
Leningrad Military District (MD)
22, 31, 37, 70
military
activities 31-3
doctrine 22, 36
issues 28-38
transit 30-1
minorities,
national 38-42
rights 57
Russian speaking 24, 26, 29,
30, 60, 62
NATO enlargement 33-8, 58
NATO-Russia charter 33, 25
near abroad 22, 36
*no first use* doctrine 22
nuclear doctrine 22
OSCE 33-5, 37, 48, 60
political dimension 23
political parties, Russian 54-7
revisionist orientation 71
security
Russia's future policy 68-71
Russo-Baltic relations since
1991 26
subsystem, Baltic/Nordic 26
status quo orientation 71
strategic allies 18
territorial disputes 42-50

and the Baltic 47-50
and Kaliningrad 44-7
and Karelia 42-4
troops withdrawal, Russian 28, 58
troubled neighbourliness 27-8
Vancouver G-7 summit, 29
Visegrad countries 18, 34, 35
Russian speaking minorities 261, 268,
269, 276

salient environment 4, 267, 269, 278
era stability 8
past salient environment 8-9, 283
scenarios 2, 275-81
environment scenarios 10-2
*see also* Estonia, Finland,
Latvia, Lithuania *or*
Poland
security
buffer 279-80
common 272, 273
community 262
comprehensive 272
grey zone 264, 268, 277, 279, 280
guarantees 228, 231, 232
hard 228, 266, 271, 275, 279
soft 228, 264, 266, 271, 273
security policy 2
selection of countries 1, 12-3
self defence capability 248, 249
soft vs. hard security 78-9
spheres of interest 7
rhetoric on 7, 88
spill-over 77
state building 228, 232, 257, 280
status quo power 275, 276, 279, 280
survival strategies, Baltic states' 234

territorial defence, Baltic states' 235,
242, 255
threat perception 269

uncertainty avoidance 77-8, 80

US-Europe relationship 75-6
  NATO annexation of WEU 76, 78

Waltz's 'Theory of International
      Politics' 292-3
WEU 271